FOYLES (£16-95/10-10-88)
(£10 TOKEN)

Systems Design with Advanced Microprocessors

John R Freer BSc, DMS, CEng, MIEE

Principal Consultant
Software Sciences Limited

Pitman

PITMAN PUBLISHING
128 Long Acre, London WC2E 9AN

First published in Great Britain 1987

British Library Cataloguing in Publication Data
Freer, John
Systems design with advanced microprocessors
——(Computer systems series)
1. Microprocessors
I. Title II. Series
004.16 QA76.5

ISBN 0–273–02679–8

Printed in Great Britain at The Bath Press, Avon

Contents

Preface

In recent years the technical press has published many articles emphasising the advantages of one variety of 32-bit microprocessor over the others and announcing several new concepts in advanced microprocessor and computer architecture. To the average reader, these articles announce the products and provide information which the manufacturer would like known but do not give a thorough, balanced understanding of how the new generation of microprocessors work or how they may be used in new system architectures.

This book attempts to rectify the absence of suitable reference material on advanced microprocessors and is intended to meet the needs of practising system designers (concerned with microprocessor hardware and software), engineering and marketing managers using microprocessors in new products, and students of electronic engineering or computer science.

The term 'advanced microprocessor' has been used to encompass 32-bit microprocessors and computer elements, digital signal processor chips, dedicated artificial intelligence microprocessors, and microprocessors which may be used to construct parallel processing systems, such as hypercube and wavefront arrays or dataflow machines. System design with these advanced microprocessors differs considerably from design with their 8 and 16-bit predecessors and parts of this book cover many aspects including architectural design, software and mechanical construction.

Readers with little previous knowledge of microprocessors should start with chapters 1, 2 and 3 plus the glossary of microprocessor terminology as an introduction, before progressing to the later chapters. Chapters 5, 9 and 11 consider new system design alternatives; chapters 4, 6 and 9 cover system design alternatives using conventional 32-bit microprocessors; and chapters 7, 8 and 10 give detailed consideration to the engineering aspects of system design.

Throughout this book, the emphasis is on practical, qualitative explanations with many explanatory diagrams, rather than an intensively theoretical treatment. In covering such a wide range of subjects in one volume, it is inevitable that many points of detail must be omitted. Other volumes in Pitman's 'Computer Systems' series are being prepared to plug these gaps, providing a more detailed treatment of many topics covered in this book and many others which are of importance in the wider applications of modern computer systems.

JRF

The author would like to thank the manufacturers referred to in the text for providing information on their products.

Information on the MC68020 contained in Chapter 4 and the material in Appendix A was provided by courtesy of Motorola Ltd.

Information on the T414 contained in Chapter 5 and the material in Appendix B was provided by courtesy of Inmos.

The photomicrograph on the cover, showing the T414 transputer, was provided by courtesy of Inmos.

Computer Systems series

Consultant Editor: John Freer Principal Consultant Software Sciences Limited

Systems Design with Advanced Microprocessors/Freer
Security in Computer and Communications Systems/Shore
Space Computing Systems
Supercomputers and Array Processors/Jones & Ron
Digital Signal Processing Design/Bateman & Yates
Computer Communications and Networks/Freer
Design and Implementation of User Interfaces/Reid & Welland
Practical Systems Development/Parker
Transputer Applications/Harp (Ed.)
Software Integrity/Sennett (Ed.)
Single-chip Microcomputer Systems/Barrow & Valentine
Communications and Control in Industrial Automation/Kochar
Systems Modelling/Staton, King & Thomas
Database Systems/Tillman
Fundamentals of Electronic Warfare/Palfreyman

These titles will be published mainly during 1988 and 1989.

1 Introduction to advanced microprocessors

1.1 Introduction

In 1985 more than six new types of 32-bit microprocessor were introduced and more than four types had been demonstrated in earlier years. The availability of these new components will revolutionise a large segment of the computer market because they offer levels of performance in excess of those which were previously achievable by super-minicomputers, at a price comparable with 16-bit microcomputers. Microcomputers (computers based on microprocessors) are therefore expected to increase their share of the computer market to more than 50% by 1995 and the computer market is expected to increase in revenue by 500% between 1985 and 1995.

Designers of systems which require greater performance than 16-bit microprocessors can provide must become familiar with the capabilities of 32-bit microprocessors. To achieve levels of performance greater than the conventional system architectures can provide, systems designers must learn how to implement new system architectures. This book provides information on all the popular 32-bit microprocessors and others which are intended for less general applications; it also describes and assesses several new types of system architecture which are made possible by the less conventional 32-bit microprocessors.

What is a 32-bit microcomputer or microprocessor? A 32-bit microcomputer includes program and data memory, input/output interfaces, and a 32-bit microprocessor chip or set of chips. A 32-bit microprocessor may lack memory and system interfaces but must use **32-bit internal registers** and a **32-bit data interface bus.** Processors which employ a bit-slice architecture, with slices less than 32-bits, do not fall into the 32-bit microcomputer classification and chips which have 32-bit internal registers and a 16-bit interface bus are not 32-bit microprocessors.

1.2 Semiconductor technology

Semiconductor technology has tended to follow a seven-year cycle of evolution since 1947 when the transistor was invented. Figure 1.1 shows the phases of development which have taken place and the increase in production volume for each phase. Thirty-two-bit microprocessors are only possible because very-large-scale integration (VLSI) is now able to put the

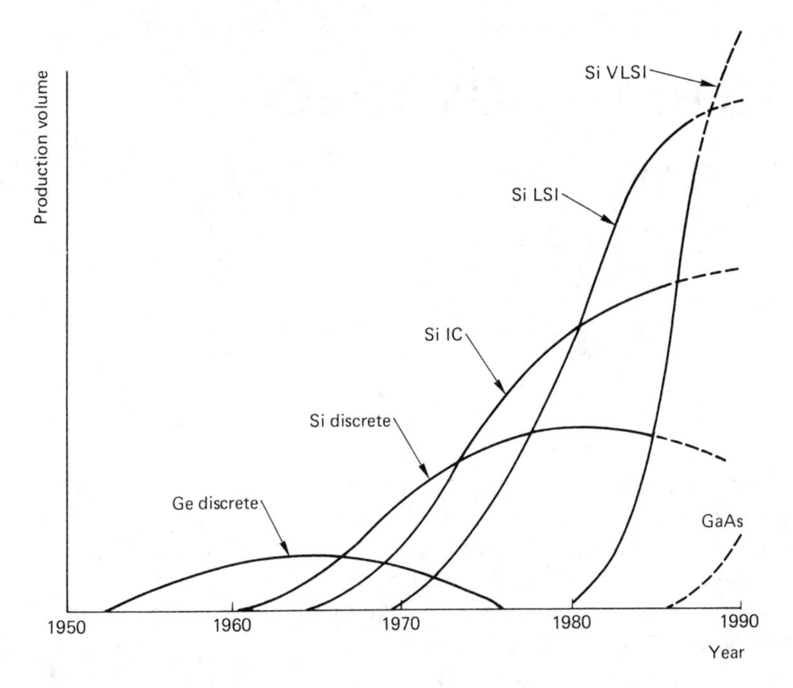

Fig. 1.1 Phases of semiconductor technology

required number of transistors on a silicon chip and achieve a yield which makes the price competitive. As the processes are developed, the yields of working microprocessors will improve and production costs will fall.

Figure 1.2 shows how the number of transistors which could be provided economically on a microprocessor chip has risen from 2300 in 1971 (for the Intel 4004) to 275 000 in early 1986 when the Intel 80386 became available. The Hewlett Packard Focus 32-bit microprocessor achieved 450 000 transistors on a chip in 1981 by the use of electron-beam lithography to produce 1.5 μm lines and 1 μm spaces on a MOS die.

The major factor in increasing the number of transistors which can be accommodated on a VLSI chip is the minimum *feature size* (called *the design rule*). The majority of 32-bit microprocessors use 2 μm design rules whereas the previous generation of microprocessors used 4 μm design rules. This difference gives a fourfold increase in transistor density. The *clock speed* may also be increased as the design rules are reduced. For example, the initial NS32032 chip used 3.5 μm design rules and had a clock speed of 6 MHz but when the chip was shrunk a 15 MHz clock speed became possible. To achieve design rules below 2 μm, manufacturers have to adopt improved lithographic techniques. By using deep ultraviolet, electron beam and X-ray lithography, design rules below 1 μm should become practical by 1990.

Power consumption is a major limiting factor in chip complexity. As the number of NMOS transistors increases on a VLSI chip, with more than 250 000 transistors the power dissipation increases exponentially. The practical limitation in the amount of power which can be dissipated from an NMOS chip by conventional means (1.5 to 2 W) makes it necessary to consider alternative types of semiconductor technology for 32-bit microprocessors with large numbers of transistors. Many manufacturers of 32-bit

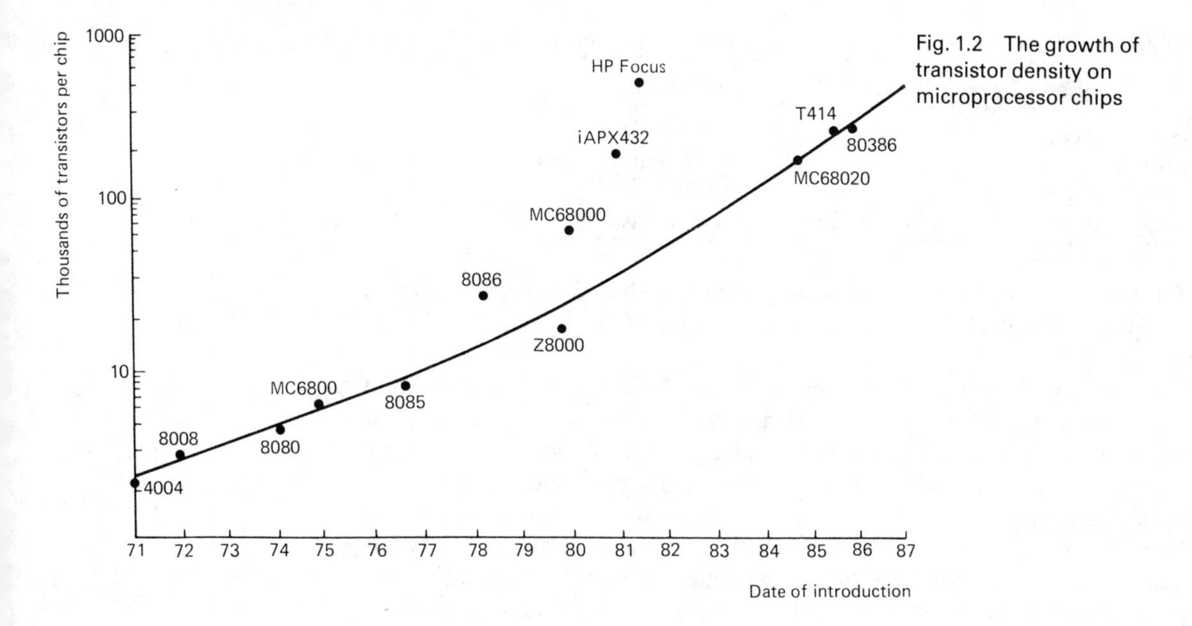

Fig. 1.2 The growth of transistor density on microprocessor chips

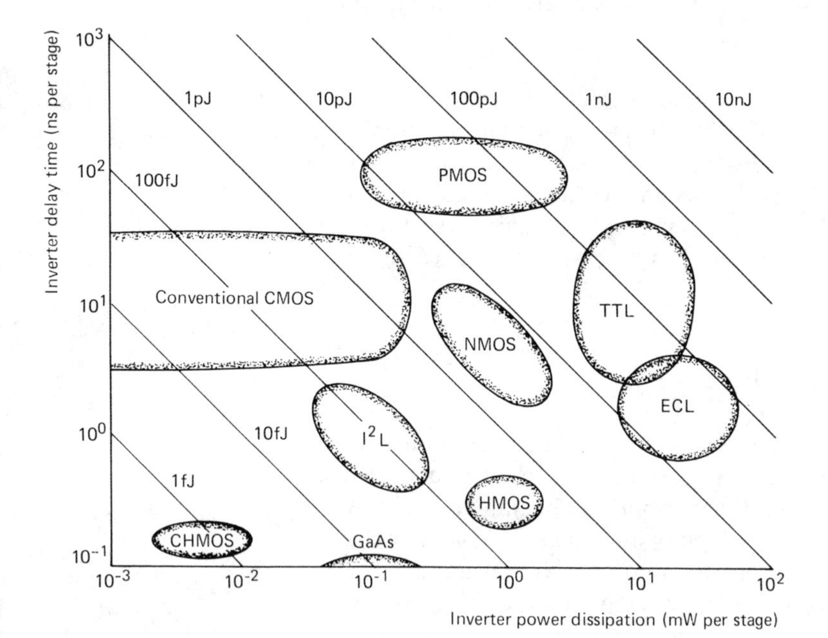

Fig. 1.3 Comparison of speed-power products for semiconductor technologies

microprocessors have adopted a fabrication technique which combines CMOS with NMOS to give the low-power dissipation of CMOS and the higher speed of NMOS.

The *speed-power product* (in Joules) for a semiconductor technology is a useful figure of merit. Intel have reduced the speed-power product of their MOS semiconductor processes as shown in Table 1.1. Figure 1.3 shows how the speed-power product of several alternative semiconductor technologies compare. Combined CMOS/NMOS technology offers a good combination of speed and low enough power dissipation to accommodate

Table 1.1 The evolution of speed-power product for Intel MOS technology

Year	*Speed-Power product* (pJ)	*Technology*
1975	2.0	NMOS
1977	1.0	HMOS (high-density NMOS)
1979	0.5	HMOSII
1983	0.04	CHMOS (CMOS/HMOS)

500 000 transistors in a package dissipating less than 2 W. An additional advantage of reduced chip temperature is that the probability of failure reduces.

An alternative means of achieving high speed with low power dissipation is to construct CMOS on a silicon-on-sapphire substrate but the cost of this technology has prohibited its use for commercial applications. In the future, gallium arsenide (GaAs) semiconductors may offer higher levels of speed and integration but the cost will be much higher than MOS because the materials are rare and the semiconductor manufacturing process has many more stages. Initial use of gallium arsenide is limited to small, high-speed components for military applications; commercial VLSI is unlikely for many years but LSI bit-slice processor elements are available in gallium arsenide.

As chips become more complex, the computer aided design and test systems must become more efficient to reduce the design and test times. No longer can the manufacturers of 32-bit microprocessors afford to perform comprehensive routine testing. New techniques have been developed to reduce test times by integrating self-testing logic on-chip. The use of redundant circuitry to improve chip yield has been adopted, particularly in memory arrays.

1.3 The evolution of microprocessors

The first microprocessor, the 4-bit Intel 4004, was launched on an unprepared market in 1971. Developed to meet a calculator manufacturer's requirement, the 4004 was offered to the world as the beginning of a new era in integrated electronics. The 4004 had very limited memory addressing capability and was slow but gained acceptance in simple control applications and arcade games. Figure 1.4 shows the increase in microprocessor power from 1971 onwards.

The success of the 4004 made Intel develop the first 8-bit microprocessor, the 8008, in 1972. Throughout the early 1970s, Intel continued to convince design engineers that the computer-on-a-chip was a viable alternative to traditional hard-wired components. An important aspect in gaining acceptance was the introduction of software development tools capable of developing linkable, relocatable, object code modules in addition to the assembler which was previously the only software tool.

In 1974 Intel introduced the 8080, an improved 8-bit microprocessor which was upward-compatible with the 8008 (it would execute all the 8008

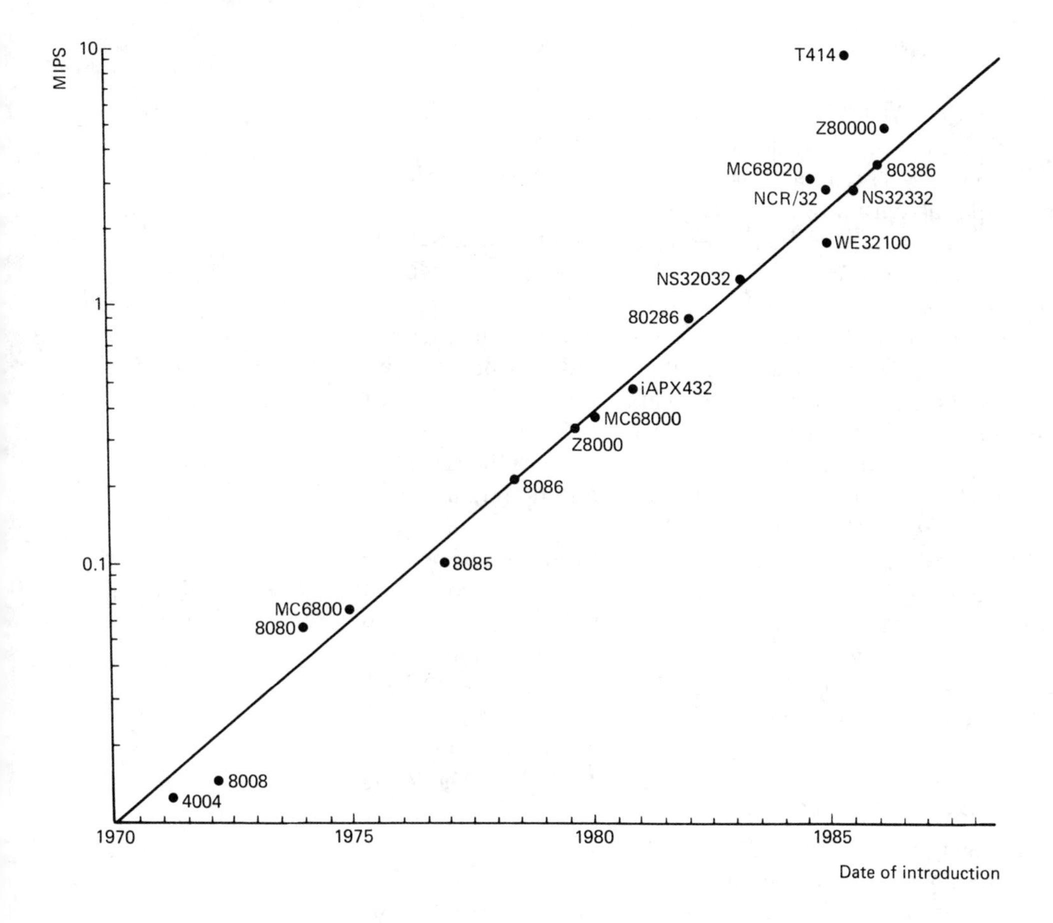

Fig. 1.4 Improvements in microprocessor power (Mips)

instructions). A wide range of 8-bit microprocessors became available by 1976 when Intel launched the 8085, an 8-bit microprocessor which required only a 5 V power supply and fewer support chips than its predecessors. Competitors included the Zilog Z80 (which has 8080 instructions as a subset of its instruction set), the MOS Technology 6802, and the Motorola 6800 followed by the 6809. Some of these microprocessors were produced in vast quantities, therefore becoming inexpensive and encouraging their use in consumer products including home computers.

Single-chip microcomputers, which include a small random access memory (RAM) and read only memory (ROM), became available for control and other consumer applications; these included the Intel 8048, Motorola 6801, Zilog Z8 and Texas Instruments TMS9940.

Sixteen-bit microprocessors were introduced in 1977. Initial devices, the National Semiconductor PACE, GIM CP1600 and Texas Instruments TMS9900, offered limited speed improvements over the 8-bit microprocessors but the more advanced 16-bit microprocessors introduced from 1978 offered much higher performance. The 8086 provided ten times the performance of the 8080 and later 16-bit microprocessors, such as the Motorola MC68000, Zilog Z8000, Texas Instruments TMS99000, National Semiconductor NS16032, Motorola MC68010 and Intel 80286, provided an increasing level of performance as the semiconductor technology and internal architectures were improved.

The Motorola MC68000 has a 32-bit internal architecture. With the exception of 32-bit multiply-and-divide, most operations can be performed on 8,16 or 32-bit values. The addressing range is 16 Mbytes, and it has 16 thirty-two-bit general registers and 7 interrupt levels.

The National Semiconductor NS16032 has a 32-bit internal architecture with a 16-bit data interface bus. The direct addressing range is 16 Mbytes and it has 8 thirty-two-bit general registers.

The Intel 80286, introduced in 1982, has a 16-bit internal architecture and an instruction set which is upward-compatible with the 8086. Extensive memory management facilities and a protection mechanism which monitors memory access from different tasks are incorporated. The direct addressing range is 16 Mbytes but a virtual memory up to 1 Gigabyte (1000 Mbytes) may be supported. The 80286 has 8 general-purpose registers and 2 interrupt levels.

The first 32-bit microprocessors, with 32-bit data interface buses, became commercially available in 1983–84; these were the National Semiconductor NS32032, a development of the NS16032, and the NCR/32 chip set. Two other 32-bit microprocessors were in production in 1983 but were not commercially available; they were the Hewlett Packard Focus and the AT&T WE32000. 1985 saw a flood of 32-bit microprocessors onto the market. At the beginning of 1985 the Motorola MC68020 became available and, towards the end of the year, the Inmos T414 and Intel 80386. The Zilog Z80000 was subsequently released in 1986.

After much publicity the Intel iAPX432 became available in 1981 but failed to be accepted by the market because of its poor performance. The iAPX432 system consists of three chips: the 43201 instruction decoder, 43202 execution unit and 43203 interface processor. Data is processed in units up to 32-bits wide and special features include data protection, multiprocessor support, multi-tasking and dynamic storage allocation. Instructions are of variable length and two processors may be coupled back-to-back, one checking the operation of the other.

1.4 Conventional 32-bit microprocessors

The four most popular 32-bit microprocessors with conventional architectures are

- Motorola MC68020
- National Semiconductor NS32032
- Intel iAPX386 (80386)
- Zilog Z80000

These chips offer several advantages over their 16-bit predecessors:

- Higher data throughput with the 32-bit-wide data bus.
- Larger direct addressing range (theoretically 4 Gbytes with 32 address bits).

- Higher clock frequencies and operating speeds as a result of improvements in semiconductor technology.
- Higher processing speeds because larger registers require fewer calls to memory and register-to-register transfers are typically five times faster than register-to-memory transfers.
- More instructions and addressing modes to improve software efficiency.
- More registers to support high-level languages.
- More extensive memory management and coprocessor capabilities.
- Cache memories and instruction pipelines to increase processing speed and reduce peak bus loads.

Each of these microprocessors has an instruction set which is an enhanced version of that employed on the manufacturer's 16-bit microprocessor; software is therefore upward-compatible. All four microprocessors compete for many 32-bit microprocessor applications but each has a bias towards certain application areas.

To construct a complete general-purpose 32-bit microprocessor, five basic functions are necessary:

1 Arithmetic Logic Unit (ALU)
2 Memory Management Unit (MMU)
3 Floating-point Coprocessor
4 Interrupt Controller
5 Timing Control.

Some manufacturers have included several of these functions on the microprocessor chip while others require individual chips for each function. Each manufacturer approached the design in a different way, adding refinements to the basic von Neumann architecture (described in Section 1.5). For this reason the system designer must become familiar with the microprocessor architectures before making a selection.

The National Semiconductor NS32032 and its Texas Instruments second-source, the TI32032, have an architecture similar to the VAX minicomputer with uniform linear addressing, demand paged virtual memory management to protect one user from another, privileged instructions to protect the operating system from unscrupulous users, and a 32-bit minicomputer-like instruction set. Addressing modes, data types and operations are encoded symmetrically to suit high-level language compilers.

The Intel 80386 can use segmented address space which is claimed to suit the organisation of modular programs and structured data better than a linear addressing space because meaningful program units can be protected from each other. A page-based memory-management mapping scheme is considered more efficient than a segment-based scheme.

The Z80000 addressing modes will support both linear and segmented addressing. Segmented addressing splits up the memory space into many small pieces; in page-based systems the logical space is broken up into the same number of pieces as the physical address space.

Figure 1.5 shows the construction of an NS32032-based general-purpose microcomputer. Separate chips are used for the five basic functions: CPU,

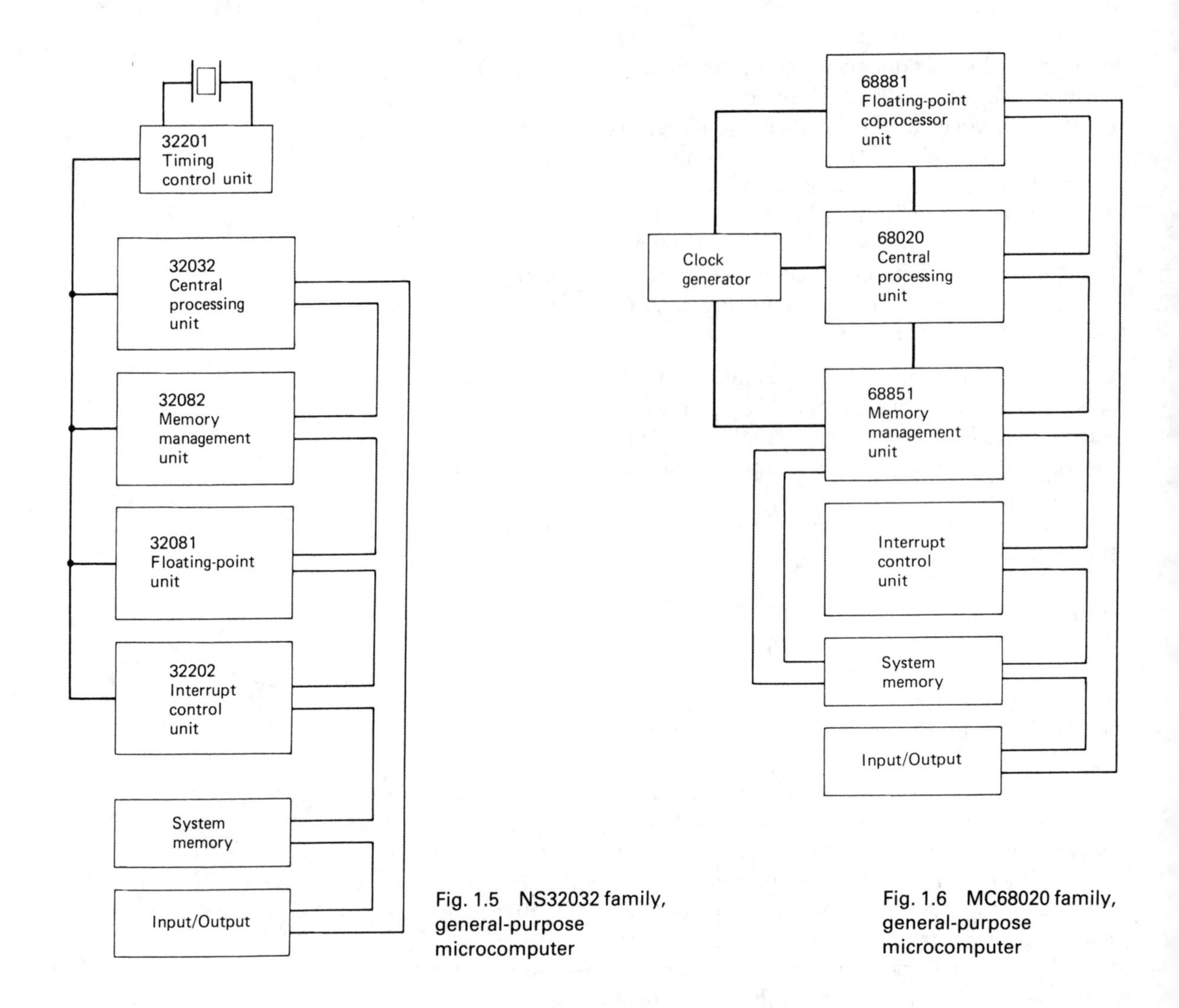

Fig. 1.5 NS32032 family, general-purpose microcomputer

Fig. 1.6 MC68020 family, general-purpose microcomputer

MMU, floating-point coprocessor, interrupt control and timing control. The NS32032 makes no provision for cache memory. An improved version of the NS32032, the NS32332, includes a number of additional capabilities:

8/16/32-bit data bus width.
Burst mode data transfers.
Higher-speed arithmetic logic unit using a barrel shifter.

The Motorola MC68020 architecture has been optimised for computationally intensive tasks. Figure 1.6 shows a MC68020-based general-purpose microcomputer. The MC68020 includes a 256-byte on-chip instruction cache memory. A clock generator, MC68881 floating-point coprocessor, interrupt controller, and an MC68851 memory management unit are required to complete the microcomputer functions.

The internal pipelined architecture of the MC68020 executes instructions faster than they can be fetched from off-chip memory. The on-chip instruction cache reduces instruction fetch time when the required instruction is held in cache. This is most effective when slower off-board memory introduces wait states in instruction execution. Dynamic bus sizing permits the processor to communicate with 8-bit, 16-bit or 32-bit external devices, selected under software control without additional overheads.

The Zilog Z80000 includes a virtual memory management unit plus a 256-byte instruction/data cache on the chip. It also includes a six-stage pipelined processor architecture and has a burst memory transfer capability to maximise bus bandwidth without requiring faster memories. Several data transfers can take place after an address transfer, thus memory bus bandwidth can effectively be doubled. The Z8070 arithmetic processing unit is available to execute floating-point arithmetic.

The Intel 80386 has a pipelined architecture and includes on-chip virtual memory management to reduce software overheads and avoid delays which are introduced by off-chip memory management units. The 80386 supports the use of an off-chip cache memory and floating-point coprocessor chip, the 80387, as shown in Figure 1.7.

The performance of a microcomputer system is determined as much by the coprocessors as by the microprocessor and some coprocessors are nearly as complex as the microprocessor chip itself. In coprocessor operations, the CPU fetches the instructions, performs any address calculations that

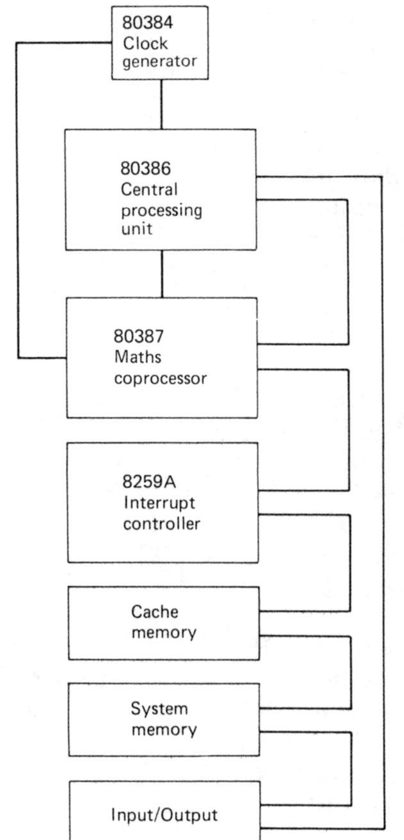

Fig. 1.7 80386 family, general-purpose microcomputer with cache memory

may be needed, and routes the instruction, with the appropriate data, to the coprocessor for execution. If the necessary coprocessor chip is not fitted to the system, the CPU generates a software trap which allows the instruction to be emulated by software at a much lower speed.

1.5 Unconventional architectures

The conventional von Neumann computer architecture has been in use for more than 30 years. Its main features are

- A single computing unit incorporating the processor, communications and memory.
- A linear memory addressing map made up of fixed size memory words.
- A low-level machine language.
- Sequential, centralised control.

The von Neumann architecture is reaching the limits in achievable processing speed because the sequential fetching of instructions and data through a common memory interface forms a bottleneck. Future types of high-performance computer will have to employ different architectures to increase processing power, and these architectures are likely to exhibit parallelism in some form to escape the von Neumann bottleneck.

One method of classifying computer architectures is Flynn's taxonomy which is based upon how the computer relates its instructions to the data being processed (see Figure 1.8):

SISD (Single Instruction-stream, Single Data-stream)
This is the conventional von Neumann computer in which there is one stream of instructions and each arithmetic instruction initiates one arithmetic operation. Techniques such as pipelining and cache memories may be used to speed up processing.

SIMD (Single Instruction-stream, Multiple Data-stream)
This type of computer has a single stream of instructions but has vector instructions that initiate many operations. Each element of a vector is regarded as a member of a separate data stream giving multiple data streams. For example, one instruction can operate on an array of data. SIMD computers include the Cray 1 pipelined vector computer and the ICL DAP processor array.

MIMD (Multiple Instruction-stream, Multiple Data-stream)
Multiple instruction streams require the existence of several processing units and therefore several data streams. Examples include multiprocessor configurations and arrays of microprocessors.

The Inmos T414 transputer is designed to operate in MIMD arrays using four high-speed serial links to communicate with adjacent processors. Two Kbytes of on-chip memory is provided and more local memory may be attached to the memory interface bus. A toroidally connected array of transputers is shown in Figure 1.9. Each additional transputer adds its own local memory bandwidth to the system so the overall memory band-

Fig. 1.8 Comparison of SISD, SIMD, MISD and MIMD architectures (MISD architecture is not in common use)

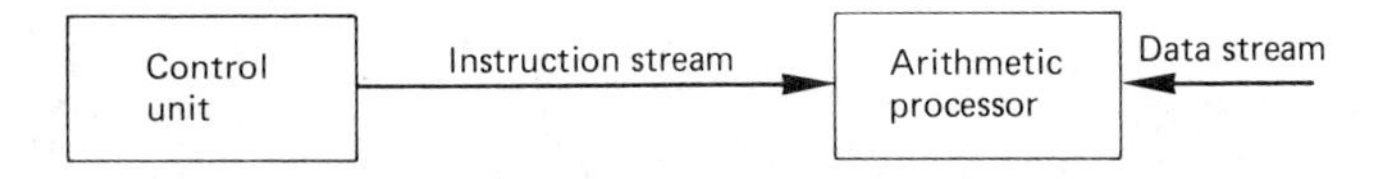

SISD – Single Instruction-stream, Single Data-stream

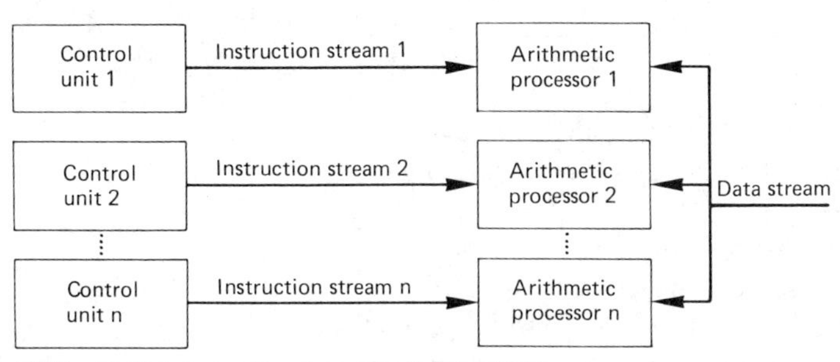

SIMD – Single Instruction-stream, Multiple Data-stream

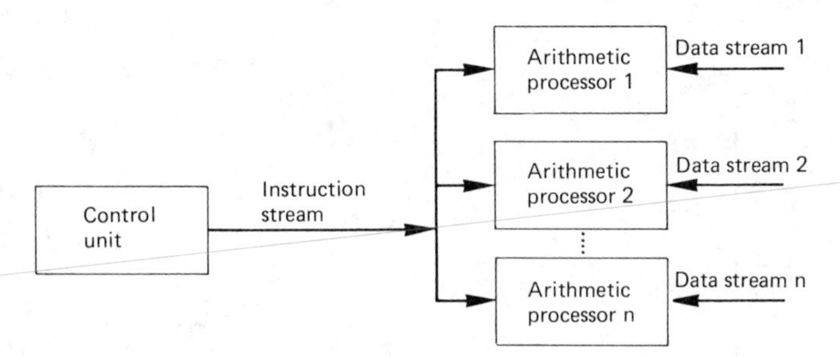

MISD – Multiple Instruction-stream Single Data-stream

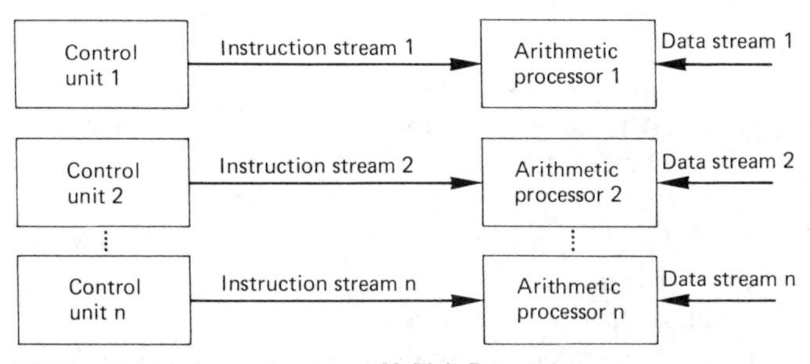

MIMD – Multiple Instruction-stream, Multiple Data-stream

width is proportional to the number of transputers in the system. Total processing power also increases in proportion to the number of transputers in the array.

In support of the transputer's parallel processing capability, special instructions are provided to share processor time between concurrent processes and to perform inter-process communication. Although the

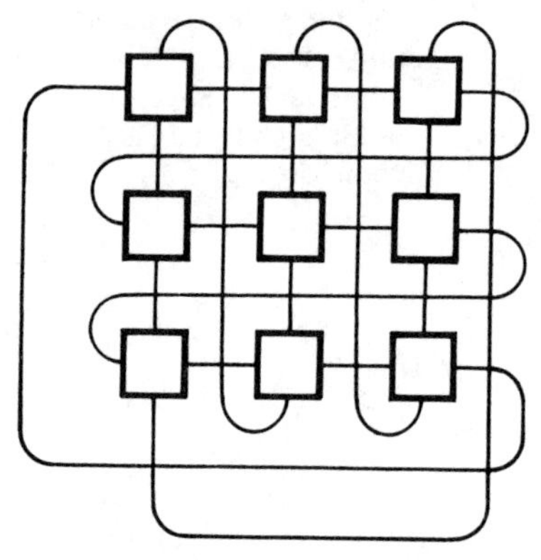

Fig. 1.9 MIMD computer architecture composed of T414 transputers in a toroidally connected array

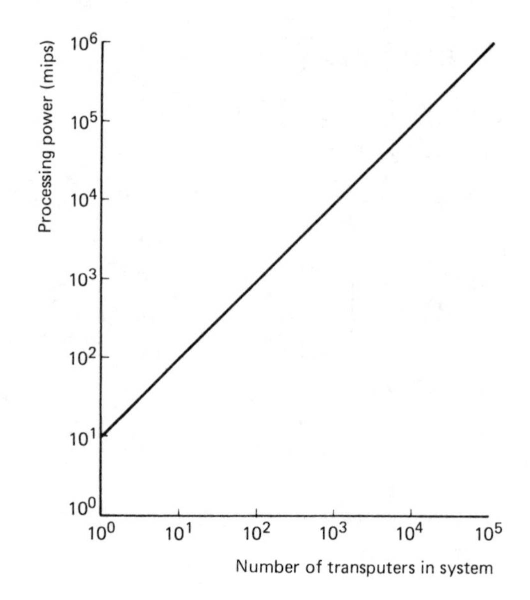

transputer can be programmed in standard high-level languages, to exploit the parallel processing capability a special language, Occam, has been developed.

The transputer and the Acorn ARM are both *reduced instruction set computers* (RISCs). Reduced instruction set computers aim to achieve faster processing through simplicity of design. This is the opposite trend to that of conventional 32-bit microprocessors which use increasingly complex instruction sets, demanding many machine cycles to interpret high-level instructions from ROM look-up tables.

A RISC CPU takes up the minimum area of silicon, and uses hard-wired instructions and wide bandwidth communications to execute instructions more rapidly. Although RISC machines may be expected to execute more instructions, this should be compensated for by the increase in execution speed. The transputer has an instruction cycle time of 50 ns and the CPU occupies only 35% of the chip area.

Another form of multiprocessing is achieved by *dataflow* machines. A dataflow architecture uses coded identifiers or tokens to guide data concurrently through the processes. Instructions are executed automatically when data is available but calculations which depend upon recursion (looping operations) are not executed efficiently. To program a dataflow processor, a graphic representation called a *directed graph* is used. This consists of a group of nodes connected by arcs. Information travels between nodes in one direction in a similar manner to activities linking events on a PERT chart. When a directed graph is executed on a dataflow machine, each node represents a processing task assigned to a processing element and the arcs represent the data paths needed to execute the task. Figure 1.10 shows a typical directed graph, for performing the calculation $f = (x \times y) + z$.

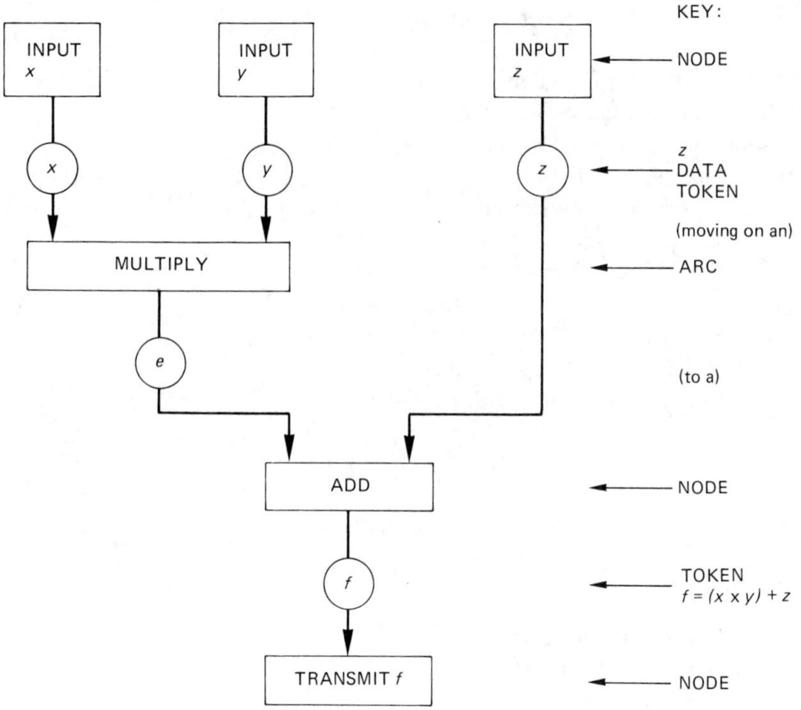

KEY:
INPUT x
INPUT y
INPUT z
NODE
x
y
z
z DATA TOKEN
(moving on an)
MULTIPLY
ARC
e
(to a)
ADD
NODE
f
TOKEN f = (x x y) + z
TRANSMIT f
NODE

Fig. 1.10 A directed graph for calculating $f = (x \times y) + z$

Host CPU
System bus
System bus interface
Host CPU memory
Host CPU I/O
μPD7281
μPD7281
μPD7281

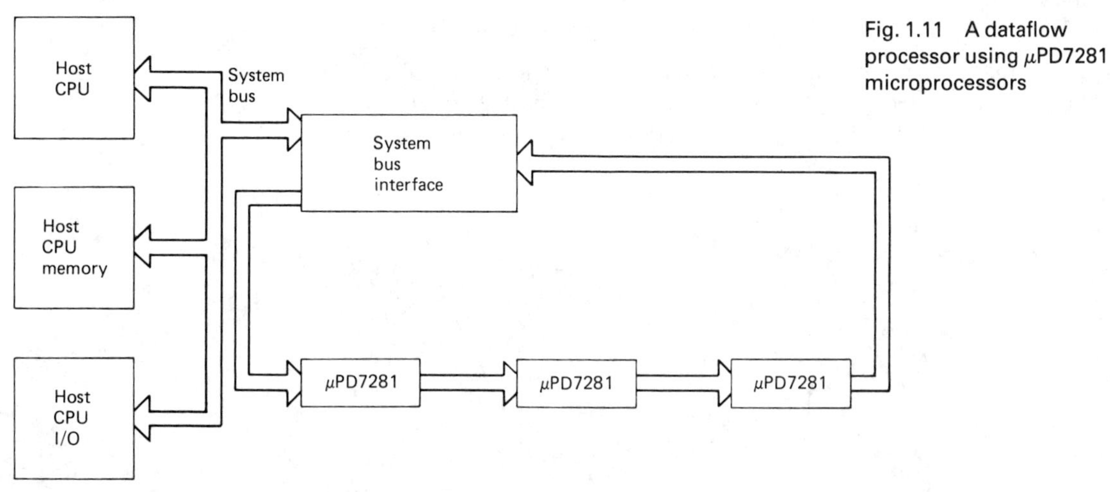

Fig. 1.11 A dataflow processor using μPD7281 microprocessors

Dataflow processors each work on different parts of a program in parallel and several dataflow processors working in parallel increase speed almost linearly. The NEC μPD7281 processor is designed primarily for image processing and is based upon dataflow and pipelining principles. Figure 1.11 shows three μPD7281 microprocessors acting as a peripheral processor, configured as a pipeline loop linked by a system-bus interface to the system bus of a host processor. Application programs are down-loaded from the host processor and data tokens for processing are fed from the system bus.

1.6 Typical applications for advanced microprocessors

The majority of applications for conventional 32-bit microprocessors are expected to be in office automation and applications currently dominated by 16-bit microcomputers and minicomputers. CAD/CAM workstations, office automation and high-performance personal computers are expected to be the first applications of general-purpose 32-bit microprocessors and compatibility with 16-bit microprocessor software will be a major selection point favouring the WE32100, NS32032, MC68020 and 80386.

Low-end minicomputer applications are expected to be taken over by 32-bit microcomputers because of their lower cost. The NCR/32 microprocessor has the advantage of being able to emulate the instruction set of a minicomputer or mainframe. The higher performance of processors constructed from the AMD 29300 or SN-74AS88XX series functional blocks will be attractive in array processors, super-minicomputers and high-speed controllers.

The third application area is in new and innovative designs which are not possible with previous microcomputers or minicomputers. These applications may include:

Expert systems	Telecommunications
Image processing	Scientific applications
Military computing	Factory automation
Engineering applications	Supercomputers constructed from arrays of microprocessors.

Unconventional 32-bit microprocessors like the transputer, μPD7281 and CLM (described in Section 3.13) are expected to concentrate on innovative application areas. A number of RISC-based personal computers and office workstations are now available.

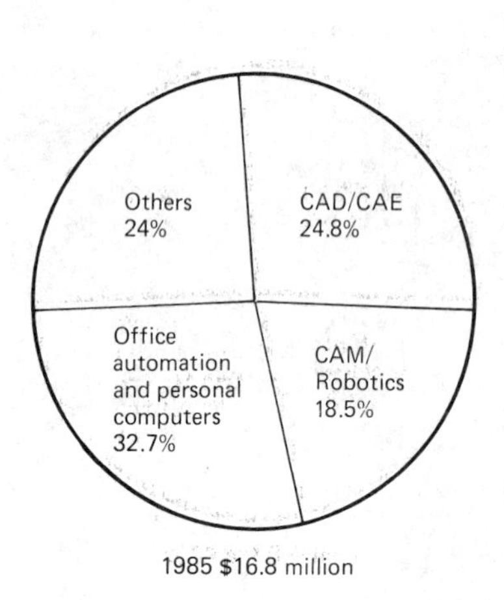

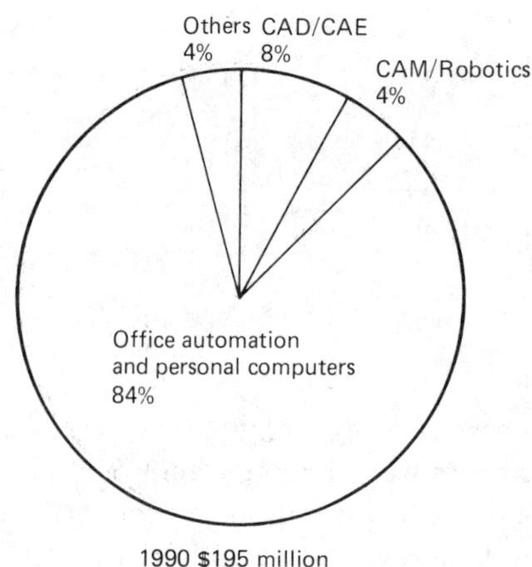

Fig. 1.12 32-bit microprocessor market share predictions for 1985 and 1990

Market predictions, shown in Figure 1.12, conclude that office automation and personal computers will dominate the market for 32-bit microprocessors by 1990 but initial sales will mostly be in scientific and technical applications.

2 New architectures and design features

2.1 Conventional computer design

2.1.1 Introduction

This chapter describes several new forms of architecture and design features which are found in advanced microprocessors and computer systems using these microprocessors.

Sections 2.1 and 2.2 consider architectural changes:

- 2.1 describes conventional computer design based upon the traditional von Neumann (SISD) architecture.
- 2.2 describes alternative computer architectures, computer classifications, program and machine organisation, multiprocessing systems, systolic and wavefront arrays.

Sections 2.3, 2.4 and 2.5 consider new design features which are used to improve the performance of microprocessors and microcomputer systems:

- 2.3 describes pipelines which are a form of fine grain parallelism employed by processors to execute multiple instructions simultaneously.
- 2.4 describes cache memory design and performance.
- 2.5 describes memory architectures including local memory bus extensions, interleaving and virtual memory management.

Sections 2.6 and 2.7 consider new forms of instruction set used by advanced microprocessors:

- 2.6 describes extended processing sets implemented by 32-bit microprocessors as coprocessors or extended processing units.
- 2.7 describes reduced instruction set computers (RISC) and compares their operation with conventional microprogrammed CPUs.

Sections 2.8 and 2.9 consider special-purpose computers:

- 2.8 describes high-integrity processors for fault tolerant, safety critical and high-security applications in addition to describing memory protection features used by advanced microprocessors.
- 2.9 describes the evolution of digital signal processor (DSP) chips and

the Harvard architecture and surveys the wide range of high-performance DSP chips currently available.

Digital computer design started in the 1940s and the first generation of vacuum tube machines were used for data processing in the 1950s. Second-generation computers, using discrete transistors, were introduced in the early 1960s and the minicomputer appeared as a more cost-effective and smaller alternative to the mainframe for a wide variety of scientific, industrial and commercial tasks.

Integrated circuits were used in the third-generation mainframes and minicomputers from the mid 1960s and, with the development of VLSI integrated circuits, microprocessors were introduced in the early 1970s. Despite these vast improvements in computer and memory technology, the basic computer architecture remained relatively unchanged because it was adequate for the level of performance required.

The first major variations in computer architecture were developed in the 1970s for supercomputers and the use of these parallel processing techniques has now reached the new generation of advanced microprocessors. General-purpose 32-bit microprocessors employ fine-grain parallelism in pipelines while concurrent processing may be achieved in systems constructed from arrays of microprocessors.

2.1.2 The von Neumann architecture

The principles of computer architectures and instruction sets remained almost static from the earliest electronic computers to the late 1970s. At that time, variations on the conventional von Neumann architecture began to appear in supercomputers and array processors. In the early 1980s the manufacturers of 16-bit microprocessors introduced pipelining in CPU designs and extended processing sets in the form of coprocessors. The von Neumann architecture has four main characteristics:

1. A single computing element incorporating a processor, communications and memory.
2. A linear organisation of fixed-size memory cells.
3. A low-level machine language with instructions performing simple operations on elementary operands.
4. Sequential, centralised control of computation.

The early computer architectures were designed for scientific and commercial calculations and were developed to increase the speed of execution of the simple instructions. To make the computers perform more complex processes, much more complex software was required. The development of semiconductor technology has increased the speed of execution of the von Neumann processors but a single communication path must be used to transfer instructions and data between the processor and memory. Large memories must be accommodated on different chips to the microprocessor and in most cases on different circuit boards. The result is that the data transfer rate on the memory interface severely constrains the processing speed.

As higher-speed memory becomes available, the delays introduced by the capacitance and transmission line delays on the memory bus and the propagation delays in the buffer and address decoding circuitry become more significant and place an upper limit on processing speed. The use of multiprocessor buses with the need for arbitration between computers requesting control of the bus exacerbates the problem and typically introduces several processor wait cycles while data or instructions are fetched from memory. One method of increasing processing speed and data throughput on the memory bus is to increase the number of parallel bits transferred on the bus. Microprocessor buses were first increased in width from 8 bits to 16 bits and then to 32 bits. Mainframe computers often use 64-bit memory buses and the next generation of microprocessors may include some 64-bit devices but these will present packaging problems.

The use of a von Neumann architecture at a system level introduces a single communication path between shared, or global, memory and a number of processors on the system bus. The global bus and the global memory can only serve one processor at a time and, as more processors are added to try to increase the speed of processing, the global bus bottleneck becomes worse. If the processing consists of several interdependent tasks, each processor will compete for global memory access and global bus transfer time. Typically only three or four times the speed of a single processor can be achieved in multiprocessor systems with global memory and a global bus. Figure 2.1(a) shows the von Neumann architecture which has a single memory bus and (b) shows a global bus in a multiple processor configuration.

To reduce the effect of the von Neumann global memory bus as a bottleneck, manufacturers of 32-bit microprocessors have incorporated *pipelines*

Fig. 2.1 The von Neumann system architecture

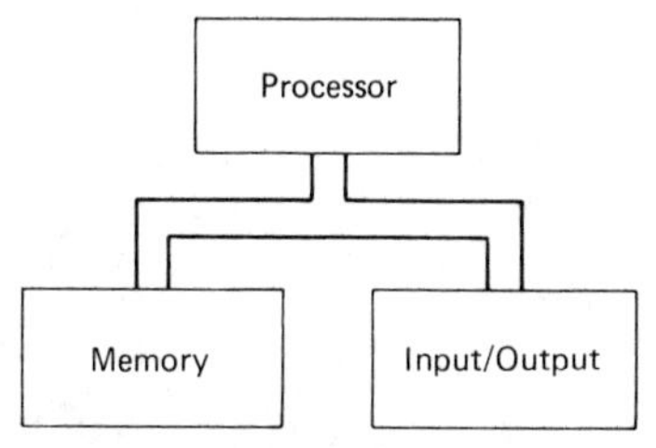

(a) *Single processor configuration*

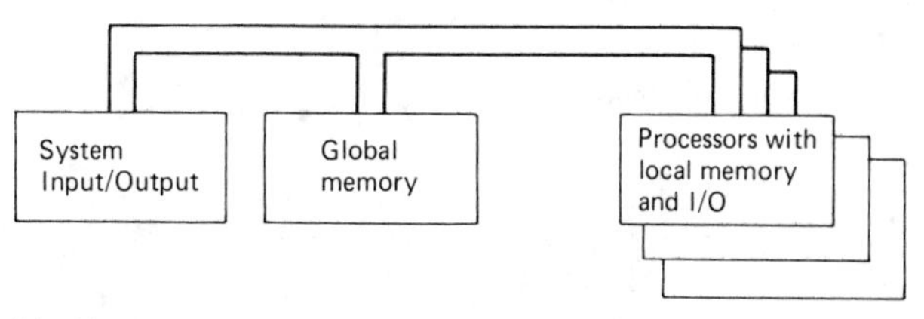

(b) *Multiple processor configuration with a global bus*

(which break each instruction down into basic elements which can be manipulated simultaneously) and *cache memories* (which pre-fetch instructions and/or data from global memory and store them in high-speed local memory until they are required for execution by the processor). Even with these enhancements, the sequential von Neumann architecture is now reaching the limits in processing speed, and future computer architectures will increasingly make use of parallel processing architectures which permit large numbers of computing elements to be programmed to work together simultaneously. The usefulness of a parallel processor does however depend upon the availability of suitable parallel algorithms.

2.2 Alternative computer architectures

2.2.1 Introduction

There are four main methods of implementing parallel processing now developed to a stage where they can be incorporated in new systems designs:

1 *Dataflow architectures* which are driven by the flow of data from a producer to a consumer, transferred by a data token. When all the necessary inputs are available, processing takes place (in contrast to the von Neumann architecture which typically exhibits control flow, directed by program instructions). Dataflow architectures are suitable for parallel processing, particularly in knowledge-based applications such as the Japanese fifth-generation computing project.
2 *Single instruction-stream, multiple data-stream* (SIMD) computers which perform the same operation simultaneously on different data. Most supercomputers are SIMD machines.
3 *Multiple instruction-stream, multiple data-stream* (MIMD) computers comprising arrays of independent computers, each with its own memory, capable of performing several operations simultaneously.
4 *MIMD computers* comprising a number of *slave processors* which may be individually connected to multi-access global memory by a switching matrix under the control of a master processor. This architecture has been used in experimental mini-supercomputers.

2.2.2 Computer classifications

Novel forms of parallel computer are under development in the USA, Europe and Japan, also in countries of the Soviet block, but no comprehensive means of classifying the designs has been established. However, the various forms may be broadly classified as having

a) Control-flow program organisation
b) Dataflow program organisation, or
c) Reduction program organisation.

Control-flow computers use explicit flows of control information to cause the execution of instructions. *Dataflow computers* use the availability of operands to trigger the execution of operations. *Reduction computers* use the need for a result to trigger the operation which will generate the required result. Several variations on each form of processor are being considered in research laboratories throughout the world.

A major objective for researchers is to develop architectures which can be implemented as simple VLSI chips which can be replicated in the computer system design. The use of VLSI is seen to be essential to achieve high performance because propagation delays in wires increase considerably as the system size increases but decrease linearly as the dimensions of VLSI circuit elements are reduced. The cost of designing and testing complex circuits makes it desirable to design only a few different types of simple computing elements and to use those elements in large quantities to construct compact, regular processing networks.

To reduce the size of microprocessor VLSI chips, the trend towards more complex instruction sets has been reversed in the reduced instruction set computers (RISCs) which aim to achieve a higher instruction rate and hence match the performance of microprocessors with conventional instruction sets.

A tree architecture, for example, may employ a collection of simple computing elements connected together as a binary tree with no global communication. Communication takes place between a parent element and its children elements in the tree and between the root of the tree and the external world. The tree architecture can be implemented as an integrated circuit with regular interconnections between repeated cell elements using predominantly local connections to reduce on-chip wiring. These integrated circuits may be assembled into regular patterns to construct large machines.

2.2.3 Computer program organisation

The three basic forms of computer program organisation may be described in terms of their *data mechanism* (which defines the way a particular argument is used by a number of instructions), and the *control mechanism* (which defines how one instruction causes the execution of one or more other instructions and the resulting control pattern).

Control-flow processors have a 'by reference' data mechanism (which uses references embedded in the instructions being executed to access the contents of shared memory) and, typically, a 'sequential' control mechanism (which passes a single thread of control from instruction to instruction). Dataflow computers have a 'by value' data mechanism (which generates an argument at run-time which is replicated and given to each accessing instruction for storage as a value) and a 'parallel' control mechanism. Both mechanisms are supported by data tokens which convey data from producer to consumer instructions and contribute to the activation of consumer instructions.

Two basic types of reduction program organisations have been developed:

a) String reduction which has a 'by value' data mechanism and has advantages when manipulating simple expressions.
b) Graph reduction which has a 'by reference' data mechanism and has advantages when larger structures are involved.

Control-flow and dataflow programs are built from fixed-size primitive instructions with higher-level programs constructed from sequences of these primitive instructions and control operations. Reduction programs are built from high-level program structures without the need for control operators. The relationship of the data and control mechanisms to the basic computer program organisations is shown in Table 2.1.

Table 2.1 The relationship of data and control mechanisms to computer program organisations

		Data mechanism	
		By value	*By reference*
Control mechanism	*Sequential*		von Neumann control flow
	Parallel	Data flow	Parallel control flow
	Recursive	String reduction	Graph reduction

2.2.4 Machine organisation

Apart from the computer program organisation, three basically different classes of machine organisation can be found:

1 *Centralised*, consisting of a single processor, communication and memory. A single active instruction passes execution to a specific successor instruction.
2 *Packet communication* using a circular instruction execution pipeline in which processors, communications and memories are linked by pools of work.
3 *Expression manipulation* which uses identical resources in a regular structure, each resource containing a processor, communication and memory. The program consists of one large structure, parts of which are active while other parts are temporarily suspended.

Examples of these organisations are

a) The traditional von Neumann microprocessors have a centralised machine organisation and a control flow program organisation.
b) The NEC μPD 7281 has a packet communication machine organisation and dataflow program organisation.
c) An expression manipulation machine may be constructed from a regular structure of T414 transputers, each containing a von Neumann processor, memory and communication links.

2.2.5 Multiprocessing systems

Multiprocessing systems make use of several processors each obeying its own instructions, usually communicating via a common memory. One way of classifying multiprocessor systems is by the degree of *coupling* they exhibit. Figure 2.2 shows the four levels at which processors may be coupled. Tightly coupled systems have processors interconnected by a multiprocessor system bus which becomes a performance bottleneck. Interconnection by a shared memory is less tightly coupled and a multiple-port memory may be used to reduce the bus bottleneck. The use of several autonomous com-

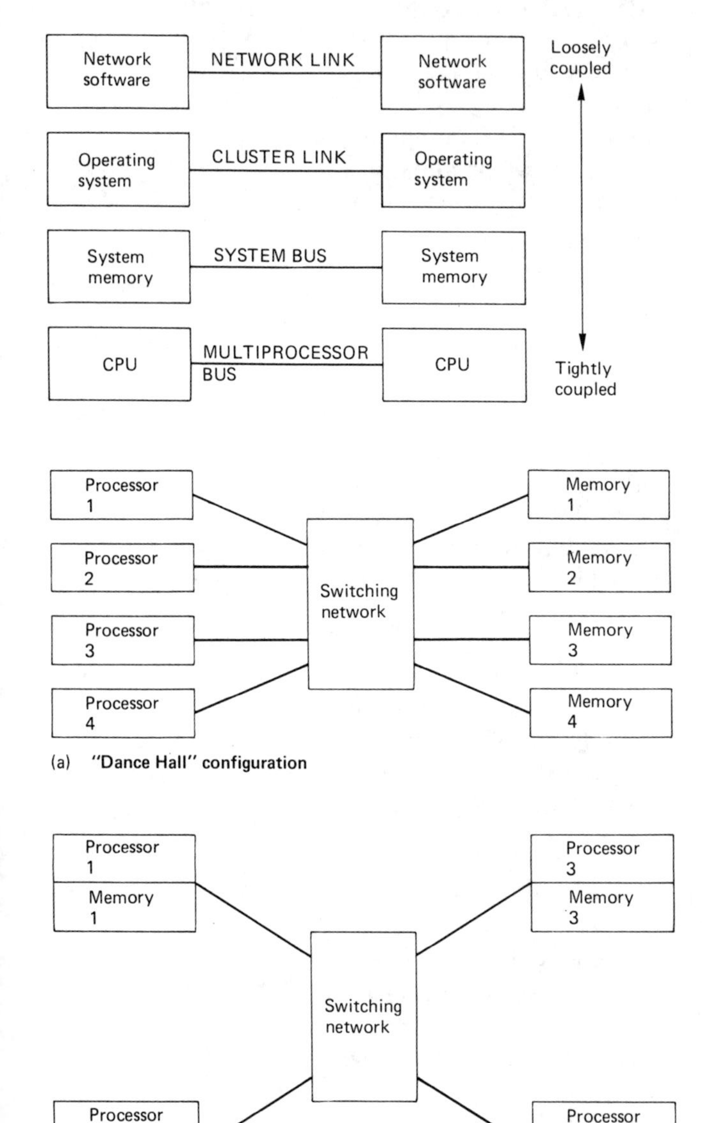

Fig. 2.2 The degree of coupling in multiprocessor systems

Fig. 2.3 'Dance hall' and 'Boudoir' multiprocessing systems

puters, each with its own operating system, in a cluster is more loosely coupled and the use of a network to interconnect computers, using communications software, is the most loosely coupled alternative.

Multiprocessors may also be classified as autocratic or egalitarian. *Autocratic control* is exhibited where a master-slave relationship exists between processors. *Egalitarian control* gives all processors equal control of shared bus access.

Multiprocessing systems with separate processors and memories may be classified as 'dance hall' configurations in which the processors are lined up on one side with the memories facing them. Cross-connections are made by a switching network (see Figure 2.3). At the other extreme are the 'boudoir' configurations in which each processor is closely coupled with its own memory and a network of switches is used to link the processor-memory pairs.

Another term which is used to describe a form of parallel computing is *concurrency* which denotes independent, asynchronous operation of a collection of parallel computing devices rather than the synchronous (or lockstep) operation of devices in a multiprocessor system.

2.2.6 Systolic and wavefront arrays

Two forms of computer array have been used for digital signal processing:

1 The *systolic processor*, which is a regular array of processing elements, each communicating with its nearest neighbours and operating synchronously under the control of a common clock with a rate limited by the slowest processor in the array. The term systolic is derived from the rhythmic contraction of the heart, analogous to the rhythmic pumping of data through an array of processor elements.
2 The *wavefront processor*, which is a regular array of processing elements, each communicating with its nearest neighbours but operating with no global clock. It exhibits concurrency and is data driven. The operation of each processor is controlled locally and is activated by the arrival of data after its previous output has been delivered to the appropriate neighbouring processor. Processing 'wavefronts' develop across the array as processors pass on the output data to their neighbours.

The wavefront processor array tends to be more efficient than the systolic processor when processing times are variable. Figure 2.4 illustrates the difference between systolic and wavefront processor arrays. The T414 transputer may be used to implement either a systolic or a wavefront processor in which each element is a 32-bit microprocessor. An alternative approach is to construct the array from single-bit microprocessors, accommodating many elements of the array on a single chip.

The NCR Geometric Arithmetic Parallel Processor (GAPP) is a two-dimensional array chip containing 72 single-bit processors, each with 128 bits of RAM. Larger arrays may be constructed from several GAPP chips for image processing, signal processing or database applications. The GAPP

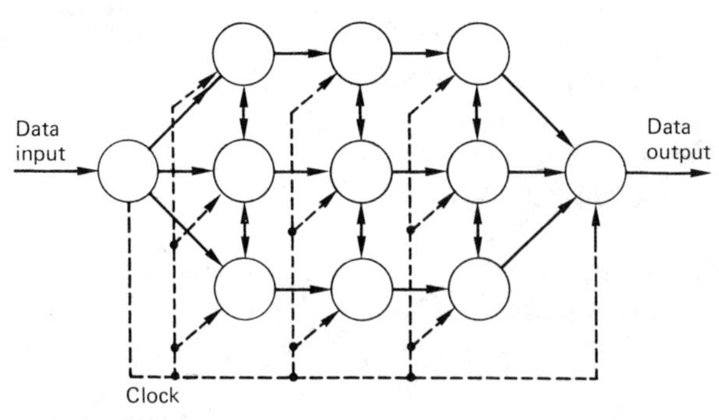

(a) **Systolic Processor Array**

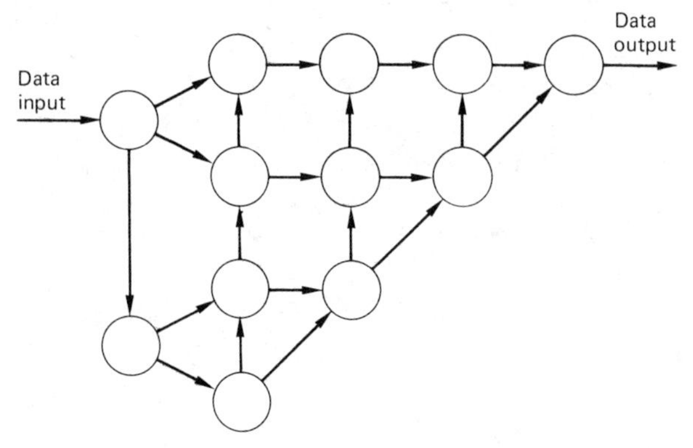

(b) **Wavefront Processor Array**

Fig. 2.4 Systolic and wavefront processor arrays

processes data words in parallel, working on words of varying lengths by sequentially processing each bit (word-parallel, bit-serial processing). The GAPP is classified as an SIMD array processor rather than a systolic array because it has the ability to broadcast data to all cells. This ability however introduces long interconnections which reduces speed. The GAPP can nevertheless be configured as a systolic array.

The Stonefield CLIP (developed at University College London in the 1970s) and the ICL DAP processors are both SIMD array processors using single-bit processing elements on LSI chips. The CLIP is primarily employed for image processing and the ICL DAP primarily for executing fast signal processing algorithms and number crunching.

A truly systolic array chip has been developed by GEC Hirst research centre. The MA717 is a pure systolic array with data input via peripheral elements and data movement through the array in the form of data streams moving from element to element. This systolic architecture is able to achieve almost twice the clock rate of the GAPP.

2.3 Pipelines

Most 32-bit von Neumann microprocessors employ instruction *pipelines* to increase performance by allowing the processor to execute multiple instructions in parallel. The processor separates each instruction into its basic operations and uses dedicated execution units for each type of operation. The most basic form of pipelining is to pre-fetch the next instruction whilst simultaneously executing the previous instruction. This makes use of bus time which would otherwise be wasted and reduces instruction execution time.

To illustrate the use of a pipeline, consider the multiplication of two decimal numbers: 3.8×10^2 and 9.6×10^3. The processor performs three operations:

a) Multiplies the mantissas ($3.8 \times 9.6 = 36.48$).
b) Adds the exponents ($2 + 3 = 5$).
c) Normalises the result to place the decimal point in the correct position (3.648×10^6).

If three execution units performed these operations, operations *a* and *b* would do nothing whilst *c* was being performed. If a pipeline were implemented, the next number could be processed in execution units *a* and *b* whilst *c* was being performed.

The operation of the Z80000 pipeline has been well publicised. The instruction cycle consists of six stages:

a) Instruction fetch.
b) Instruction decode.
c) Operand address calculation.
d) Operand fetch.
e) Execution.
f) Operand store.

As the preceding instruction completes a stage in the pipeline, it releases the execution unit and the next instruction can advance to that stage. Under ideal conditions, one instruction will have been clocked into the pipeline as the last instruction leaves, increasing the performance by six times.

However, if instructions are not always executed in sequence, or if each instruction does not always use every stage of the pipeline, or if each stage of the pipeline is not of the same duration, the optimum performance is not achieved. Non-sequential events occur with jump and call instructions or during context switches; these cause the pipeline to be partly or fully emptied. Shorter instructions do not use all stages of the pipeline and some stages of the pipeline are slower than the others, thus reducing the overall pipeline speed.

Figure 2.5 shows the loss of performance caused by instructions which do not use all stages of the pipeline and by stages which take more time than others. The instruction sequence is

INC R2 (Increment register 2)
MOVE R3, @ R2 (Move operand in R3 to address in R2)
DIV R4, R3 (Divide contents of R4 by contents of R3)

The increment instruction uses only the fetch, decode and execute stages leaving three stages unused. The move instruction uses the content of R2 which only becomes available when the increment instruction has finished

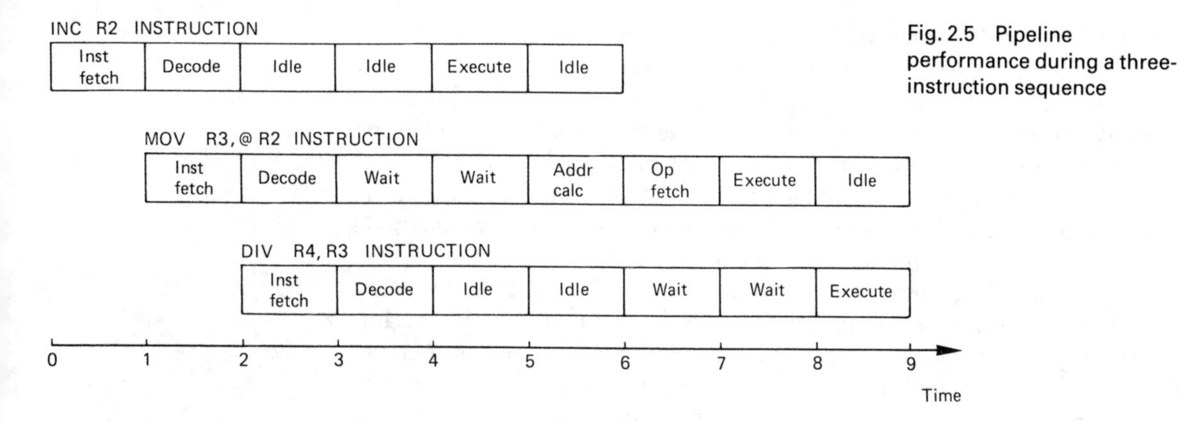

Fig. 2.5 Pipeline performance during a three-instruction sequence

with it, so it must wait for two operation execution periods. The pipeline effectively stops while the arithmetic operations are performed in the execute stage of the divide instruction.

To get a rough indication of performance increase through the use of a pipeline, the stage execution interval may be taken to be the execution time of the slowest pipeline stage. The performance increase from pipelining is roughly equal to the sum of the average execution times for all stages of the pipeline, divided by the average value of the execution time of the slowest pipeline stage for the instruction mix considered. Non-sequential instructions cause the instructions behind in the pipeline to be emptied and filling to be re-started. Non-sequential instructions typically comprise 15 to 30% of instructions and they reduce pipeline performance by a greater percentage than their probability of occurrence.

2.4 Cache memory

2.4.1 Introduction

Von Neumann computer system performance is considerably affected by memory access time and memory bandwidth (maximum memory transfer rate). These limitations are especially tight for 32-bit microprocessors with high clock speeds. While static RAMs with 25 ns access times are capable of keeping pace with processor speeds, they must be located on the same board as the processor to minimise delays, thus limiting the amount of high-speed memory available. Dynamic RAM has a greater capacity per chip and a lower cost than static RAM but even the fastest dynamic RAMs with 80 ns access times are unable to keep up with high-speed microprocessors, especially if they are located on a separate board attached to a memory bus. When a processor requires instructions or data sent to/from memory faster than the memory can read or write, the processor enters a wait state until the instruction or data is available. This considerably reduces the performance of the processor.

A *cache memory* consisting of a high-speed memory, either on the microprocessor chip or external to the chip but on the computer board, provides a fast-acting local storage buffer between the processor and the slower main memory. Some memory accesses cause values to be stored in the cache and subsequent read operations to the same address access the cache memory without the wait states required for main memory access. Off-chip but on-board cache memory may require several memory cycles whereas on-chip cache may only require one memory cycle, but on-board cache can prevent the excessive number of wait states imposed by memory on the system bus and it reduces the system bus load.

The cost of implementing an on-board cache can be lower than the cost of faster system memory required to achieve the same memory performance. Figure 2.6 shows the cost break-even points for types of memory which introduce different numbers of processor wait states. At all memory sizes, memory access time is reduced for memory which introduces wait states.

Cache memory can be used to hold instructions, data or both. Caches can be accessed randomly and therefore it may be possible to contain instruction loops with jump instructions within the cache address limits.

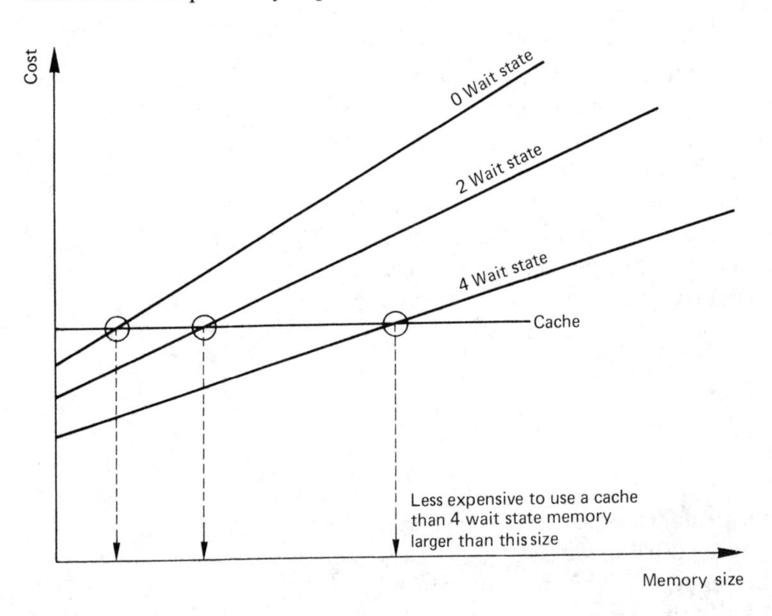

Fig. 2.6 Break-even points for a cache versus main memory with different numbers of wait states

2.4.2 Cache performance

Cache performance depends on *access time* and the *hit ratio*, which is dependent on the size of the cache and the number of bytes brought into the cache on any fetch from main memory (the line size). Increasing the line size increases the chance that there will be a cache hit on the next memory reference. If a 4 Kbyte cache with a 4-byte line size has a hit ratio of 80%, doubling the line size might increase the hit ratio to 85% but doubling the line size again might only increase the hit ratio to 87%.

Overall memory performance is a function of cache access time, cache hit ratio and main memory access time for cache misses. A system with an 80% cache hit ratio and 120 ns cache access time may access main memory 20% of the time with an access time of 600 ns. The average access time in nanoseconds would be

$$(0.8 \times 120) + [0.2 \times (600 + 120)] = 240$$

The reduction in bus bandwidth required for processor-to-memory transfers resulting from the use of a cache can be calculated for the MC68020:

$$\text{Bus bandwidth (Mbytes)} = \frac{\text{Bus utilisation} \times \text{Bytes transferred}}{\text{Clock cycles/transfer} \times \text{Cycle time in ns}}$$

Four bytes are transferred on each memory access which takes three clock cycles with a 60 ns clock cycle and 82% bus utilisation. The bus bandwidth required with no cache is

$$\text{Bus bandwidth (no cache)} = \frac{0.82 \times 4}{3 \times 60} = 18.2\ \text{Mbyte/s}$$

For the MC68020 with a cache hit ratio of 100%, a bus utilisation of 60% is typical, giving a bus bandwidth requirement of

$$\text{Bus bandwidth (with cache)} = \frac{0.65 \times 4}{3 \times 60} = 14.4\ \text{Mbyte/s}$$

The reduced bus bandwidth is available for other processors or bus users.

2.4.3 Cache design

Microprocessors with demand-paged virtual memory systems require an *associative cache.* Virtual memory systems organise addresses by the start addresses for each page and an offset which locates the data within the page. An associative cache associates the offset with the page address to find the data needed. When accessed, the cache checks to see if it contains the page address (or tag field); if so, it adds the offset and, if a cache hit is detected, the data is fetched immediately from the cache. Problems can occur in a single-set associative cache if words within different pages have the same offset. To minimise this problem a two-way associative cache is used. This is able to associate more than one set of tags at a time allowing the cache to store the same offset from two different pages. A fully associative cache allows any number of pages to use the cache simultaneously.

A cache requires a replacement algorithm to find replacement cache lines when a miss occurs. The Z80000 uses a 'least recently used' algorithm to put the least recently used cache line at the top of the stack, for replacement when the next cache miss occurs and the next line is read from main memory.

Microprocessors such as the MC68020, which do not use demand paged virtual memory, can employ a *direct-mapped cache* which corresponds exactly to the page size and allows data from only one page to be stored at a time. Figure 2.7 shows the MC68020 direct-mapped cache. It comprises a 256-byte buffer organised as 64 cache lines. Each cache line consists

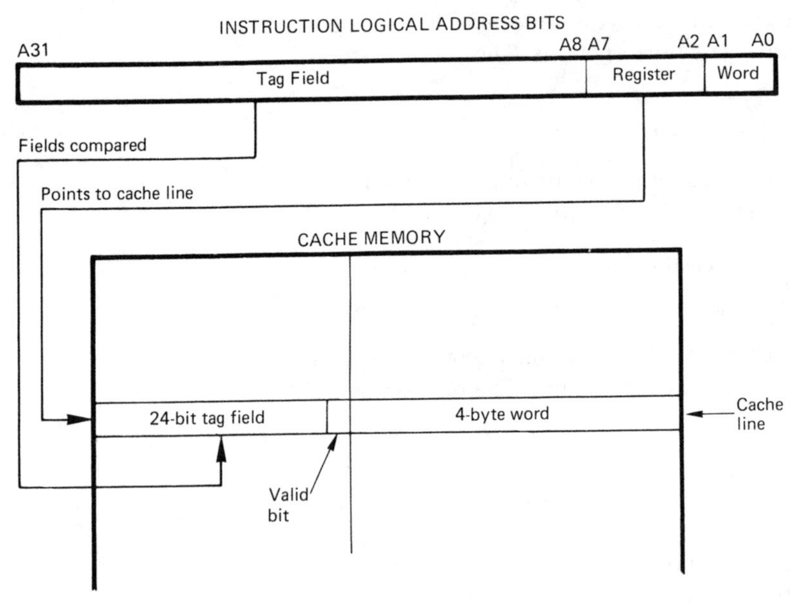

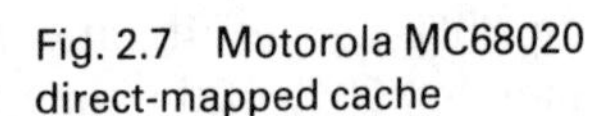
Fig. 2.7 Motorola MC68020 direct-mapped cache

of a 24-bit tag field and valid bit plus a 4-byte data word. When an instruction is required, address bits 2 to 7 provide a pointer to one of the 64 cache lines. The most significant 24 bits of the address are compared with the tag field of that line and if a match occurs the valid bit is set and the instruction fetch is performed from cache. If a miss occurs, because the comparison failed or the valid bit was reset, the instruction is fetched from memory and the cache entry is updated automatically.

In multiprocessor systems with a data cache, if one processor reads data from a shared memory and stores that data in a cache, subsequent reads may come from the cache rather than shared memory. If other processors modify the data in shared memory meanwhile, incorrect data will be obtained from cache. This problem does not occur with an instruction-only cache such as that employed by the MC68020 but this does not provide the advantages of a cache on repetitive reads from data buffers. The cache-coherence problem with shared memory is overcome in the Z80000 by restricting shared memory and preventing 1 Kbyte pages of shared memory from being read into the cache.

2.5 Memory architectures

2.5.1 Introduction

Thirty-two bit microprocessors have introduced three new concepts in the way memory is interfaced:

1 *Local memory bus extensions* permit larger local memories to be connected without the delays caused by bus requests and bus arbitration found on multiprocessor buses.

2 *Memory interleaving*, common on large mini and mainframe computers, has been used in some 32-bit microcomputer systems to speed up sequential memory accesses.

3 *Virtual memory management* has been introduced to exploit the power of 32-bit microprocessors for multi-user, multi-task applications by relieving users from implementing complicated overlay procedures when using disk memory. It provides a means of exploiting the processor's physical address space by using semiconductor memory in part of the address space and implementing the rest as virtual addresses on disk.

2.5.2 Local memory bus extensions

Local memory bus extensions have been provided to increase the size of the local memory above that which can be accommodated on the processor board. Multiprocessor system buses such as VME and Multibus II provide 32 address and data lines to increase their bandwidth over previous 16-bit buses but the need to request the bus and go through arbitration with other potential bus users considerably reduces effective memory bandwidth. The solution is to define new local bus extension standards such as iLBX II and VMX32. These 32-bit wide private memory channels offer a high bandwidth for access to private memory boards without using the main system bus.

The iLBX II bus which has a 48 Mbyte/s bandwidth may also be used to link two processor boards to main memory avoiding the main system bus which becomes an input/output and control bus. By overlapping the local memory bus and the system bus cycles it is possible to achieve higher memory access rates from microprocessors with pipelines which permit the address of the next memory reference to be generated while the previous data word is being fetched.

2.5.3 Memory interleaving

Pipelined microprocessors with the ability to generate the address of the next memory reference while fetching the previous data word would be slowed down if the memory were unable to begin the next memory access until the previous memory cycle had been completed. The solution is to use *two-way memory interleaving*. This uses two memory boards, one for odd addresses and one for even addresses. One board can begin the next memory cycle while the other board completes the previous cycle.

The speed advantage is greatest when multiple sequential memory accesses are required for burst input/output transfers by direct memory access. DMA defines a block transfer in terms of a starting address and a word count for sequential memory accesses. Two-way interleaving may not prevent memory wait states for some fast signal processing applications and systems have been designed with four (or more) way interleaving, in which the memory boards are assigned consecutive addresses by a memory controller.

2.5.4 Virtual memory management

The earlier microprocessor systems used a form of memory management known as the 'bare machine'. The user had access to the entire real memory for execution of any program and had to use complicated overlay schemes to run large programs in the restricted memory space. Later memory management schemes with resident monitors could operate in user mode, where the user executes the program, or the monitor mode, where the operating system runs the program with access to the entire memory space. Fixed-partition and variable-partition memory management schemes were developed to make multi-user operation possible (that is to allow several programs of varying sizes to execute simultaneously).

These earlier memory management systems (the bare machine, resident monitor, fixed and variable partition memory management schemes) managed real memory and the size of the program was equal to the size of the memory segment into which it was loaded for execution. The more modern virtual memory management schemes do not require programs to be loaded into contiguous memory and allow the system memory to appear much larger than it is.

Two forms of *virtual memory management* are implemented by 32-bit microprocessors: paging and segmentation. *Paging* involves the division of memory into fixed-size pages, typically 512 bytes, and programs are loaded into non-contiguous memory areas called frames which are managed by the operating system. As shown in Figure 2.8, the processor generates a logical address consisting of a page number and an offset. The page number is an index to the page table which gives the number of the frame containing the page. The physical address location of the frame, together with the offset, determine the physical address of a memory word. The page table translates from the logical memory map to the physical memory map. The translation takes place in two stages, first referencing the page table, then computing the physical address of the word using the physical

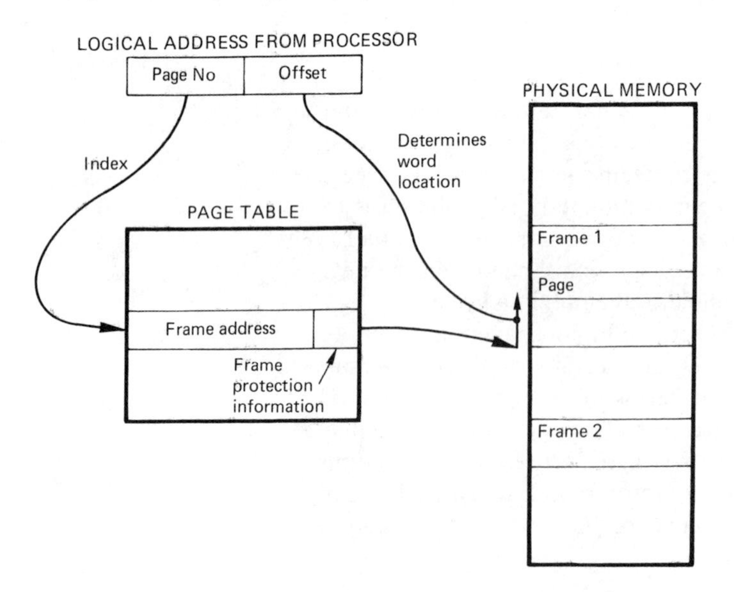

Fig. 2.8 Paged virtual memory access procedure

address of the frame with the offset. User protection such as the ownership and read/write access for each frame can be specified in the page table. The address translation imposes a time overhead which can slow down memory access considerably.

Segmentation is popular for modular programming applications. Modular programming uses a module for each function to simplify understanding, writing and testing of each piece of the program. Each module is defined by the function it performs rather than its size which varies from one module to another. Segmented virtual memory lets each module occupy its own contiguous piece of memory whereas paging breaks the module down into pages.

The logical address generated by a processor with a segmented virtual memory system consists of a segment number and an offset. A segment table provides a base value (which defines where the segment begins in physical memory) and a limit (which identifies the size of the segment). The offset must not exceed the limit. Protection is provided simply by defining the ownership and read/write access rights once, for the segment which contains the whole software module.

Segmented virtual memory systems suffer from holes of unused memory which must be compacted occasionally. This process can be inconvenient in real time systems. A fit algorithm must be provided in a segmented system; this must search for an unused piece of memory to accommodate each segment. Paged systems do not require such complex algorithms, do not suffer from holes between programs (external fragmentation), and limit holes within programs (internal fragmentation) to one frame per program.

Demand paged virtual memory takes a page from disk to main memory on-demand (that is, when the processor makes a reference to a location in that page). This form of paged virtual memory has been implemented in several 32-bit microprocessors and is similar to the method used in many multi-user minicomputer and mainframe systems. A simple paged virtual memory system specifies, in advance, the required areas of logical address space but a demand paged system can produce a page from an area of logical address space which is not specified in advance of the demand.

2.6 Extended processing sets

2.6.1 Introduction

Since the conventional von Neumann 32-bit microprocessors have to meet the widest possible range of applications, the instruction set is a compromise between adding instructions which will speed up processing in particular applications and the additional chip complexity which each instruction introduces. A common method of adding more specialised instructions without increasing the complexity and cost of the basic microprocessor is to add coprocessors or extended processing units which provide the additional instructions for those users who need them.

The most common *extended processing unit* (EPU) is the *floating-point coprocessor* which is made available by most 32-bit microprocessor manufacturers. The complexity of the floating-point coprocessor is comparable with that of the 32-bit microprocessor but it can offer an improvement of about 100 times in the execution speed for floating-point instructions and much greater precision. The details of extended processing unit implementations vary from one manufacturer to another but many basic principles are common to all implementations.

The 32-bit microprocessor uses an instruction template to make use of special instructions implemented by the EPU. The template is a set of reserved op-codes which is identified by the processor as a particular bit pattern in certain bit positions. The remaining bit positions define the particular extended instruction.

The EPU is usually connected to the address and data lines of the processor and decodes the template op-code at the appropriate time, but an alternative method can be employed which requires external logic to decode a separate EPU address space where the EPU is not able to decode the template instruction. Some coprocessors are able to take control of the processor bus to directly access memory, while others rely on the main processor providing appropriate addresses for the coprocessor to read or write the data. While all 32-bit microprocessors support the direct memory access method, the coprocessor chips available to-date rely on the processor providing memory addresses. Some coprocessor boards for array processing or analog input/output use direct memory access.

The processor must be able to use a software emulation of the coprocessor for systems which have no coprocessor fitted. A bit in the CPU control register may be set if a coprocessor is fitted. If this bit is not set, an extended instruction template will cause the CPU to jump to a specific address where equivalent software routines are located to emulate the EPU instruction. If no provision is made for a software trap, a jump instruction must replace any EPU instruction when the coprocessor is not fitted,

Some coprocessors operate in non-concurrent (or synchronous) mode which makes the CPU wait for the coprocessor to complete its instruction execution before executing the next instruction. Others operate in concurrent (or asynchronous) mode which permits the CPU to execute other instructions while the coprocessor completes its instruction execution. Concurrent operation is obviously faster but, if the CPU modifies memory before the coprocessor has read it, or if the coprocessor modifies memory without the CPU knowing, problems can occur. These synchronisation problems can be avoided by preventing direct memory access in concurrent mode.

2.6.2 Z80000 extended processing units

The Z80000 extended processing architecture does not include memory management because on-chip memory management is used and this is allocated a separate privileged I/O space. Figure 2.9 shows the format of the Zilog EPU instructions. The EPU ID code can select one out of four coprocessors. The EPU is connected to the address/data bus and can decode its own instructions but the CPU controls all addressing and data passing. Concurrent operation is supported.

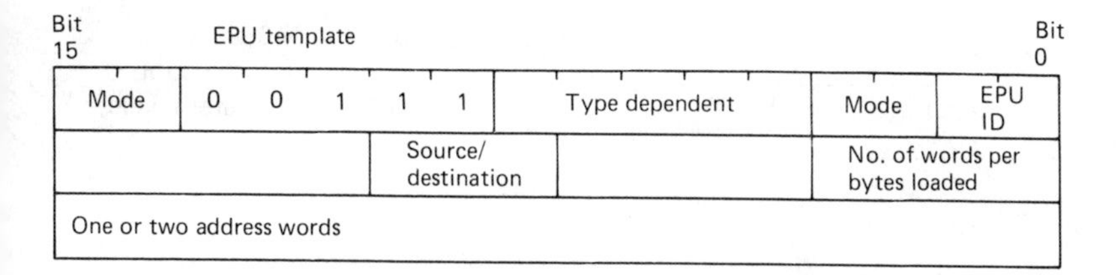

Fig. 2.9 Zilog EPU instruction format

2.6.3 NS32032 slave processors

The NS32032 refers to its extended processing units as slave processors because the CPU performs all addressing and data transfers. The slave processors are connected to the address/data bus and use the ID byte (see Figure 2.10) to identify an EPU instruction. The NS32032 contains 3 bits in the configuration register which define whether custom, memory management or floating-point slave processors are fitted. If none are set, the EPU instructions will trap to software routines.

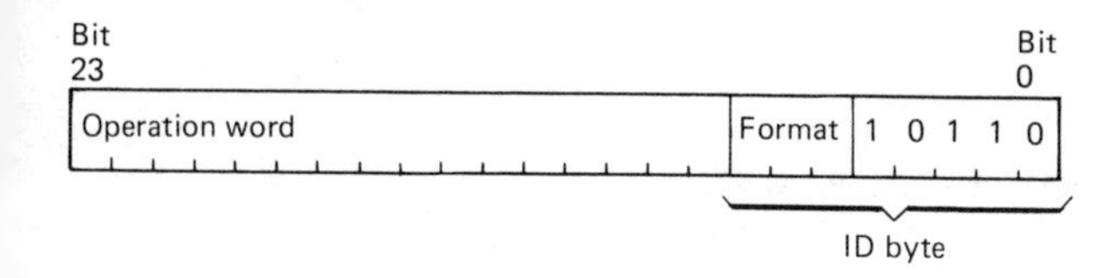

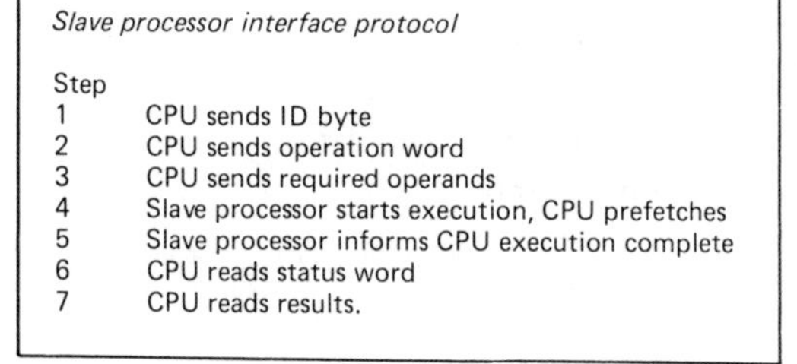

Slave processor interface protocol

Step
1 CPU sends ID byte
2 CPU sends operation word
3 CPU sends required operands
4 Slave processor starts execution, CPU prefetches
5 Slave processor informs CPU execution complete
6 CPU reads status word
7 CPU reads results.

Fig. 2.10 NS32032 slave processor instruction format and interface protocol

2.6.4 MC68020 coprocessors

The MC68020 coprocessors are peripherals on the address/data bus but operate non-concurrently in the CPU address space. Decoding logic is required to recognise the status line code to address up to eight coprocessors. Two identity codes may be user-defined: one specifies the 68851 Paged Memory Management Unit and one specifies the 68881 Floating Point Coprocessor, while the remaining four are reserved for future Motorola products. The CPU recognises EPU instructions and goes into supervisor mode, produces the appropriate status line code, and receives a data transfer and size acknowledge signal from the coprocessor. If the coprocessor is not fitted, a bus error occurs and the CPU generates a jump to a specific address where a software emulation can be located. The MC68020 coprocessor instruction format and register space are shown in Figure 2.11.

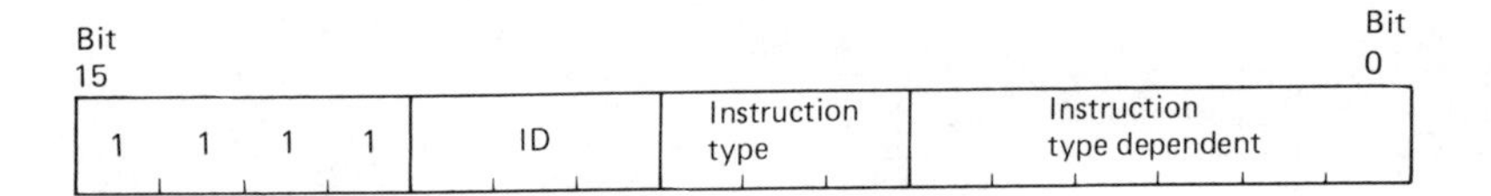

Fig. 2.11 MC68020 coprocessor instruction format and register space

REGISTER	USE
Response	by coprocessor to request action.
Control	to acknowledge or abort instruction.
Save	to initiate save operation.
Restore	to initiate restore operation.
Operation	to save coprocessor operation word.
Command	for general instructions.
Condition	for branch and conditional instructions.
Operand	passes 32-bit data operands.
Register	optional: register primitives
Instruction	optional: instruction address
Operand Address	optional: operand address

2.6.5 80386 coprocessors

The Intel 80386 coprocessors are connected directly to the address/data bus and the status lines to permit the coprocessor to track the instruction pipeline. The 80287 Numerics Coprocessor, designed for use with the 80286 processor, may be used with the 80386 but the later 80387 offers a 32-bit bus interface and enhanced floating-point arithmetic and performs at 1.8 million double-precision Whetstones/second compared with 0.3 for the 80287. (The Whetstone is a floating-point benchmark unit.) The coprocessor and CPU can operate concurrently but precautions must be taken to ensure that, for some instructions, the coprocessor has finished before the CPU proceeds. Synchronisation problems can be resolved by the programmer or by the compiler which must insert wait instructions after every ESC instruction. A trap mechanism is provided on the 80386 to emulate coprocessor functions in software.

2.7 Reduced instruction set computers

2.7.1 Introduction

The development of most conventional microprogrammed computers and microprocessors has resulted in more complex chips with large instruction sets which execute more microinstructions for each complex instruction, thus increasing programmer productivity. An alternative approach is to reduce the complexity of the instruction set, which results in a less-complex and less-expensive computer. Reduced instruction set computers (RISCs) can provide comparable or superior performance to complex instruction set computers by using a simple, regular instruction set which allows the combination of instructions to be executed faster than the equivalent complex instruction.

RISCs operate faster because the instructions are optimised for execution within one machine cycle while other computers generally require several machine cycles. RISCs normally use register-to-register operations accessing main memory with simple load and store instructions, therefore executing simple operations faster. Complex operations are converted into a series of simple instructions which run faster than with complex instruction sets. The reduction in the number of logic gates or microcode ROM required to decode and execute complex instructions makes a RISC microprocessor much smaller and potentially less expensive than a complex instruction set microprocessor.

To be successful, a RISC chip must have a high bandwidth memory to permit high-speed instruction execution and a compiler which can efficiently re-formulate high-level languages in terms of the more simple instructions. Research work at Berkeley University evaluated the frequency with which instructions were called, then tried to eliminate the dispensable ones and speed up the instructions most often used. Table 2.2 shows the frequency of some common instructions executed on a complex instruction set computer. A RISC tries to enhance performance by speeding up the most time-consuming operations in typical high-level programs such as procedure call/return and loop.

Table 2.2 Frequency of instructions executed on a complex instruction set computer

	% of high-level instructions		*% of machine instructions*		*% of memory references*	
Instruction	PASCAL	C	PASCAL	C	PASCAL	C
Call, Return + Set up, Save & Restore	15	12	31	33	44	45
Loop	5	3	42	32	33	26
Assignment	45	38	13	13	14	15
If	29	43	11	21	7	13
Other	6	4	2	1	2	1
Total	100	100	100	100	100	100

RISC central processor units typically use about 30 to 50 instructions compared with more than 90 for a conventional microprocessor (and 303 for a VAX 11/780 super-minicomputer) and require less than 50 000 transistors compared with more than 150 000 for a conventional 32-bit microprocessor. The development time required for a RISC microprocessor is typically less than for a conventional microprocessor; the Acorn ARM chip was designed in just 18 months.

One school of thought defines a RISC as having single-cycle operation, hard-wired (rather than microprogrammed) control, few instructions and addressing modes, and a fixed instruction format. Many RISC machines however do not meet all these requirements. Memory reference instructions consisting of load and store operations, and register-to-register operations which permit optimisation of compilers through re-use of operands, are typical in RISCs.

The control of a microprogrammed CPU consists of a control read only memory. Each ROM word is read on a specific clock cycle and each bit is associated with a particular processing function. By changing the microinstructions stored in the ROM, the instruction set is changed. Typically a microcoded machine has a fixed-size control ROM of between 256 and 4K words which is addressed by a microcode sequencer. This has the ability to use microcode instructions to generate the next address in jump instructions.

The instructions in a hard-wired RISC CPU (without microprogramming) are not taken from a fixed size ROM but from any location within the large virtual-address space of the computer.

2.7.2 Operation of a conventional microprogrammed CPU

Figure 2.12 shows the operation of a basic microprogrammed CPU. Data is taken from the main memory on the CPU memory bus into the arithmetic logic unit via the register file. Processed data results are returned to main

Fig. 2.12 Basic microprogrammed CPU architecture

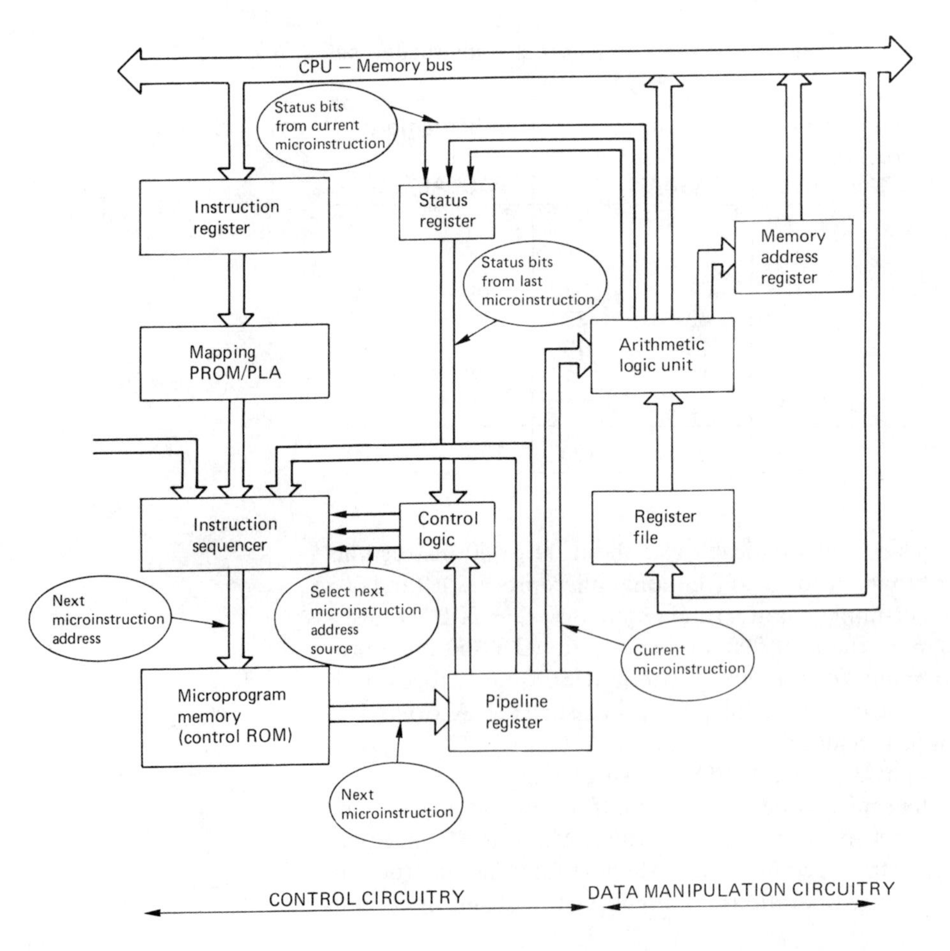

memory on the CPU memory bus and memory addresses from the arithmetic logic unit are output to the memory address register. Status bits are stored in the status register after each operation.

The control circuitry is centred around a control ROM which stores long microinstruction words (about 40 bits). Each microinstruction contains bits which control the data manipulation elements. Each microinstruction is accompanied by a clock pulse which causes a small operation such as a data transfer or a register-to-register add to occur. A machine instruction is performed by executing several microinstructions in sequence. Microinstruction bits therefore have to define the next microprogram memory address by causing the control logic to make the sequencer take inputs from the appropriate source.

2.7.3 Operation of a RISC CPU

Figure 2.13 shows the operation of the Ridge System 32 RISC. The instruction fetch and execution units are independent but share a common CPU memory bus. The instruction fetch unit pre-fetches instructions from the main memory or the cache and places them in a pre-fetch buffer. The instruction unit takes instructions from the pre-fetch buffer and performs the required operation, then stores the result in a register to enable subsequent register-to-register operations. Recently executed instructions remain in cache for quick access in loop instructions. Pipelining is used

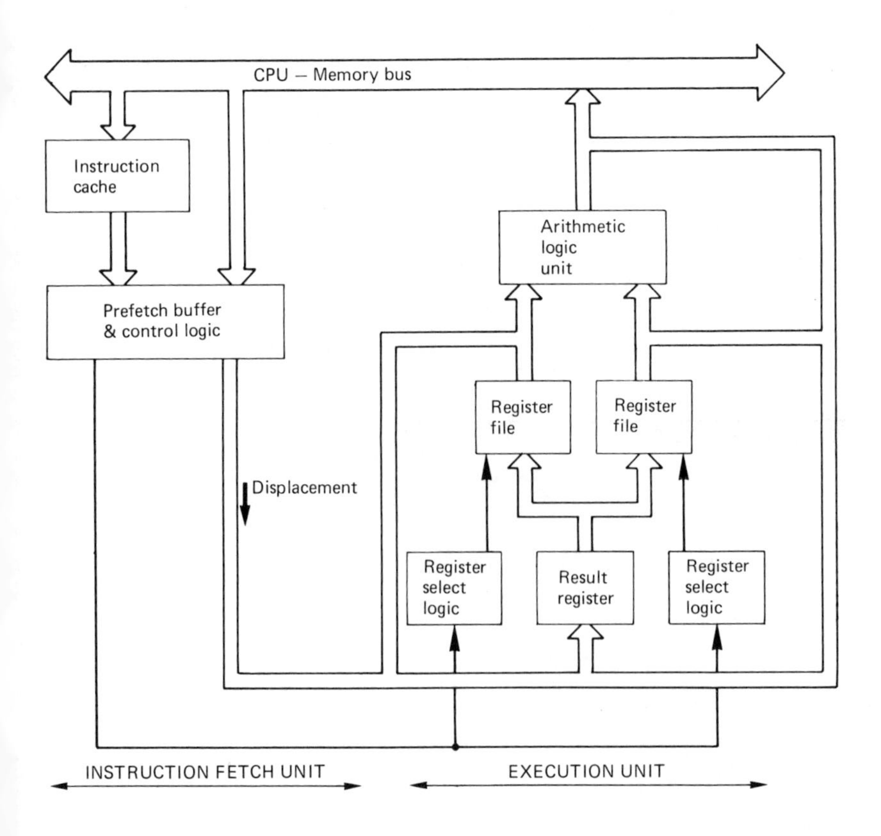

Fig. 2.13 Basic reduced instruction set computer architecture

to overlap fetch, decode and execute operations resulting in an effective rate of one simple instruction per cycle.

A branch-prediction technique may be used to pre-fetch instructions because conditional branch instructions can slow down processing when the outcome of a branch must be determined before the next instruction can be fetched. If a branch is correctly predicted, the next instruction is loaded into the pipeline but if not predicted correctly the pipeline must be cleared, and after a delay, the real target instruction is loaded.

The need to store variables in local registers in a RISC requires large numbers of registers, which can increase the time taken for procedure calls. One solution to this problem is to divide the set of registers into overlapping windows. Each procedure call is allocated a new window of registers and a return restores the window of registers to the set. By overlapping the register windows (low registers in the calling procedure *equal* high registers in the called procedure), the passing of parameters between procedures is speeded up and the need to physically move data is avoided.

2.7.4 The transputer instruction set

The T414 transputer uses a simple 8-bit basic instruction but multi-byte instructions can be created as shown in Figure 2.14. An evaluation stack eliminates the need for instructions to specify registers explicitly. The registers used and the way data must be moved between registers is implicit in the instructions.

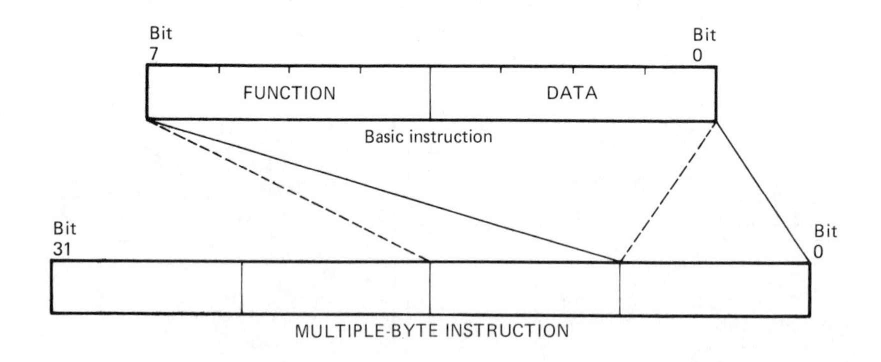

Fig. 2.14 Transputer single-byte instruction format

The four function bits in the transputer instruction define 16 functions, each with a data value up to 16. The 13 basic instructions include:

a) Load constant
b) Add constant
c) Load local
d) Store local
e) Load non-local
f) Store non-local
g) Jump
h) Conditional jump
i) Call
j) Load local pointer

Table 2.3 Summary of reduced instruction set computers

Model	*Manufacturer*	*Estimated Mips*	*ALU width bits*	*Year introduced*	*Technology*	*Country of origin*
T414	Inmos	10	32	85	CMOS chip	UK
ARM	Acorn	3	32	85	NMOS chip	UK
VIPER	RSRE	1	32	85	Gate array	UK
ROMP	IBM	5	32	86	Two VLSI chips	USA
SPECTRUM	Hewlett Packard	7	32	86	CMOS chip	USA
System 32	Ridge	2	32	84	Bit-slice	USA
R2000	MIPS	10	32	86	CMOS chip + Floating Point Chip	USA
R2100	MIPS	3	32	86	Board	USA
R2300	MIPS	5	32	86	Board	USA
R2600	MIPS	8	32	86	Board	USA
GaAs RISC	TI & CDC	200 (pipelined)	32	88	GaAs chip	USA

Two more basic function codes, prefix and negative prefix, are used to allow the operand of any instruction to be extended in length. The prefix instruction loads its four data bits into the operand register and shifts the register up four places. The negative prefix instruction is similar but also complements the operand register before shifting it up. Consequently operands may be extended to 32 bits by a sequence of prefixing instructions.

The operate instruction causes its operand to be interpreted as an operation on the values held in the evaluation stack. Up to 16 operate functions can be encoded in a single byte instruction. When prefix instructions are combined with operate, any number of new instruction codes can be created and software from earlier transputer types may be re-used on later generations which may use new instructions. In a typical program more than 80% of instructions executed may be of only one byte. A 64 Kbit control ROM is used to implement multi-cycle instructions.

The transputer form of RISC has permitted a 50 ns cycle time to be achieved and the processor occupies only about 25% of the chip area. While most RISCs use more code space than complex instruction set computers, the transputer uses *less* code space because of its single-byte basic instruction with multi-byte instruction capability.

Table 2.3 gives basic information on several RISC computers and microprocessors.

2.8 High integrity processors

2.8.1 Introduction

The Concise Oxford dictionary defines integrity as 'wholeness, soundness, uprightness, honesty'. There are four major aspects of integrity affecting microcomputers:

a) Fault tolerance.
b) Predictable performance for safety critical applications.
c) Memory protection in multi-user/multi-tasking systems.
d) Security protection mechanisms to partition information within a system.

2.8.2 Fault tolerance

Fault tolerance in a computer system has the ultimate goal of increasing the probability that a task or process will be successfully completed. This can be achieved in two ways:

1 By increasing the electronic reliability of the equipment using redundant components to bypass failed components.
2 By altering the task or process when a failure has been detected with the objective of reducing the likelihood of a disaster.

The use of fault tolerant computer systems is now spreading from expensive military or air traffic control systems to many commercial applications such as on-line transaction processing, and a number of relatively inexpensive multi-microprocessor systems are now available to meet this requirement.

There are three main approaches to fault tolerance:

1 The *software-based approach* as used originally by Tandem. The application software must provide resilience with an overhead of up to 30% in processor loading but there are few redundant hardware components.
2 *Hardware-based* fault tolerance using redundant hardware but imposing no constraints on the application software.
3 The use of *back-to-back duplicate processors* of conventional design in a loosely coupled configuration. This is not the most cost effective and efficient solution and often constrains application software.

The use of hardware-based fault tolerance using multiple microcomputers is becoming the favoured approach to fault tolerance because the cost of components is falling rapidly and the relative cost of software production is increasing.

To configure a fault-tolerant multi-micro computer system, a mechanism for checking the output of each processor is required. This may be a separate comparator board, perhaps performing a majority vote of three processor boards, or it may make use of less-expensive internal error detection facilities on the computer boards.

Another requirement in a fault-tolerant system is to transfer the peripherals and system interfaces from a failed processor to its replacement processor. This can introduce a large amount of switching circuitry or can use a single vulnerable bus. A fault-tolerant configuration of T414 transputers, shown in Figure 2.15, takes advantage of the Error Out signal on the T414 and the transputer serial links to switch peripherals and system interfaces between computer boards. The use of the parallel processing capability

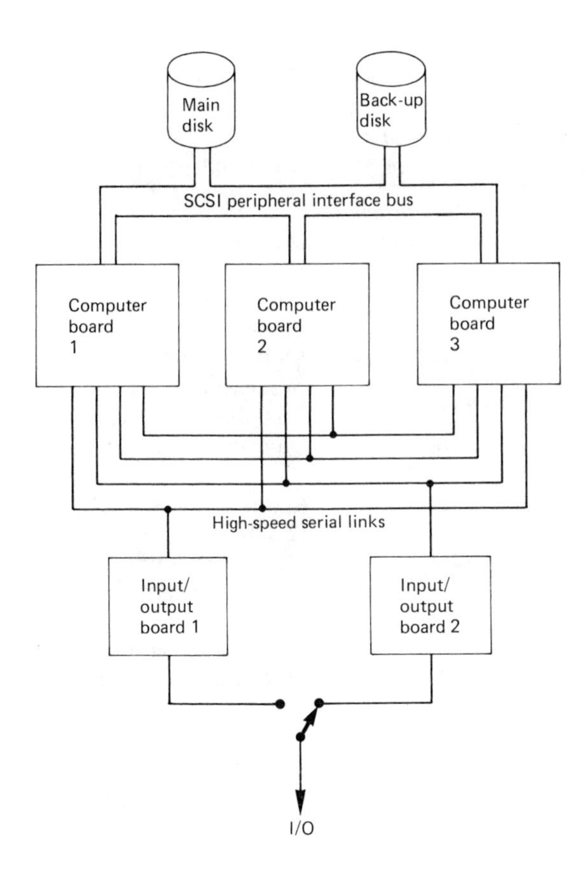

Fig. 2.15 A transputer-based fault-tolerant system

of the transputer also makes it possible to redistribute processing tasks between processors when part of the system fails, thus giving graceful degradation in system capability and taking advantage of the full system's performance when all processors are available.

Data integrity may be ensured in computer systems by adding parity bits, checksums, or error detection and correction codes to the data before storage or transmission and subsequently checking the redundant code for corruption.

Table 2.4 gives basic information on several fault-tolerant computers.

2.8.3 Safety critical applications

It has long been realised that commercial microprocessors have several failings for safety critical applications:

a) The instruction sets are not fully defined and unpredictable actions can occur. Particular problems occur with carry and overflow functions.

b) Chips, said to be second sources of the same type and available from different manufacturers, can have functional differences.

c) Later versions of the same chip may have changes in internal details, introduced to correct errors or improve performance, without notifying the user.

d) In the race to improve functionality, instruction sets and internal

Table 2.4 Summary of fault tolerant computers

Model	*Manufacturer*	*Estimated Mips*	*Date introduced*	*Maximum memory* (bytes)	*Architecture*
FT200	Stratus	0.9	82	8M/node	
FT250	Stratus	0.9–2	85	8M/node	Multiple 68000 processors (2–4)
XA400	Stratus	2	84	8M/node	Multiple 68010 processors
XA600	Stratus	3	84	16M/node	Multiple 68010 processors
3B20D	AT&T	1.0			Dual (hot standby)
3200 Resilient	Concurrent (Perkin-Elmer)	4 (Single CPU)	82	16M	Dual 32-bit processors
Eternity	Tolerant Systems Inc	1+	85	12M	Redundant NS32032 (2–20)
Non Stop 1+	Tandem	1.4–11.2	86	2M	Multiple redundant 16-bit processors
Non Stop EXT	Tandem	1.6–3.2	85	32M	(2–4) multiple redundant 16-bit processors
Non Stop 2	Tandem	1.6–12.8	81	128M	(2–4) multiple redundant 16-bit processors
Non Stop TXP	Tandem	4–32	83	256M	Multiple redundant 32-bit processors
Reliant 2	No Halt	0.6–4	85	2–16M	Multiple 8086 (4–18)
300 XR	Parallel	0.9+	85	16M	Multiple 68010

architectures become extremely complicated which can result in unpredictable behaviour.

In order to specify the operation of software and microprocessors in a more rigorous way, several formal design methods and tools have been developed including LCF-LSM (Logic of Computable Functions, Logic of Sequential Machines) produced by the University of Cambridge Computing Laboratory. LCF-LSM has been used to define the arithmetic of a special 32-bit microprocessor developed for safety critical applications by the Royal Signals and Radar Establishment (UK), known as VIPER. A special structured assembly language (VISTA) has also been developed and a program validation facility has been set up.

The VIPER design has been implemented on a gate array containing 200–300 latches and 2000–3000 combinatory cells. A fully ruggedised version is expected to be available to industry in mid-1989. The VIPER architecture is very simple, containing an accumulator (A), two index registers (X, Y) and a program counter (P) as shown in Figure 2.16. Register B holds the results of the carry and compare functions and a STOP signal is generated if an illegal operation, invalid output or out-of-range address is generated. No interrupts are provided and all software will be validated before use making a STOP signal an indication of disastrous failure of the system.

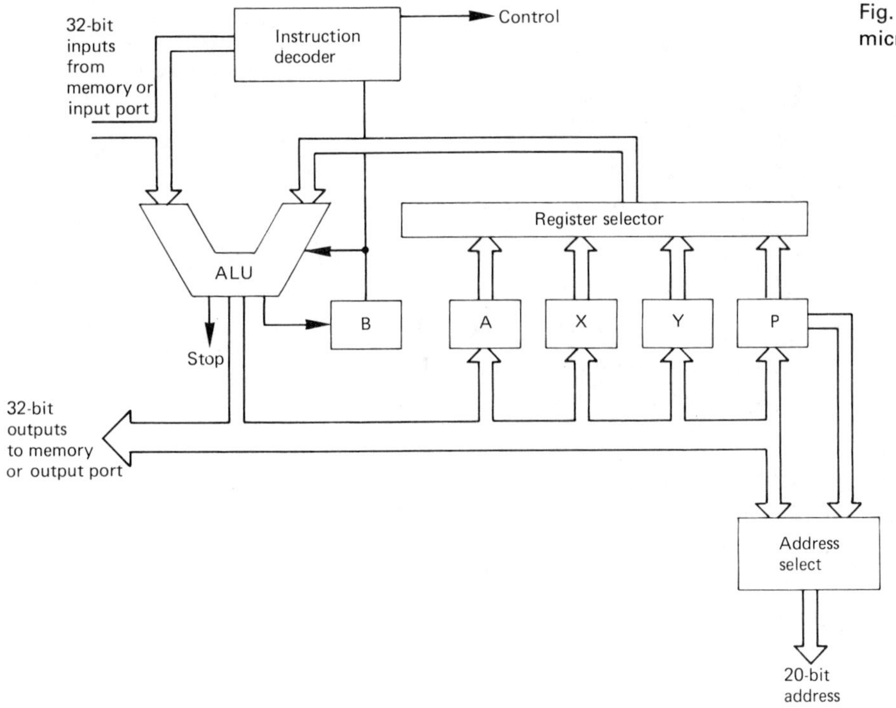

Fig. 2.16 The VIPER 32-bit microprocessor architecture

2.8.4 Memory protection

Multi-user and multi-task computer systems are susceptible to corruption of data belonging to one task or user by another task or user. System crashes frequently result from the processor jumping out of program and accidentally corrupting program or data before halting or entering an endless loop of instructions. A particular problem with multi-user systems is the unauthorised access of one user to data belonging to another user. A banking system for example would find this situation unacceptable. Some of the 32-bit microprocessors have implemented a memory protection mechanism to reduce the occurrence of these unwanted actions.

Two main forms of *error containment* are found in microprocessors:

1 Access attribute checking before access is granted to a particular task or to ensure that instruction and data segments are accessed only at the appropriate time in the instruction cycle. Typically, each task in a multi-task system has both a private and a shared memory space.
2 A ring structure of hierarchical privilege levels to prevent errors from the more error-prone outer levels of application-related software corrupting the more trustworthy and crucial software at the centre. (Sometimes referred to as firewalls.)

A four-level hierarchical memory protection scheme as used in the Intel 80386 is shown in Figure 2.17. This is an extension of the user and supervisor

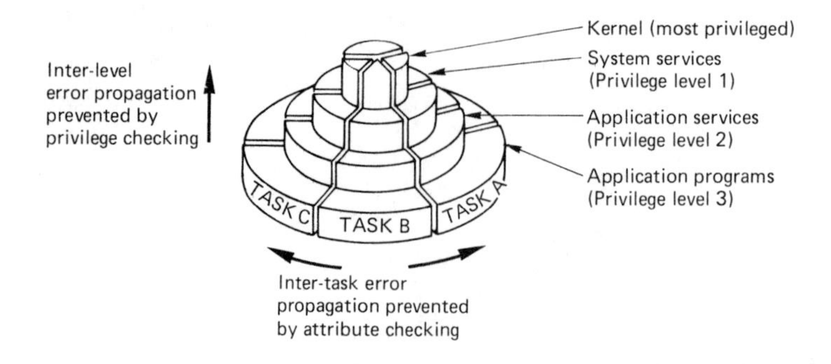

Fig. 2.17 Memory protection by task/user and privilege level

privilege modes commonly used by minicomputers. The 80386 controls access to both data and procedures between levels of a task using two rules:

a) Data stored in a segment with privilege level P can be accessed only by code executing at a privilege level equal to or greater than P.
b) A code segment/procedure with privilege level P can only be called by a task executing at the same or a lower privilege level than P.

The on-chip implementation of hierarchical memory protection and attribute checking, implemented in the operating system to prevent inter-task error propagation, can result in a high level of error containment. According to one estimate, 95% of system crashes in multi-user/multi-task systems can be avoided by these mechanisms.

2.8.5 Security protection mechanisms

Preventing unauthorised access to data stored in computers is a common requirement in defence, security, government and financial systems. The data is a valuable asset which must not be read or modified either unintentionally or by covert programming or by unauthorised users gaining access to the data.

Data security is usually provided by special operating system software which controls access to computer resources and data by using a set of tables listing authorised users and their access rights. In practice this approach is vulnerable because operating systems are composed of many complex programs which are frequently modified and contain errors. The more patches a computer operating system has, the more susceptible it is to exploitation.

To prevent the exploitation of errors resulting from software patching, systems have been developed with a validated security kernel which enforces the security mechanism and controls all access in the system. Trusted software provides the other user interface functions. Trusted software must undergo a checking procedure using an accepted verification methodology to ensure that it contains no errors or additional code within legitimate programs to trigger unauthorised actions (the Trojan Horse ploy).

A ring structure of privilege levels can be used to protect files and to protect the computer security kernel from attack. Ring numbers of files associated with each application can only be changed by authorised users and the security kernel may be employed to check every attempt to modify ring numbers.

Discretionary access to a secure computer system may be controlled by an access control list and all users will have a personal identification code which may be authenticated by an encrypted password. Encryption should use one-way algorithms to prevent the password being recovered in clear form.

The highest class of trusted computer system is referred to as class A1 in the US Department of Defense Orange Book. Computers of this type make use of hardware security protection mechanisms to enforce the separation of users with different security characteristics (that is, to provide multi-level security).

2.9 Digital signal processing chips

2.9.1 Introduction

A digital signal processor (DSP) is a system which accepts digitised signal information, performs some mathematical operations on the information, and delivers the result to a host system or output device. Most digital signal processing systems take in analog signal information using an analog-to-digital converter, process the data using a digital signal processing chip with associated memory, and output the results to a host computer bus or to a digital-to-analog converter (see Figure 2.18).

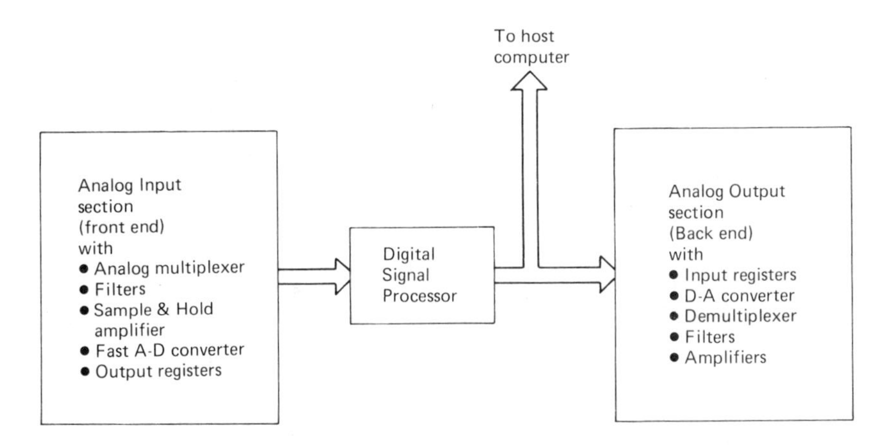

Fig. 2.18 A typical digital signal processing system

The first purpose-designed digital signal processing chip was the Intel 2920 which included analog-to-digital and digital-to-analog converters on the chip. The 2920 had four analog input channels, eight analog/digital output channels, and a 24-bit processor with 192 × 24-bit ROM words and 40 × 25-bit RAM words. Most applications of early DSP chips were to replace purely analog systems thereby giving better precision and accuracy.

Later DSP chips excluded the analog input and analog output sections because these were best implemented with different types of technology.

Table 2.5 Summary of digital signal processing chips

Model	*Manu-facturer*	*Cycle time*	*On-chip memory*	*Off-chip memory range*	*Tech-nology*	*Data bits*	*Estimated 1024-point complex FFT time*	*Year introduced*	*Country of origin*	*Special facilities*
TMS32010	TI	200 ns	1532 × 16 ROM 144 × 16 RAM		NMOS	16/32	42 ms	1982	USA	
TMS32020	TI	200 ns	544 × 16 RAM		NMOS	16/32	14.18 ms	1985	USA	
TMS320C25	TI	100 ns	4 KW ROM 512 W RAM	80 KWords	CMOS	16/32	13.2 ms	1986	USA	2 buses
µPD7720	NEC	250 ns	1024 × 23 ROM 128 × 16 RAM		NMOS	16	77 ms	1981	Japan	
µPD77230	NEC	150 ns	3K × 32 ROM 1K × 32 RAM	4 + 8 KW	CMOS	32 bit FP 24/47	10.8 ms (floating point)	1986	Japan	Floating point
MC56000	Motorola	100 ns	2 KW ROM 1K RAM	128 + 64 KW	CMOS	24/56	5 ms	1986	USA	Serial interface
DSP128	STC	320 ns	512 × 16 bits RAM	64 Kbytes	NMOS	16/32	70 ms	1984	UK	
S2811	AMI	300 ns	376 × 16/17 ROM 128 × 16 RAM		NMOS	16		1983	USA	
2920	Intel	400 ns	192 × 24 ROM 40 × 25 RAM		NMOS	25		1980	USA	Analog input/output
ADSP2100	Analog devices	125 ns	16 × 24 inst cache	16 + 32 KW	CMOS	16/40	7.6 ms	1986	USA	2 buses
LM32900	National	100 ns	—	64 + 64 KW	CMOS	16/32	13.4 ms	1986	USA	3 buses
PCB5010	Philips	125 ns	1.5 KW ROM 160 W RAM	64 + 64 KW	CMOS	16/40	6.85 ms	1986	USA	
TS68930	Thomson	160 ns	1792 W ROM 256 W RAM		NMOS	16/32		1986	France	
DSP32	AT&T	250 ns	512 W ROM 1 KW RAM		NMOS	32 bit FP 40	19.2 ms	1986	USA	Floating point
NSM6992	OKI	100 ns	1 KW ROM 256 W RAM		CMOS	22 bit FP 16/22		1986	Japan	Floating point
MN1900	Matsushita	250 ns	2 KW ROM 66 W RAM		CMOS	20/24		1986	Japan	
MB8764	Fujitsu	100 ns	1024 × 24 ROM 256 × 16 RAM		CMOS	16/26		1984	Japan	

Instead they concentrated on increasing the arithmetic speed of the processor, adding more instruction ROM and data RAM, improving the bit manipulation capability and adding floating-point processing capability.

2.9.2 Survey of DSP chips

The most popular 16/32-bit DSP chips were the Texas Instruments TMS32010 and NEC μPD7720. The TMS32010 has a 16-bit data word with a 32-bit accumulator, 1536-word instruction ROM and 144-word RAM. The instruction cycle time is 200 ns giving an instruction execution rate of 5 million instructions per second (Mips).

Complex mathematical operations in the analog domain, such as differentiation and integration, are implemented by DSP chips as multiplications and additions. The speed at which a DSP chip executes multiplications and additions is therefore a good indicator of overall arithmetic capability. To achieve high-speed multiplication, DSP chips use dedicated multiplier hardware rather than software routines.

As shown in Table 2.5, many new DSP chips were introduced in 1986, some with 32-bit external data buses and some with floating-point arithmetic capability. The time to execute a 1024-point complex fast Fourier transform (FFT) is a good measure of performance for a DSP chip because it is a well defined benchmark for a typical application. The manufacturer of a DSP chip which has only 512 bytes of on-chip RAM may be reluctant to quote the execution time for a 1024-point complex FFT because performance will be lower than an equivalent DSP with more on-chip RAM.

2.9.3 The Harvard architecture

Whilst most DSP applications use fixed-point arithmetic and require only small amounts of RAM and ROM, the later chips include barrel shifters which speed up floating-point operations and bit manipulation. Many DSP chips, including the TMS32010, STC DSP128 and Fujitsu MB8764, use a Harvard architecture. The Harvard architecture is an enhancement of the von Neumann architecture in which the data and instruction memory have separate data paths, thus avoiding the single bus bottleneck of von Neumann processors and speeding up instruction execution. Figure 2.19 shows the basic architecture of a TMS32010 based upon the Harvard architecture but modified by the addition of a bridge between the program and data buses to permit crossovers between program and data memories.

The use of pipelining also improves processing speed and some DSP chips (MB8764 and DSP128) include circuitry which enables up to eight chips to be cascaded for higher performance requirements. The DSP128 can address up to 64 Kbytes of ROM off-chip but maximises the size of on-chip RAM making larger digital signal processing algorithms possible. The architecture of the DSP128 CRISP is shown in Figure 2.20.

The NEC μPD77230 incorporates both a 32×32-bit floating-point parallel multiplier and a 55-bit output floating-point arithmetic logic unit and is capable of over 6 Mips performance. Other DSP chips with floating-point arithmetic capability are the DSP32 and MSM6992. Floating-point

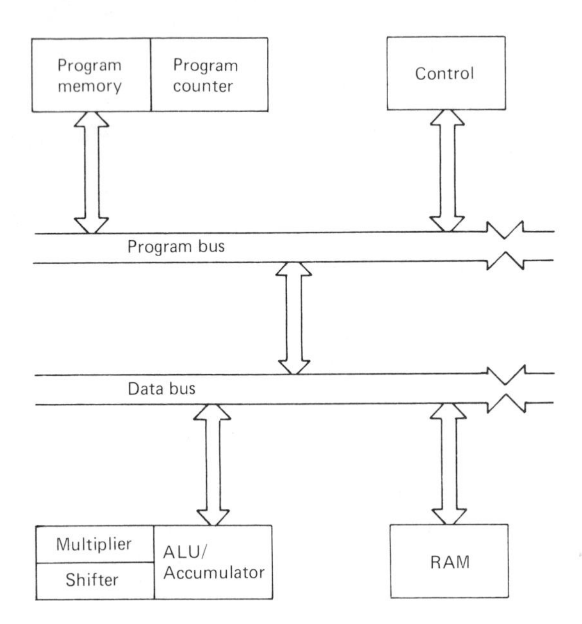

Fig. 2.19 Modified Harvard architecture of the TMS32010 digital signal processor chip

capability makes applications which require a wide dynamic range of signal value possible.

2.9.4 Special-purpose DSP chips

A variety of special-purpose DSP chips have been developed including the NEC μPD7281 dataflow processor which may be used for image processing in loops of up to 14 μPD7281s connected in series. Systolic arrays can also be used for real time image processing or speech recognition where high processing power is required and global communication is not necessary between the processing elements. A systolic 'elevator' chip developed by Hewlett-Packard and the University of Strathclyde assigns an upward and a downward path to the bottom and top N/2 sets of input data for an FFT. The lack of global communication between elements in a systolic array makes the FFT difficult to execute but the systolic elevator assigns two separate arrays to the upward and downward movements.

Many other systolic array chips have been developed, some with built-in delay and arithmetic stages to execute particular DSP functions such as finite-impulse-response filters. A lot more work is required on suitable algorithms for systolic array implementation. Fault tolerance can be designed into systolic arrays using parity on inputs to detect faulty connections and transient errors. Redundant input/output linkages can then be activated to reconfigure the array without the faulty elements. Another approach to fault tolerance is to build redundant circuitry into each processing element and to compare the output of the redundant element with the output of the active element, subsequently re-configuring the array when a fault is detected.

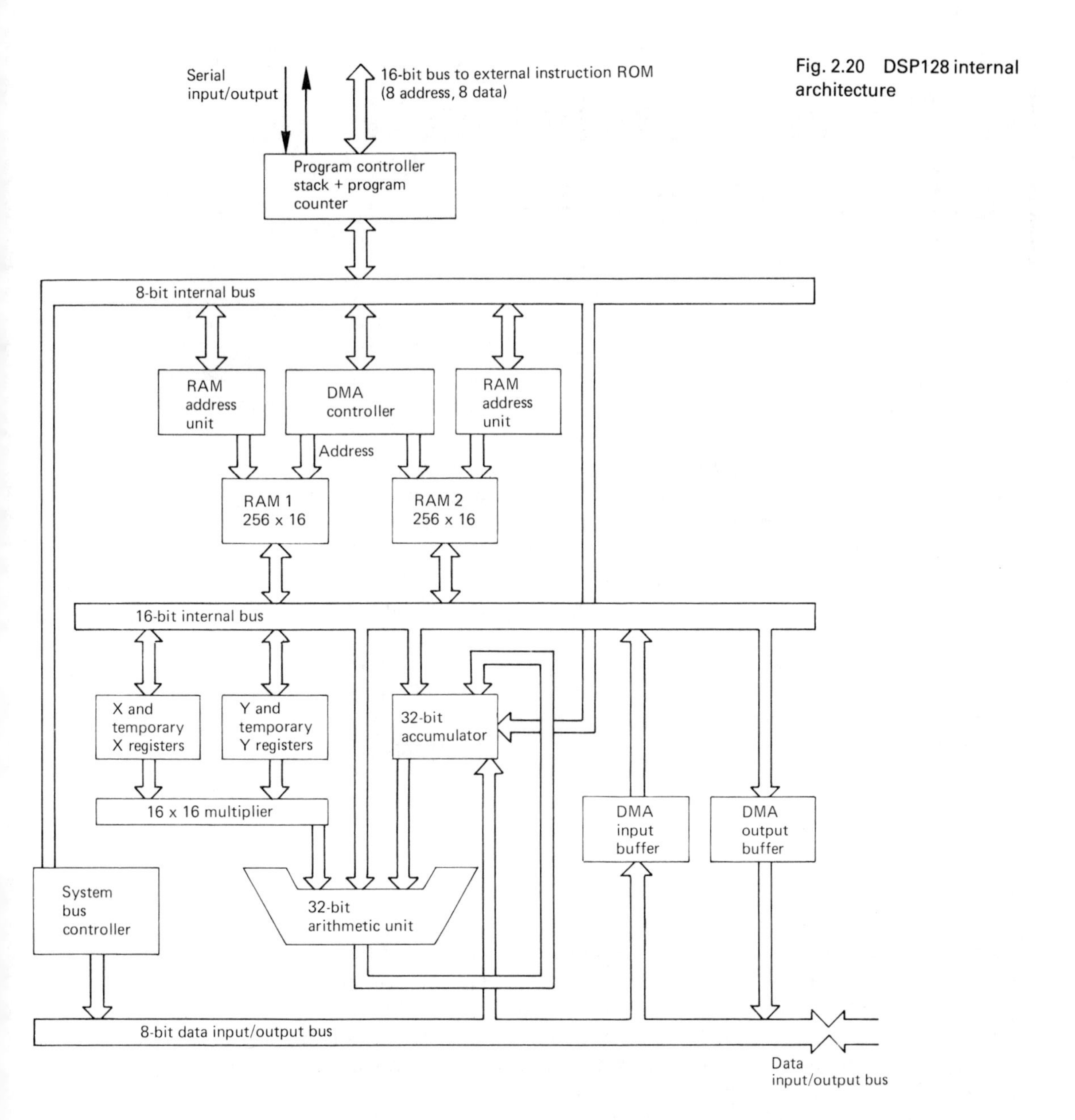

Fig. 2.20 DSP128 internal architecture

3 Survey of advanced microprocessors

3.1 Introduction

This chapter provides a description of each general-purpose 32-bit microprocessor currently on the market and a number of other advanced microprocessors currently available or under development. Table 3.1 summarises the more significant features of the general-purpose microprocessors. These all use the von-Neumann architecture although the T414 transputer has features which make it suitable for use in multiprocessor arrays for parallel processing.

Many of the figures given in Table 3.1 are approximate because they vary considerably from one application to another and, in addition, some manufacturers may introduce a series of enhancements which will improve the performance but also alter other parameters. Some aspects are not directly compatible between all types of microprocessor; the RISC aspects of the T414 architecture make comparisons with other processors imprecise.

3.2 NS32032

The NS32032 was the first truly 32-bit microprocessor when launched on the market in 1983. It is a development of earlier National Semiconductor microprocessors which had 32-bit internal architectures but 8 or 16-bit data interface buses. The NS32032 is both upward and downward compatible with its predecessors and is second-sourced by Texas Instruments as the TI32032. Each NS32000 series processor has the same internal 32-bit architecture and a two-operand symmetrical instruction set which is capable of working with bytes, words or double words.

Figure 3.1 shows the family of support chips configured with the NS32032; these include:

a) NS32201 Timing Control Unit (TCU)
b) NS32082 Memory Management Unit (MMU)
c) NS32081 Floating Point Unit (FPU)
d) NS32202 Interrupt Control Unit (ICU).

The 32081 FPU and 32082 MMU are slave processors. Unlike coprocessors which can decode their own instructions, the CPU decodes operations and

Table 3.1 Comparison of 32-bit microprocessors

FEATURE	PROCESSOR NS32032	NS32332	MC68020	Z80000	80386	WE32100	NCR/32-000	T414
Semiconductor process	NMOS	NMOS	HCMOS	NMOS	HCMOS	Domino CMOS	NMOS	HCMOS
Design rules (μm)	3.5	2	2.25	2	1.5	1.5	3	1.5
Clock rate (MHz)	4/6/10	10/15	12.5/16.67/20/24	10/18/25	12/16	10/14/18	13.3	12.5/15/20/30
Maximum performance (Mips) approximate	1.2	3	3.5	5	4	3	3 in native mode	6–20
Power consumption (W)	1.5		1.5	2	2.5	0.7	3	0.5
Pins/chip	60	84	114	64	132	132	68	84
Second source(s)	TI		Hitachi Rockwell Thompson-CSF		AMD Siemens			
On-chip cache/memory (bytes)	0	0	256 Inst. cache	256 Data+ 256 Inst.cache	0	256 Data cache	0	2048 RAM
On-chip interfaces	0	0	0	0	0	0	16-bit ISU interface	4 serial 20 Mbit/s
Address bits (multiplexed/not)	24 (mux)	32 (mux)	32	32 (mux)	32 (mux)	32	24 (mux)	32 (mux)
Addressing modes	9	9	20	9	24	9	6	2
Memory management On/Off chip: Paged/Segmented	Off/Paged	Off/Paged	Off/Paged	On/Paged/Seg.	On/Paged/Seg	Off/Paged/Seg	Off/Paged	None
Number of instructions	86	86	65	110	111	169	179 microinstructions	13 basic instructions 45 other
Instruction queue	8 bytes	20 bytes 3 stages	2 words 3 stages	6 stages	4 stages	4 stages	3 stages	4 instructions
General-purpose registers	8	8	16	16	8	9	16	0
Dedicated registers	8	8	7	11	24	7	22	6
Burst memory transfer	No	Yes	No	Yes	No	No	No	No
Dynamic bus sizing	No	Yes	Yes	Yes	No	No	Yes	No

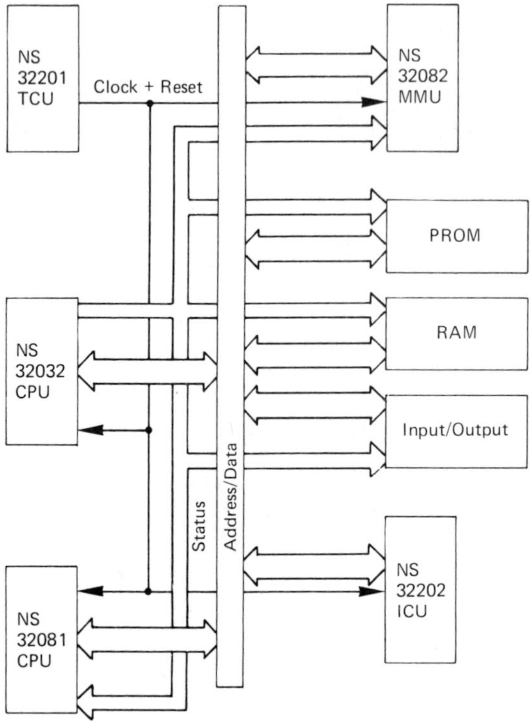

Fig. 3.1 NS32032 microcomputer configuration

stops while instructions or data are sent to the slave processor (without additional lines of program code).

Figure 3.2 shows the functional block diagram of the NS32032. The instruction set and addressing modes were strongly influenced by the VAX super-minicomputer reflecting the chip designer's emphasis on features which improve the efficiency of high-level language compilers.

The eight 32-bit-wide general-purpose registers can handle byte, word or double-word data and eight dedicated registers are provided to support the high-level language addressing modes:

a) Program counter.
b) Two stack pointers for user and interrupt stacks.
c) Frame pointer which allows access to parameters and local variables on the stack.
d) Static base register which points to relocatable global variables.
e) Interrupt base register which locates the dispatch table for interrupts and traps.
f) Module register which holds the descriptor address of the currently executing module.
g) Processor status register.

Support of stack-based addressing simplifies re-entrant code procedures. This is particularly useful for block structured languages such as Pascal.

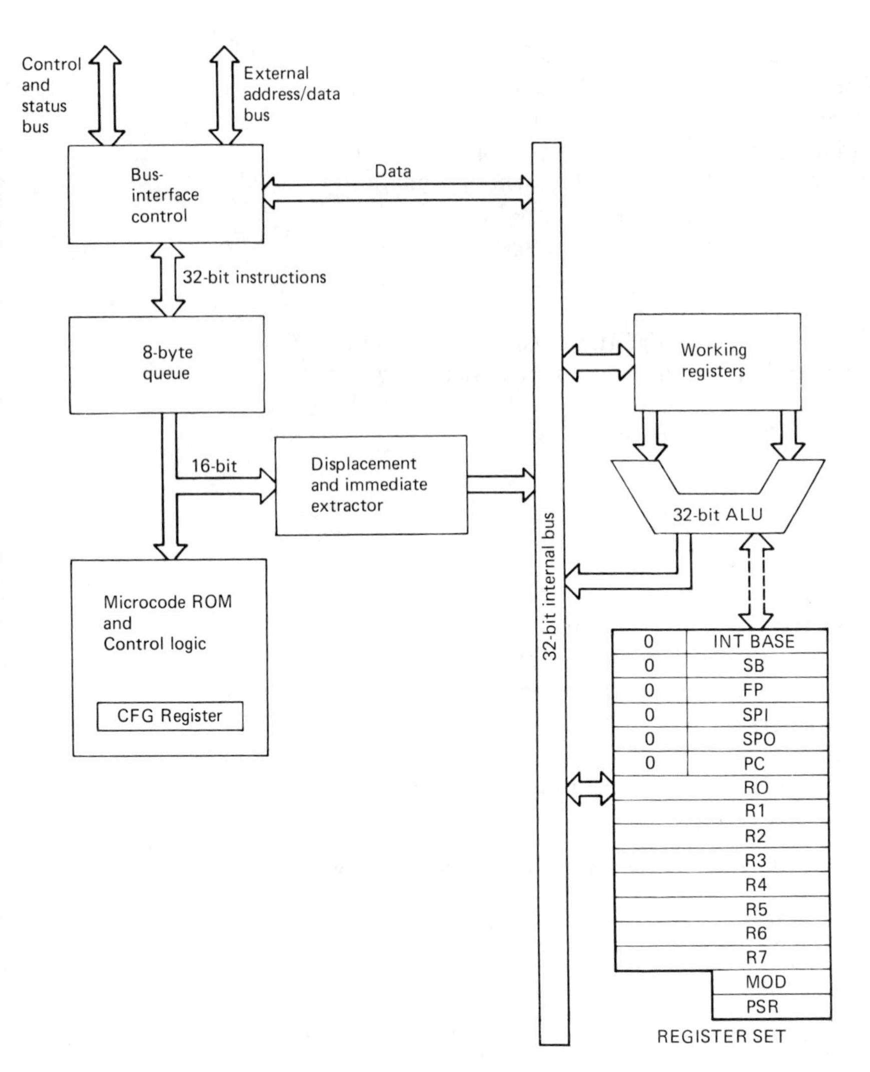

Fig. 3.2 NS32032 functional block diagram

A 16 Mbyte uniform (non-segmented) linear addressing space is used. All registers and therefore all addressing modes use the same addressing form, which simplifies compiler writing (because different types of code generation are not required for static variables, local variables and stack variables). In addition to the typical immediate, absolute register and register-relative modes, five memory addressing modes are provided to support high-level languages:

a) Memory-space.
b) Memory-relative.
c) External (allows modules to be relocated without linkage editing).
d) Scaled-index.
e) Top of stack (permits the selected stack pointer to specify operand selection.)

To protect the operating system, a user operating mode is available which prevents user programs from executing some instructions or accessing some registers. The alternative supervisor mode has no limitations.

The NS32082 Memory Management Unit maintains an internal cache of the 32 most recent translations and updates the cache automatically when a page that is not in cache is requested. Demand paged virtual memory management is provided which describes the logical address space in tables which are stored in memory. The MMU has automatic direct access to these tables.

The NS32081 Floating Point Unit uses the IEEE standard for single (32 bit) and double (64 bit) precision floating-point numbers and contains eight general-purpose 32-bit registers which may be accessed by the CPU in the same way that it accesses its own internal registers.

3.3 NS32332

The second generation of the NS32032 processor, the NS32332, was first sampled in late 1985 and a CMOS version, the third-generation NS32C532, is forecast for 1987. Each new generation has the same architecture but includes features which improve performance.

The new features introduced in the NS32332 retain complete software compatibility but are estimated to increase the performance to three times that of the NS32032. These features include:

a) A 32-bit-wide address bus which increases the physically addressable memory space from 16 Mbytes to 4 Gbytes.
b) An improved ALU with a barrel shifter and improved microcode to speed up address and index computing.
c) The instruction queue is extended from 8 to 20 bytes.
d) Bus cycle timing is upgraded to allow the processor to work at 15 MHz with a no-wait state external cache and to run normal bus cycles in 4 clocks with the MMU fitted.
e) A dynamically configurable bus width of 8, 16 or 32 bits depending upon the memory or I/O area addressed.
f) Burst mode bus transfers were added, capable of giving memory access in 2 clock cycles to speed up transfers to the queue or to slave processors.
g) The slave processor interface was given the ability to select 16 or 32 bit data paths to allow faster execution of slave instructions.
h) Two separate bus error and abort protocols were added using a separate bus line, and an instruction restart scheme was added.
i) The semiconductor technology was improved to permit clock rates to be increased from 10 MHz to 15 MHz.

The claimed threefold increase in performance results from a 50% performance improvement from the fast adder and improved microcode (which speed up execution of in-line code), a 30% improvement from the new bus interface and enlarged queue, and a 50% increase in clock speed:

$1.5 \times 1.3 \times 1.5 = 2.93$ times the power of the 32032

The NS32C532 is expected to increase processing power further by using a higher clock speed and including an on-chip cache memory.

3.4 MC68020

The MC68020 is the first member of the Motorola M68000 family to have external 32-bit data and address buses. It will execute all the object code written for previous members of the M68000 family with a higher execution rate because it operates at a higher clock rate (16 MHz compared with 8 to 12.5 for the 68000 and 68010). It has a pipeline and includes an instruction cache.

The MC68020 was adopted in many early 32-bit designs because it was one of the earliest high-performance 32-bit microprocessors to become available on the market. Earlier M68000 series processors had 32-bit user registers, operands and internal registers but the MC68020 added 32-bit data paths, two internal 32-bit address paths, a 32-bit execution unit, three 32-bit arithmetic units and an on-chip instruction cache. In executing MC68000 code, for a Pascal benchmark, performance of a 16 MHz MC68020 has been measured to be 3.2 times greater than an 8 MHz MC68000 with the cache disabled, and 3.8 times faster with a cache hit. With optimised MC68020 code, the 16 MHz MC68020 has been measured to be 4.9 times faster than an 8 MHz MC68000 with the cache disabled, and 6.6 times faster with a cache hit. (See Table 3.2.)

Table 3.2 Pascal benchmark performance comparison

	MC68000 code	*Optimised MC68020 code*
8 MHz MC68000	1	1
16 MHz MC68020 cache disabled	3.2	4.9
16 MHz MC68020 with cache hit	3.8	6.6

The instruction set enhancements in the MC68020 are mostly associated with giving 32-bit displacements and supporting 32-bit operands for a few instructions which did not already have them. The same virtual memory facilities included in the MC68010 are included in the MC68020 and a coprocessor interface has been added to provide instruction set extensions.

The coprocessor interface is based on external bus cycles. The coprocessor interface registers are memory-mapped into the CPU address space and coprocessor operation is controlled by a sequence of writes and reads of these coprocessor interface registers. Coprocessor instructions from the MC68020 may be passed to one out of eight types of coprocessor. The first two types available were the MC68881 Floating Point Coprocessor Unit and the MC68851 Programmable Memory Management Unit.

The MC68881 is rated at 400K floating-point operations per second, conforms to the IEEE floating-point standard (P754), and includes eight 80-bit floating-point data registers and a microcoded processor with a 67-bit ALU and barrel shifter. The MC68881 will operate at 12.5 or 16.67 MHz and is constructed in 2-μm HCMOS with 155 000 transistors. Heat dissipation is up to 1 watt. The MC68851 provides demand paged virtual memory management and a multiple protection/privilege level capability for operating system support.

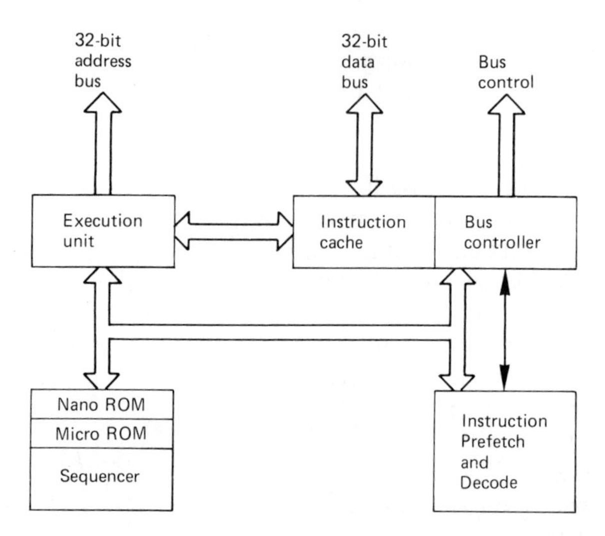

Fig. 3.3 MC68020 functional block diagram

Figure 3.3 shows the functional block diagram of the 68020. The instruction prefetch controller loads instructions from the data bus into the decode unit and the instruction cache. The sequencer control unit provides overall chip control managing the internal buses, registers and functions of the execution unit. Sixteen 32-bit general-purpose registers, a 32-bit program counter, a 16-bit status register, a 32-bit vector base register, two 3-bit alternate function code registers and 32-bit cache address and control registers are provided.

Seven basic data types are supported:

a) Bits.
b) Bit fields (string of consecutive bits 1–32 bits long).
c) BCD digits (packed 2 digits/byte or unpacked 1 digit/byte).
d) Byte integers (8 bits).
e) Word integers (16 bits).
f) Long-word integers (32 bits).
g) Quad-word integers (64 bits).

The asynchronous external bus is non-multiplexed with 32 address bits and 32 data bits. The processor supports dynamic bus sizing which allows operands to be transferred to or from external devices, automatically determining device port size (8/16/32 bit) on a cycle-by-cycle basis, eliminating data alignment problems.

Eighteen addressing modes of nine basic types are provided:

1 *Register Direct*
  Data Register Direct
  Address Register Direct
2 *Register Indirect*
  Address Register Indirect
  Address Register Indirect with Post-increment
  Address Register Indirect with Pre-decrement
  Address Register Indirect with Displacement
3 *Register Indirect with Index*
  Address Register Indirect with Index (8-bit Displacement)
  Address Register Indirect with Index (Base Displacement)
4 *Memory Indirect*
  Memory Indirect Post-indexed
  Memory Indirect Pre-indexed
5 *Program Counter Indirect with Displacement*
6 *Program Counter Indirect with Index*
  PC Indirect with Index (8-bit Displacement)
  PC Indirect with Index (Base Displacement)
7 *Program Counter Memory Indirect*
  PC Memory Indirect Post-indexed
  PC Memory Indirect Pre-indexed
8 *Absolute*
  Absolute Short
  Absolute Long
9 *Immediate*

The MC68020 has been employed in many CAD/CAE workstations. Twenty-five MHz versions of the MC68020 became available in 1986 together with 20 MHz versions of the MC68881 and the MC68030 which integrates the MC68020 and many functions of the MC68851 on one chip. A RISC version of the MC68020 is scheduled to be introduced in 1987.

3.5 Z80000

In contrast to the NS32332, MC68020 and 80386, the Z80000 design was not constrained by an overwhelming need to be upward-compatible with earlier 16-bit designs. The result has been an extremely advanced architecture using an advanced NMOS process thought to be capable of producing 25 MHz operation with smaller and less expensive chips than CMOS processes. Zilog have made embedded military applications a high priority for the Z80000 and plan to offer the Z80000 as part of large custom integrated circuits. The late introduction of the Z80000 has limited its commercial application.

The Z80000 is the only first-generation general-purpose 32-bit microprocessor with both instruction and data caches on-chip and this is claimed to generally improve performance by about 20%. Other features which increase speed of operation and reduce the need for support chips are a six-stage pipeline and on-chip memory management.

A hardware interface control register and six on-chip programmable wait-state generators make it possible to specify selected characteristics of the support circuitry including bus speed, data-path widths and the number of wait states. External bus speed may be the same as the CPU or half or quarter speed, thus making it possible to run the Z80000 on a 25 MHz clock with lower speed memory and I/O devices.

The Z80000 instruction set allows Z8000 programs which do not use the Z8000 privileged instructions, address and control field encodings to be run. Many of these reserved encodings have been used to extend the Z80000 register file, address range and instruction functionality.

The Z80000 has a general-purpose register file with sixteen 32-bit registers, a frame pointer and stack pointer plus a 32-bit program counter and 16-bit flag and control word. Nine other special-purpose registers are used for memory management, system configuration and other CPU control.

The instruction set provides a regular combination of nine general addressing modes with operations on numerous data types including bits, bit fields, bytes (8 bits), words (16 bits), longwords (32 bits) and variable-length strings.

The 32-bit logical address space permits direct access to 4 Gbytes of memory. Three modes of address representation are provided:

1 *Compact mode* which permits denser code for applications with less than 64 Kbytes of address space by using 16-bit addresses.
2 *Segmented mode* which supports either a maximum of 32 768 64-Kbyte segments or to up to 128 16-Mbyte segments. Address calculations do not affect the segment number only the offset within the segment.
3 *Linear mode* which provides uniform and unstructured access to 4 Gbytes of memory.

The memory management facility performs address translation and access protection for memory which is concerned with the operating system functions. Demand paged virtual memory allows programs to execute from a combination of primary and secondary memory. The page translation mechanism uses translation tables created in memory by the operating system. The CPU automatically refers to these tables to perform address translation and access protection.

The logical address space is divided into 1 Kbyte pages and similarly the physical address space is divided into 1 Kbyte frames. The memory management mechanism maps logical pages into an arbitrary physical frame and the information for the sixteen most recently used pages are stored in a Translation Lookaside Buffer. When the information is not available from the buffer the CPU uses tables in memory to translate the address and the information is loaded into the buffer.

The Z80000 supports four types of multiprocessor configuration:

a) Coprocessors
b) Slave processors

c) Tightly-coupled multiple CPUs
d) Loosely-coupled multiple CPUs.

Coprocessors such as the Z8070 Arithmetic Processing Unit work synchronously with the CPU to execute the same instructions using the Extended Processing Architecture. Slave processors such as the Z8016 DMA Transfer Controller perform dedicated functions asynchronously with the CPU. Tightly-coupled multiple CPUs execute independent instruction streams. Separate bus request protocols are provided to support slave processors and tightly-coupled multiprocessors. Loosely-coupled multiple CPUs generally communicate through a multi-ported interface using the interrupt and I/O facilities of the CPU.

Figure 3.4 shows the functional block diagram of the Z80000. The external interface logic controls bus transfers. The Z-BUS external interface is a 32-bit multiplexed address/data bus. The cache stores 256 bytes of

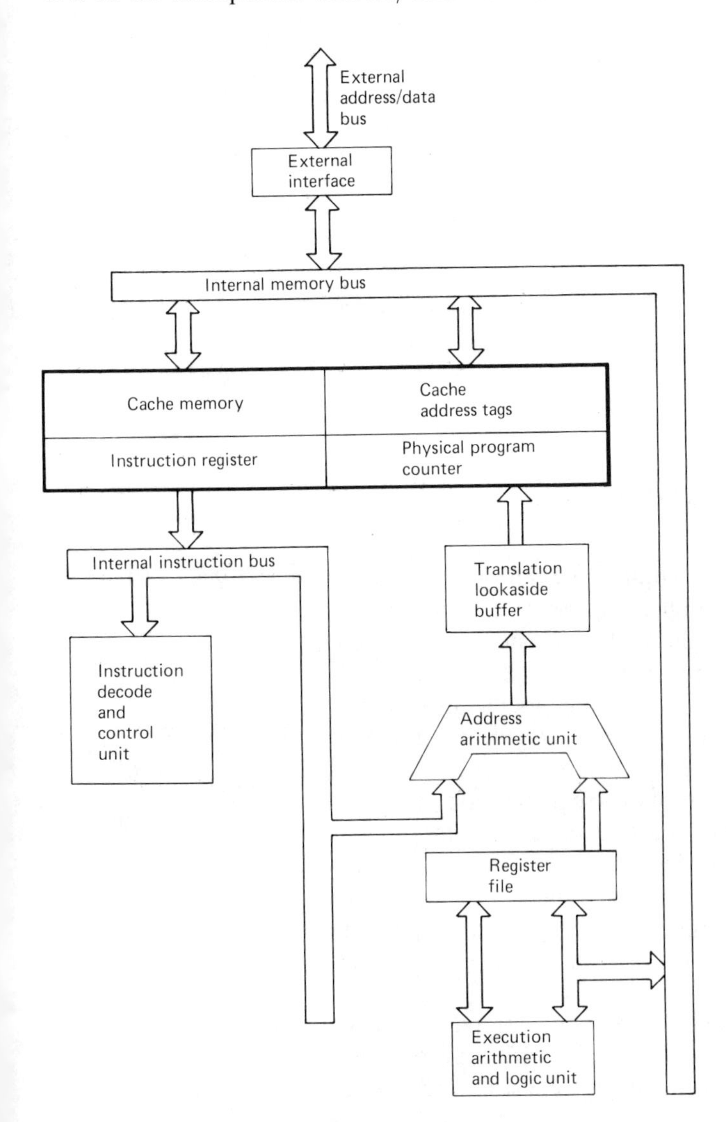

Fig. 3.4 Z80000 functional block diagram

instructions and 256 bytes of data, read from the instruction or data buses. The translation lookaside buffer translates logical addresses calculated by the address arithmetic unit to physical addresses for the cache. The address arithmetic unit performs all address calculations; it reads base and index registers from the register file, and displacements and direct addresses from the instruction bus. The register file contains general-purpose registers and special registers used to store values temporarily during instruction execution. The execution arithmetic and logical unit calculates the results of instruction execution. Two operands may be read from the register file simultaneously or one can be written. One path is multiplexed with a path from a memory bus. The instruction decode and control unit includes two programmable logic arrays for separate microcoded control of the arithmetic logic units. Its function is to decode instructions and control the operation of the other functional units.

3.6 Intel 80386

The 80386 is a 32-bit extension of the 16-bit 80286 architecture with additions including:

a) 32-bit registers and data paths.
b) Up to 4 Gigabytes of physical addresses.
c) Up to 64 Terabytes (2^{46}) of virtual memory.
d) 32-bit data bus with a throughput of up to 32 Mbyte/s using a 16 MHz clock.
e) More instruction pipelining.
f) More on-chip memory management facilities which support both segmentation and paging.
g) On-chip address translation cache.
h) Four breakpoint registers and other self-test facilities.
i) Higher clock speeds (12.5 and 16 MHz).

The 80386 has object code compatibility within the 8086 family making it possible to run the large number of applications programs written for the 8086, 80186 and 80286. It also has the ability to run existing 8086 series applications in a protected environment. For example, in protected mode, PC-DOS and MS-DOS applications can be run under a Unix, Xenix or proprietary operating system in a virtual 8086 environment. In real mode the 32-bit extensions may be used for higher-speed operation.

The on-chip memory management unit supports segmentation, in which large blocks of main memory are allocated for individual programs or data structures. The maximum segment has been increased from 64 Kbytes as on the 80286 to 4 Gbytes per segment. Page addressing is also supported with a fixed page size of 4 Kbytes. A paging cache stores the last 32 entries and, at 4 Kbytes per page entry, 128 Kbytes of memory may be directly addressed.

Segmented and paged, segmented only, linear only or paged linear memory addressing architectures may be implemented with the 80386. As shown in Figure 3.5 the memory management unit consists of separate

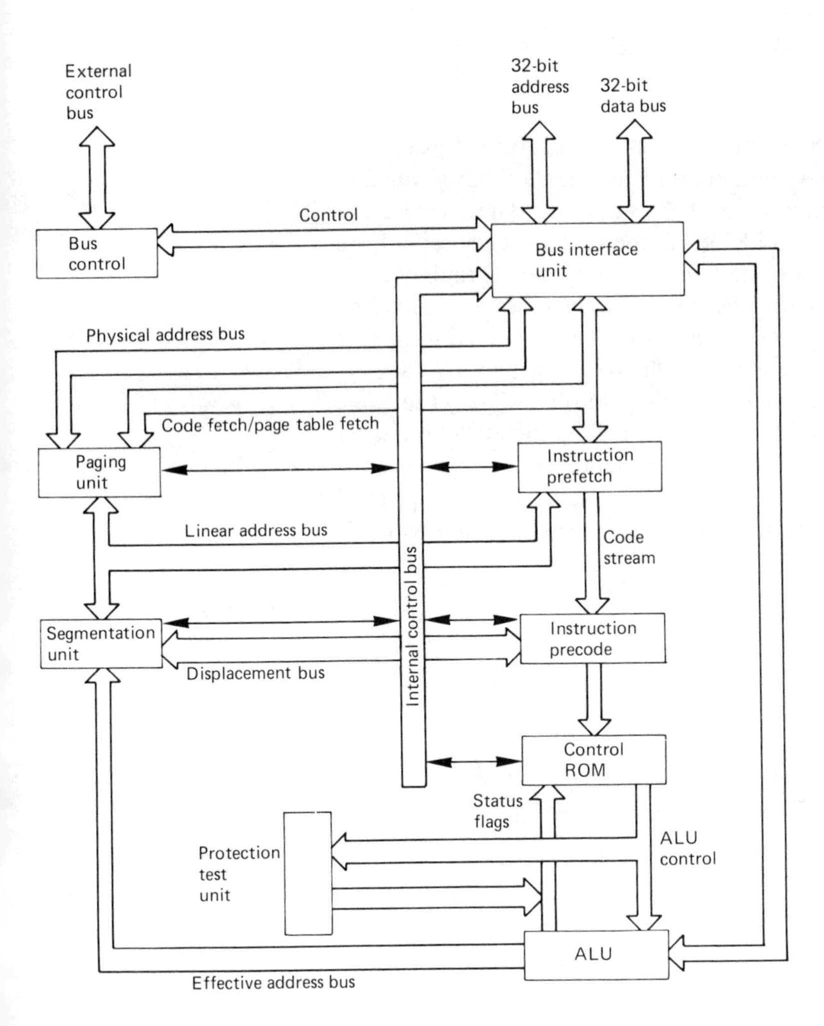

Fig. 3.5 80386 functional block diagram

paging and segmentation units. The paging mechanism operates beneath and is transparent to the segmentation process, to allow management of the physical address space.

The memory protection features of the 80286 have been retained and protection is supported in both the segmentation and paging units. Each task has a separate segment descriptor table and task-to-task isolation is enforced by hardware. Privilege levels for more trusted code are provided in the segmentation and paging units and each segment descriptor contains type codes which may be used to prevent data from being executed, code from being written into, and read-only data from being written.

The 80386 has 32 registers which have many functions including:

a) Eight 32-bit general-purpose registers
b) Segment registers
c) Instruction pointers and flags
d) Control registers
e) System address registers

f) Debug registers
g) Test registers.

The registers are a superset of the 16-bit 8086, 80186 and 80286 registers.

The bus interface offers address pipelining, dynamic data bus sizing and direct byte enable signals for each byte of the data bus. The coprocessor interface will support the 80287 and 80387 numeric coprocessors and the 82786 graphics/display coprocessor which converts high-level graphics commands into the necessary pixel updates and display functions including windowing. The 82586 LAN coprocessor may also be connected to handle the protocols and error handling aspects of high-speed local area networks.

All normal data types are supported including: 16 bit and 32-bit integer, bit field, byte strings, binary coded decimal; and when the 80287 or 80387 is fitted, signed 32, 64 or 80 bit real number representation.

Rather than incorporate an instruction and/or data cache on-chip, Intel decided to put a 32 entry address translation cache on-chip and to leave

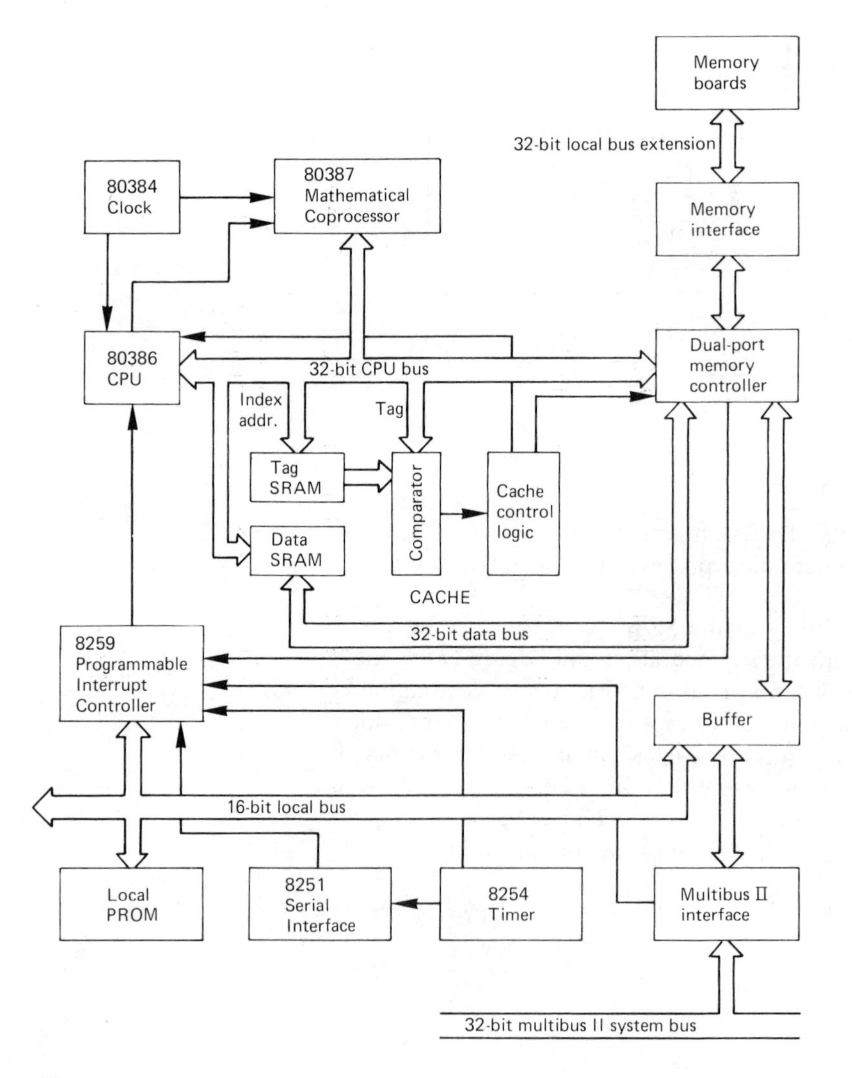

Fig. 3.6 80386 microcomputer configuration

the user to implement an on-board instruction/data cache. Intel claim that the available chip area is best used for segmentation and paging address caches instead of an instruction cache because about 55% of instructions require address translation. A special 2-clock bus cycle is provided for fast access to larger external caches for instructions and data. This compares with 3 clock periods for an MC68020 to access an external cache (or 4 clock periods with a memory management unit) and 4 clock periods for an NS32032 to access an external cache (or 5 clock periods with a memory management unit).

Figure 3.6 shows a microcomputer configuration with an 80386 CPU, 80387 mathematical coprocessor, an on-board direct-mapped cache memory and a dual port memory controller, giving the CPU and the Multibus II system bus access to the memory on the local bus extension.

3.7 WE32100

The WE32100, manufactured by AT&T, is a second-generation 32-bit microprocessor. Its predecessor, the WE32000, originally known as the Bellmac-32, was used by AT&T in its own products. The WE32100 has three times the speed of its predecessor and includes a 64-word instruction cache. Versions of the WE32100 were put on the open market with 10 MHz and 14 MHz clock speeds in 1985, followed by an 18 MHz version said to have four times the power of a VAX.

Figure 3.7 shows a microcomputer configuration constructed from WE32100 series chips. The WE32100 CPU has separate 32-bit address and data buses. The data bus can use word (32-bit), half-word (16-bit) or byte

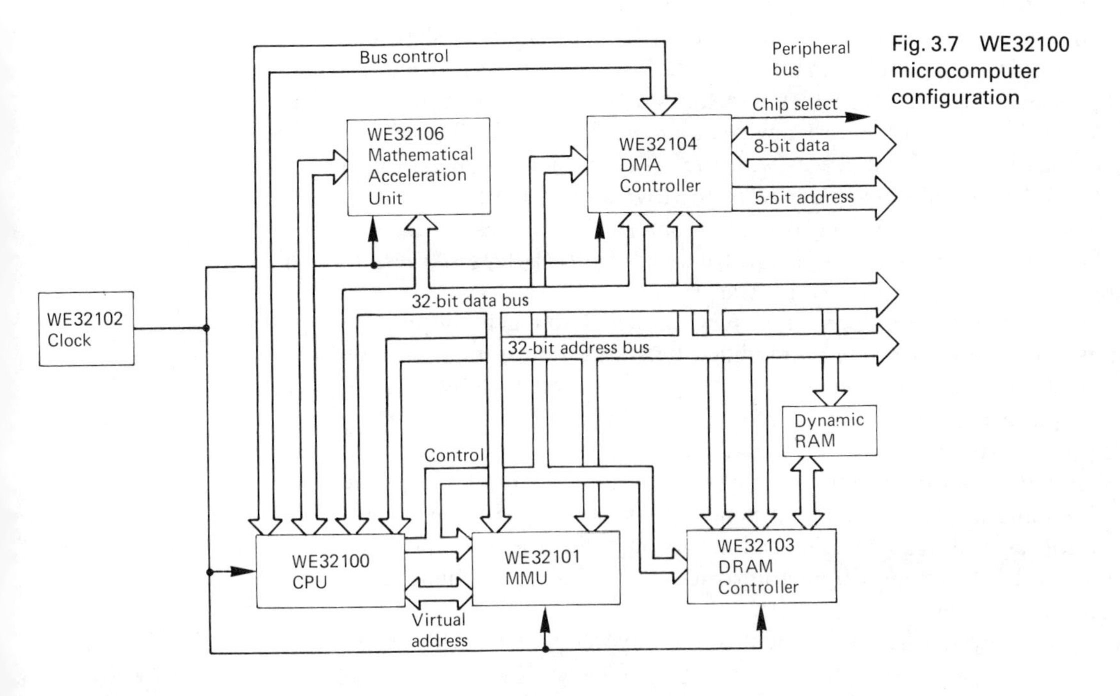

Fig. 3.7 WE32100 microcomputer configuration

(8-bit) transfers. Direct memory addressing capacity is 4 Gbytes and the WE32101 memory management unit supports a 4 Gbyte virtual address space with either paged or segmented virtual memory. The WE32101 also handles miss processing and other routine memory management functions. The CPU supports four levels of execution privilege (kernel, executive, supervisor and user mode) and fifteen interrupt levels.

The WE32106 Math Acceleration Unit carries out single, double and 80-bit floating-point arithmetic to the IEEE P754 standard at a rate exceeding one million Whetstone instructions per second. Addition or subtraction can take place in 1.4 μs.

The WE32104 Direct Memory Access Controller can perform high-speed 32-bit memory-to-memory or memory to/from 8-bit peripheral bus DMA transfers, performing a memory fill operation at 23.9 Mbyte/s.

The WE32103 Dynamic RAM Controller can be programmed to optimise memory speed and supports double-word and quad-word memory fetches.

The CMOS chip set is designed to minimise the device count and the power supply requirements. The system architecture is designed to mirror, in hardware, the model of a Unix System V process. A highly optimised C language compiler is available in addition to compilers for Fortran, Cobol, Pascal and Basic.

3.8 NCR/32-000

The NCR/32-000 is unique in its ability to be microprogrammed to emulate another microprocessor or a minicomputer/mainframe instruction set using an external microinstruction program PROM.

The NCR/32-000 Central Processor Chip (CPC) operates at 13.3 MHz clock speed with two non-overlapping clock phases to form a system cycle period of 150 ns. The functional block diagram of the CPC is shown in Figure 3.8. Two independent external multiplexed buses are provided: a 32-bit processor-memory bus which interfaces with the main memory, I/O ports and other system support devices and the 16-bit ISU (instruction storage unit) bus which interfaces with the off-chip microinstruction program PROM. The addressing range is 16 Mbytes of direct real memory and 128 Kbytes of direct microinstruction memory. The processor-memory bus supports data transfers at rates in excess of 50 Mbyte/s. Access to the bus is controlled by a priority arbitrator.

The register storage unit incorporates sixteen 32-bit general-purpose registers. These registers may be modified by status indicators to provide conditional operations at the microinstruction level and eight 16-bit microinstruction jump registers are provided. The 32-bit ALU will operate on nibble (digit), byte, halfword, word and file (string) data types with decimal, binary and Boolean operations. A three-stage microinstruction pipeline is provided and up to 179 microinstructions plus variants with register-to-register format are available. Special set-up microinstructions speed up execution of IBM System 370 microinstructions, including the building of program status words.

During each cycle, the CPC executes microinstructions from the three

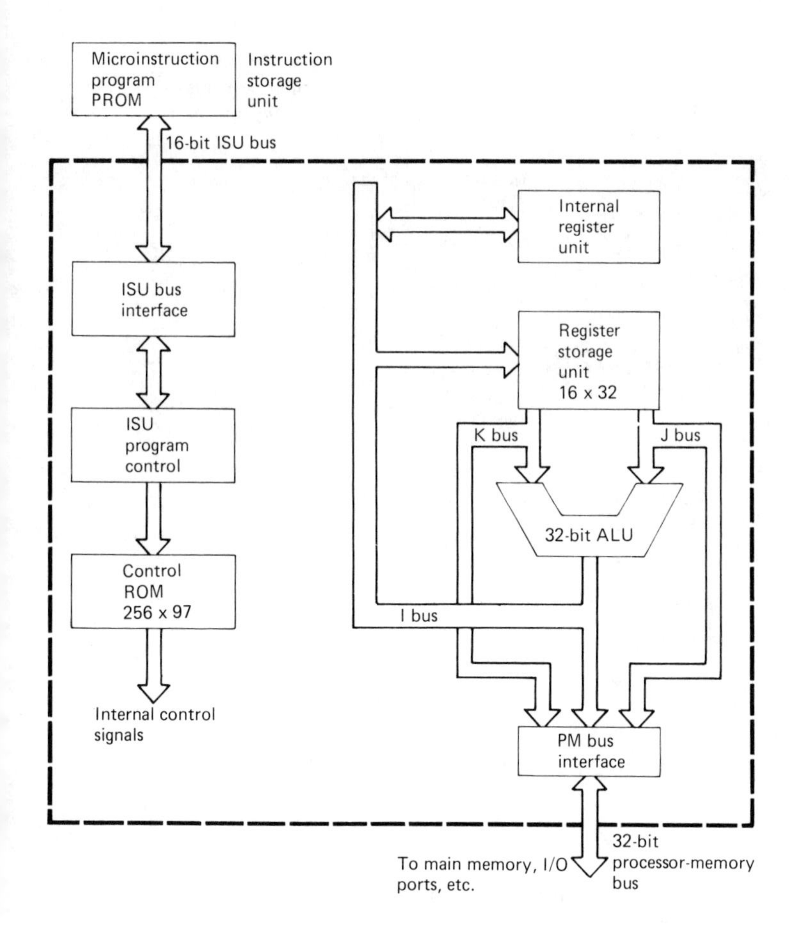

Fig. 3.8 NCR/32-000 CPC functional block diagram

pipeline stages, fetch, interpret and execute. More than 95% of instructions execute in one cycle. During fetch, the CPC control register contents are used as the address for the microinstruction program PROM and the next microinstruction is loaded into the instruction register. During interpret, the microinstruction is decoded to set up execution controls and to read the execution operands from the register storage unit. During execute, the operands selected during the interpret stage are processed, written into the register storage unit and routed externally over the processor-memory bus.

External transfers on the processor-memory bus use three types of cycle:

a) Real memory transfers (partial byte and full 32-bit word).
b) Virtual memory transfers (using the ATC for address translation).
c) External register transfers (primarily for I/O operations).

Figure 3.9 shows an NCR/32 microcomputer configuration. The NCR/32-010 Address Translation Chip (ATC) provides memory management functions for real and virtual memory, a time-of-day clock plus error checking and correction for system memory. Virtual memory management uses a dynamic address translation unit containing sixteen entries, each consisting of a 22-bit virtual page number and a 25-bit page descriptor.

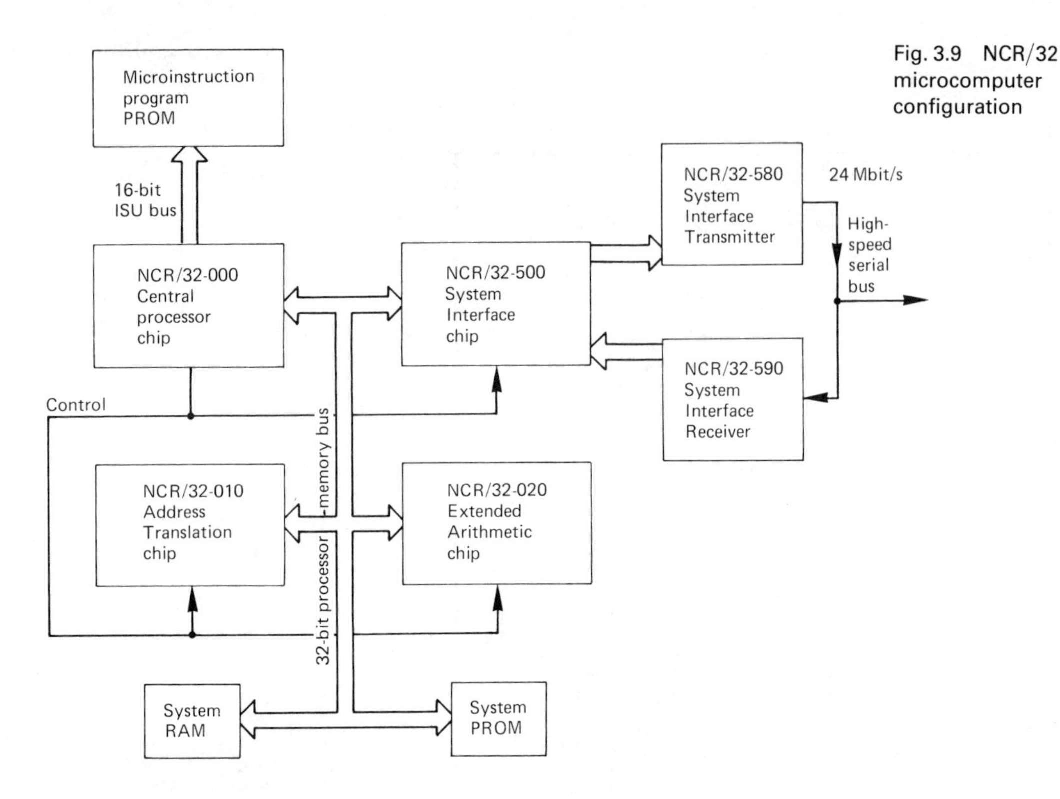

Fig. 3.9 NCR/32 microcomputer configuration

The virtual memory addressing range is 4 Gbytes and three page sizes (1024, 2048 or 4096) may be used with either a 24-bit or 32-bit virtual address.

Memory protection facilities are provided by eight access permit bits (four for privilege and four for non-privileged mode). A processor interrupt is generated by logic which compares the current virtual address with the address in the virtual monitor register to prevent data being written into the address in the monitor register. The time-of-day clock has a 4 μs resolution and is accessed by the processor as a 32-bit external register. Time intervals may be measured and an interrupt is generated on completion.

Single error correction and double error detection are provided for main memory using seven error correction code bits stored with each 32-bit word. If, on reading the data, the newly calculated error correction code bits do not match the stored bits, a single error would be corrected but if more than one bit is in error a fault signal is generated and further memory references aborted until the error is processed in the trap service routine.

The NCR/32-500 System Interface Controller interfaces the processor-memory bus to slow-speed peripherals and long-distance communications. The NCR/32-580 System Interface Transmitter and NCR/32-590 System Interface Receiver chips may be used to provide a serial CSMA/CD communication network interface with a data rate up to 24 Mbit/s and up to 248 stations on a multidrop bus. The system interface controller acts as a DMA controller taking messages from a memory buffer, adding flags and CRC characters, and controlling the transfer to the system interface transmitter, byte-by-byte as a single packet. Channel selection, channel acquisition and CSMA/CD arbitration or retry are performed by the system interface controller and, on receive, it monitors the communication channels for messages addressed to its sub-system and stores the messages in the buffer after checking and stripping off the CRC.

The NCR/32-020 Extended Arithmetic Chip provides a complete set of IBM-compatible arithmetic operations including single and double precision binary, floating point, packed and unpacked decimal and format conversions. Floating-point addition, single precision, typically takes 1.6 μs.

3.9 Inmos T414

The T414 transputer went into production in 1985. The T414 differed from the later T800 in the size of on-chip RAM, 2 Kbytes on the T414 compared with 4 Kbytes for the T800. Both are 32-bit machines with a von Neumann RISC architecture but the T800 has a floating-point processor on-chip. As shown in Figure 3.10, the T414 has a 32-bit multiplexed external memory bus with a physical address space up to 4 Gbytes. Various memory configurations may be added including mixed fast and slow devices. Dynamic RAM refresh signals are available. Data rates up to 25 Mbyte/s may be achieved on the external memory bus.

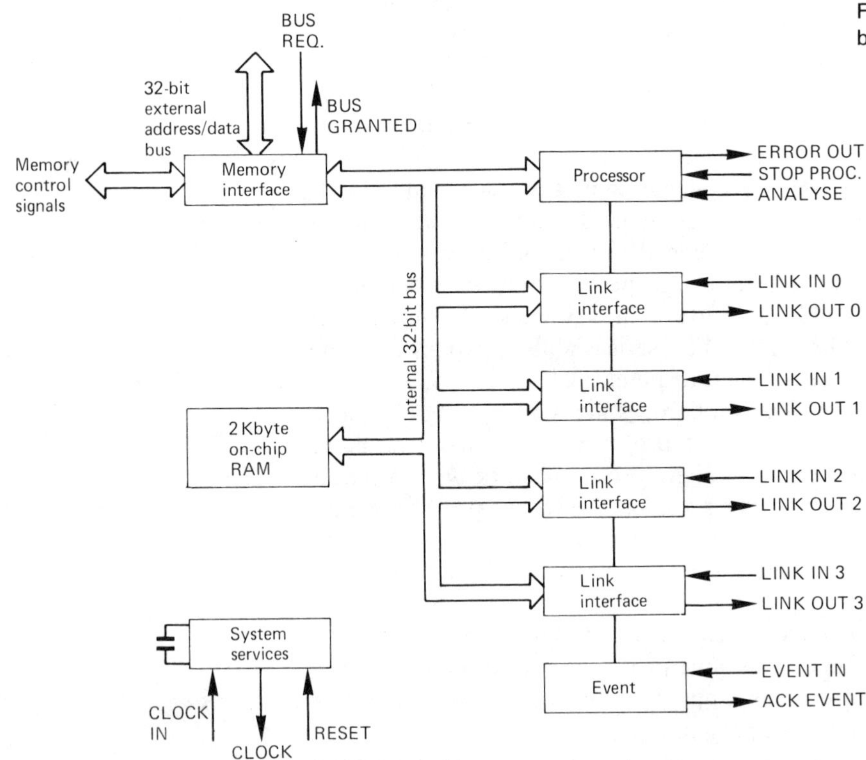

Fig. 3.10 T414 functional block diagram

The transputer is intended for connection to other transputers or peripherals by the four communications links which are included on-chip. A DMA block transfer mechanism is used to transfer messages from on-chip or off-chip local memory through the serial links. The link interfaces and the processor operate concurrently without significantly reducing the power of the processor. The use of point-to-point serial links to interconnect computers avoids the need for arbitration as required on multiprocessor buses, avoids capacitive loading problems, and prevents the communications bandwidth saturating as more processors are added to the system.

Each serial link provides two channels, one in each direction. Data is transmitted at 10 or 20 Mbit/s as a series of bytes, each byte preceded by the two 1 bits and followed by a 0 bit. After transmitting a data byte, the sending transputer waits until a two-bit acknowledge signal is received to signify that the receiving transputer is ready to receive more data. Communication is possible between independently clocked systems if the clock frequency is the same.

A number of link adaptor chips are available to interface the transputer serial links to non-transputer devices or communications interfaces. Peripheral controllers may also be connected to the memory bus where they may access the whole of the memory space for direct memory access transfers.

No conventional interrupt structure is provided but equivalent facilities are provided by the two levels of priority which may be assigned to waiting processes on serial links and an event request input. To assist in fault detection and analysis in a multi-transputer system, an error flag is connected to an error output pin. System state may be preserved for subsequent analysis by connecting the analyse (input) pin to the error (output). The error outputs from several transputers may be connected to an OR gate and the output connected to the event request input of a system control transputer.

The transputer may be used as a single chip taking advantage of its 10 Mips performance and it may be programmed in a variety of standard high-level languages because it has been designed for efficient compiler operation. To take full advantage of the transputer's ability to be connected in networks or arrays to build high-performance systems, the Occam programming language should be used because it is able to exploit fully the concurrent processing features of the transputer.

Occam eases the design of concurrent processing systems using one transputer or arrays of transputers because a program running in a transputer is equivalent to an Occam process. Therefore, a network of transputers can be described directly as an Occam program. An Occam program breaks the task into a series of concurrent tasks, and each parallel task is then written as a separate Occam process including the points of communication between processes.

In a multiprocessor system Occam can be used to spread the load according to the resources available. The same program may be run on a single processor or on several processors simply by changing some configuration statements at the beginning of the program.

A transputer continues with each Occam process until it reaches a point where it needs more information from another process or has information waiting for another process. It then stops the process, stores the process pointer number, and puts the process into a dormant mode. The processor then continues with other processes until the information is available for the first process (possibly from a serial link).

If the processes are on separate transputers, each process proceeds until it is ready to transmit and then waits until its receiving transputer has reached the point in its process where it is ready to receive. When both are ready they will exchange data and continue. Some processes could be exchanging messages and continuing their part of the overall process independently of those which were in a dormant state. By this mechanism the vast processing power of a transputer array and the vast bandwidth of its communications links is derived.

3.10 Acorn RISC Machine (ARM)

The British personal computer manufacturer, Acorn, developed the ARM in 18 months to meet a need for a low-cost high-power processor for artificial intelligence and high-level language applications. The ARM, launched in late 1985, embodies the common attributes of a RISC:

a) A small hard-wired instruction set.
b) A heavily pipelined processor.
c) Context switching registers to handle interrupts.
d) A small chip size.
e) A large memory bandwidth.

The functional block diagram of the ARM is shown in Figure 3.11. The flow of data through the 32-bit internal buses is controlled by a number of separate functional units rather than a central microcode ROM. The instruction decoder is a programmable logic array in which the instructions are hard-wired and bits in the instruction word provide most of the control information. A heavily pipelined architecture and a barrel shifter permit the ARM to achieve 3 Mips. All instructions except for load-and-store multiple register instructions are completed in a single 150 ns multiple clock period. While executing consecutive register-to-register instructions one instruction controls the data path while a second instruction is being decoded for the following cycle.

The instruction set consists of 44 basic instructions which can be divided into five basic instruction types:

a) Register-to-register instructions
b) Arithmetic and logic operations
c) Single register load and store
d) Multiple register load and store
e) Branch operations.

There are no multiply or divide instructions. Each 32-bit instruction has a 4-bit condition-code field to define up to sixteen conditions on instruction execution.

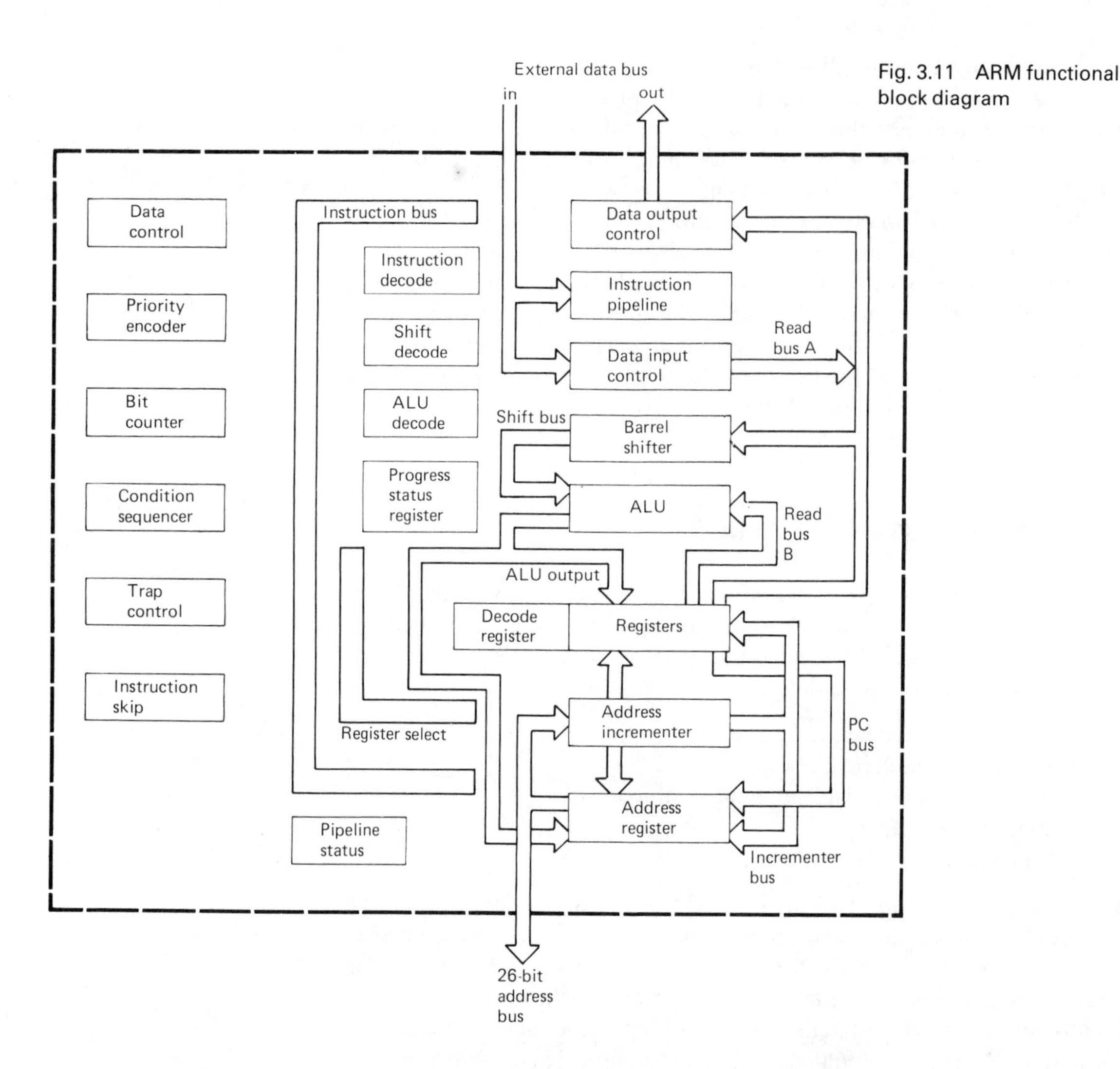

Fig. 3.11 ARM functional block diagram

The ARM has a 26-bit address bus and a separate 32-bit data bus to help achieve an 18 Mbyte/s memory bandwidth, and an optional burst mode can increase data transfer rates by another 30% compared with page mode. The addressing range is 64 Mbytes. The ARM has two addressing modes:

a) Base relative, which permits either a 12-bit immediate value or a second register to be used as the offset.
b) Program relative.

The ARM has twenty-five 32-bit registers but only 16 registers are available to the programmer. During interrupts the other registers are used to simulate a DMA channel without saving the user's registers. Register 14 is the subroutine link register and register 15 contains the program counter and processor status word. There are two data types: 8-bit bytes and 32-bit words which must be aligned to a multiple of 4 bytes.

3.11 NEC μPD7281

The μPD7281 image pipelined processor is a high-speed digital signal processor specifically designed for digital image processing applications such as restoration, enhancement, compression and pattern recognition but it may also be employed to implement fast Fourier transforms or numeric processing. It is also significant because it is the first VLSI device to embody a practical dataflow architecture. The μPD7281 employs a token-based dataflow and pipelined architecture to achieve a processing speed of about 5 Mips and several μPD7281 chips may be wired in series to produce an almost linear increase in processing power.

The μPD7281 is designed to be used as a peripheral to a host processor, relieving the host of time-intensive computations. A minimum amount of interface hardware is required to configure up to fourteen μPD7281 chips in a multiprocessor system. Each chip is given a module number during reset and the output data bus of one chip is connected to the input data bus of the next, while the $\overline{\text{OREQ}}$ and $\overline{\text{OACK}}$ output handshake lines are cross-connected to the equivalent input handshake lines on the next chip.

The functional block diagram of the μPD7281 is shown in Figure 3.12.

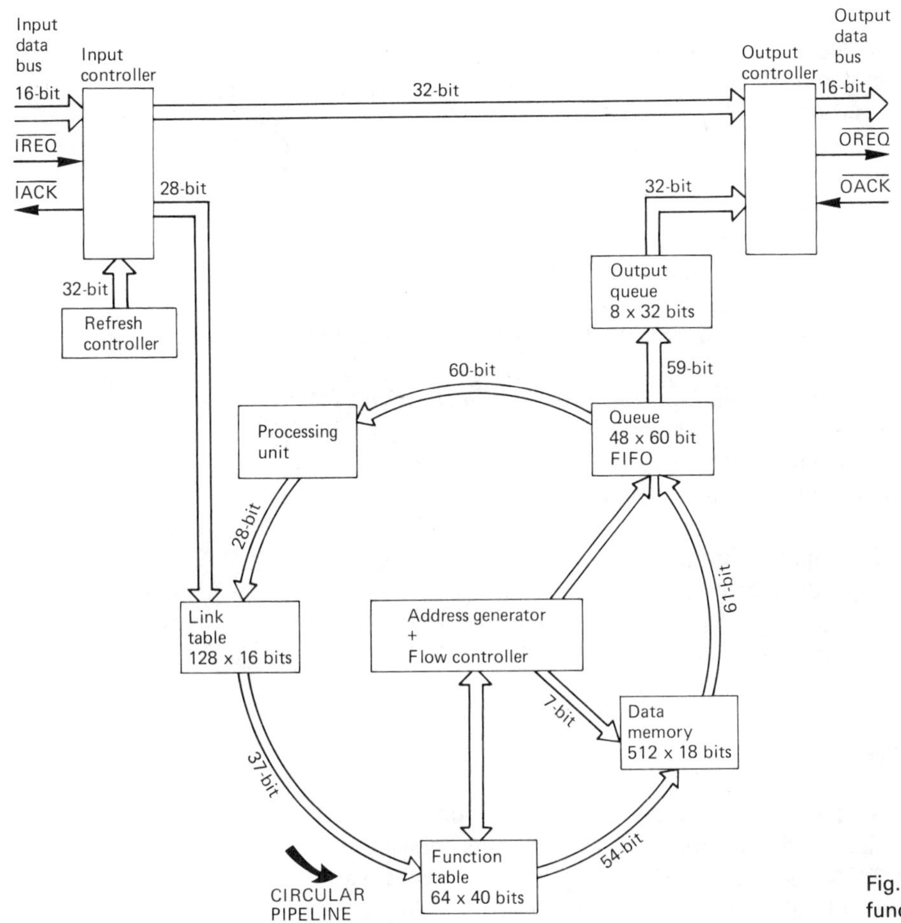

Fig. 3.12 μPD7281 functional block diagram

The processing unit includes a fast multiplier capable of performing a 17×17 bit multiply in 200 ns. The internal architecture can perform several operations concurrently and does not need to fetch instructions, perform subroutine stack operations, or transfer data between registers as would be required in a von Neuman processor.

An internal circular pipeline is formed from

a) The link table
b) The function table
c) The data memory
d) The queue
e) The processing unit.

Tokens entering through the input controller pass onto the link table to be processed around the circular pipeline as many times as are required. When the token is fully processed it is put into the output queue and passed to the output controller for transfer to the next μPD7281 or the host processor interface.

Before any processing occurs, the host processor down-loads the object code and any constants into the link table and function table using special input tokens. The object code is closely related to the information on the directed dataflow graph. The arcs represent the entries in the link table and the nodes represent the entries in the function table. An arc between two nodes passes a data token which is identified by a corresponding entry in the link table. A node on the directed dataflow graph represents an operand and the type of operation is logged into the function table along with identification information for the outgoing arc.

The input controller checks whether an entering token is to be processed by checking the module number field of the token. If the module number field of the token is not the same as the μPD7281 module number, the token is passed directly to the output controller but, if it is the same, the token has the module number field removed and is passed to the link table for processing.

It takes seven pipeline clock cycles for a token to pass fully around the circular pipeline and thus up to seven tokens may be processed in parallel. The format of a token changes significantly as it passes around the circular pipeline. Each token must have at least a 7-bit identifier field and an 18-bit data field. The identifier field is used as an address to the link table memory and is renewed with data from the link table memory every time the token passes the link table. The data field consists of a control bit, a sign bit and sixteen data bits. A token may have up to two data fields plus output code, control and other fields if necessary.

3.12 Fairchild Clipper

The Fairchild Clipper is a 32-bit microprocessor consisting of one arithmetic logic unit chip and two identical cache/memory management chips for data and instructions. The 3 CMOS chip set (with a total of 846 000 transistors) was introduced in 1986 and uses a hard-wired RISC design to achieve over

5 Mips (33 Mips peak). The initial version has a 30 ns cycle time (33 MHz clock). Early applications for the Clipper are expected to be in engineering and scientific workstations.

One cache memory is used for operands and one for data. To increase memory bandwidth, separate 32-bit buses are used to connect the data and instruction memories to the ALU chip as shown in Figure 3.13. Burst mode updating of cache memories allows the next four 32-bit words to be placed on the buses in sequence thus significantly increasing throughput. The bus bandwidth to the CPU is 133 Mbyte/s.

The CPU chip has four major elements:

a) A 32-bit ALU with an integer pipe, a three-port 32×32-bit register file and a serial 64-bit shifter.

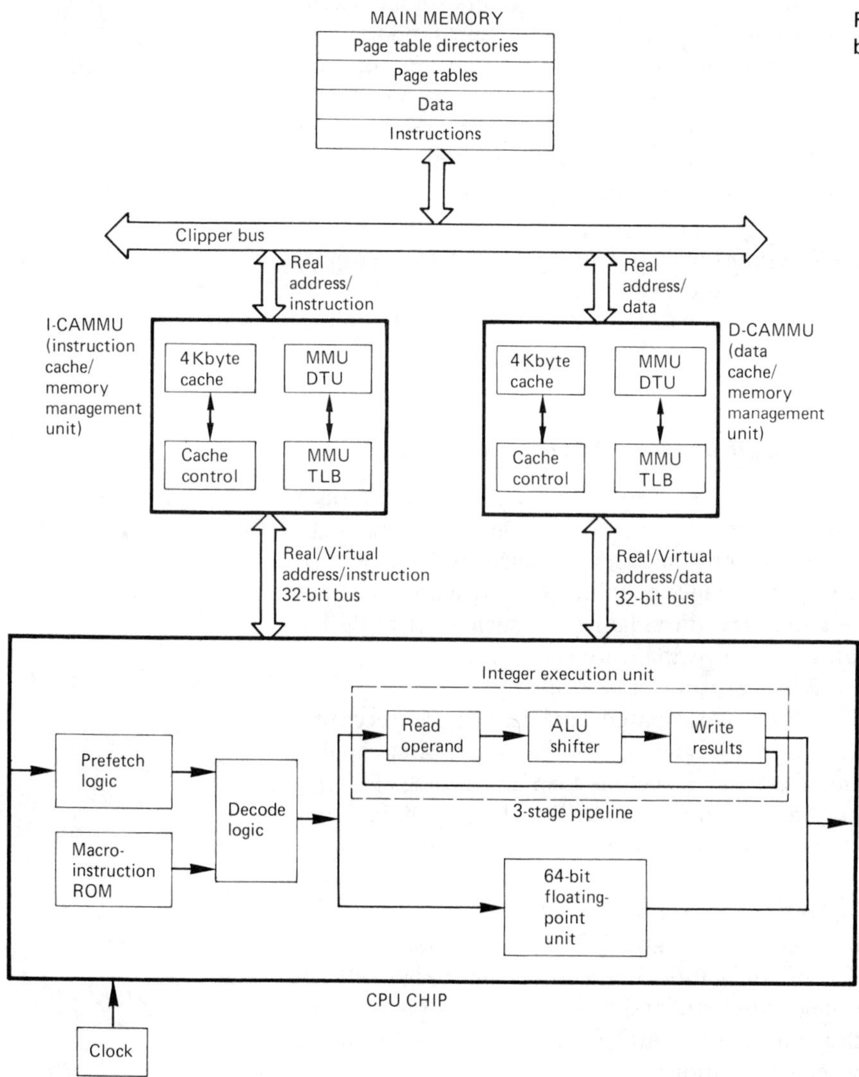

Fig. 3.13 Clipper functional block diagram

b) A 64-bit floating-point unit with eight 64-bit registers. (IEEE P754 Standard.)
c) Prefetch logic to support an 8-byte instruction buffer.
d) A macroinstruction ROM to execute sequences of standard machine instructions as high-level instructions.

Extensive pipelining is employed. The fetch, decode and execute processing phases are overlapped and up to three instructions may be processed simultaneously during the execute phase in the integer execution unit.

The 101 basic instructions are hard-wired allowing most instructions to execute in one 30 ns clock cycle. Sixty-seven high-level macroinstructions are currently implemented but more can be added in the 2048 instruction ROM.

Each cache/MMU chip has a 4 Kbyte RAM organised as a two-way associative cache with 16-byte lines read from main memory. The caches are expected to have a hit ratio greater than 90% and an average access time of 90 ns in most applications. Each cache/MMU chip supports two 32-bit virtual address spaces, one for supervisor mode and one for user mode. A 256-entry two-way associative translation lookaside buffer (TLB) holds most recently used address translations and supplies the physical page address given a virtual address. When a cache miss occurs two-level page tables carry out the virtual to physical address translation and update the buffer.

The Clipper is designed to support from one to eight standard microprocessors as input/output processors and the design has been optimised for high-performance scientific applications such as CAD and simulation in a Unix environment using the C programming language.

3.13 Texas Instruments Compact LISP Machine (CLM)

One of the first high-level language processors to be implemented on a chip was the Compact LISP machine. With conventional processors, high-level languages are transformed into machine language by compilers or interpreters with substantial performance penalties. Such penalties increase with the problem-oriented non-procedural languages such as Lisp, Prolog and Ada; thus they execute more slowly than more conventional procedure-oriented languages such as Basic, Fortran and Pascal.

Artificial intelligence and knowledge-based applications are becoming increasingly important and they demand high-power processors capable of executing non-procedural languages such as Lisp and Prolog. For this reason Texas Instruments, under contract to DARPA, developed the Compact LISP Machine, a 32-bit microprocessor microprogrammed to support common Lisp.

The CLM is a 32-bit CMOS processor with a 40 MHz clock frequency constructed using sub-2μm technology to give 550 000 transistors. As shown in Figure 3.14 the CLM is of conventional von Neumann design with an ALU capable of performing arithmetic and logic operations on typed or un-typed data. The shifter and masker are provided to rotate up to 32 positions in support of bit-field operations.

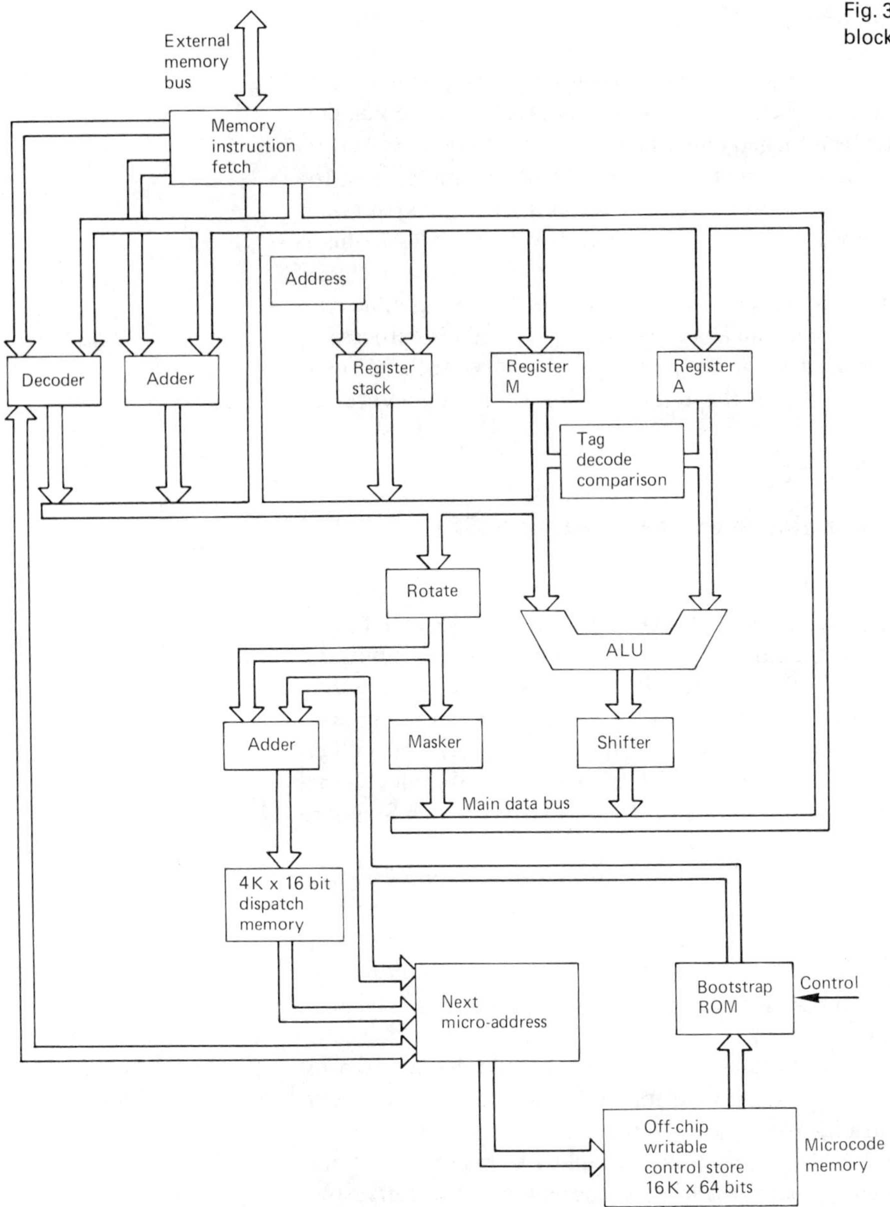

Fig. 3.14 CLM functional block diagram

About half the chip is used by the on-chip RAM (over 114 Kbits); the rest is CPU logic based upon the circuits used in the Explorer processor, previously constructed from many integrated circuits by Texas Instruments.

The microcode memory of the CLM is very large, 16 Kbytes by 64 bits, and was therefore made external to the chip together with the memory mapper. The chip does, however, include a normaliser which improves the floating-point performance. The A and M register files and a data bus drive the ALU, which in turn drives the control section of the CLM and feeds back data to the ALU inputs. The dispatch memory is used for macroinstruction decoding and generic operations; it contains the starting addresses of specific microcode routines.

The 40 MHz clock is too fast to make a large memory possible using standard DRAM, so a data cache is accessed in parallel with the mapper. For a cache hit, the data is returned immediately and the memory operation aborted. For a cache miss, the memory operation is completed and the memory is accessed over the system bus. A special high-speed system bus with a large address range was developed for use with the CLM; this is the Nubus.

The CLM executes a superset of common Lisp which is compatible with Explorer Lisp. The CLM chip makes possible small symbolic processing systems which may be used as embedded expert systems such as smart instruments which participate in the interpretation of the data received and in the diagnosis of their own faults.

3.14 TMS34010 Graphics System Processor (GSP)

The GSP is a 32-bit CMOS microprocessor with an architecture which is specifically designed for graphics display applications, combined with a graphics display unit on the same chip. In addition to a general-purpose instruction set, the TMS34010 has special instructions for pixel processing including raster operations, bit boundary block transfers to manipulate two-dimensional arrays, and Boolean operations on arrays. The GSP is programmable in high-level graphics languages such as the Graphics Kernel System (GKS) or Programmer's Hierarchical Interactive Graphics Standard (PHIGS).

As shown in Figure 3.15 the TMS34010 incorporates a 32-bit CPU with an ALU, adder, barrel shifter, thirty-one 32-bit registers and a 256-byte instruction cache. Pipelining permits the processor to perform calculations while the memory control unit accesses memory and the CRT control section executes graphics commands to control the display timing and dynamic RAM refresh functions.

The address space is 4 Gbytes and each bit may be addressed to permit bit field management, for example data may be taken from a 3-bit field, expanded and placed in a 12-bit field anywhere in memory. Moving variable-size pixel arrays about in display memory is typical in raster operations. The bit addressable memory permits various combinations of screen resolution and number of bit planes per pixel to be selected.

The CPU is capable of operation at 6 Mips with an external bus cycle time of 320 ns for accessing the local memory and the video interface. A pixel resolution of 1024×1280 is practical using a 320 ns cycle time and multiple GSPs can be connected to a bit map to increase the array size. The maximum pixel drawing rate is 48 million per second. Power consumption of the TMS34010 is 0.5 W when operating at 6 Mips.

The same local memory space is used to store the instructions, the display data and several screens of pixel data. If necessary the host memory address space can overlap the GSP address space, share the same memory space, or use a separate memory array.

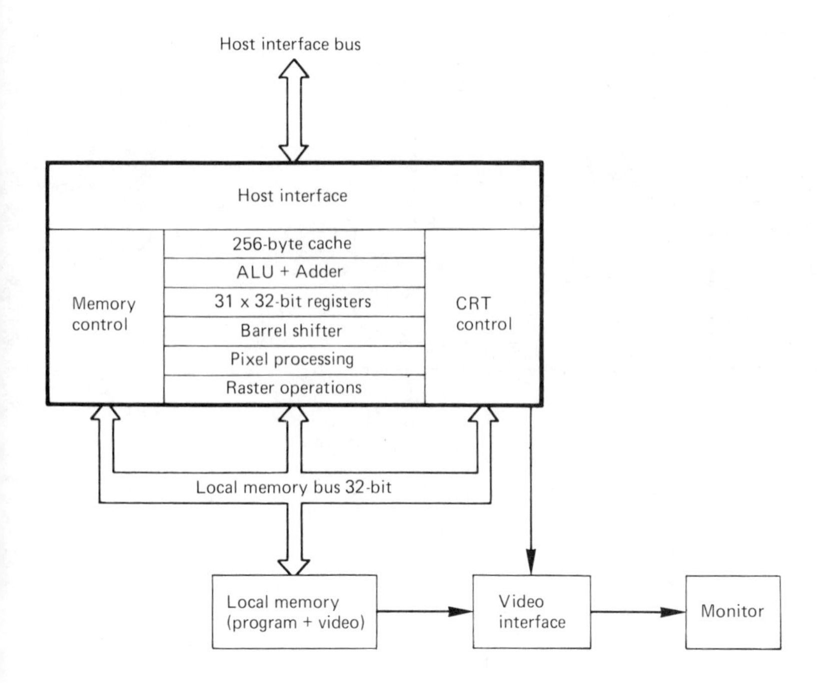

Fig. 3.15 TMS34010 graphics system processor block diagram

3.15 Thomson–CSF SCQM

The SCQM is an object-oriented capability-based RISC processor with the ability to access a large distributed virtual memory space. It is currently under development for applications requiring data consistency and protection for large databases plus stored information models such as may be required by expert systems.

The virtual memory space is made up of objects, each given a 48-bit name plus a 22-bit offset address in a 70-bit virtual address. The 70-bit address can access a 32-bit data word and it is intended that object names will remain for the life of the system rather than be reused. When an object is created, a capability is generated which can be duplicated to give either full or partial access rights to the named object. Objects are designated a particular function and may not be used for other purposes.

Figure 3.16 shows the SCQM system configuration. The CPU chip is a reduced instruction set computer and six support chips will be developed:

a) Cache memory module
b) Main memory controller

with the system bus interface comprising four chips:

c) Cache directory
d) Bus arbiter
e) Bus monitor
f) Bus controller.

All the chips are in CMOS technology.

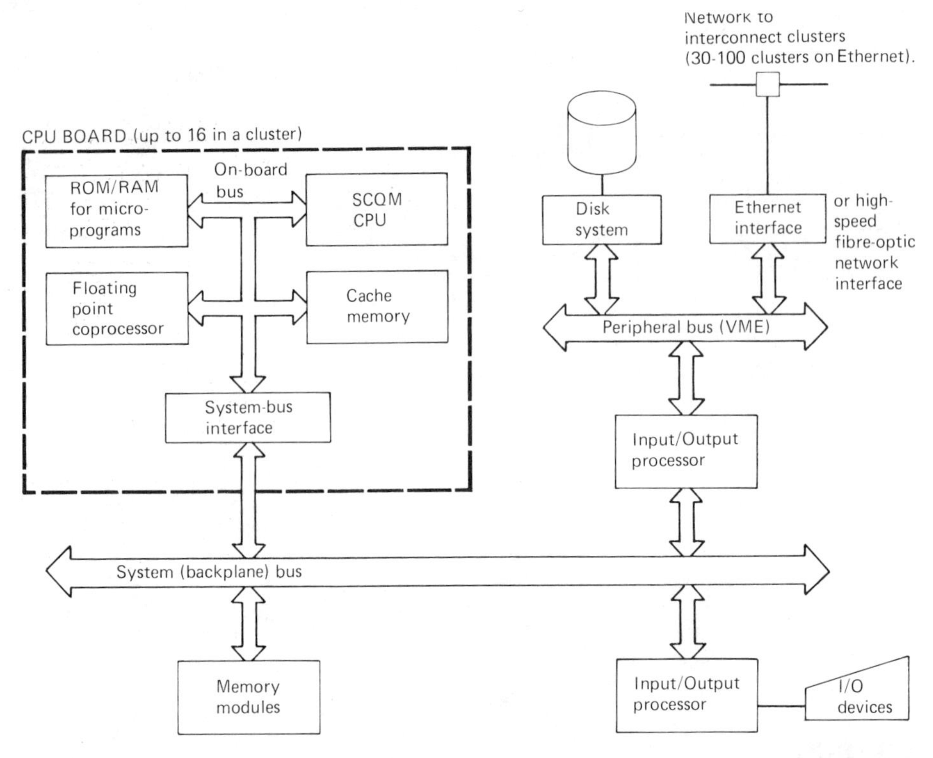

Fig. 3.16 SCQM system configuration

An SCQM system will be composed of clusters, each cluster including between one and sixteen CPU cards, an input/output processor and a number of memory modules all connected to the system bus. Distributed systems may be constructed by interconnecting the clusters through a network. Data may be accessed from anywhere in the network using the same 70-bit virtual object address. A prototype Ethernet network is expected to support up to 100 clusters but higher-speed fibre-optic networks will support many more clusters.

The CPU chip will be used in both the CPU board and the input/output processors. It is designed with a fixed 32-bit instruction format and a 64-bit data path executing one instruction in each 50 ns cycle giving a peak performance of 20 Mips. Speed is maintained by an on-chip instruction cache and a 256-entry address translation lookaside buffer. A single SCQM board is expected to have a worst-case performance of 8 Mips and a sixteen CPU board cluster is expected to operate at 60 Mips under the worst-case constraints.

The CPU architecture emphasises loading, storing and register-to-register operations using 32 programmable registers mapped by a window mechanism onto a bank of 122 registers. The software kernel supports a Unix-like operating system, giving network transparency and direct access to the object management level, and an Ada run-time system.

3.16 Am29300

The Am29300 family of bipolar 32-bit microprocessor building blocks, manufactured by Advanced Micro Devices, permit a high-performance 32-bit processor to be constructed with a high-level of design flexibility. For example, a RISC or a microcoded design may be implemented; alternatively, specialist array processors, peripheral controllers, graphics processors or digital signal processor architectures may be constructed. A typical microcoded CPU using the Am29300 series is shown in Figure 3.17.

The Am29300 family consists of

a) Am29323 32-bit parallel multiplier
b) Am29325 32-bit floating point controller
c) Am29331 16-bit microprogram sequencer
d) Am29332 32-bit arithmetic logic unit
e) Am29334 four-port dual access register file.

The Am29300 family offers many advances on the earlier 2901 series of bit slice processors; these include:

a) Many data types are supported using a combination of the three ALU types: AM29332 for 32-bit integers, BCD and bit fields, AM29323 for integer multiplications, and Am29325 for floating-point operations.

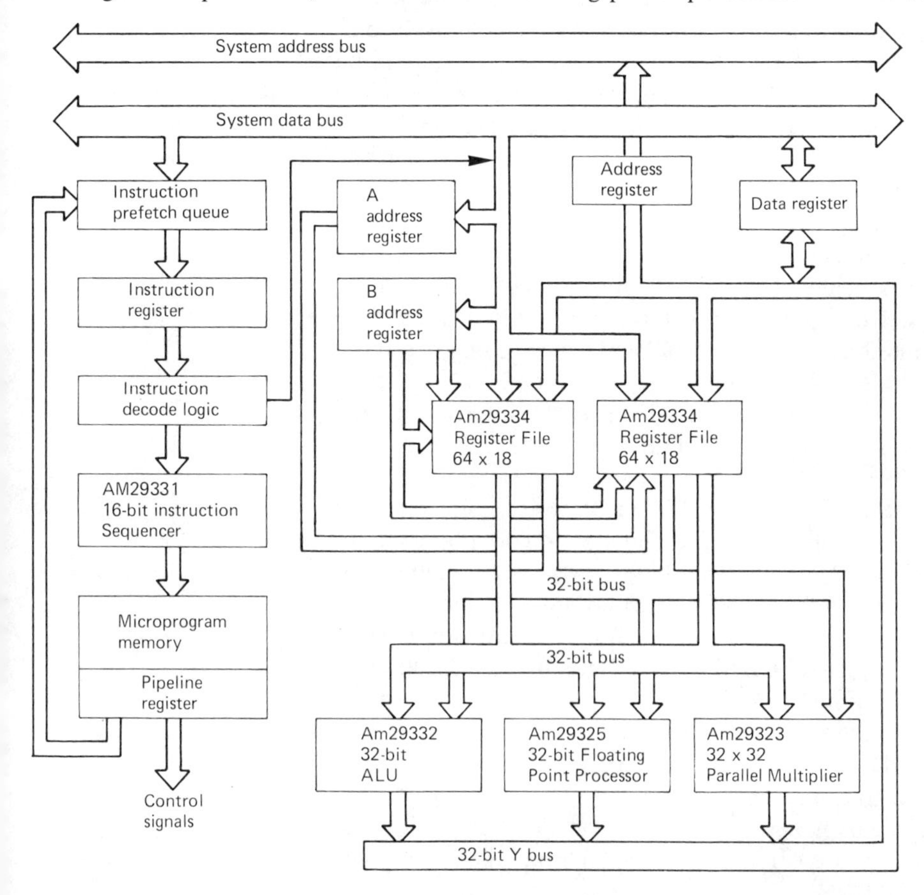

Fig. 3.17 Am29300-based CPU block diagram

b) Three buses are used to increase bandwidth; one for output and two for input.
c) The use of a 'flow-through' architecture enables many operations to be completed in one microcycle.
d) The microcycle time of all the building blocks has been balanced to prevent one element holding up the rest of the system.
e) The partitioning of the family does not require several vertical bit slices to construct a 32-bit processor; this reduces the number of interconnections and reduces inter-chip delays as well as permitting more data types. The Am29300 series are termed horizontal slices of the CPU.

The Am29332 arithmetic logic unit has two 32-bit input buses and one 32-bit output bus. Two Am29332 chips may be wired together, one as the master and the second as a redundant slave with its normal outputs disabled and using the same inputs as the master to permit the same operations to be carried out. Outputs from the master are compared with the internal results in the slave and, when they do not match, an error signal is generated. Other diagnostic features include parity generation and checking of all data in the Am29332.

The register file is included on a separate chip (the Am29334), rather than on the ALU chip, to permit greater speed using the higher power budget available on a separate chip. This also permits more than one register file. The second register file may for example act as a mailbox to pass data between processors. The Am29334 is configured as sixty-four 18-bit registers, including a parity bit with each byte. Two are therefore required with a 32-bit system bus. All registers are identical and two read ports and two write ports are provided. The write control allows each separate byte of a register, or both bytes simultaneously, to be written.

The Am29331 microprogram sequencer can address up to 64K words of microcode and the internal stack supports up to 33 levels of subroutine nesting. Address sources include the program counter, stack, loop counter, and two address buses. The second address bus input is provided to reduce delays caused by tristate bus turn-on and turn-off times. Using two buses it is possible to pre-enable address sources and switch buses when the address is valid. Interrupt requests are supported by separate interrupt request and acknowledge pins on the Am29331. Traps are generated by internal system errors.

The CPU shown in Figure 3.17 is typical of a microcoded minicomputer using the Am29300 series building blocks. The system could be made to achieve an 80 ns microcycle time by using high-speed system memory or a cache attached to the system bus. The instruction prefetch queue speeds up instruction decoding and instructions are fed to an instruction register and decode logic. When register-based addressing is used, the addresses are fed to the Am29334 register files. When immediate addressing is used, the decode logic feeds address field data to the ALU data path where it is used directly. In the case of indirect addressing it is used to form an address which is fetched from memory.

The arithmetic logic unit is constructed from an Am29332 ALU, an Am29325 floating-point processor and an Am29323 parallel multiplier.

Communication between these units is via the Y bus. Data is transmitted between the ALU and the system data bus via a bidirectional data register.

3.17 SN-74AS88XX

Texas Instruments manufacture a range of 32-bit microprocessor building blocks similar to the Am29300 series. The SN-74AS88XX series includes bipolar and CMOS parts to implement a four-bus processor architecture claimed to be capable of processing speeds up to 20 Mips.

The family consists of seven processing functions:

a) 74AS8832 32-bit registered ALU
b) 74AS8833 64 to 32-bit funnel shifter
c) 74AS8834 64-word × 20-bit register file
d) 74AS8835 16-bit micro-sequencer
e) 74AS8836 32-bit multiplier
f) 74AS8837 64-bit floating-point processor
g) 74AS8838 32-bit barrel shifter.

Although they consume up to 4 W, the Schottky transistor logic members of the SN-74AS88XX family produce certain system benefits: faster switching speeds are achievable because the bipolar devices can charge and discharge capacitive loads much faster than CMOS devices and the greater drive and fan-out capability of bipolar chips makes it possible to interface directly with large system buses. The power consumption of the CMOS members of the family (74AS8836 and 74AS8837) is considerably lower than that of the bipolar parts. CMOS parts use 1 μm feature size and bipolar parts use 1.5 μm features.

The AS8836 will perform a 32 × 32-bit signed multiply in 75 ns and will also execute 32 × 16, 16 × 32 and 16 × 16 operands. The AS8837 supports IEEE and DEC floating-point, double or single-precision formats and will convert between the formats. Two floating-point numbers can be multiplied in 75 ns and both pipelined or flow-through architectures are supported.

To simplify debugging, the AS8835 microsequencer incorporates a window comparator which can be programmed to trap attempted instruction accesses outside the expected microcode address range. The AS8835 can quickly dump and reload the stack allowing unlimited stack depth expansion for recursive microcode programming.

The AS8832 registered ALU has a separately clocked register file which permits a single processor, in a multiprocessor system, to store the results of a calculation in its own register file and to update the registers of other processors in a single clock cycle. This improves interprocessor communication by increasing interprocessor communication speeds and reducing the amount of microcode required.

The AS8832 may be microprogrammed to configure the chip dynamically as a 32-bit processor, two 16-bit processors or four 8-bit processors operating independently on separate data. This facility is useful where the same instructions are executed on different pieces of data such as SIMD or array processors.

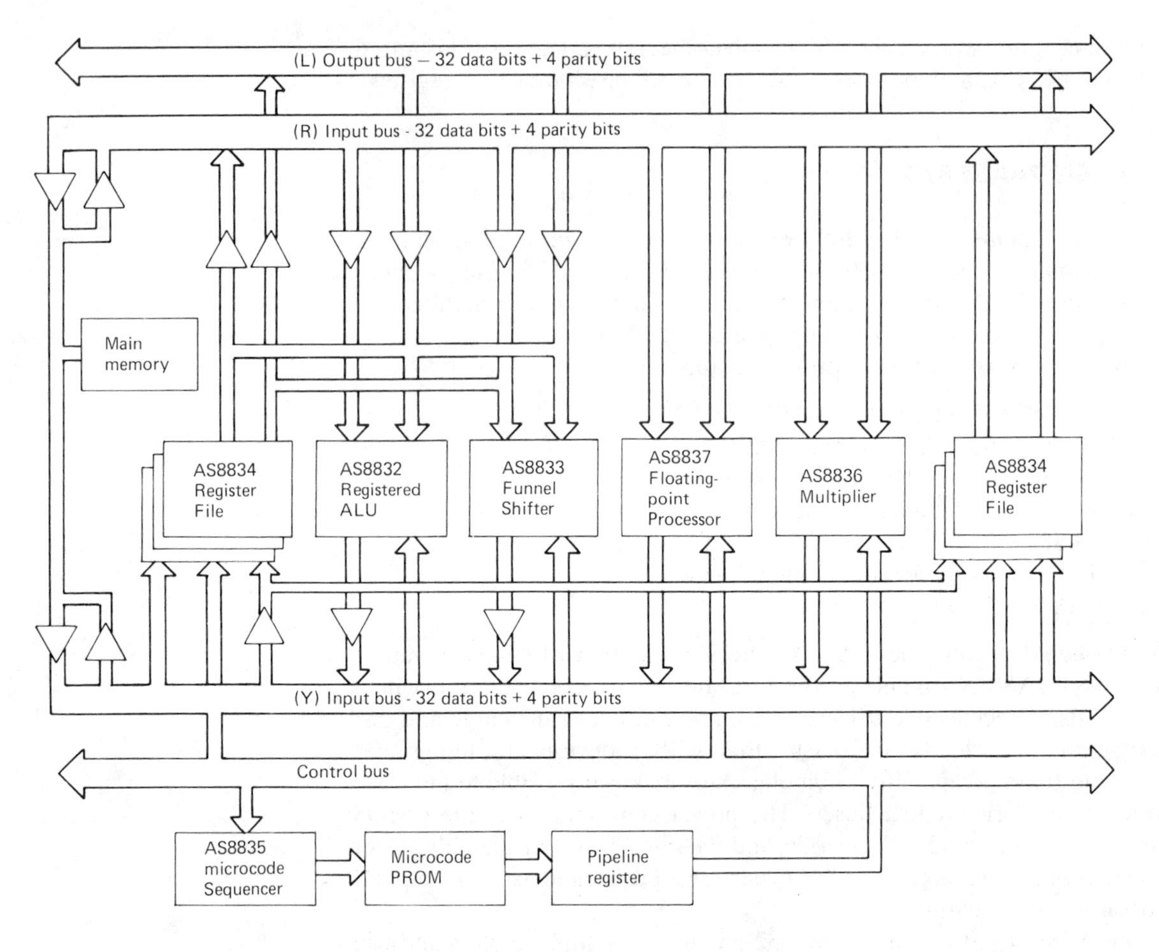

Fig. 3.18 SN-74AS88XX-based CPU block diagram

The AS8833 funnel shifter is used to perform single (32-bit) or double (64-bit) floating-point normalisation in a single clock cycle. This may be carried out independently in parallel with ALU operation.

Figure 3.18 shows the SN-74AS88XX family of building blocks in a CPU with three bi-directional I/O buses (32-bits of data plus 4 parity bits) and a control bus which is used to transfer the microword from the micro-sequencer to other processing elements for execution. All members of the AS88XX family except the barrel shifter support parity generation and checking as well as master/slave error detection. Pin grid array packages are employed ranging from 84 to 208 pins.

4 Motorola MC68020

4.1 MC68020 architecture

4.1.1 The M68000 family

The MC68020 has been selected for more detailed treatment because it has several features which are typical of many general-purpose 32-bit microprocessors and at the time of writing there was a good base of applications knowledge.

The first model in the M68000 range was the MC68000 and several other models have now been added; these include:

a) MC68008 which is an MC68000 with an 8-bit external data bus in place of a 16-bit data bus; this permits 8-bit support chips to be used and reduces the size and cost of the package.
b) MC68010 which is similar to the MC68000 but includes features which improve operating system support and increase the processing speed.
c) MC68020 which has all the features of the MC68010 but has a 32-bit external data bus, on-chip instruction cache and many new instructions.
d) MC68030 which integrates an MC68020, a subset of the MC68851 programmable memory management unit (using a 22-entry translation lookahead buffer) and separate 256-byte instruction and data caches. Performance is thus increased by 1.5 to 2.5 times when these new facilities are used but the improvement in performance is approximately 50 per cent for MC68020 compiled code run on a 20 MHz MC68030. The cache is reorganised as 16 entries of four 32-bit words, the same as the Z80000, and the internal bandwidth is increased to 80 Mbyte/s. Other improvements include 1.2 μm CHMOS (300 000 transistors) and a burst mode for filling the caches from memory.
e) A RISC version of the MC68020 is also planned and the future MC68040 is expected to have a larger data bus and internal 128-bit registers.

The MC68010 includes an additional vector base register which stores the interrupt vector base addresses. This register may be set to zero for compatibility with the MC68000 and may be set to other values to allow different operating system processes to handle their own traps.

Other changes incorporated in the MC68010 modify stack information stored after an exception (caused by program errors or external events).

One change permits an instruction which caused a bus error to be restarted. This makes virtual memory systems possible by using a bus error to indicate when a memory location, which has not been copied into real memory, is addressed.

Two new instructions were included in the MC68010:

a) MOVEC which is used to access control registers including the vector base pointer.
b) MOVES which permits address spaces which would otherwise be unaccessible to be read.

The current privilege level determines data access to the user data and supervisor data address spaces. Three-bit function code generators for source and destination may be set by MOVEC to permit a program running in supervisor mode to use MOVES to read or write to locations in a supervisor program, user program or user data address space.

The MC68020 has many new 32-bit operations including 32-bit offsets in branch instructions, 32-bit displacements in indexed addressing modes, and 32-bit operands in CHK, LINK, UNLK, MUL and DIV instructions. New instructions include one which moves blocks of data between address spaces.

Privileged instructions, those which may potentially compromise the integrity of the computer, such as RESET, can only be executed in supervisor mode, with the S bit (bit 13) in the status register set prior to execution. This capability is fundamental to the virtual machine concept which permits one operating system to be run in user mode and another operating system to be run in supervisor mode. The MC68010 and MC68020 differ subtly from the MC68000 in the use of privileged instructions affecting access to the status register.

Two features are included in the design of the MC68020 to increase overall processing speed:

a) Instruction prefetch unit or pipeline
b) An instruction cache.

These features also make it difficult to estimate processing times because instruction execution overlap is caused by the instruction prefetch unit, and the cache hit rate must be taken into account.

The instruction prefetch unit is a three-word-deep on-chip instruction store which anticipates the next instruction address; thus external memory fetches are anticipated and overlapped with current processor execution. Instruction addresses are calculated independently from data addresses to permit simultaneous access when data is read from external memory and the instruction is read from the on-chip cache.

4.1.2 Instruction cache

The 256-byte instruction cache reduces the number of bus cycles required for instruction fetches from main memory. The instruction cache may be disabled by the cache disable pin or by using the cache control register. Entries to the cache may be cleared by use of the cache control register and the cache address register. The cache must be cleared when a context switch between tasks takes place and the cache entry must be invalidated when an operating system executes a breakpoint instruction (BKPT).

The enable bit in the cache control register disables the cache when set to 0 causing the processor to fetch all instructions from external memory. Writing a 1 to the clear bit clears all the cache entries and causes the cache to refill with new data. When the freeze bit is set, the valid data in the cache may not be replaced. When the clear entry bit is set to 1, the location in the cache corresponding to the address in the cache address register is invalidated.

When the cache is enabled, to fetch an instruction the CPU always checks the cache using address bits A7 to A2 to locate a 32-bit-long word in cache memory (see Figure 4.1). It then compares address bits A31 to A8 and the function code bit FC2 with the 25-bit tag of the entry which is also stored in the cache. If the function code and the address bits match the tag, a cache hit occurs and the CPU sets the valid bits for the cache entry. Using address bit A1 the CPU selects the 32-bit instruction from the cache. When a cache miss occurs (because the tag for an instruction does not match the tag in the cache or when the valid bit is clear), the CPU puts the instruction address bits A31 to A8 in the tag field, sets the valid bit,

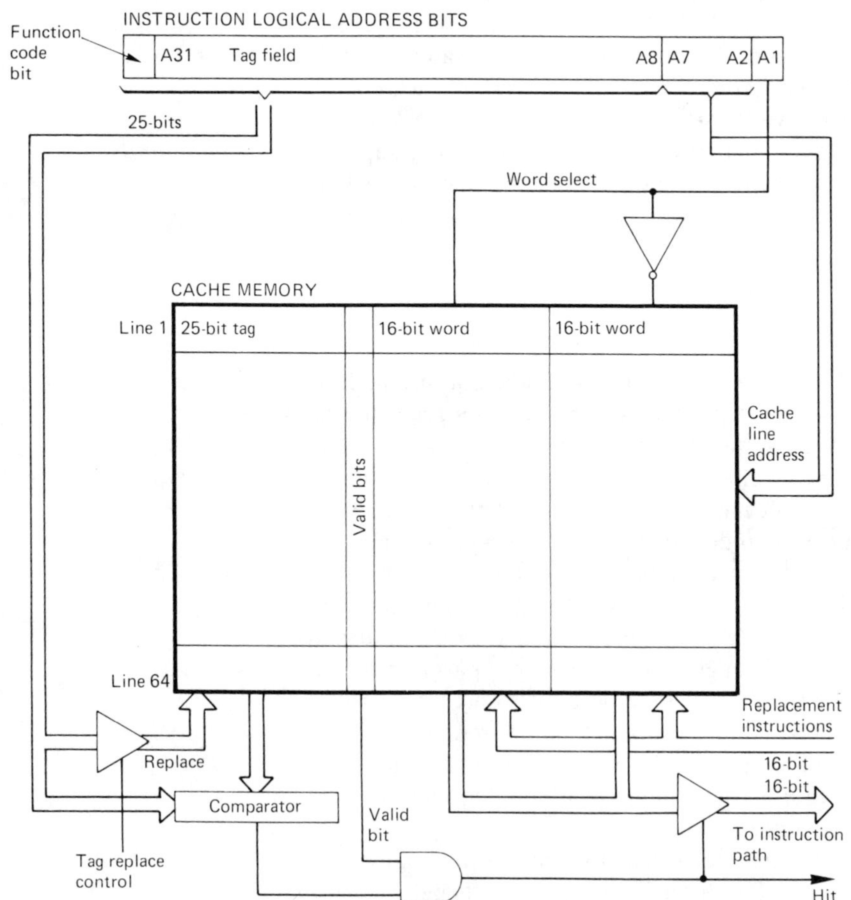

Fig. 4.1 MC68020 cache

then fetches one 32-bit-long word from main memory and places it in the cache.

To calculate the overall performance of the processor with a cache memory the following formula may be used:

$$P_o = P_m + [(P_h - P_m) \times H_r]$$

where P_o is overall performance in Mips (million instructions per second)
P_m is performance of cache misses
P_h is performance of cache hits
H_r is the hit ratio (between 0 and 1).

Figure 4.2 shows the performance of a 16 MHz 68020 with 0% and 100% cache hits against total system access time (address-to-data delay in nanoseconds).

4.1.3 MC68020 registers

As shown in Figure 4.3, the MC68020 has eight 32-bit general-purpose data registers (D0 to D7), seven 32-bit address registers (A0 to A6), three 32-bit stack pointers (user, master and interrupt), a 32-bit program counter, a 32-bit vector base register, a 32-bit cache address register, a 32-bit cache control register, a 16-bit status and a 3-bit alternate function code register.

The master stack pointer, cache control register and cache address registers are additions to the MC68000 register set. The interrupt stack pointer is similar to the MC68000 supervisor stack pointer. The master stack pointer has been added to simplify task switching for operating systems and supports multiprocessing by giving each process a small master stack area where process-specific exception data is stored, in addition to a common large interrupt stack area.

4.1.4 Addressing modes

The addressing modes were listed in section 3.4. Some routine address calculations required by high-level languages were not supported by the MC68000 but have been added to the MC68020. Program counter memory indirect addressing is similar to memory indirect addressing but the address register is usually added to the calculation using the current program counter contents. This results in position-independent code in which the memory pointer is accessed relative to the current program counter.

Indirect pre-indexed addressing uses the contents of the index register in the address calculation before memory indirection is performed and can be used to access operands through a pointer which is part of a record or an array of records. Alternatively it may be used to access operands through an array of pointers. Indirect post-indexed addressing adds the contents of the index register after performing memory indirection to calculate the effective address. Indirect post-indexed addressing may be used to access a pointer addressed array element.

The address index registers may be scaled (by shifting the contents of the register by zero, one, two or four bit positions to the left) before being

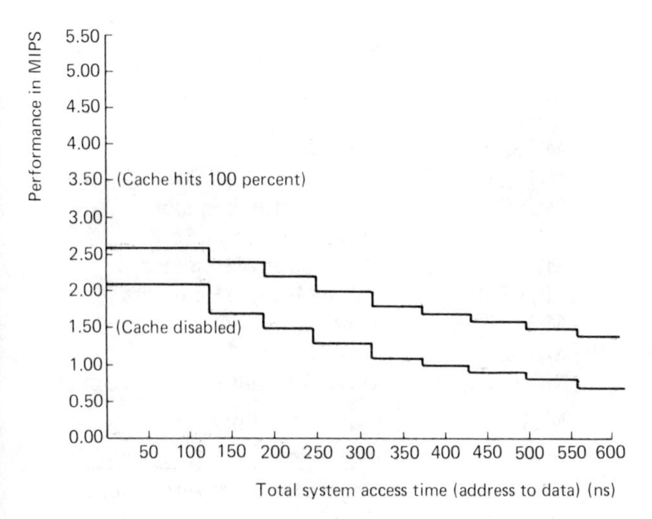

Fig. 4.2 Performance (Mips) of a 16 MHz MC68020

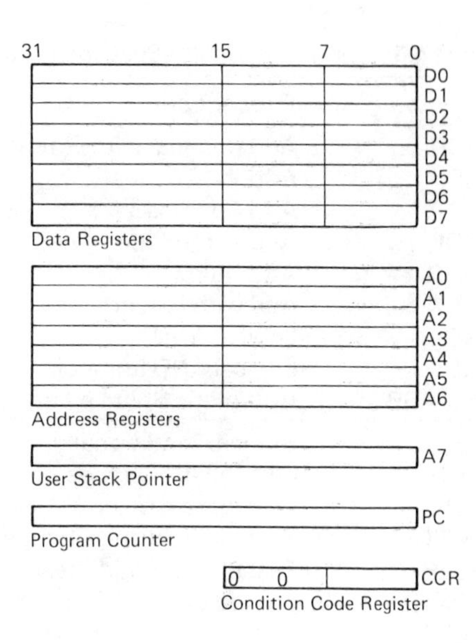

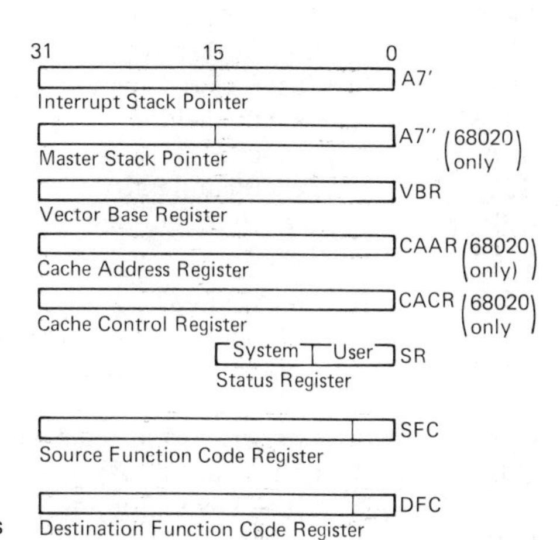

Fig. 4.3 MC68020 registers

used, giving the effect of multiplying the contents by zero, two, four or eight. Scaling may be used to permit the same address index register to point to individual bytes, words, long words, and quad words.

The base address register or program counter may be suppressed to permit the use of any index register in place of the base register. This makes it possible for the MC68020 to put addresses in data registers and, by suppressing the program counter, to give the user access to program space.

4.1.5 The MC68020 instruction set

Table 4.1 summarises the MC68020 instruction set. All the 56 instruction types of the MC68000 are included and several instructions were enhanced in the MC68020 to support 32-bit operands. Bit-field instructions were added to improve support for compilers and graphics applications.

Table 4.1 Summary of MC68020 Instructions

Mnemonic	Description
ABCD	Add Decimal with Extend
ADD	Add
ADDA	Add Address
ADDI	Add Immediate
ADDQ	Add Quick
ADDX	Add with Extend
AND	Logical AND
ANDI	Logical AND Immediate
ASL, ASR	Arithmetic Shift Left and Right
Bcc	Branch Conditionally
BCHG	Test Bit and Change
BCLR	Test Bit and Clear
BFCHG	Test Bit Field and Change*
BFCLR	Test Bit Field and Clear*
BFEXTS	Signed Bit Field Extract*
BFEXTU	Unsigned Bit Field Extract*
BFFFO	Bit Field Find First One*
BFINS	Bit Field Insert*
BFSET	Test Bit Field and Set*
BFTST	Test Bit Field*
BRA	Branch
BSET	Test Bit and Set
BSR	Branch to Subroutine
BTST	Test Bit
CALLM	Call Module*
CAS	Compare and Swap Operands*
CAS2	Compare and Swap Dual Operands*
CHK	Check Register Against Bound
CHK2	Check Register Against Upper and Lower Bounds*
CLR	Clear
CMP	Compare
CMPA	Compare Address
CMPI	Compare Immediate
CMPM	Compare Memory to Memory
CMP2	Compare Register Against Upper and Lower Bounds*
DBcc	Test Condition, Decrement and Branch
DIVS, DIVSL	Signed Divide
DIVU, DIVUL	Unsigned Divide
EOR	Logical Exclusive OR
EORI	Logical Exclusive OR Immediate
EXG	Exchange Registers
EXT	Sign Extend
JMP	Jump
JSR	Jump to Subroutine
LEA	Load Effective Address
LINK	Link and Allocate
LSL, LSR	Logical Shift Left and Right
MOVE	Move
MOVEA	Move Address
MOVE CCR	Move Condition Code Register
MOVE SR	Move Status Register
MOVE USP	Move User Stack Pointer
MOVEC	Move Control Register
MOVEM	Move Multiple Registers
MOVEP	Move Peripheral
MOVEQ	Move Quick
MOVES	Move Alternate Address Space
MULS	Signed Multiply
MULU	Unsigned Multiply
NBCD	Negate Decimal with Extend
NEG	Negate
NEGX	Negate with Extend
NOP	No Operation
NOT	Logical Complement
OR	Logical Inclusive OR
ORI	Logical OR Immediate
PACK	Pack BCD*
PEA	Push Effective Address
RESET	Reset External Devices
ROL, ROR	Rotate Left and Right
ROXL, ROXR	Rotate with Extend Left and Right
RTD	Return and Deallocate
RTE	Return from Exception
RTM	Return from Module*
RTR	Return and Restore Condition Codes
RTS	Return from Subroutine
SBCD	Subtract Decimal with Extend
Scc	Set Conditionally
STOP	Stop
SUB	Subtract
SUBA	Subtract Address
SUBI	Subtract Immediate
SUBQ	Subtract Quick
SUBX	Subtract with Extend
SWAP	Swap Register Words
TAS	Test Operand and Set
TRAP	Trap
TRAPcc	Trap Conditionally*
TRAPV	Trap on Overflow
TST	Test Operand
UNLK	Unlink
UNPK	Unpack BCD*

Table 4.1 (continued)

COPROCESSOR INSTRUCTIONS	
cpBcc	Branch Conditionally
cpDBcc	Test Coprocessor Condition, Decrement, and Branch
cpGEN	Coprocessor General Instruction
cpRESTORE	Restore Internal State of Coprocessor
cpSAVE	Save Internal State of Coprocessor
cpScc	Set Conditionally
cpTRAPcc	Trap Conditionally

The 32-bit instruction enhancements include:

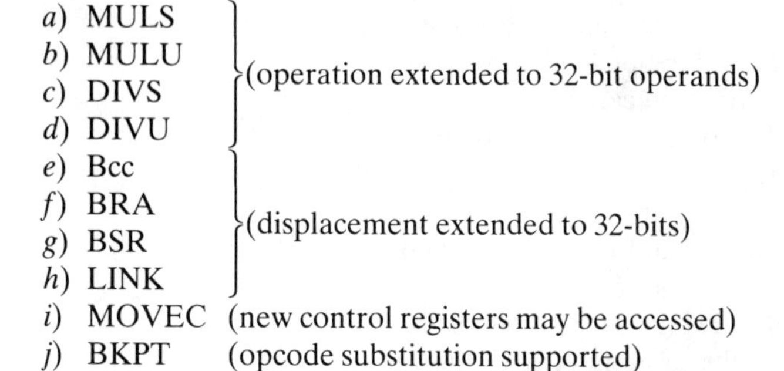

a) MULS
b) MULU
c) DIVS
d) DIVU
(operation extended to 32-bit operands)
e) Bcc
f) BRA
g) BSR
h) LINK
(displacement extended to 32-bits)
i) MOVEC (new control registers may be accessed)
j) BKPT (opcode substitution supported)

New MC68020 instructions are marked * in Table 4.1. Of particular interest are the bit field instructions which support the use of the MC68020 in a Unix environment using the C language. Variables are often packed in memory through the use of bit fields. For example, one 6-bit, one 4-bit and two 3-bit variables can be packed into a 16-bit integer rather than using an entire integer for each variable, thereby conserving memory.

The MC68020 has eight additional bit field instructions compared with the MC68000; these instructions may be used to manipulate individual bits in memory or in registers. A bit field is an array of bits which may fit into a single register or may consist of large amounts of memory used for bit-mapped graphics, communications buffers using packed data or assembler op-codes. A bit field instruction specifies the field selection by a field offset, which denotes the first bit in the field relative to the base address, and a field width, which determines the number of bits in the field.

The bit field instruction syntax consists of the instruction mnemonic followed by the effective address of the base for the bit field, followed by the field offset and the field width. For example:

BFCHG ⟨EA⟩ (offset : width)

The new PACK and UNPK instructions can be used to store binary coded decimal (BCD) data, packed with two digits per byte and to unpack it into one BCD digit per byte. A user-defined constant may be added by both the PACK and UNPK instructions to allow conversion to or from ASCII, EBCDIC or other data formats.

The new CHK2 (check 2) and CMP2 (compare 2) instructions are used to compare the upper and lower bounds in either signed or unsigned format. The CMP2 instruction sets condition codes according to the result of the operation. CHK2 sets the condition codes and causes a system trap if either boundary condition fails.

The new CAS (compare and swap) instruction compares the contents of a data register to the operand at the effective address and, if they are equal, the contents of a second data register are used to update the operand at the effective address. If the register contents and the operand are not equal, the operand remains unchanged but the value in the register is updated with the operand at the effective address. The CAS2 instruction is similar to CAS but uses two compare registers (for upper and lower bounds), two update registers and two operands at different effective addresses. CAS and CAS2 instructions are non-interruptible to ensure data security in single and multiprocessor systems. Typical applications are for updating system counters and for insertion and deletion from linked lists.

The new TRAPcc (trap conditionally) instruction can use any condition code as the trapping condition and can be followed by a word or long word which conveys information to the trap handler such as a high-level language statement number or other debugging information.

The MC68020 has several enhanced multiply and division instructions including two which give 32-bit results which are the same size as the 32-bit operands. This is intended to support high-level languages such as Pascal or C where an integer times an integer results in an integer of the same size.

4.1.6 Virtual machine

A virtual memory system is supported to permit a relatively small main memory with a low access time to be directly accessed by the processor while maintaining an image of a much larger virtual memory on slower secondary storage devices. An attempted access of a location in the virtual memory map, which is not in physical memory, is referred to as a page fault. This causes the access to be temporarily suspended while the data is fetched from the secondary store and placed in physical memory; then the suspended access is completed.

The MC68020 supports virtual memory by suspending an instruction's execution when a bus error is produced by a page fault. The instruction is completed after the physical memory has been updated.

A typical use of a virtual machine system is to develop software, such as an operating system, for use on a different machine. To do this the host operating system emulates the hardware of the target system and allows the new operating system to be executed and debugged as it would on the target system. The new operating system must execute at a lower privilege level than the host operating system in order to trap any attempts by the new operating system to use virtual resources which are not present and to permit them to be emulated by software.

The MC68020 fully supports a virtual machine by running the new operating system in the user mode and the host operating system in the supervisor mode. This causes the host operating system to trap any attempts by the new operating system to access supervisor resources or execute privileged instructions.

4.2 Performance calculations

4.2.1 Factors which influence performance

MC68020 instruction timing calculations are made difficult due to

a) Instruction prefetch and the on-chip instruction cache.
b) Operand misalignment.
c) Instruction execution overlap.

These factors make timing calculations on a single instruction basis untypical of performance when executing performance benchmark programs.

The MC68020 User's Manual includes a set of instruction timing tables which may be used to calculate the best and worst case bounds for an instruction stream. It is not possible to calculate exact timing from these tables because they cannot anticipate the combination of factors which will influence a particular sequence of instructions. Absolute instruction timing must be measured by using the microprocessor to execute the target instruction stream.

Instruction prefetches which result in a cache hit occur with no delay in instruction execution. Instruction prefetches which result in a cache miss cause one external memory cycle to be performed. The MC68020 always prefetches long words. If, for example, a branch to an odd word location causes the instruction prefetch to fall on an odd word boundary, the even word associated with the long word base address will be read at the same time as the odd word is read (with 32-bit memory). An instruction prefetch normally falls on an even word boundary and the MC68020 reads both words at the long word address, effectively prefetching the next two words.

Operand misalignment occurs when the address of a word operand falls across a long word boundary or a long word operand falls on a byte or word address which is not a long word boundary. Additional bus cycles are required to carry out transfers where operand misalignment occurs.

Concurrent operation of the bus controller and sequencer within the MC68020 introduces ambiguity into the calculation of instruction timing due to potential overlap of instruction execution. For example, the sequencer may request a bus cycle which the bus controller cannot perform immediately, causing the bus cycle to wait until the current cycle is complete.

Instruction overlap is the number of clock periods for which two instructions execute simultaneously. It is possible for the execution time of an instruction to be absorbed by the overlap with a previous instruction, resulting in a net execution time of zero clock periods.

4.2.2 Instruction execution time examples

Figures 4.4 to 4.7 show the activity of the bus controller, sequencer and bus while executing a simple sequence of instructions:

```
MOVE.L  D4, (A1)+
ADD.L  D4, D5
MOVE.L  (A1), – (A2)
ADD.L  D5, D6
```

It is assumed that a 32-bit memory data path is used. Figure 4.4 assumes that the cache is disabled and the first instruction is prefetched from an odd word address. Memory is accessed with zero wait states. Figure 4.4 shows instruction overlap during clock periods 3 to 6 as the bus controller performs a write to memory as part of the first MOVE instruction. The sequencer performs the ADD instruction during clock periods 4 and 5 and begins the source effective address calculation for the second MOVE instruction during clock period 6. The bus controller activity overlaps the execution of the first ADD instruction causing the attributed execution time for the first ADD to be zero.

Fig. 4.4 Processor activity with no cache, no wait states and odd instruction alignment for the first instruction

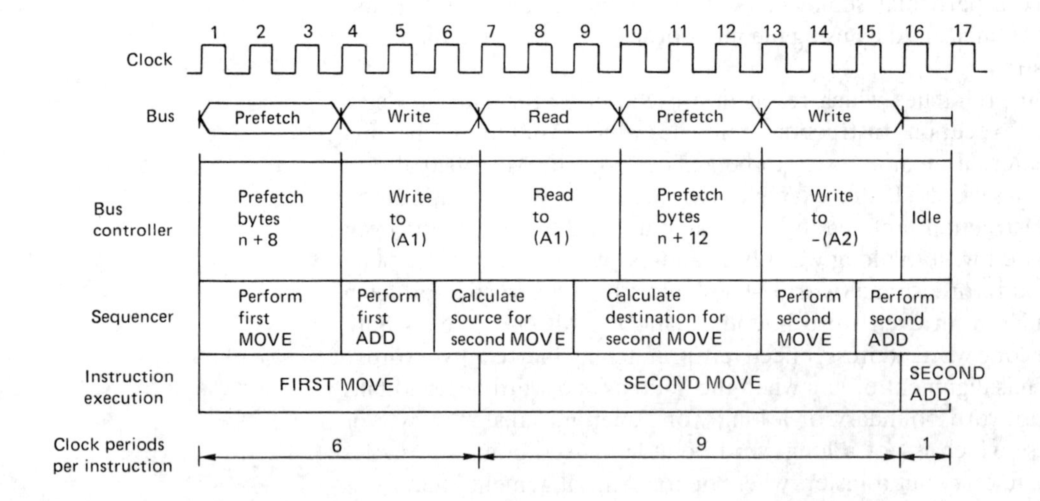

The second MOVE instruction has an effective execution time of 9 clocks which has been shortened by one clock period because of overlap with the bus controller which completes the write operation of the first MOVE instruction while the sequencer begins the effective address calculation of the second move instruction. During clock cycle 15 the sequencer performs the second ADD instruction while the bus controller is writing to the second MOVE instruction destination. The effective execution time of the second ADD instruction is shortened by one clock period because of overlap with the second MOVE instruction and has an attributed execution time of one clock period.

Figure 4.5 shows the execution of the same instruction stream under the same conditions except that the instructions are placed differently in

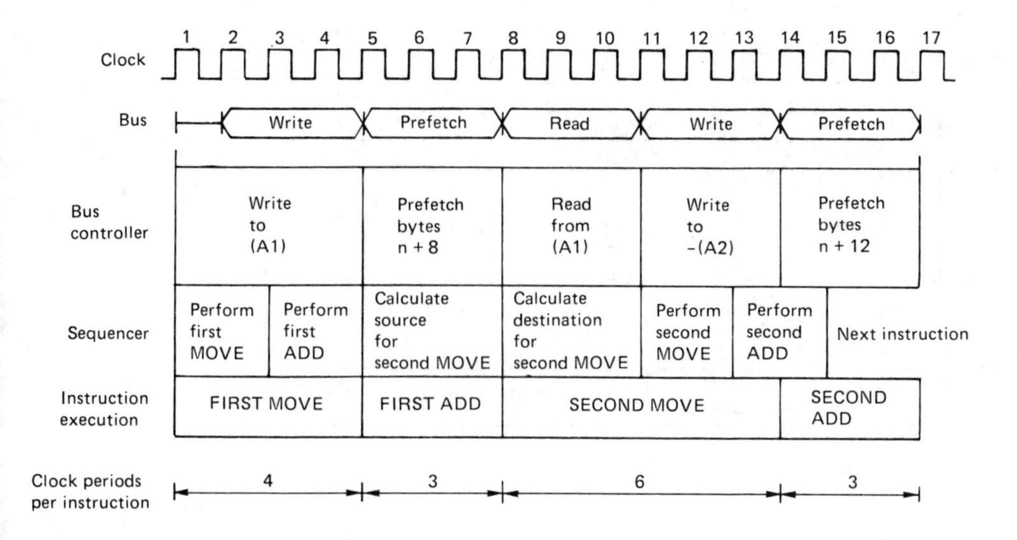

Fig. 4.5 Processor activity with no cache, no wait states and even instruction alignment for the first instruction

memory with the first instruction prefetched from an even word address. The total execution time is not changed but the individual instruction execution times are different to those shown in Figure 4.4 demonstrating that the effects of overlap are dependent on the alignment of instructions in memory.

Figure 4.6 shows the execution of the same instruction stream with the cache enabled, all instructions in cache and zero memory wait states. Because the instructions are in cache the alignment of the original instructions in memory is not relevant to timing. The total number of clock cycles is reduced from 16 to 12 clock periods. No external bus cycles are required for instruction prefetch because the instructions are in cache. Prefetch occurs without delay and the bus controller is often idle.

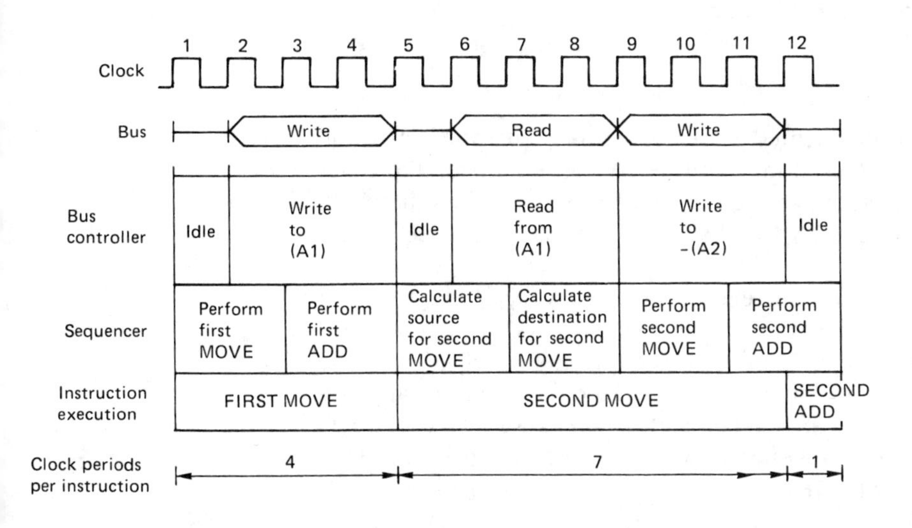

Fig. 4.6 Processor activity with instructions in cache and no wait states

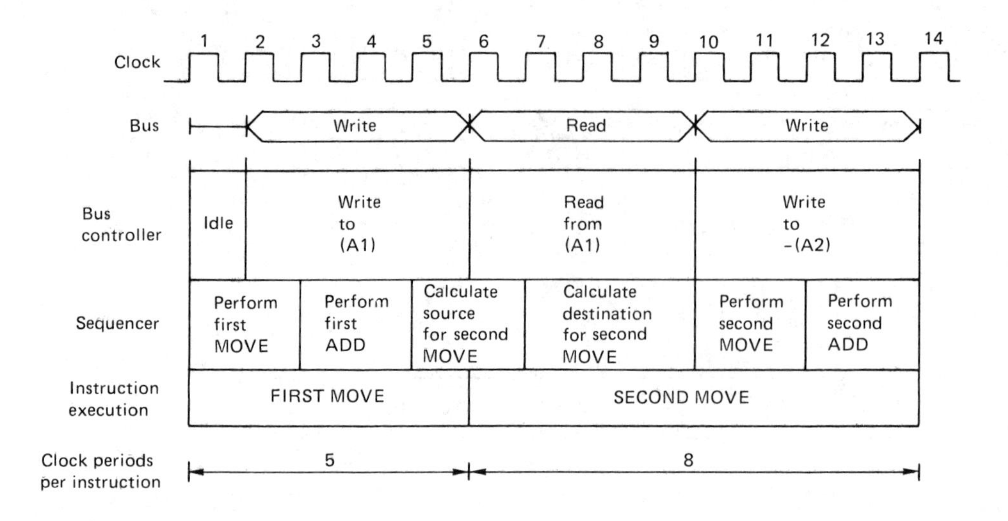

Fig. 4.7 Processor activity with instructions in cache and 1 wait state

Figure 4.7 shows the execution of the same instruction stream with the cache enabled, all instructions in cache but with one memory wait state, making four clock periods necessary for every read or write. Because the idle bus cycles gained by the use of a cache coincide with the memory access wait states, the total execution time, 13 clock periods, is only one more than required with no wait states.

As demonstrated by these four examples, it is not possible to calculate the exact number of clock cycles required for individual instructions because of the effects of the instruction sequence and alignment, cache hits and memory wait states. The best timing predictions which can be made are in terms of the best, average and worse case limits for a string of instructions. Performance ratios for similar tasks and appropriate benchmarks are the best way of comparing the performance of one 32-bit microprocessor with another.

4.3 Floating-point coprocessor

4.3.1 Basic functions

The MC68881 is a register-oriented processor which extends the instruction set of the M68000 family but it may also be used as a peripheral to other processors. The architecture has been designed to permit integration with future processors. Figure 4.8 shows how the MC68881 is connected in a MC68020 system.

Figure 4.9 shows the internal registers of the MC68881. Eight 80-bit floating-point data registers are provided to hold numbers in extended precision data format. Numbers may be transferred to the MC68881 in single (32-bit), double (64-bit) or double extended (80-bit) format but are converted into an extended real number and all operations take place in extended precision. Table 4.2 shows the sizes of each field in the three floating-point formats of the IEEE P754 floating-point standard.

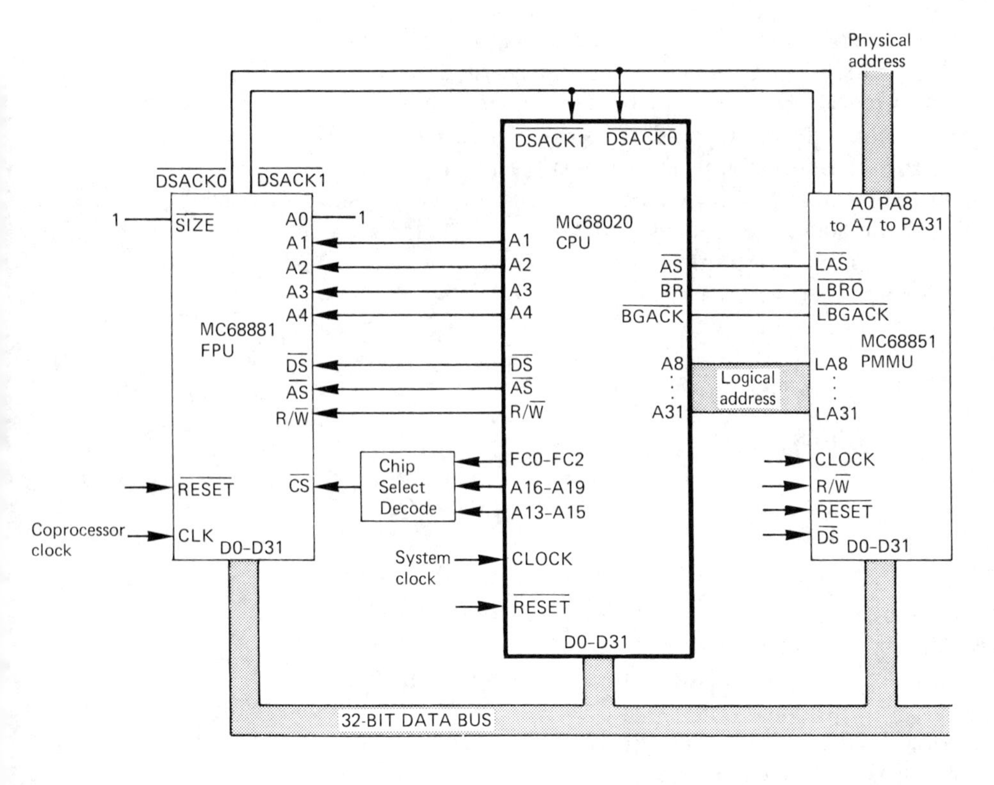

Fig. 4.8 MC68881 connected in a MC68020 system

Table 4.2 Number of bits in each field for three types of floating-point data size

	Single	*Double*	*Double Extended*
Sign	1	1	1
Exponent	8	11	15
Mantissa	23	52	64
Total	32	64	80

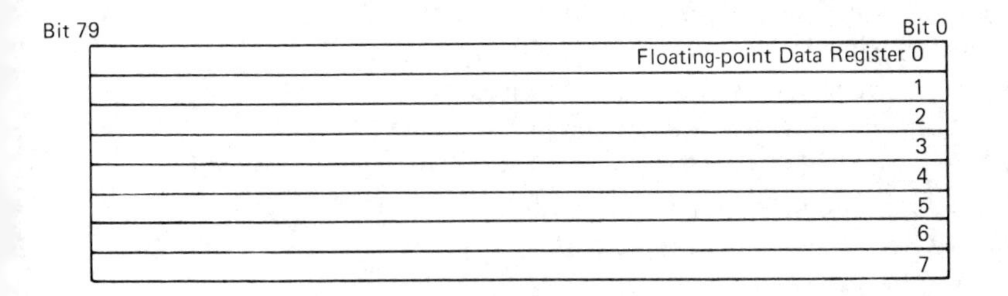

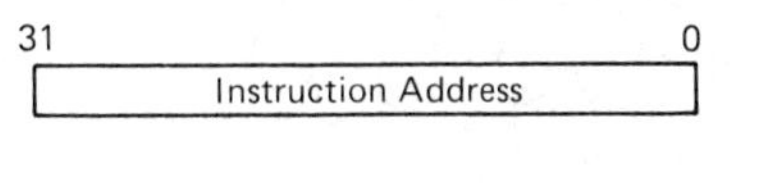

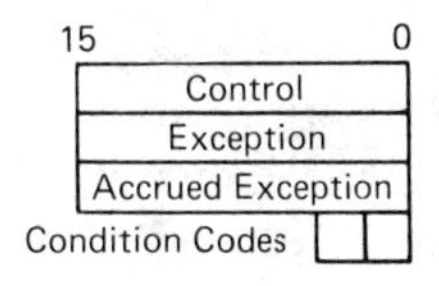

Fig. 4.9 Internal registers of the MC68881

The 16-bit accrued exception word contains the logical exclusive OR of exceptions for all operations since the last clear of the accrued exception register. The exception register contains only the exceptions from the last operation and the condition code register holds the result of the last compare instruction. The instruction address register contains the main processor memory address for the last instruction executed by the coprocessor. The purpose of the instruction address register is to determine the address of the faulty instruction during an error trap.

The arithmetic operations performed are

a) Add (3 μs)
b) Subtract
c) Multiply (4 μs)
d) Divide (6 μs)
e) Remainder
f) Compare (2 μs)
g) Square root
h) Integer part.

(Figures in brackets are single precision execution times for an MC68020 with an MC68881 coprocessor using a 16 MHz clock.)

More than 40 instructions are provided including transcendental functions (sin, e^x, log, etc.).

In addition to normalised numbers, some special data types are recognised from the largest and smallest exponents:

a) Positive True Zero
b) Negative True Zero
c) Plus Infinity
d) Minus Infinity
e) Denormalised Numbers
f) Not-a-Number.

The MC68881 includes a 67-bit arithmetic logic unit for manipulating mantissa bits and a barrel shifter which can shift from 1 to 67 bits in one machine cycle. The coprocessor interface tasks are shared between the MC68881 and the MC68020 with the tasks which are executed most efficiently in the MC68020 being carried out in the MC68020 at the request of the coprocessor. The MC68020 and MC68881 will only execute concurrently on an instruction-by-instruction basis as determined by the MC68881. The MC68020 coprocessor interface is described in section 2.6.4.

A 16.67 MHz MC68020 and MC68881 give a combined floating-point benchmark performance of 1.2 MWhetstones/second. The higher-performance MC68882 floating-point coprocessor uses 1.2 μm CHMOS. The 10% reduction in chip size helps to improve performance by 2 to 4 times.

4.3.2 System integration

A major performance bottleneck with floating-point coprocessors is the time taken to transfer data between the main processor and the coprocessor. Earlier types of floating-point processor used standard I/O operations for communication with the main processor. The standard MC68020 coprocessor interface handshake offers an improvement in total execution time of about four times that which may be achieved using conventional I/O instructions. Even if the floating-point processor executed instructions in zero time, the net improvement in total execution time would only be about a factor of two using conventional I/O instructions.

Silicon Graphics have employed a novel method of improving the total execution time for floating-point instructions using an MC68881 with an MC68020 in their Iris 3030 Workstation. To reduce total floating-point instruction execution times by a factor of two to three times compared with the standard MC68020 coprocessor interface procedure, they treat the MC68881 as a memory location on the microprocessor bus. The four most significant address bits are used to create sixteen memory segments which are used for special purposes including the passing of data between the MC68020 and the MC68881.

The four most significant address bits are decoded and, when four 1 bits are detected, a floating-point operation is performed using the least significant 15 address bits to send control information to the MC68881 with each 32-bit data transfer. Using the MC68020's fastest addressing mode, absolute short address, the control information in the lower 15 bits is sign-extended to generate automatically the four 1 bits in the most significant address bits.

This approach to integrating the MC68881 into the system has resulted in single-precision additions being executed in 1 μs and double precision addition being executed in 1.5 μs including all data and control information transfers. This scheme does however impose two limitations which may be unacceptable in some applications:

a) The direct memory addressing range of the MC68020 is reduced from 4 Gbytes to 250 Mbytes.
b) The compilers and operating system must be modified to take the design into account by passing control bits in the address.

4.4 Paged memory management unit

4.4.1 Basic functions

The MC68851 Paged Memory Management Unit (PMMU) is a coprocessor chip designed for use with the MC68020 in applications where a paged memory management system is required. The PMMU performs virtual memory management, that is it translates logical addresses from the MC68020 into physical addresses within the range of the primary and secondary memory fitted to the system. It also provides paging and access control for memory.

The physical to logical address map is stored in tables, located in memory which both the MC68020 and MC68851 can access. The PMMU has an internal 64-entry translation cache which stores the most recently used translation table entries to avoid the need for additional bus cycles every time a translation takes place. When the logical address being accessed by the

MC68020 matches an entry in the translation cache, the translation occurs in less than 45 ns. When there is no valid entry, external memory is accessed to load the translation into cache. Typically the time required to search for the mapping descriptor is less than 1 μs where two table levels are used.

The translation cache is fully associative and a pseudo least recently used algorithm is employed for replacement of the 64 entries. An average hit rate of greater than 98% can be expected with a typical operating system and application code. Descriptors for time-critical code or data sections may be locked into the cache to avoid any possibility of table searching.

The register set of the MC68851 and the M68000 family instruction set extensions are shown in Appendix A. Ten registers control the translation and protection features, and instructions are provided for PMMU control functions, loading and storing PMMU registers, and testing access rights and conditional bits set by tests.

4.4.2 System connections

Figure 4.10 shows how the MC68851 is connected into a memory system. Communication between the PMMU and the MC68020 is via the standard coprocessor interface. This makes the MC68851 registers appear as an

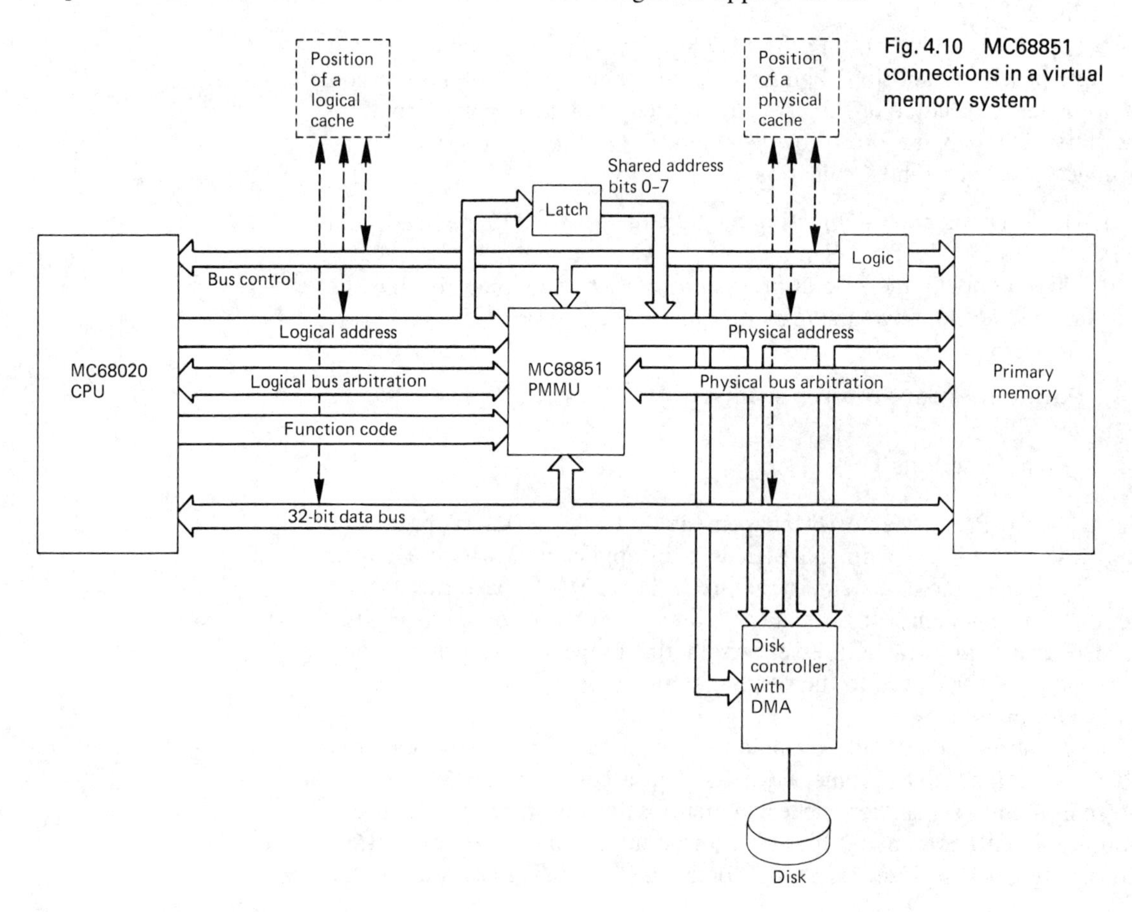

Fig. 4.10 MC68851 connections in a virtual memory system

extension of the MC68020 programming model and the PMMU instruction set becomes an extension of the MC68020 instruction set and so may be mixed with standard MC68020 code. Pages may be set to one of eight values between 256 bytes and 32 Kbytes, the number of table levels may be set, the privilege level may be set to one of 8 protection levels, and the number of address lines may be set up to a maximum of 32.

Figure 4.11 shows the main signals on the MC68851 which is packaged in a pin grid array. The microprocessor bus interface operation is asynchronous and has separate address and data lines. The PMMU has the same dynamic bus sizing capability as the MC68020, permitting communication with 8, 16 or 32-bit wide memory on a cycle-by-cycle basis. Multiple bus masters are supported using bus request and acknowledge arbitration circuitry in the PMMU.

When an off-chip instruction and data cache is included in a memory system, it may be placed on either the logical or physical side of the PMMU. A physical cache will introduce wait states unless extremely fast memory is used because the PMMU translation time is added to the cache access time. A logical cache does not have PMMU translation time added to its access time but it suffers from the problem of differentiating between tasks using the same logical addresses in a multi-tasking operating system.

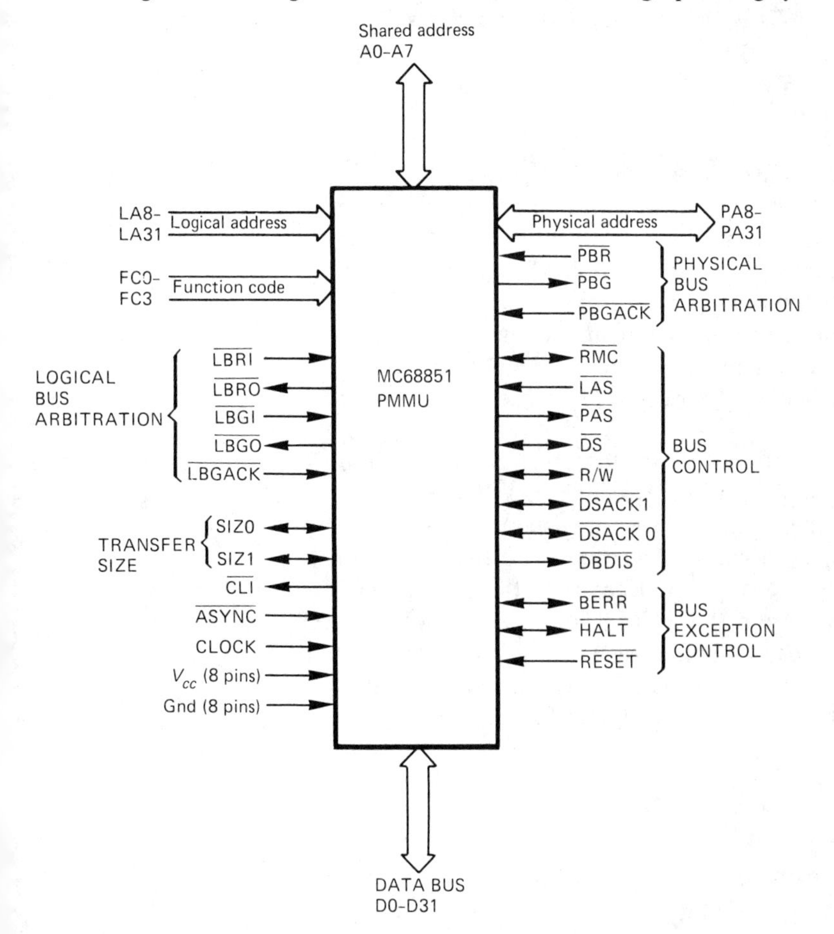

Fig. 4.11 Main signal groups of the MC68851

It may also hold stale data in multiprocessor systems or systems with multiple bus masters.

To help reduce the PMMU-induced delays in a physical cache system the cache may signal the completion of a transfer cycle by asserting DSACK before the cache access has been fully validated. Thus tag validation logic in the cache has more time to function; if an error is found up to one clock cycle later the BERR will invalidate the access.

A cache in a multiprocessor system must prevent areas of memory used by different processors being cached and modified locally making the data in main memory stale. A physical cache may use a DMA monitor to detect accesses by other processors and to invalidate entries which have been modified by different processors. A logical cache is unable to use a monitor because the monitor would not be aware of the physical address map. An alternative solution is to make the operating system designate shared global address pages, identified by a cache-inhibit bit in the page descriptor, which are not read into the cache.

The problem of task differentiation with logical caches and multi-tasking operating systems may be overcome by using a task alias value which the PMMU uses to identify tasks within its own translation cache. The MC68020 can read this value and incorporate it in the tag field of the logical cache. The task alias value for a cache enquiry is compared with the value in the tag field for the stored entry.

4.4.3 Breakpoint facilities

Breakpoint facilities are incorporated in the PMMU for system development purposes. When one of the eight M68000 breakpoint op-codes is detected, the MC68020 informs external hardware of the breakpoint by performing a breakpoint acknowledge cycle. The PMMU contains eight pairs of breakpoint registers at appropriate addresses which contain replacement op-codes for the breakpoint instruction and control information (including a breakpoint skip count to determine the number of times a replacement op-code is returned to the MC68020 before a bus error is signalled).

Counting breakpoints may be used in loops to detect error conditions in timers and counters or to compile statistics on code usage. Eight sections of code may be monitored by the eight breakpoint registers. An instruction in each section of code is replaced with a breakpoint and the instruction is stored in the PMMU breakpoint register. Each time the breakpoint is accessed, the opcode is loaded from the PMMU into the MC68020 and executed while the skip count is decremented. When the skip count reaches zero a bus error is generated and a trap handler can add the count to an accumulated count held by the operating system for each segment of code.

4.4.4 Address translation

The address translation table, stored in external memory, is tree structured and uses the logical address as an index to the branches of the tree. The translation control register can configure the translation mechanism to suit a variety of applications. A wide address range with sparse use of memory, as may be required for artificial intelligence applications, may be achieved without using large translation tables.

The PMMU may be used to implement either paged or segmented memory management by setting the variable parameters appropriately. If a mapping descriptor indicates that the table search should end before all the fields are used, a segment is assumed to exist and the descriptor contains the addresses of the contiguous set of pages which comprise the segment.

4.4.5 Protection mechanisms

The protection mechanisms of the PMMU include five protection classes which may be applied to individual pages or sets of pages:

a) No access, which denies access to pages or groups of pages in the logical address space.
b) Read only, which prevents overwriting.
c) Supervisor only, which prevents access by user code and is useful when the supervisor and user share the same address space.
d) Program only, which permits only program code in areas of the logical address space.
e) Data only, which permits only data in areas of the logical address space.

The user/supervisor mode distinction is applied to all address translations and different tables are used to provide user to user protection. In addition, a ring-like protection mechanism for user tasks may be constructed by the PMMU. Zero, two, four or eight levels of protection may be applied to code modules and access rights are granted to other levels through gates which are authorised by the operating system. Level 0 has highest priority.

The upper bits of the logical address indicate the access level and each bus cycle run by the logical bus master is checked for adequate privilege levels by the PMMU. For example, eight levels of protection use bits 29–31 of the logical address as access level bits to indicate the protection level of the code module rather than being used as table indexes. If the access level bits indicate a priority level which is higher than that stored in the current access level register of the PMMU and an access to the user space is attempted, a bus error signal is generated by the PMMU and the cycle is terminated.

5 Inmos T414 transputer

5.1 T414 architecture

The T414 transputer has been selected for more detailed treatment because it is the first commercial 32-bit microprocessor to make parallel processing a reality.

The T414 transputer is a 32-bit microprocessor with a RISC CPU, 2 Kbytes of on-chip RAM, four high-speed serial communications links and a timer with 1 μs resolution (see Figure 5.1). The internal architecture follows the von Neumann design with a single address and data bus linking the CPU to the on-chip and off-chip memory. The transputer includes many features which make it capable of being employed in parallel processing applications and of being connected, with few additional components, in two-dimensional processor arrays.

When employed as a single microprocessor, the T414 outperforms most other 32-bit microprocessors and typically requires half the amount of instruction code but it does not support virtual memory and it does not have an elaborate interrupt structure to support many memory mapped peripherals. In parallel multiprocessor applications the transputer with its Occam programing language has no serious competition but compilers have been produced for C, Pascal, Fortran, Ada and Lisp to support more conventional applications.

5.1.1 The transputer family

The first member of the transputer family to become generally available (in 1985) was the T414 which is a 32-bit machine with a 2 Kbyte memory. A similar 16-bit chip, the T212, provides a 2 Kbyte RAM and four high-speed serial communications links but it has a 16-bit address/data bus which limits the direct memory addressing range to 64 Kbytes. A specialised 16-bit transputer, the M212, provides a dedicated disk interface for ST506 or several other disk interface standards and has two serial communication links.

The G412 graphics controller is a 32-bit transputer with a graphics output interface including a colour look-up table with red, green and blue video outputs. A floating-point version of the 32-bit transputer, the T800, includes a 4 Kbyte on-chip memory, four serial communications links capable of 20 Mbit/s and an on-chip floating-point processor operating in parallel

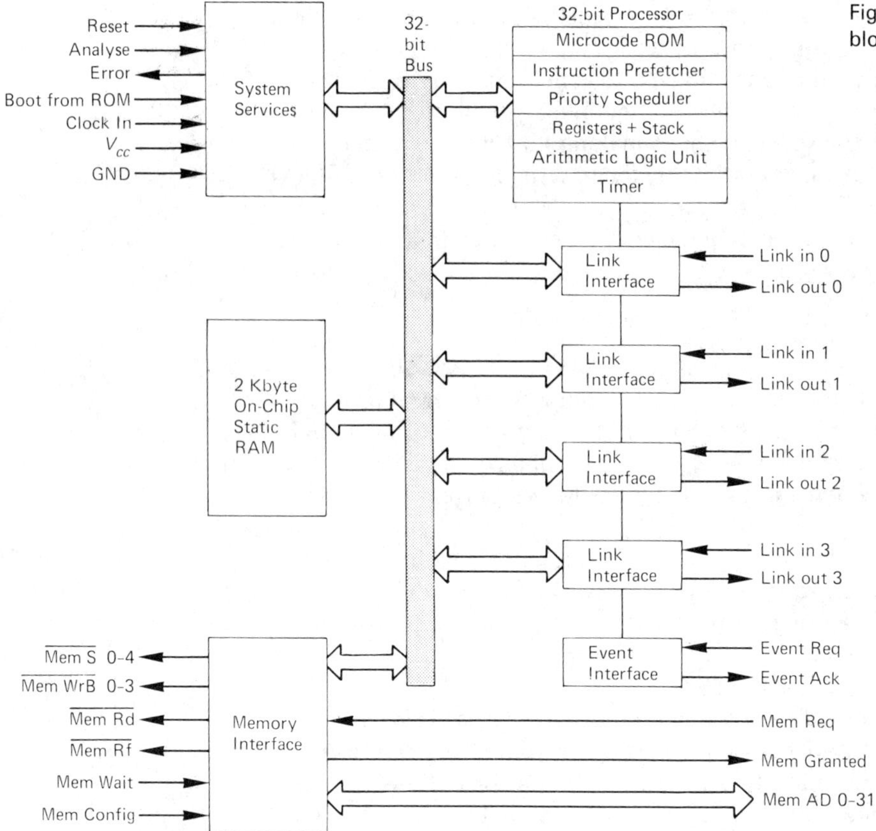

Fig. 5.1 T414 functional block diagram

with the CPU.

The 20 MHz version of the T800 is capable of sustaining 1.5 million floating-point operations per second (Mflops) with 32-bit calculations and 1.1 Mflops with 64-bit calculations, an improvement of 5 to 10 times on the T414. A 30 MHz version will be capable of 2.25 Mflops. Single-precision floating-point additions or multiplications take 350 ns at 20 MHz while multiplication takes 850 ns and division takes 950 ns. Performance with a Whetstone benchmark is 4 MWhetstones/second, about four times faster than the MC68020 with an MC68881 and estimated to be about twice the speed of the MC68030 with an MC68882 coprocessor.

Support chips for the transputer family include the C011 serial link adaptor which produces one byte-wide input interface and one byte-wide output for interface purposes. The C012 serial link adaptor provides an interface between a serial link and an 8-bit bi-directional system bus. Data on the T414, M212, C011 and C012 is provided in Appendix B. A crossbar switch chip (C004) is available to switch 32 serial link inputs to 32 serial link outputs under the control of a 33rd serial link. This may be used to reconfigure transputer networks and may be cascaded to switch larger networks.

Early versions of the transputer executed instructions at 10 Mips but later versions provide 20 Mips performance using the same 5 MHz external clock which is frequency multiplied on-chip to generate the required clock frequency. By this means it is possible to upgrade a system to use higher-speed versions of the transputer without making any changes to the circuitry. Transputers are available with 20 Mbit/s serial links but retain the option of switching to 10 Mbit/s for compatibility with slower parts of the system. The configuration of off-chip memory types and their access times may be selected during a system reset.

5.1.2 Serial links

The means by which the transputer family implements concurrent processing on several transputer chips is determined by the design of the serial links and the use of Occam channels. A basic description of the architecture is given in Section 3.9 and the use of Occam for concurrent processing is described in Section 9.4.

Each serial link provides two Occam channels, one in each direction. Communication may take place simultaneously on all four serial links while the CPU is busy. A T414 using a 50 ns cycle time with four links operating at 10 Mbit/s in both directions, using internal memory, has a maximum load on CPU performance of about 8%.

Messages are transmitted as a sequence of bytes. Each eight-bit byte is preceded by two 1 bits and followed by a 0 bit. An acknowledge consisting of a 1 and a 0 bit is returned to signify that the receiving transputer is ready to receive another byte (see Figure 5.2). Both links carry data and acknowledgements. To permit continuous transmission, the receiving transputer should transmit the acknowledgement as soon as it begins to clock in the data byte.

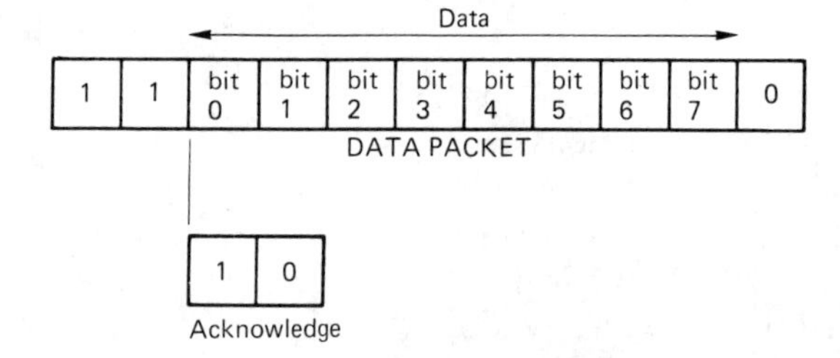

Fig. 5.2 Serial link message format

All types of transputer will provide a 10 MHz data rate option in order to permit link compatibility. Communication is wordlength-independent to permit communication between the 16-bit T212 and the 32-bit T414. Transputers with independent clocks may communicate using serial links if the clock frequencies are within 400 parts per million. This permits the use of inexpensive crystals. To extend the length of the serial links, RS-422 or similar balanced line drivers and receivers may be employed. Unbalanced drivers and receivers are unsuitable because the positive-going transition time of the link waveform must closely match the negative-going transition time.

5.1.3 Registers

Six registers are used in the execution of sequential processes:

a) The workspace pointer which points to an area of store containing local variables (W ptr).
b) The instruction pointer which points to the next instruction to be executed (I ptr).
c) The operand register which is used to form instruction operands (O reg).
d) Three registers A, B and C, which form an evaluation stack used for expression evaluation, holding the operands of scheduling and communication instructions and parameters of procedure calls (A reg, B reg, C reg).

5.1.4 Communications and concurrent processing

For concurrent processing, the optimum method of programming the T414 is in Occam. The Occam model of concurrency and communication is directly supported by the transputer hardware. A scheduler permits any number of concurrent processes to be executed together, sharing processor time. Process switching time is less than 1 μs and inter-process communication uses I/O memory block moves. Active processes awaiting execution are held on a linked list of workspaces which is implemented by two registers, one pointing to the first process on the list and the other to the last process (see Figure 5.3). Whenever a process is unable to proceed, its instruction pointer is saved in its workspace and the next process is taken from the list.

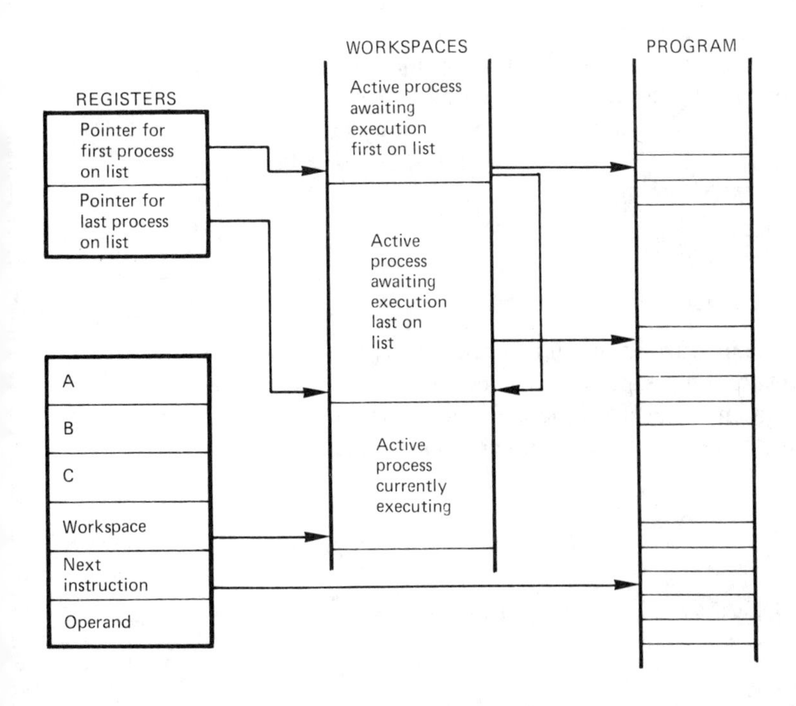

Fig. 5.3 Registers and workspaces for concurrent processes

The two levels of priority, known in Occam notation as PRI and PAR (Priority Parallel), are supported. Processes may be either low priority or high priority. Low-priority processes must wait to be executed until no high-priority processes are active. Low-priority processes are periodically time-sliced to provide an even distribution of processor time between tasks which demand large amounts of processing time. Each time-slice period lasts for 4096 cycles of the 5 MHz clock-in (about 800 μs). High-priority processes should not be allowed to occupy the processor continuously for a full time-slice period.

Occam channels provide links between processes. Internal channels are implemented by single words in memory but channels between processes executing on different transputers are implemented by serial links. The address of the channel determines whether a channel is internal or external; this permits a process to be written and compiled without constraining the connection of its channels.

A process prepares for input or output by loading the evaluation stack with

a) The identity of the channel
b) The number of bytes to be transferred
c) A pointer to a buffer.

An internal channel passes a message by storing the identity of the first process to become ready (either the inputting or outputting process) in the channel word and the pointer is stored in the workspace. The processor then executes the next process from the scheduling list. When the second process using the channel is ready, the message is copied, the waiting process is added to the active process list, and the channel is reset to the empty state.

When the message is passed by an external channel the processor passes the transfer to an autonomous link interface and deschedules the process. When the link interface has transferred the message by a direct memory access mechanism it causes the processor to reschedule the waiting process. The processor can execute other processes while the external message transfer takes place.

The *link interface* has three registers containing:

a) A pointer to the workspace for the process
b) A pointer to the message
c) The number of bytes to be transferred.

These registers are initialised and the instruction pointer stored in the process workspace when the input or output message is to be executed. When both processors have initialised both link interfaces, the message is copied and both link interfaces add the process to the end of the local active list.

5.1.5 Memory organisation

The directly addressable memory space is 4 Gbytes with the 2 Kbyte on-chip memory addresses in the range

80000000 to 80000800 (octal)

Off-chip memory is accessed by a 32-bit multiplexed address/data interface capable of transfering up to 25 Mbyte/s. An on-chip configurable memory controller provides all timing, including control signals and dynamic RAM refresh signals for a variety of mixed memory configurations.

The address space is linear and any byte is identified by a pointer which is a single word of data containing a word address and a byte selector in the least significant two bits. Pointer values are signed, starting at the most negative integer and passing through zero to the most positive integer. The use of a signed address space permits the comparison functions to be used on pointer values as well as on numerical values.

The memory interface controller may be reconfigured on reset to provide one of 13 preset configurations or an externally generated configuration type loaded from a PAL or ROM. The *memory interface* has six states (T states):

(T1) Address set-up time before address valid strobe
(T2) Address hold time after address valid strobe
(T3) Read cycle tristate/write cycle data set-up
(T4) Read or write data
(T5) Read or write data
(T6) End tristate/data hold

Each T state may be configured to have 1 to 4 T_m periods to suit the memory used, where T_m is half the processor cycle time. T4 may also be extended to produce wait states by holding the MemWait input high as shown in Figure 5.4. When dynamic RAM is used the refresh can be enabled with a refresh every 18, 36, 54, or 72 periods of the input clock signal. A refresh cycle outputs a 9-bit refresh address on MemAD2-10. This is decremented after each refresh cycle.

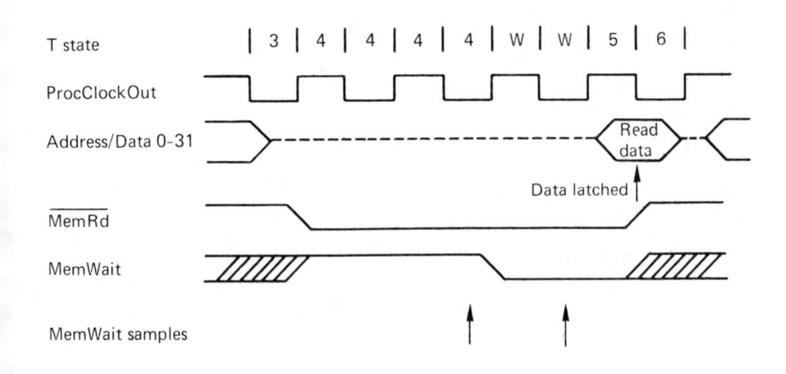

Fig. 5.4 Memory cycles with MemWait extending T4 by two periods

5.1.6 The instruction set

The principles of the transputer instruction set were described briefly in Section 2.7.4. The instruction set was designed to give the most frequently used instructions the most compact representation and to make compilation most efficient. The instructions are all multiples of 8-bits in length and are independent of the wordlength of the transputer, thus the same code may be run on 16 or 32-bit transputers.

Each instruction is one byte long with the four most significant bits forming the function code and the four least significant bits forming the data value. Thirteen of the functions, the direct functions, encode the most important operations.

Two other short instructions, the prefix and negative prefix instructions, are used to extend the length of any instruction's operand. This simplifies language compilation by providing a standard method for giving any instruction an operand of any size up to the processor wordlength (32-bits for the T414). To optimise object code the number of prefix instructions should be kept to a minimum.

The OPR instruction causes its operand to be interpreted as an operation on the values held in the stack. By this method, up to 16 operations may be encoded in a single byte instruction.

The W ptr register is used as a base to address the local variables and channels of a process. The three registers A reg, B reg and C reg form a three-word evaluation stack which holds the source and destination of most arithmetic and logical operations. When a value is loaded into the stack, the contents of B reg are pushed into C reg and A reg into B reg before A reg is loaded. The evaluation of operators with two operands is performed by instructions which combine the values of A reg and B reg.

The most common operations are loading and storing variables and literal values. The ldc (load constant) instruction is a single-byte instruction which loads values between 0 and 15 into the stack. The ldl (load local variable), stl (store local variable) and ldlp (load pointer to local variable) instructions identify locations in memory relative to the workspace pointer. A local variable held in location x can be pushed onto the stack by the ldlx instruction and its address pushed by ldlpx. By using stlx, the value of the variable can be set to a value popped from the stack.

Single-length signed arithmetic with overflow is provided by these instructions:

add	addition	(cumulative)
sub	subtraction	
mult	multiplication	(cumulative)
div	division	
rem	remainder	
adc	add constant	

Single-length arithmetic without overflow is provided by

sum	addition	(cumulative)
diff	subtraction	
prod	multiplication	(cumulative)

Logic and shift instructions include:

and	bitwise and	(cumulative)
or	bitwise or	(cumulative)
xor	bitwise exclusive or	(cumulative)
not	bitwise not	
shl	shift left	
shr	shift right	

Shift operations shift the operand in B reg by the number of bits specified in the A reg

Comparisons and conditional behaviour are provided by

diff	difference
eqc	equal to constant
gt	greater
j	jump
cj	conditional jump

The jump instruction deschedules the process if the current time-slice period has been exceeded to ensure that the opportunity to deschedule arises once in each loop. Conditional jump never deschedules the process.

Single-byte addressing instructions which provide access to items in data structures include:

bcnt	byte count
wcnt	word count

bcnt multiplies A reg by the number of bytes in the word and wcnt decomposes an address into its component word part and byte selector.

Input of a variable uses the instruction:

C ? V = (address(V); address (C); length(V); input)

Output of a variable uses the instruction:

C ! V = (address(V); address(C); length(X); output)

Single-word outputs for a value e use the instruction:

C ! e = (address(C); e; outword)

Procedures may be implemented using the instructions:

call	call
gcall	general call
adj	adjust
gadj	general adjust
ret	return

The call instruction adjusts the workspace pointer storing the instruction pointer and three evaluation stack registers. The return instruction restores the instruction pointer and deallocates the four locations using the workspace pointer. A complete list of instructions is given in Table 5.1.

Table 5.1 T-series Transputer Instructions

Direct, Prefixing and Indirect Functions

Code	Abbreviation	Name
#07	ldl	load local
#0D	stl	store local
#01	ldlp	load local pointer
#03	ldnl	load non-local
#0E	stnl	store non-local
#05	ldnlp	load non-local pointer
#0C	eqc	equals constant
#04	ldc	load constant
#08	adc	add constant
#00	j	jump
#0A	cj	conditional jump
#09	call	call
#0B	ajw	adjust workspace
#02	pfix	prefix
#06	nfix	negative prefix
#0F	opr	operate

Operations

Code	Size	Abbreviation	Name
#00	short	rev	reverse
#20	long	ret	return
#1B	long	ldpi	load pointer to instruction
#3C	long	gajw	general adjust workspace
#06	short	gcall	general call
#42	long	mint	minimum integer
#21	long	lend	loop end
#13	long	csub0	check subscript from 0
#4D	long	cont1	check count from 1
#29	long	testerr	test error false and clear
#10	long	seterr	set error
#55	long	stoperr	stop on error
#57	long	clrhalterr	clear halt-on-error
#58	long	sethalterr	set halt-on-error
#59	long	testhalterr	test halt-on-error
#02	short	bsub	byte subscript
#0A	short	wsub	word subscript
#34	long	bcnt	byte count
#3F	long	wcnt	word count
#01	short	lb	load byte
#3B	long	sb	store byte
#4A	long	move	move message
#46	long	and	and
#4B	long	or	or
#33	long	xor	exclusive or
#32	long	not	bitwise not
#41	long	shl	shift left
#40	long	shr	shift right
#05	short	add	add

Operations

Code	Size	Abbreviation	Name
#0C	short	sub	subtract
#53	long	mul	multiply
#2C	long	div	divide
#1F	long	rem	remainder
#09	short	gt	greater than
#04	short	diff	difference
#52	long	sum	sum
#08	short	prod	product
#0D	short	startp	start process
#03	short	endp	end process
#39	long	runp	run process
#15	long	stopp	stop process
#1E	long	ldpri	load current priority
#07	short	in	input message
#0B	short	out	output message
#0F	short	outword	output word
#0E	short	outbyte	output byte
#12	long	resetch	reset channel
#43	long	alt	alt start
#44	long	altwt	alt wait
#45	long	altend	alt end
#49	long	enbs	enable skip
#30	long	diss	disable skip
#48	long	enbc	enable channel
#2F	long	disc	disable channel
#22	long	ldtimer	load timer
#2B	long	tin	timer input
#4E	long	talt	timer alt start
#51	long	taltwt	timer alt wait
#47	long	enbt	enable timer
#2E	long	dist	disable timer
#3A	long	xword	extend to word
#56	long	cword	check word
#1D	long	xdble	extend to double
#4C	long	csngl	check single
#16	long	ladd	long add
#38	long	lsub	long subtract
#37	long	lsum	long sum
#4F	long	ldiff	long diff
#31	long	lmul	long multiply
#1A	long	ldiv	long divide
#36	long	lshl	long shift left
#35	long	lshr	long shift right
#19	long	norm	normalise

Table 5.1 (continued)

Operations Code	Size	*Abbreviation*	*Name*
#2A	long	testpranal	test processor analysing
#3E	long	saveh	save high priority queue registers
#3D	long	savel	save low priority queue registers
#18	long	sthf	store high priority front pointer
#50	long	sthb	store high priority back pointer
#1C	long	stlf	store low priority front pointer
#17	long	stlb	store low priority back pointer
#54	long	sttimer	store timer
#63	long	unpacksn	unpack single length fp number
#6D	long	roundsn	round single length fp number
#6C	long	postnormsn	post-normalise correction of single length
#71	long	ldinf	load single length infinity
#73	long	cflerr	check single length fp infinity or NaN
#72	long	fmul	fractional multiply

5.1.7 Booting, resetting, analysing and error detection

Transputers are able to boot from any of the serial links; alternatively they may execute code in external ROM. If the Boot from ROM pin is low, the processor interprets the first message to arrive on any link after a reset, as a bootstrap program to be read into memory and executed. This facility permits a large array of transputers to be reconfigured by a control processor via the serial links which interconnect the transputers.

To reset the T414, the Reset pin is pulsed while the Analyse pin is low. This initialises the internal state losing all state information, configures the external memory interface and boots the system. If the transputer is active when reset, it halts immediately,

When the Reset pin is pulsed while the Analyse pin is low, the processor halts but preserves internal state information. Dynamic RAM continues to be refreshed and debugging software may be bootstrapped when the Analyse pin is taken low.

A system containing several transputers may be analysed by asserting Analyse on all transputers simultaneously in response to an Error output (see Figure 5.5). The processors continue until the current active processes are completed, then halt, ignoring any scheduling requests. The internal timer stops and output links only respond to inputs by sending acknowledgements.

Information which is booted after an Analyse includes:

a) Processor workspace pointer value
b) Processor instruction pointer value

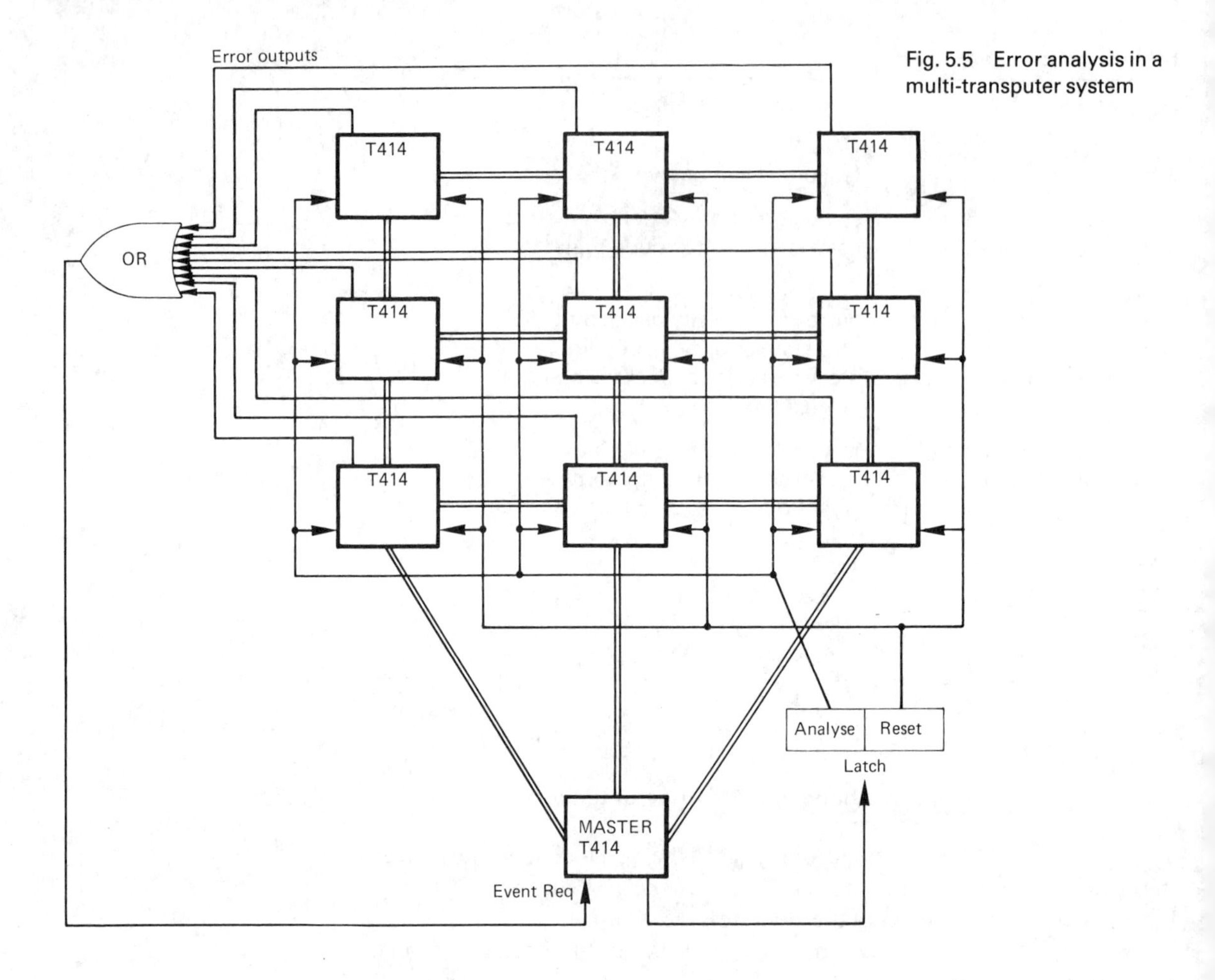

Fig. 5.5 Error analysis in a multi-transputer system

c) Error Flag and Halt On Error Flag values
d) Link Input/Output, Link Ready and Link Count register contents in some circumstances
e) Waiting message held in queues
f) Timer list pointer words
g) Process queue pointers.

When run-time errors such as arithmetic overflow or array bounds are detected, the Error flag is set and its output is available on the Error pin. When the Halt On Error flag is set the processor may be halted when the Error flag becomes set; this permits the processor to be booted and analysed. The instruction pointer will point to the byte of memory which is two bytes beyond the last byte of the instruction which generated the error. After a normal Analyse the instruction pointer indicates the byte of memory following the final byte of the instruction which caused the process to halt.

5.1.8 Peripheral interfacing

Peripheral devices may be connected to the T414 by using a C011 or C012 link adaptor or by accessing the external memory address space for direct memory access transfers. DMA is supported by the MemReq and MemGranted pins. The processor and links can access internal memory while DMA takes place to external memory.

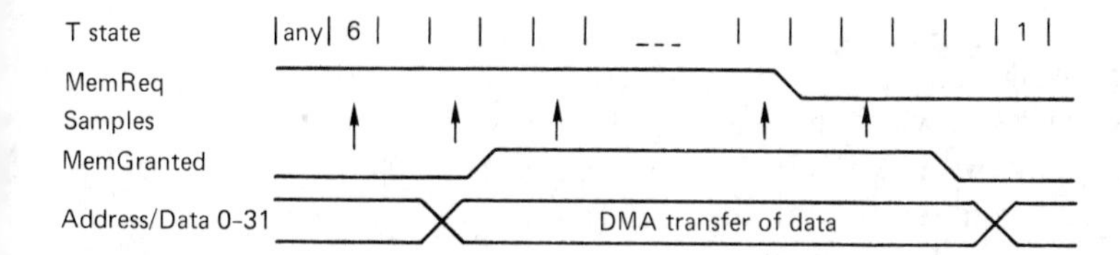

Fig. 5.6 Handshake for direct memory access

Figure 5.6 shows the DMA handshake. MemReq is sampled during the last period of the memory interface cycle (T6) and in every alternate idle clock period. When MemReq is detected and no DRAM refresh cycles are required, the memory address/data lines are taken to the high impedance state within two T_m periods and MemGranted is taken high one T_m period later. While MemGranted is high, MemReq is sampled every alternate clock period and, if it is found to be low, the MemGranted signal is taken low two T_m periods later and transputer interface cycles can restart.

The T414 has no interrupt facilities but instead it has two event signals, EventReq and EventAck which provide a means of communicating external events to Occam processes within the transputer. The rising edge of the EventReq input makes an external channel available for communication with the process (in addition to the four serial links). When the channel is ready and the process is ready to input from the channel, the EventAck output is taken high and the process is scheduled. When EventReq goes low the processor will take EventAck low in response.

5.2 Performance calculations

Because the transputer does not use cache memory or extensive pipelining, it is possible to predict the number of processor cycles required to execute a sequential program with reasonable accuracy. Concurrent processes are less predictable and may require detailed simulation.

Several speed selections of the T414 are available. Each uses the same 5 MHz input clock frequency but the internally generated processor clock speed and processor cycle time varies as shown in Table 5.2.

The Inmos Transputer Reference Manual gives a set of average figures for each operation which permit program size and execution time to be estimated. This list is reproduced in Appendix B. The transputer development system includes provision for estimating performance of Occam programs in addition to compiling, checking and debugging Occam programs and loading a target system.

Table 5.2 T414 speed selections

Designation	*Internal clock*	*Cycle time*	*Instruction throughput*
T414-12	12.5 MHz	80 ns	6 Mips
T414-15	15 Mhz	67 ns	7.5 Mips
T414-20	20 MHz	50 ns	10 Mips

The T414 does not implement floating-point arithmetic so these operations are provided by a run-time package which uses about 400 bytes of memory for single-length floating-point arithmetic. To speed up the execution of floating-point arithmetic and eliminate the memory required, the T800 transputer has been developed; this includes floating-point instructions in the standard instruction set and includes 4K of RAM in place of the 2K provided on the T414.

When the program or data is held in external memory, extra processor cycles may be required, depending on the speed of the external memory and the instruction executed. When an external memory access occurs in a processor cycle, the processor continues to execute other cycles at full speed until the next memory access is reached. This overlap in processor operations when external memory is involved reduces the accuracy of performance estimates.

Two extra processor cycles per external memory access are introduced by the fastest available external memory and a typical value would be five additional processor cycles. Program stored in external memory which introduces 2 to 3 additional processor cycles per memory cycle does not significantly slow down the execution of linear code sequences. If more processor cycles are introduced, the number of extra memory cycles required for linear code sequences may be estimated from

$$\text{Number of additional memory cycles} = \frac{(e-3)}{4}$$

where e is the number of additional processor cycles.

A transfer of control requires $(e + 3)$ memory cycles.

If e has a value of 6 or greater, the effective rate of the serial links may be reduced if all four are operating in both directions simultaneously.

Table 5.3 shows the effect of external memory speed on execution time for the sieve benchmark which includes many small data access loops but no concurrency, multiplication, division or communication. Table 5.4 shows the effect of external memory speed on execution time for a pipeline algorithm which computes a square root.

The performance of a short input-output program has been estimated to take 113 processor cycles (and to require 36 bytes of memory) using the statistics given in Appendix B. This compares closely with the figures produced by a low-level simulator which estimated 108 processor cycles and 33 bytes of code. The Occam program is

Table 5.3 The effect of external memory on execution time for the sieve benchmark

Number of extra processor cycles	*0*	*2*	*3*	*4*	*5*
Program + data on-chip	1				
Program off-chip		1.3	1.5	1.7	1.9
Data off-chip		1.5	1.8	2.1	2.3
Program and data off-chip		1.8	2.2	2.7	3.2

Table 5.4 The effect of external memory on execution time for the square root benchmark

Number of extra processor cycles	*0*	*2*	*3*	*4*	*5*
Program + data on-chip	1				
Program off-chip		1.1	1.2	1.2	1.3
Data off-chip		1.2	1.4	1.6	1.7
Program and data off-chip		1.3	1.6	1.8	2.0

```
CHAN            C:
PAR
        INT     a:
        SEQ
          a := 0
          C !  a
        INT     x:
          C ?  x
```

5.3 IMS M212 disk processor

Most microcomputer systems need to include a winchester disk or floppy disk drive. Systems based upon transputers are no exceptions but the design of a disk controller with serial link interfaces is a major task and the disk controller boards available for VME or Multibus II are not easily adapted for use with a transputer-based system. For this reason a special version of the 16-bit transputer has been developed, including the necessary circuitry and software to interface with winchester and floppy disk drives.

Figure 5.7 shows the major functional blocks in the M212. In the basic system configuration the only circuitry required to interface with a disk drive consists of buffers and the two serial links are provided to interface with host transputers.

5.3.1 Processor and memory

The processor is identical to the 16-bit T212 transputer; this is capable of up to 10 Mips performance using the same instruction set as the 32-bit transputers. The M212 is available in various speed selections, all using a 5 MHz input clock:

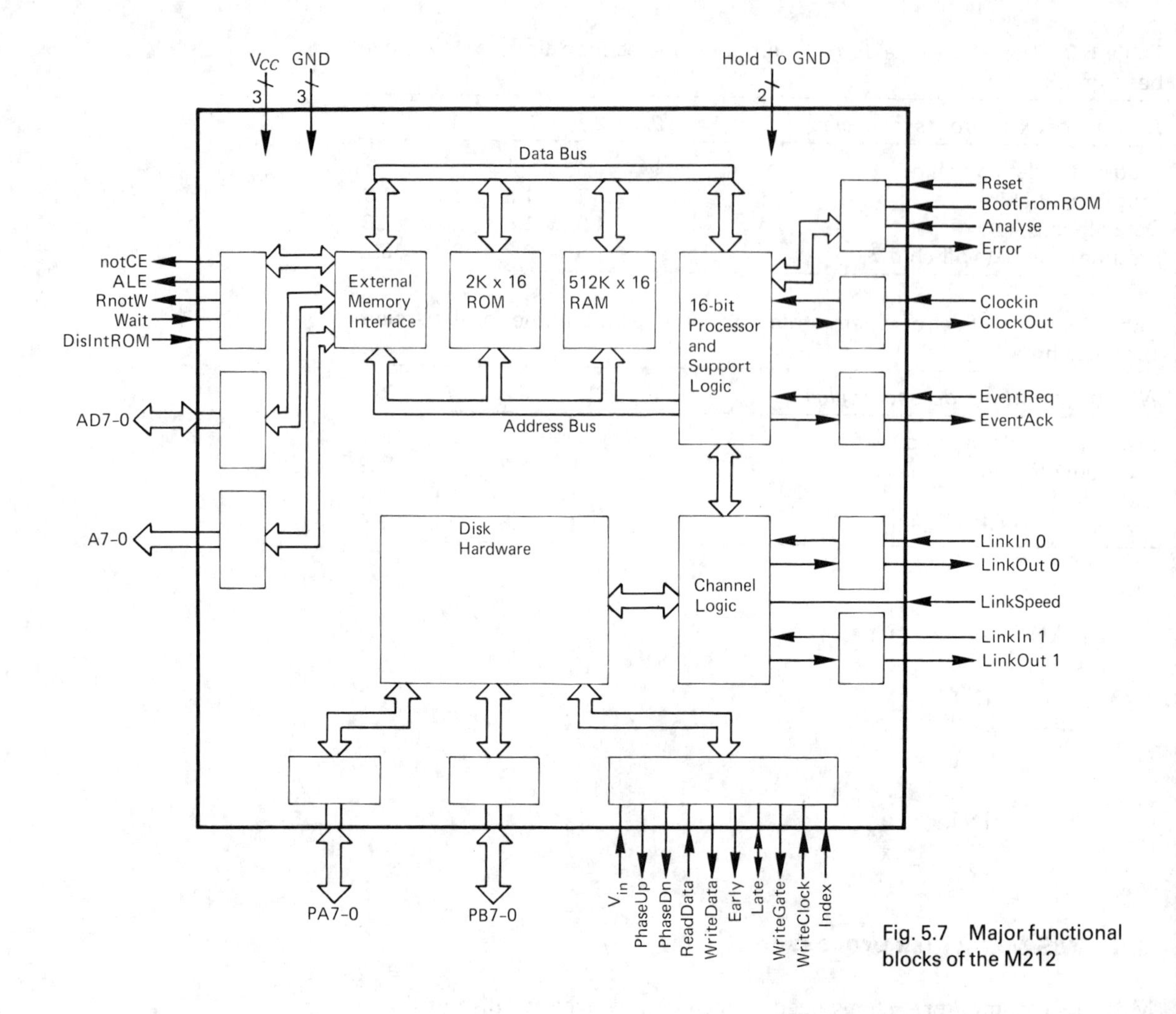

Fig. 5.7 Major functional blocks of the M212

M212–10 for 100 ns processor cycle time giving 5 Mips
M212–12 for 80 ns processor cycle time giving 6 Mips
M212–15 for 67 ns processor cycle time giving 7.5 Mips
M212–20 for 50 ns processor cycle time giving 10 Mips

The on-chip memory consists of a 1 Kbyte static RAM capable of supporting a combined data rate of 40 Mbyte/s from the processor, two serial links and two peripheral interfaces. A 4 Kbyte on-chip ROM contains the software which makes the M212 function as an autonomous disk controller.

An external memory interface is provided to support enhanced systems with up to 64 Kbytes of external RAM or PROM. An 8-bit data path and 16-bit address are multiplexed onto 16 pins on the 68-pin package. The interface is designed to provide a simple interface to byte-wide fast static RAM with a maximum data transfer rate of 8 Mbyte/s. Slower memory may be employed by using the wait pin.

5.3.2 Disk interface

Two programmable 8-bit bi-directional ports and a data transfer control port are provided to interface with soft-sectored winchester and floppy disk drives with the minimum amount of external circuitry. The disk control circuitry interfaces with the rest of the M212 through a transputer link. The disk control logic performs data separation, precompensation, programmable CRC/ECC generation and checking, FM/MFM encoding and decoding, and address recognition.

The two 8-bit bi-directional ports are used for the less time-critical interfaces such as:

a) Head select
b) Drive select
c) Direction of head movement
d) Track zero indication.

The data transfer control port supports the more time-critical signals such as those associated with connection of a filter for the data separation phase locked loop, a filter for the pre-compensation phase locked loop, disk read and write data, a reference clock and timing signals. Data rates between 125 kHz and 10 MHz are possible.

Simple interconnection of ST506/ST412 and SA450 compatible disk drives is provided by the Occam procedures stored in the on-chip ROM. For other types of disk drive or peripheral interfaces such as SCSI, the internal procedures may be replaced with Occam code in external ROM/PROM. The external software can make use of those parts of the on-chip software which are common to the desired application.

Sixteen commands for *disk control* are implemented by the on-chip ROM:

a) End of sequence
b) Initialise
c) Read task
d) Write task
e) Select drive
f) Poll drive
g) Restore
h) Seek
i) Step in
j) Step out
k) Read buffer
l) Write buffer
m) Read sector
n) Write sector
o) Format
p) Select head.

Disk control commands may be received from either of the two serial links but one link will be ignored until an end-of-sequence command has been received from the other link. Figure 5.8 shows the basic disk interface system and Figure 5.9 shows an enhanced peripheral interface system using

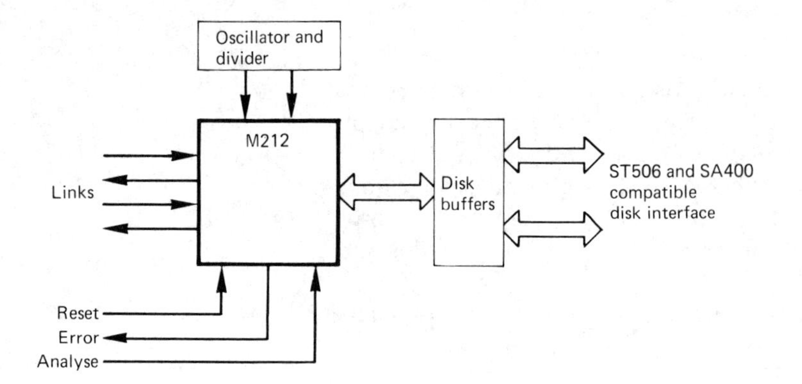

Fig. 5.8 Basic M212 configuration

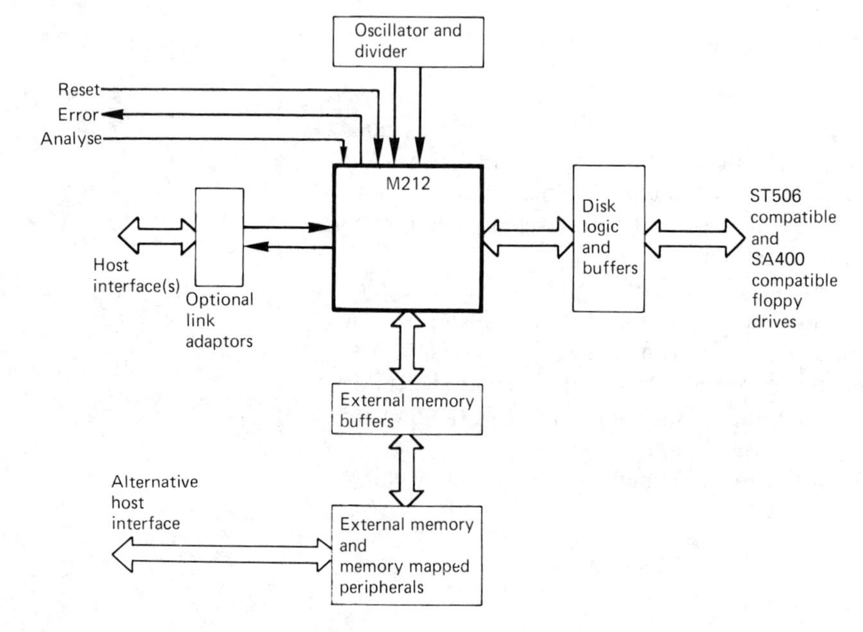

Fig. 5.9 Enhanced M212 configuration

external memory for peripheral control commands and additional buffer memory.

6 32-bit backplane buses

6.1 The evolution of backplane buses

Modular computer systems using the standard von Neumann architecture need a backplane to interconnect the circuit boards. The backplane almost certainly employs at least one common data bus to carry information and electrical power between the components. By using a popular standard for the bus, the system designer is able to make use of compatible circuit boards from several manufacturers and thus can have a fair degree of confidence that the boards will work together with a pre-defined level of performance.

For a system which requires no boards from other manufacturers it is still advantageous to use a popular backplane bus standard to interconnect the circuit boards. The designer can take advantage of a wide range of support chips, connectors, racks, test equipment, etc. and is relieved of the lengthy process of defining and proving the bus design.

The use of standard backplane buses began in the early 1970s when microprocessors began to offer the possibility of constructing a system from plug-compatible boards based on parallel buses. Early buses included the STD bus, S100 and Multibus I. These first-generation products were typically oriented towards a particular microprocessor family. The use of 8-bit data paths, 64 Kbyte addressing ranges and single-master operation soon made the early buses such as S100 and STD unsuitable for the more advanced 16-bit microprocessors, though both of these buses have now been extended.

Multibus I was extended to support higher system performance by adding the iLBX memory bus and was adequate for most 16-bit microprocessor applications. Multibus I has a 16-bit data path and a 16 Mbyte addressing range, but the 6.75 inch × 12 inch cards with complex edge connectors are unsuitable for rugged applications.

The form factor (dimensions) of a board is a compromise between size and ruggedness, and the use of a double Eurocard (IEC 240.2) form factor has become popular because it makes rugged applications possible where shock and vibration are a problem with larger boards. The use of two part connectors such as the DIN 41612/DIN 41494 connector are inherently more reliable than edge connectors.

Versabus was the first bus standard to cater for 8, 16 and 32-bit data transfer and overcame the limited addressing range of contemporary buses by offering 4 Gbytes of addressing range. The Versabus has two major points against it becoming a popular standard:

a) It uses a large, 9.25 inch × 14.5 inch form factor with edge connectors.
b) It is proprietary to Motorola.

While Multibus I dominated the 16-bit backplane market in 1981, a triumvirate comprising Motorola, Signetics and Mostek proposed an open specification for an asynchronous 16/32-bit bus with a double Eurocard form factor and 4 Gbytes addressing range. This VME standard was accepted as IEEE P1014 and rapidly gained acceptance with manufacturers who wanted a simple evolution path from 16-bit processors to 32-bit processors or who wanted to take advantage of the more rugged construction.

As the popularity of the VME bus increased, Intel rapidly developed the Multibus II standard which has a 32-bit data path, 4 Gbyte addressing capability and an extended-length double Eurocard form factor. The Multibus II standard was announced three years after the first VME boards became available and will take some time to catch up with the VME bus in popularity. The ability of Multibus II to carry out parity checks may make it more popular than the VME bus for the types of application which have previously used large computers.

Two other 32-bit backplane bus architectures are now available, Futurebus and Nubus, but in 1987 neither had attracted extensive backing. In 1979 the IEEE sponsored the development of a 32-bit bus standard which would be independent of any particular microprocessor or architecture, would be optimised for 32-bit processing, and would promote fault tolerance. The IEEE P896.1 sub-committee formed a joint US/European working group with the European Distributed Intelligence Study Group in 1980. The Futurebus standard was publicly released in early 1986 and has been supported by a few US and European manufacturers.

Nubus started as a research project at the Massachusetts Institute of Technology and was developed by Western Digital Corporation and Texas Instruments before being adopted by the IEEE Nubus standardisation committee as IEEE P1196. Nubus supports 8, 16 and 32-bit data transfers with 4 Gbytes direct addressing range and has a memory mapped architecture treating I/O commands and interrupts as locations in memory. This feature has made Nubus suitable for use in artificial intelligence workstations produced by Texas Instruments.

Table 6.1 summarises the major features of the four 32-bit buses: VME, Multibus II, Futurebus and Nubus. Table 6.2 compares the family of buses which provide dedicated functions in support of the VME bus and Multibus II. The use of local memory bus extensions such as iLBX and VMX were discussed in Section 2.5.2.

Thirty-two-bit system buses such as VME and iPSB are not generally used to link processors to memory. The speed of memory required by a 32-bit microprocessor can be provided better by local memory, on the processor board, or by a local memory bus extension which does not have the arbitration delays necessary on a multiprocessor system bus. The bulk of traffic on the system bus is typically block transfers between peripherals, global memory and processors. To take advantage of the high processing

Table 6.1 Major features of 32-bit backplane buses

	VME bus	*Multibus II*	*Futurebus*	*Nubus*
Originator	Motorola, Mostek, Signetics	Intel	IEEE	MIT
Data paths:	Non-multiplexed	Multiplexed	Multiplexed	Multiplexed
(primary, bits)	16	32	32	32
(secondary, bits)	32, 24, 16, 8	32, 24, 16, 8	32, 24, 16, 8	32, 16, 8
Primary addr. range	2^{24}	2^{32}	2^{32}	2^{32}
Secondary addr. range	2^{32}	None	Expandable	None
Communications type	Async.	Sync. (10 MHz)	Async.	Sync. (10 MHz)
Data rate (Mbyte/s)	Max. 57, Typ. 24	40, 20, 13, 10	Max. 117.7	37.5, block trans.
Broadcast capability	No	Yes	Yes	No
Max. no. of processors	1 + 4 + chain	20	21 or 32	16
Interrupt levels	7 + chain	None	None	None
Virtual interrupts	Yes	Yes	Yes	No
Standardisation	IEEE P1014	IEEE P1296	IEEE P896.1	IEEE P1196
Message passing	No	Yes	Yes (P896.2)	No
Arbitration	Parallel, Daisy chain 4 levels	Parallel, Distributed 32 levels	Parallel, Distributed 32 levels	Parallel, Distributed
Board dims. (mm)	233.4 × 160	233.4 × 220	366.7 × 280	366.7 × 280
Board area (cm^2)	373	514	1027	1027
Connectors (pins)	Indirect 96 + 96	Indirect 96	Indirect 96	Indirect 96
Cache support	No	Some	Yes	Some
Support for tagged architecture	No	No	Yes	No
Support for fault tolerance	No	No	Yes	No
Bus drivers	TTL	TTL	Special (BTL)	TTL
Non-aligned transfers	Yes	Yes	Yes	No
Max. bus length		426 mm		
Separate serial bus	Yes	Yes	Yes	No
Error detection	No	Parity	Optional	Optional
Power supply	+5 V, ±12 V	+5 V	+5 V	+5 V

power and data throughput of 32-bit microprocessors it is essential to use 32-bit local memory buses and separate system buses. Where data can be provided in 32-bit format, a 32-bit bus offers twice the bandwidth available on a 16-bit bus, all other things being equal.

Most system manufacturers are now finding that their major investment in a new computer system is the operating system, applications software and peripheral driver hardware rather than the processor and memory hardware which is available from several sources at a relatively low price. To keep their systems at the forefront of technology, system manufacturers must be able to replace each individual part of the system as new products are introduced. The best way of achieving this objective is to select a backplane bus standard which has adequate expansion capacity and is manufacturer independent, processor independent and as independent of a particular technology as possible.

Table 6.2 VME and Multibus II multiple bus types

Bus	*Function*	*Maximum byte/s*	*Data path*	*Communication type*
VME	Parallel system bus	40 M	32-bit non-multiplexed	Async.
VMX	Local high-speed memory and I/O extension	80 M	32-bit non-multiplexed	Async.
I/O channel	Local I/O extension	2 M	8-bit	Async.
VMS	Low-cost serial system bus	3 M	1-bit	Token passing
iPSB	Parallel system bus	40 M (10 MHz)	32-bit multiplexed	Sync.
iLBX	Local high-speed memory extension	48 M (12 MHz)	32-bit non-multiplexed	Sync.
iSBX	Local I/O expansion	10 M	16-bit non-multiplexed	Async.
Multi-channel I/O	Remote DMA	8 M	16-bit multiplexed	Async.
iSSB	Low-cost serial system bus	2 M	1-bit	CSMA/CD
Bitbus	Local industrial I/O	2.4 M	Two signal pairs	SDLC sync/ self-clocked

6.2 VME bus (IEEE P1014)

The VME bus has two 96-pin connectors (DIN 41612 and DIN 41494 type) on a double Eurocard. Unlike the other 32-bit systems buses the VME bus does not multiplex the address and data lines, and therefore more interface driver/receiver chips and connector pins are required. A 16-bit VME bus may be implemented using only the upper connector (P1) but a 32-bit system bus requires both connectors (P1 and P2) as shown in Figure 6.1. When the 16-bit system bus is used, the lower (P2) connector may be used for the 32-bit VMX local extension bus or for input/output. One advantage of a non-multiplexed bus with a single bus master is that read and write operations may be pipelined in a single cycle but a multiplexed bus must use two bus cycles.

The family of buses which make up the VME bus architecture is shown in Figure 6.2 and the characteristics of each bus type are summarised in Table 6.2. The VME system bus provides communications between processor, peripheral and global memory boards. The VMX bus provides high-speed communication between a processor board and local memory extension boards. The VMS bus provides a lower-cost and lower-performance serial alternative to the parallel system bus. An I/O channel is available to provide local I/O expansion using bus cables up to 12 feet in length.

The VME system bus and VMX bus, in common with Futurebus, use asynchronous communications which contrasts with the synchronous com-

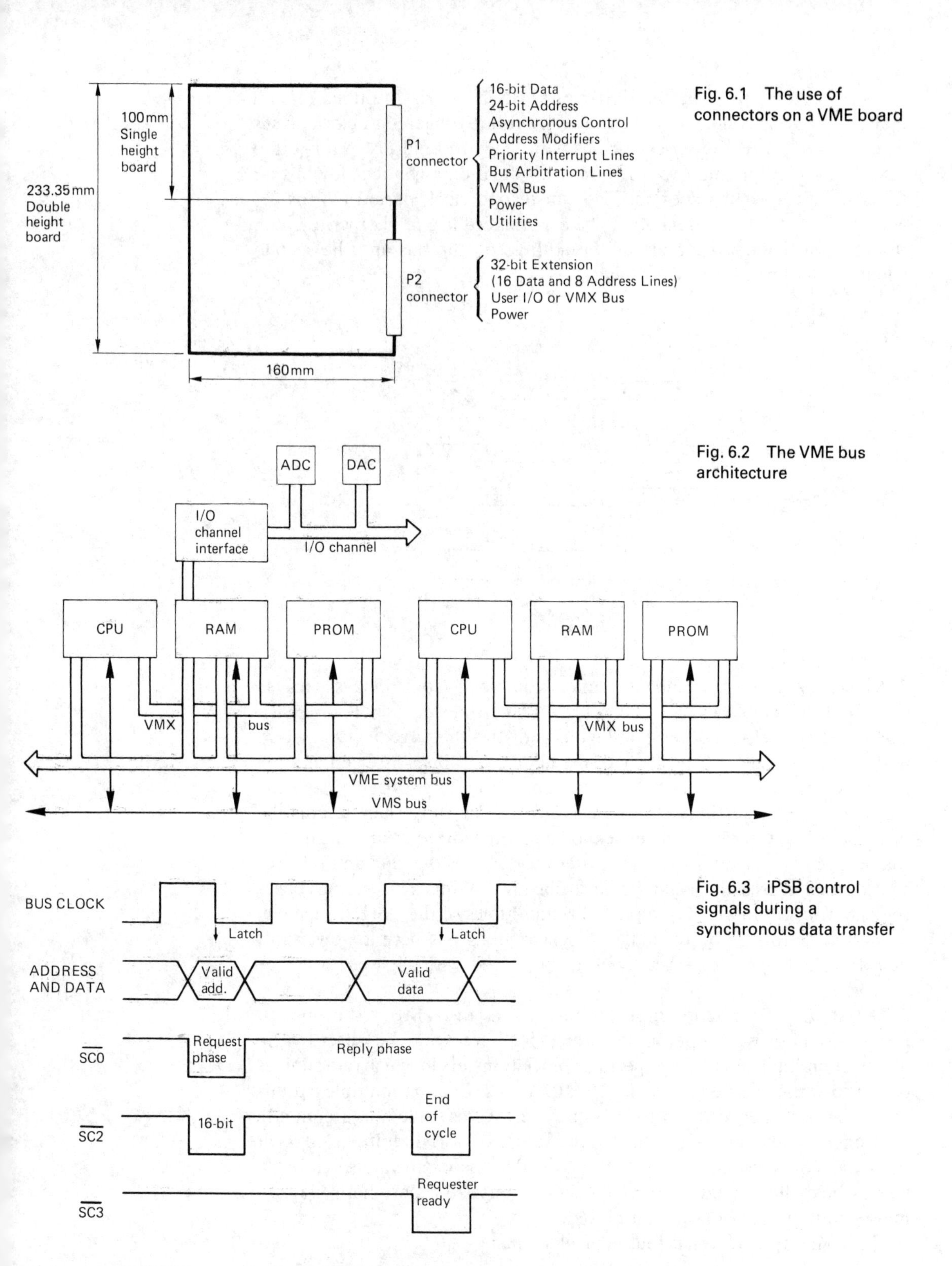

Fig. 6.1 The use of connectors on a VME board

Fig. 6.2 The VME bus architecture

Fig. 6.3 iPSB control signals during a synchronous data transfer

munications employed by the iPSB and iLBX buses (in Multibus II) and Nubus. In a synchronous system, data transfers are triggered by clock pulses (see Figure 6.3). If the processor has data ready to send just prior to the clock edge the minimum wait is imposed but, if data is not ready at that time, a wait may be experienced of up to one clock period (100 ns for Multibus II). Two such delays may be experienced in a read or write cycle, the first when the master places the address on the bus and the second when the master reads or writes data.

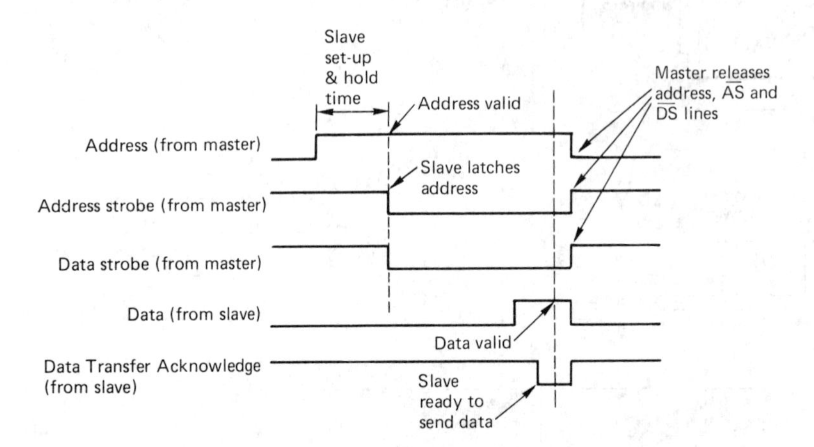

Fig. 6.4 VME bus control signals during an asynchronous data transfer

Asynchronous systems do not suffer from such latent delays because no periodic clock pulses are used to trigger data transfers (see Figure 6.4). The master places an address on the bus and after the slave device's set-up and hold times have been satisfied, the address strobe is asserted and the slave latches in the address. Next the data strobe is asserted to tell the slave that the master is ready to receive data. The slave then accepts the data and drives the data-transfer acknowledge line low to inform the master that it is ready to send data. The master then latches the data and releases the address, address strobe and data strobe lines. With asynchronous buses the data transfer rate is not locked to submultiples of the clock frequency, as with synchronous buses, and an asynchronous bus permits lower-cost boards with longer response times to be mixed with high-performance boards.

The ability of a non-multiplexed bus such as the VME system bus to perform read or write operations in one clock cycle may be offset by the ability of multiplexed buses to perform block transfers in which one address is sent to retrieve an entire block of data, thus giving the multiplexed bus an average time per read or write of one cycle. Access to memory frequently uses single reads and writes; therefore the use of a non-multiplexed local bus extension such as the VMX bus or iLBX bus is advantageous but a system bus which handles many block transfers from peripheral devices may be multiplexed or non-multiplexed.

The VME system bus has four main elements:

a) Data transfer (8, 16 or 32 bits in parallel)
b) Arbitration (4 levels)

c) Interrupt handling (7 levels)
d) Utility.

The ability to support address paths of 16, 24 or 32 bits makes it possible for 8, 16 and 32-bit processors to share the VME system bus.

The arbitration scheme used on the VME system bus is centralised to the extent that one board acts as a global arbitrator using four bus request lines. Boards may be designed to use the release-when-done-request procedure or the release-on-request procedure. Processor cards usually use release-on-request to keep tight control of the bus and to give up control only when another master processor requests the bus. DMA controllers usually use release-when-done because they generally use the bus only for a short period before releasing control.

Bus arbitration logic can be implemented in three ways:

a) Priority arbitration with priorities given to the four request levels.
b) Round-robin which lets each level have the same priority but taking turns to use the bus.
c) Single-level arbitration which monitors only one level for bus requests.

Within each level a number of sub-level requests may be designated. Bus control is granted by a daisy chain linking any number of bus requesters. The requester closest to slot 1 has the highest priority at that level.

The seven interrupt request lines may be used to support from one to seven interrupt handlers in the system. An interrupt handler can service from one to seven interrupt lines. In response to an interrupt request, an 8-bit status identification vector number is passed from the interrupter to the interrupt handler. Seven times 256 different status identification vector numbers can exist in a VME system.

The utility lines include:

a) A 16 MHz clock source.
b) 5 V and ±12 V lines plus an optional 5 V standby supply line.
c) An AC fail line which gives a minimum of 4 ms warning that DC power is going outside limits.
d) A system fail line which informs the system master or monitor of a failure on one of the boards using an open collector pull down.
e) A system reset line.

6.3 Multibus II (IEEE P1296)

Multibus II consists of a family of buses as shown in Figure 6.5. The iPSB is the parallel system bus which differs from the VME systems bus by using synchronous transmission and multiplexed address and data lines to make only one 96-way DIN connector necessary. The iLBX is a 32-bit high-speed bus for extending the local memory. As shown on Table 6.2 the iLBX is a synchronous bus like the iPSB but is non-multiplexed to permit read or write operations in one cycle for single memory accesses.

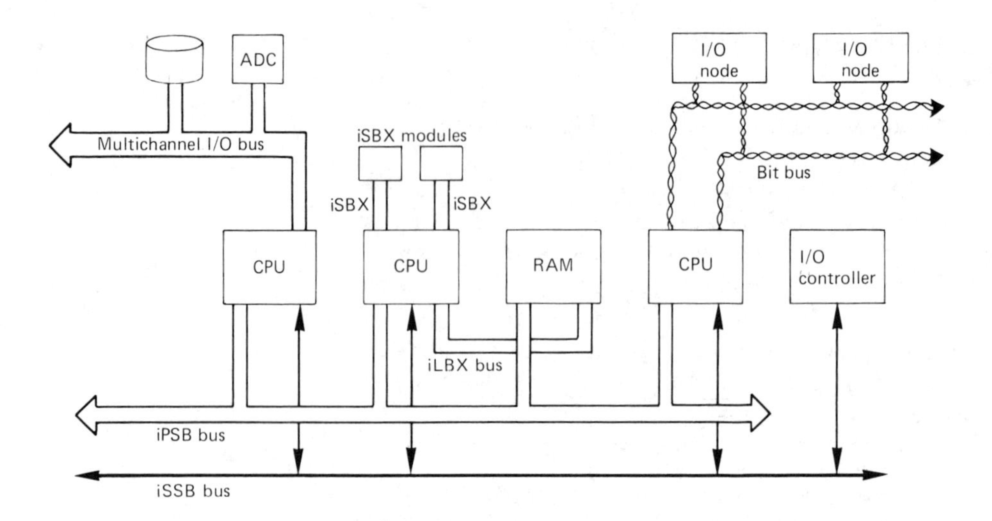

Fig. 6.5 The Multibus II architecture

The iSSB bus is a low-cost low-data-rate serial link which may be used as an alternative to the iPSB. The CSMA/CD control permits any board to gain access to the bus immediately but, if more than one user tries to access the iPSB simultaneously, the collision is detected and the two users re-try after a random delay period to prevent a second collision.

The iSBX bus is an I/O expansion bus which permits small interface modules to be added to the processor and other intelligent boards. The multichannel I/O bus permits DMA block transfers between intelligent I/O devices. Bitbus is an industrial local I/O bus using two twisted pairs to transmit data between up to 250 stations. In synchronous mode, 28 stations can transmit data at speeds between 500 kbit/s and 2.4 Mbit/s over distances up to 30 metres. In self-clocked mode, up to 28 stations may communicate over 300 metre segments at 375 kbit/s or over 1200 metre segments at 62.5 kbit/s. By interconnecting segments via repeaters, up to 250 stations may communicate over several thousands of metres. The protocol is based on SDLC and a master station controls access to the bus by the slave stations.

The 12 MHz clock speed of the iLBX bus limits the speed of data transfers because all transfers are synchronous. Asynchronous buses are able to increase speed as technology improves but the speed of any backplane bus is limited by two factors:

a) The time (about 25 ns) taken for a signal to propagate along the length of the bus and back with all the slots filled.

b) The speed of bus drivers and receivers. A TTL driver requires about 40 ns to produce a stable drive current and the receiver requires a set up and hold time of about 30 ns. The VME bus and Multibus II use TTL drivers but Futurebus employs faster drivers.

Adding all three delay factors gives a total propagation time of 95 ns for a TTL bus which limits the transfer rate to a little over 10 MHz using the technology available when VME and Multibus II were developed.

The iPSB bus uses block transfers to give an average time of one 100 ns cycle to complete a read or write operation.

The noise immunity of the Multibus II synchronous transmission is claimed to be superior to that of asynchronous buses because a single clock signal is used to trigger a transfer whereas several lines could pick up noise spikes in an asynchronous bus. The clock line of Multibus II is protected by using a lower termination impedance and higher drive current, 68 mA compared with 48 mA on other lines. The clock line is also shielded by surrounding it with decoupled power supply lines which ground noise spikes.

Noise can also effect data and address lines so the iPSB uses a parity scheme to detect errors. One parity line is provided for each data or address byte and one parity bit is added for each four bits of control data. Parity is checked at the receiving boards and, if corruption is detected, the data is rejected and retransmitted. Parity calculation can however add a 100 ns wait state to each data transfer and the system may still be vulnerable to corruption in the 8 ns period before data is clocked in (compared with a 35 ns period per cycle if parity was not implemented). To reduce the parity calculation delay Intel introduced a message-passing controller chip (MPC).

The VME system bus does not impose a particular means of passing messages between processors in a multiprocessor system. The most common method is to use a shared part of global memory and an interrupt to pass messages but Multibus II uses a message-passing protocol implemented by a special MPC chip which is capable of passing a 32-byte data block (four bytes of which are address data) in 900 ns. When the message is ready in local memory the DMA controller must load it alternately into the two 32-byte FIFO buffers in the MPC chip (see Figure 6.6). The MPC

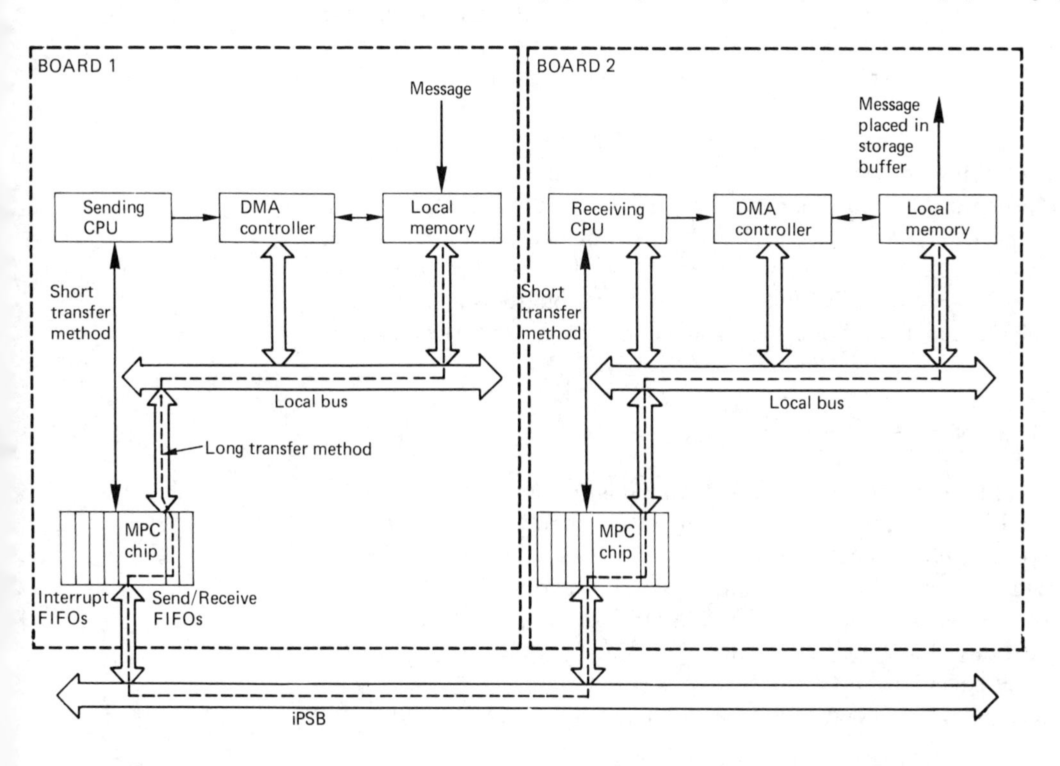

Fig. 6.6 Multibus II message passing system

chip then transmits the data in a burst to the 32-byte buffers on the receiving board's MPC chip which passes the data by DMA to local memory. An alternative, short transfer mode is available to directly move the message from the CPU to the MPC chip without accessing the local bus.

The MPC chip includes four 32-byte deep interrupt FIFO buffers which are used in place of bus interrupt lines. Short messages are transferred directly to the MPC chip from the CPU. At the receiving MPC chip, instead of being loaded into the receive FIFO buffer, the sending MPC writes into one of the interrupt FIFO buffers. The receiving MPC then interrupts the receiving CPU which moves the message out of the interrupt FIFO and either sends it to an interrupt handler or executes the message directly.

The message handling facility of the iPSB provides a high degree of decoupling between activity on the iPSB and activity on the local bus. Once the DMA controller has moved data from local memory to the MPC chip, the CPU is free to access the local bus and local memory. A shared memory system, however, only leaves the CPU free to access its local bus, not its local memory, while the DMA controller is moving data out of its local dual ported memory onto the main system bus. With shared memory the CPU is unable to execute programs from local memory for a longer period than with the iPSB message handling facility. The MPC is normally used in conjunction with a single chip microcomputer to implement the message-passing protocol, this makes iPSB unsuitable for use with low cost, non-intelligent boards.

Multibus II uses a distributed arbitration scheme in which bus master boards arbitrate amongst themselves for bus access. Each board is given a prioritised arbitration identification number by the central service module. During the resolution phase of the arbitration cycle, the board with the highest priority (lowest identification number) usually gets control of the bus first. During the last data transfer the remaining potential bus masters arbitrate for control. When in high priority mode, a potential bus master can force itself into the next resolution phase of the arbitration cycle to gain control before other requesting boards, regardless of their priority. Up to 20 potential bus masters may be handled in multiprocessor systems without requiring large numbers of dedicated bus lines. All boards have an equal opportunity of gaining bus access on the iPSB, unlike the scheme with the VME system bus which allows an active board near the top of the daisy chain to lock out bus access from boards lower down the chain.

6.4 Futurebus (IEEE P896.1)

The major benefits of Futurebus are that it is a high-performance asynchronous bus and it is independent of any particular manufacturer, processor or technology. Futurebus achieves higher bandwidths than the other 32-bit buses because it uses higher-performance transceivers than the TTL buses. The National Semiconductor DS-3896 and DS-3897 have been developed to meet the Futurebus specification and reduce the problem of capacitive loading on the backplane as more boards are attached.

As more boards are added to a bus the capacitance increases and more

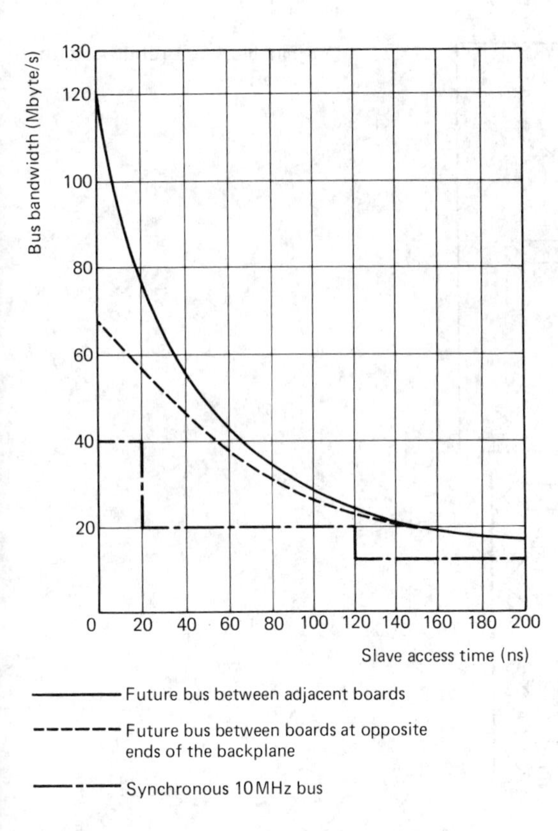

Fig. 6.7 Futurebus bandwidth and slave access time compared with a synchronous 10 MHz bus

drive current is required which causes more noise, cross-talk and power consumption. The National transceivers need only a 1 V signal swing to operate satisfactorily; this reduces power consumption, noise and cross-talk without reducing the data rate. Trapezoidal drive waveforms reduce the cross-talk and the driver circuitry reduces the capacitance of bus driver outputs. Future improvements in technology will permit increased bus performance without going outside the specification. Figure 6.7 shows that the bus bandwidth between adjacent boards can reach 117.7 Mbyte/s and an ultimate bandwidth up to 280 Mbyte/s is anticipated.

Figure 6.8 shows how a local memory bus is connected to the Futurebus. A serial input/output bus forms part of the bus together with 8, 16, 24 or 32 multiplexed address/data lines, arbitration and control lines. The asynchronous protocol permits bandwidth improvements and avoids the need for any centralised components on the backplane or constraints on board positions in the backplane.

Two data transfer modes are provided:

a) Single transfer mode for flexibility
b) Block transfer mode for speed.

The current bus master selects the operating mode and informs the slave by a 5-bit command code transmitted on each bus cycle which also selects the direction of data flow and identifies which bytes are to be accessed.

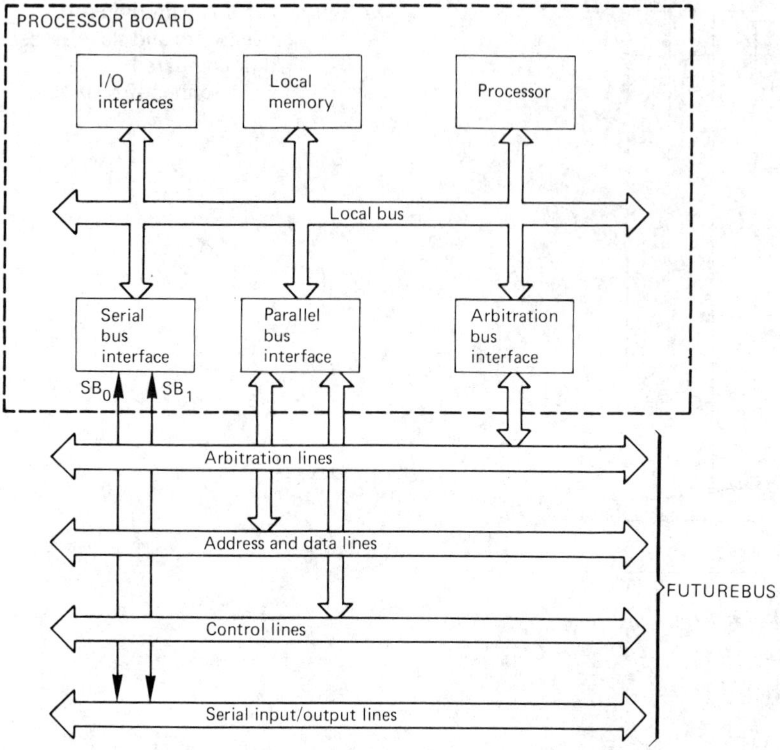

Fig. 6.8 Futurebus system interface

A broadcast mode permits a master to talk to several slaves simultaneously. Data may be written to, or read from, all slaves at the same time. Read data reaches the master as a logical OR of all slave outputs. The broadcast data transfer speed is determined by the slowest module involved in the transfer.

Most 32-bit buses justify data transfers to simplify the connection of 16-bit processors but Futurebus uses a non-justified data path to eliminate the need for byte switches. A 32-bit processor would not require additional byte switching hardware but 8 or 16-bit processors need some form of byte switching hardware for use with Futurebus.

Each data/address byte has a parity bit and the 5-bit command code has a parity bit. The generation of a valid parity bit is not mandatory because some users would prefer higher speed rather than error detection. A separate bus signal indicates on a cycle-by-cycle basis if a valid parity bit is present. To support multiprocessing with multiple processor boards, a locking mechanism is provided to prevent indivisible bus transactions being separated. The interlock protocol ensures that no other device can perform an operation between parts of an indivisible bus transaction such as a read-modify-write bus operation.

Arbitration between boards wanting to become bus master is achieved without any central control elements. Each board which may become a bus master includes control and arbitration logic which stores a 6-bit arbitration number. Each contending bus master puts its arbitration number on the 6-line open collector arbitration bus. The OR combination of bits on the arbitration bus is monitored by each board and, if the pattern does not match the one it applied, it removes its bits which were less significant than the line which did not match its own output. The arbitration lines will, after settling down, carry the highest arbitration number requesting bus control.

To avoid the possibility of boards with low arbitration numbers being disadvantaged under heavy traffic conditions a fairness scheme was adopted. This requires a board which has used the bus to refrain from issuing any further bus requests until all others have been fulfilled. Potential bus masters are classified as either fairness modules, which obey the fairness scheme, or priority modules, which compete for the bus when they need it. Priority modules are always given higher arbitration numbers.

The P896.2 version of Futurebus implements a message-passing protocol similar to Multibus II.

7 Memory and storage devices

7.1 Semiconductor memory

7.1.1 General

The same trends in semiconductor technology which make more complex microprocessors possible also make larger and faster random access memory (RAM) and read only memory (ROM) chips available. Figure 7.1 shows the approximate dates when each generation of dynamic RAM chip and microprocessor were introduced and the approximate number of transistors per chip which are required to make these devices possible.

In 1986 the first 1 Mbit dynamic RAM chips became available in commercial quantities and the first 4 Mbit dynamic RAM chips were at the laboratory development stage with production anticipated in 1988. Where cost is a major consideration, the use of 256 Kbit dynamic RAM chips became preferable to 64 Kbit devices in 1986 and consequently the proportion of 64 Kbit dynamic RAM chips sold began to decline. If the usual trends continue, it will be in 1990 that the proportion of 256 Kbit dynamic RAM chips declines in favour of the 1 Mbit components.

7.1.2 Comparison of static and dynamic RAM

Dynamic RAM (DRAM) is sold in greater volume than any other memory component because it is the most economical form of RAM. Static RAM (SRAM) chips have a lower capacity than dynamic RAM chips of the same generation because more transistors are required to produce each memory cell. A typical SRAM cell uses six transistors in a flip-flop circuit but a DRAM cell uses a capacitor to store the data bit and a transistor which connects the capacitor to a data line for reading or writing.

Static RAM can achieve lower access times and CMOS SRAM may be used more easily for battery back-up storage which retains the memory contents when the computer power supply is removed.

SRAM is more popular in byte-wide organisation which makes it less expensive to implement a small amount of RAM in a computer system. Only four 8 K by 8-bit SRAM chips are required to implement an 8 K by 32-bit memory but, using dynamic RAM, additional control chips are necessary and therefore their use is not generally considered cost-effective for memory sizes below 64 Kbytes. When 256 Kbit SRAM chips become available this threshold will probably increase to 256 Kbytes.

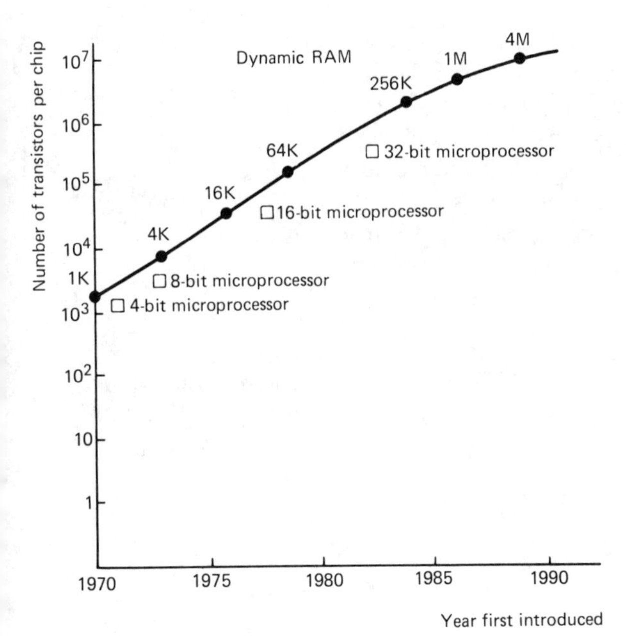

Fig. 7.1 The trend in DRAM chip density compared with microprocessor development trends

Other advantages of static RAM are that there is no need for regular refreshing of stored data and the packages are frequently compatible with byte-wide Electrically Programmable Read Only Memory (EPROM). This makes it possible to design microprocessor boards with several sockets which will accommodate either SRAM or EPROM according to the particular requirements of an application.

7.1.3 Support circuitry for dynamic RAM

Dynamic RAM is the most economical means of constructing larger RAM arrays but it is less convenient to use than static RAM. The additional interface requirements for dynamic RAM over static RAM include:

a) Driving the capacitive loads presented by DRAM chips.
b) An external refresh counter or refresh facility in the microprocessor to replace leaked charge in the storage capacitors within each cell every few milliseconds.
c) Control logic to multiplex addresses from the rows and columns in which the DRAM cells are organised during refresh and external access cycles. These functions are frequently provided by a DRAM controller chip.

Dynamic RAM is addressed by strobing the intersecting row and column of the desired cell location. Dynamic RAM may be operated in several addressing modes including:

a) Paging mode
b) Ripple mode
c) Nibble mode
d) Static column decoding.

These addressing techniques use either a Row Address Strobe (RAS) or Column Address Strobe (CAS) to access data. The row address is latched in first, then strobes enter the column addresses. In *paging mode*, new column addresses are provided for each bit as shown in Figure 7.2. Paging mode is typically only capable of reading part of a page before the memory needs refreshing. *Ripple mode* strobes in new column addresses at a much greater rate which permits a 256-bit page to be read before refresh is required. As shown in Figure 7.3, ripple mode can reduce access time to about one third of the standard read/write time.

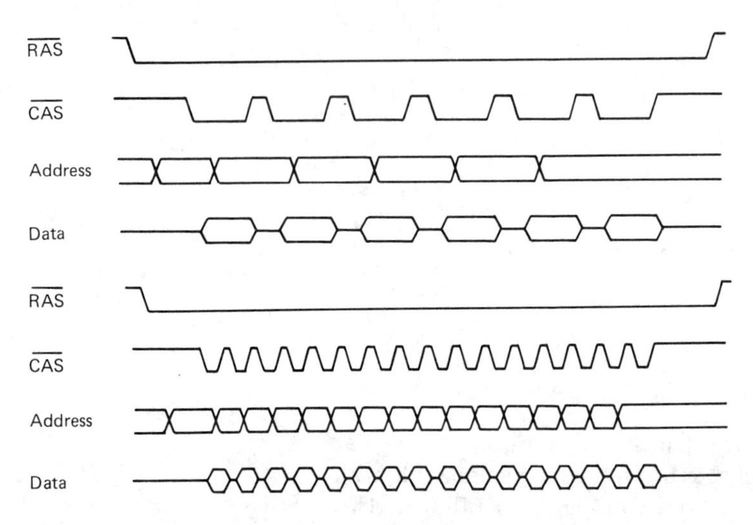

Fig. 7.2 Timing relationships for DRAM paging mode addressing

Fig. 7.3 Timing relationships for DRAM ripple mode addressing

Nibble mode permits four bits to be read out in a rapid sequence while the $\overline{RAS}$ pin is low; the $\overline{CAS}$ pin is pulsed low for each bit. Row and column addresses are set before data becomes available, a few microseconds after $\overline{CAS}$ goes low. The least significant row and column addresses are internally incremented to address the 4 nibble bits. Extended implementations of nibble mode can permit eight bits to be read out in a rapid sequence. The memory cycle time may be about one third of the standard read/write time during the nibble sequence but the average memory cycle time is only about one half of the standard read/write time (see Figure 7.4).

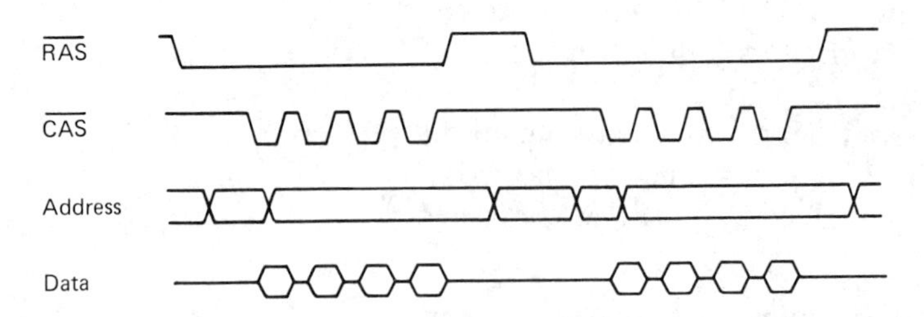

Fig. 7.4 Timing relationships for DRAM nibble mode addressing

Static column decoding uses the $\overline{RAS}$ signal to latch the row address; then column addresses are read directly from the address bus as shown in Figure 7.5. Output data follows the column addresses. The $\overline{CAS}$ pin is no longer required and may be replaced by a chip enable control pin.

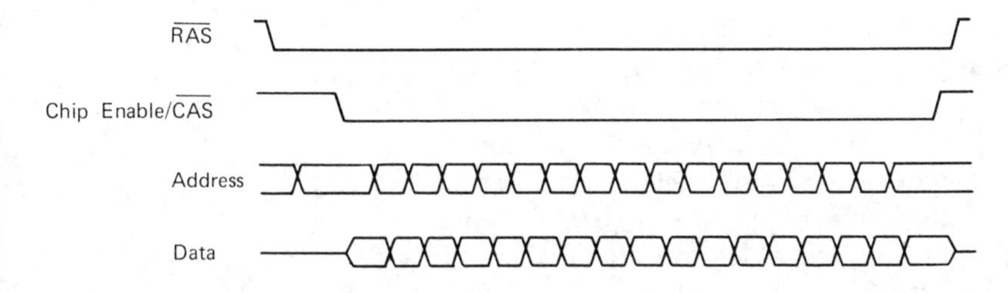

Fig. 7.5 Timing relationships for DRAM static column addressing

Several refresh options exist. The $\overline{RAS}$-only system supplies a refresh address to each row of the memory which is latched by $\overline{RAS}$. Automatic $\overline{CAS}$ before $\overline{RAS}$ refreshing requires no external refresh clocks and takes place after $\overline{RAS}$ has precharged followed by an active $\overline{CAS}$ and a falling $\overline{RAS}$.

7.1.4 Battery back-up RAM systems

Although it is possible to provide a battery back-up system to prevent dynamic RAM losing data when the system power is removed, the amount of power which must be stored in the batteries is much greater than that required by an equivalent CMOS SRAM. The need for continuous refreshing of DRAM makes it necessary to keep the entire memory support system active, whereas static CMOS SRAM only requires a small residual voltage on the V_{CC} of each RAM chip to retain stored data.

Figure 7.6 shows a diode coupled circuit and Figure 7.7 shows a transistor switching circuit which may be used to provide battery back-up for a CMOS

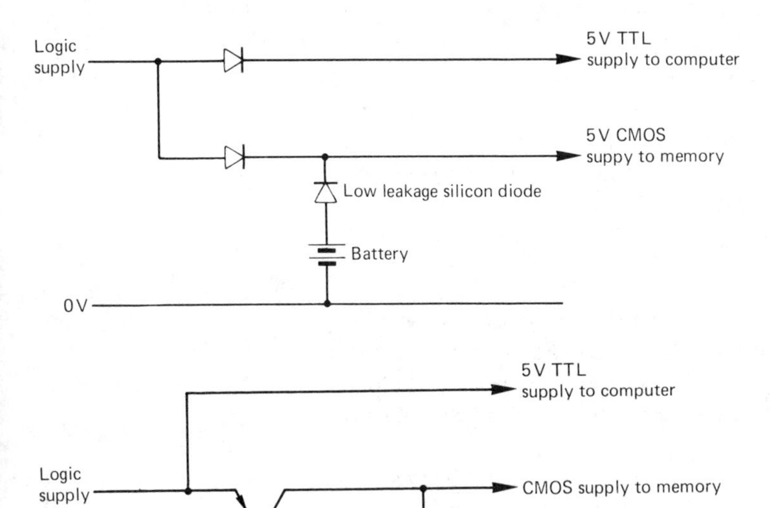

Fig. 7.6 Diode coupled battery back-up circuit for CMOS RAM

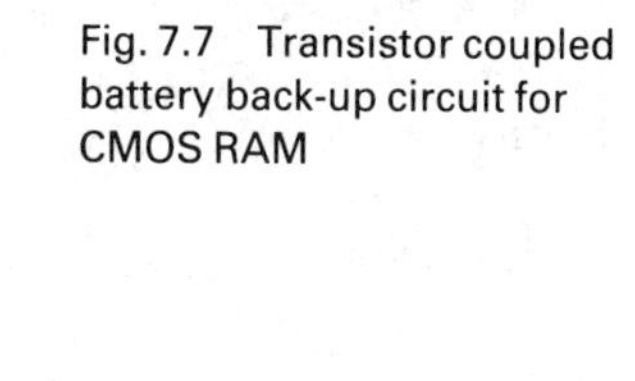

Fig. 7.7 Transistor coupled battery back-up circuit for CMOS RAM

SRAM. It is necessary to power up and power down the interface and power lines in the correct sequence to prevent data corruption or permanent damage to the CMOS SRAM chips. A parasitic SCR which is present on the input of junction isolated CMOS devices may be activated if the input or output voltages exceed the specified voltage limits which are related to V_{CC}. To prevent damage to inputs or outputs it is necessary to prevent external circuitry applying input voltages which are higher than V_{CC} or lower than the ground voltage of the CMOS RAM chips.

CMOS SRAM can typically operate on a 2 V standby supply and in this mode may draw less than 0.1 μA per chip. This compares with a current of several mA/MHz from a 5 V supply during normal operation. Normal operating current is directly related to the input switching or enable switching frequency because current flows only when inputs are taken through their linear operating region between logic 1 and logic 0 thresholds. Another cause of power consumption is the charging of capacitive output loads. This factor increases with switching frequency according to the relationship:

$$P = CV^2f$$

where P = power consumption
C = load capacitance
V = power supply voltage
f = switching frequency.

Despite the rapid increase in power consumed when CMOS SRAM operates at high speed, the power consumption of CMOS SRAM is, on average, much lower than that of other forms of RAM. The largest CMOS SRAM devices available in 1986 were 64 Kbits, organised 64K by 1 bit or 8K by 8 bits.

These 64 Kbit chips have an active power consumption of 200 mW to 300 mW and a standby power consumption of 0.1 mW. They use a merged process which combines NMOS and CMOS to achieve access times down to 45 ns but the standby current is greater than that of pure CMOS devices.

7.1.5 Non-volatile memory

Most systems require some form of non-volatile semiconductor memory to store the program. Where the program is down-loaded from a disk into RAM at power up, a small non-volatile memory is required to hold the bootstrap program which initialises the support chips and reads data from the peripheral storage device.

Masked ROM is available in NMOS or CMOS with 256 Kbit capacity but it suffers from a lack of flexibility which makes its use impractical in all but high volume applications. The mask-making charge and the time required to fabricate a ROM make it unsuitable when the software may contain undetected bugs and when short timescales are required.

Fusible-link bipolar PROM may be programmed once by blowing fusible links to form a memory pattern. High-speed operation, down to 20 ns, is available but the highest capacity available is 32 Kbits. The high cost of fusible-link PROM has led to the introduction of a less-expensive alternative form of one-time programmable EPROM. These are in fact CMOS EPROM chips in an inexpensive package without a quartz window.

The most popular form of non-volatile semiconductor memory is the *electrically programmable read only memory* (EPROM) which uses a quartz window to let in ultra-violet light for erasure of the entire contents. The ability to erase the contents makes the EPROM suitable for use in software development or early production, and where large production volumes are not required it may not be worthwhile converting to less expensive one-time programmable devices or ROMs for production.

The 512 Kbit EPROM chips became available in 1984 and 1 Mbit CMOS EPROMs became available in 1986. The organisation of the Am-27C1024, 1 Mbit EPROM is 64K by 16-bit words and versions with a maximum access time of 170 ns are available. By programming two words simultaneously the entire 1 Mbit chip may be programmed in 49 seconds.

Power supply current when operating at 5 MHz is 50 mA at 5 V which falls to 1 mA when the chip is deselected. In standby mode the supply current falls to 150 μA. These low power requirements make single card EPROM storage practical for memory requirements up to 4 Mbytes. Figure 7.8 shows how two 128 Kbyte Am-27C1024 EPROMs may be interfaced with an MC68020.

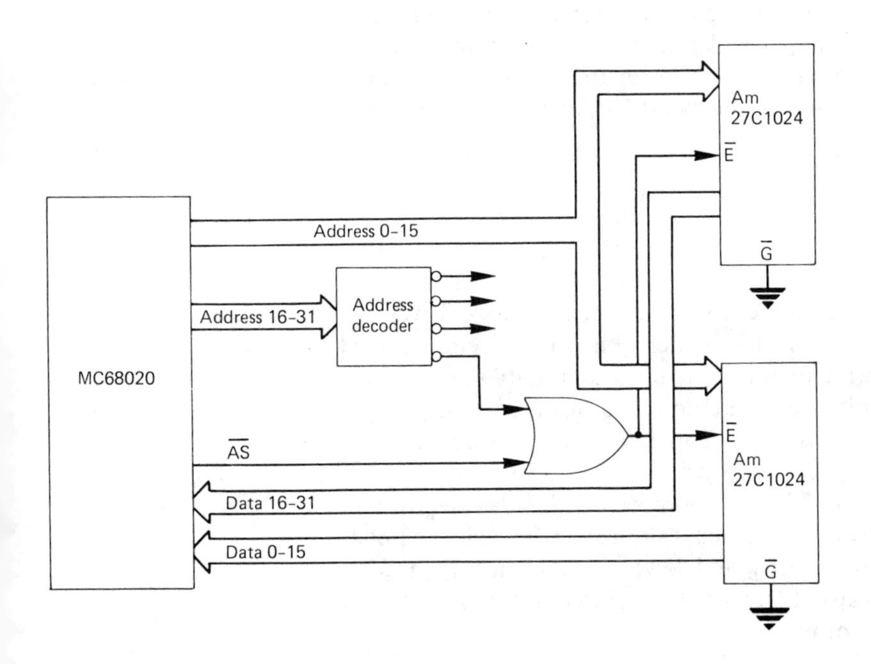

Fig. 7.8 Interfacing an MC68020 with 64K × 32-bit EPROM comprising two 64K × 16-bit devices

Electrically erasable PROM (E^2PROM) may be totally erased or re-written on a word-by-word basis without being removed from the system (as is necessary with UV erasable devices). E^2PROM is therefore suitable for applications which require frequent erasure or modification but the limited number of write cycles (about ten thousand to one million) may limit component life in some applications.

Earlier E^2PROM devices required high-voltage programming pulses and external latches for address and data but later devices incorporate on-chip pulse generators and latches for address and data which release the system bus during the write period. Current E^2PROM devices using two transistor cells have a capacity of 64 Kbits organised as 8K by 8 bits and are capable of operation from a single 5 V supply. Ten-year data retention is provided and components with access times down to 200 ns are available. New E^2PROM devices using single transistor cells are available with 256 Kbit capacity; these are capable of block erasure only and can only perform about 100 erase/write cycles.

Bubble memory is a non-volatile solid-state memory media which uses cylindrical magnetic bubbles in a film of magnetic garnet material. Data is shifted into and out of the device in serial form and constantly travels around loops within the garnet under a revolving magnetic field. Current bubble memory devices have 4 Mbit capacity but 16 and 64 Mbit devices are under development.

Bubble memory is similar to disk drives in the method of access but it has a lower average access time than flexible disk (50 ms compared with about 200 ms for flexible disk). The data transfer rate is lower (about 100 Kbit/s compared with over 200 Kbit/s for flexible disk) but the average latency is much lower (about 7 ms compared with over 70 ms for a flexible disc). Bubble memory is frequently designed as a removable cassette containing the chip and sense amplifier which may be inserted into the host part of the system. Power consumption is lower than that of mechanical mass storage devices and reliability is much better than disk or tape drives.

7.2 Disk drives

7.2.1 General

Winchester (fixed, rigid media) disk drives and flexible disk drives are the dominant mass storage media for 16-bit microcomputer systems. Optical disks are not yet available with an erase capability and, until these devices are available, magnetic media will be the dominant form of mass storage. Only limited archive applications are anticipated for present optical disks with a write-once capability.

The greater performance of 32-bit microprocessors demands equivalent improvement in the performance of the mass storage devices and a number of new devices offer higher capacity and lower access time. Figure 7.9 shows the trend for storage capacity required by computer systems to follow the increase in processor performance.

7.2.2 Winchester disk drives

Several new techniques are being applied to winchester disks to increase their capacity; these include:

a) Thin film coatings on disks to increase the number of tracks and bits which may be recorded per inch.

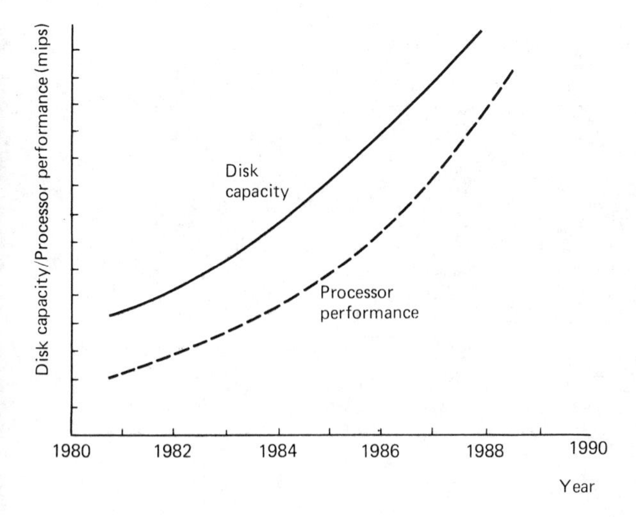

Fig. 7.9 The trend in disk capacity compared with processor performance

b) Perpendicular recording to increase recording density on the disk.
c) New types of head and reduced head/media spacing to read and record more densely packed data on disk.
d) Higher-speed disk interface standards to increase data transfer rates.
e) Higher-speed head-positioning mechanisms to reduce access times.

Using these techniques, storage capacities of up to 6 Gbytes may be possible on a 14 inch diameter disk surface before 1990, while an equivalent 8 inch surface would accommodate 3 Gbytes, a 5.25 inch surface 2 Gbytes, and a 3.5 inch surface 1 Gbyte. Access times are also expected to be reduced to less than 20 ms for an 8 inch disk. Data transfer rates may be as high as 24 MHz with the higher bit densities on 8 inch disks and up to 50 MHz on 14 inch disks.

Table 7.1 compares the capacity and performance of rigid and flexible disk drives available in 1986.

When selecting a disk drive for high system performance it is necessary to compare the *seek time*, which is the average time required to perform a seek to a cylinder of stored information. A cylinder is made up of the sum of data from a particular track on all disk surfaces. Seek time is made up of

a) Head positioning time (to move the head from one track to another)
b) Head settling time
c) Latency
d) Servo lock time
e) Track capacity.

In comparing seek times it is important to establish whether maximum or typical values are given and between what points the timing data is measured because this can vary from one manufacturer to another.

Latency is the time taken for one revolution of the disk. Half a revolution is the average time taken to reach a desired sector after the head has been positioned on the right track. To calculate total access time, half

Table 7.1 Capacity and performance of disk drives available in 1986

Type	*Surfaces*	*Diameter* (inches)	*Unformatted capacity* (Mbytes)	*Average access time* (ms)
Winchester	8	3.5	51	40
Winchester	15	5.25	143	30
Winchester	5	8	80	25
Winchester	11	8	516	20
Winchester	8	14	857	16
Removable cartridge	5	9	83	30
Removable cartridge		5.25	20	30
Removable cartridge	19	14	300	30
Flexible	2	3.5	1	96
Flexible	2	5.25	1.6	90
Flexible	1	8	28	35

the maximum latency period should be added to the seek time but in most cases seek time will be the dominant factor.

7.2.3 Disk interface standards

The de-facto industry standard interface for 5.25 inch winchester disk drives has been the ST506/412 interface which resembles a flexible disk interface. Higher-capacity disk drives make use of increased numbers of tracks per inch, increased numbers of flux reversals per inch and increased recording area. The ST506/412 interface cannot cope with increases in those parameters and alternative standards have been developed.

Figure 7.10 shows the range of data transfer rates which the ST506 and several alternative interface standards can support. Two interface standards, Small Computer Systems Interface (SCSI) and Intelligent Peripheral Interface (IPI), provide system level interfaces which permit several host computers to share several disk or tape drives. They do however require more complex, intelligent controller/interfaces which may be embedded in each disk or tape drive.

SCSI is an 8 or 16-bit parallel bus which permits host computers, each using a single host adaptor, to be connected to a variety of disk and tape drives or even modems and printers. This reduces the cost of peripheral interfaces in the host computer and reduces the processing load on the host computer. The cost of SCSI controllers in the peripherals is minimised by the use of special-purpose chips. As shown in Figure 7.11, several peripherals may be connected to each SCSI controller if an embedded SCSI interface is not available. Multiple overlap of peripheral device operations and direct copy between devices are supported by SCSI.

An 8-bit asynchronous SCSI bus has a peak data transfer rate of 1.5 Mbyte/s with 15 metres cable length. The 8-bit synchronous version

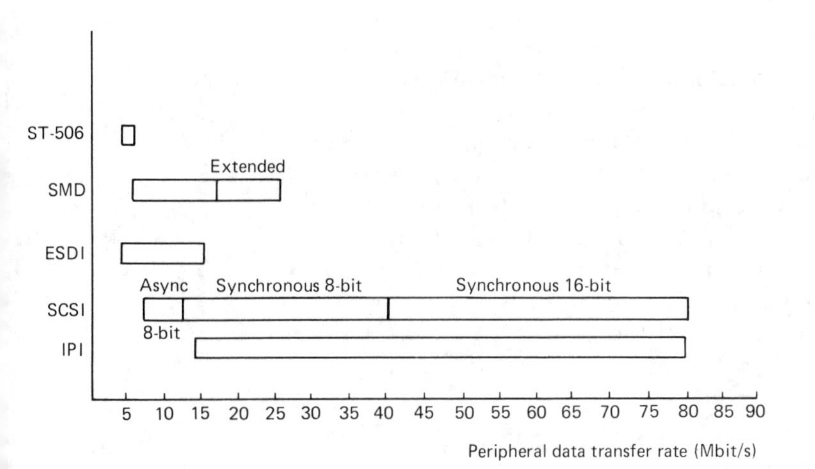

Fig. 7.10 Data rates supported by peripheral interface standards

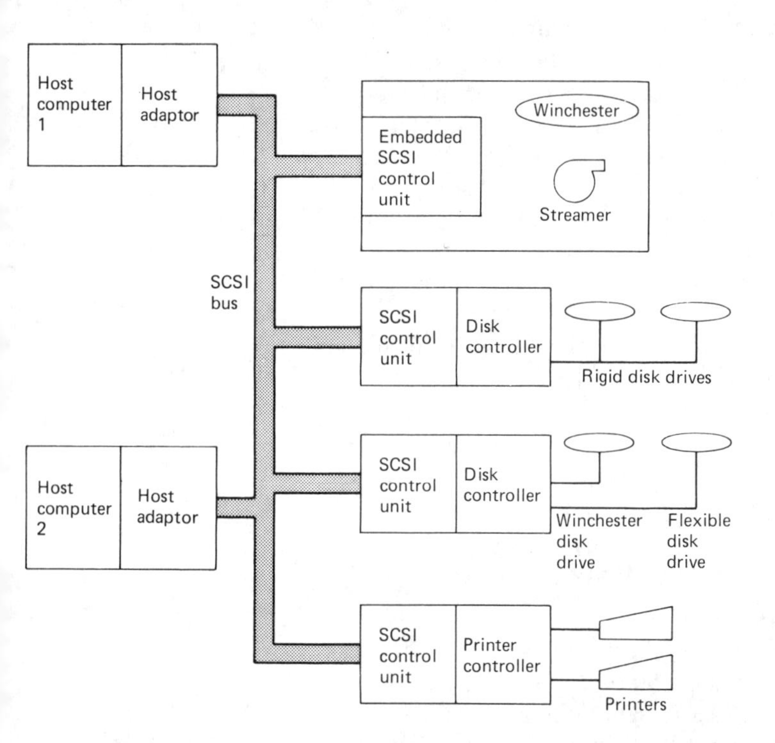

Fig. 7.11 Peripheral sharing using an SCSI bus

has a peak data transfer rate of 4 Mbyte/s with 15 metres cable length. The single-ended option has a maximum cable length of 6 metres and the differential option (RS-485) has a maximum cable length of 15 metres.

The IPI interface was developed by an ANSI committee to provide an interface with greater power and flexibility than SCSI. IPI can be expected to replace the Storage Module Drive (SMD) interface for high-performance disks while SCSI is expected to become the standard for medium and low-performance drives.

IPI is a multi-level interface with a double-byte transfer path capable of transfer rates up to 10 Mbyte/s at distances up to 125 metres. IPI level 2 is the peripheral device physical interface and chip sets are available to support this level of interface. IPI level 3 adds intelligence to the interface but, unlikle SCSI, the intelligence is defined in a general sense as protocol layers to permit customised interfaces and proprietary designs.

The ESDI interface is a device-level specification which permits a disk or tape drive manufacturer to obtain maximum performance from a peripheral. Data transfer rates up to 10 Mbit/s may be supported by ESDI compared with a limit of 5 Mbit/s for ST506 and ESDI offers greater control over the drive. Equivalent device level interfaces for tape drives are QIC-36 and QIC-02. ESDI requires only relatively simple electronics to convert the analog signals from the drive to digital form but the host computer requires a complex controller.

7.3 Tape drives

Magnetic tape drives are the most popular medium for high-volume back-up or data transfer between computers. Two varieties of tape media are available for high-capacity data storage: half-inch reel-to-reel drives and quarter-inch tape cartridges. Both forms of tape drive are available for start-stop recording, in which the tape can halt between any two blocks of data, and for streaming operation where the tape does not need to stop between data blocks, therefore making higher data transfer rates and higher storage capacity available. Start-stop recording makes it possible to search for particular blocks of data but streaming operation is suitable only for bulk data transfers.

Where tape is used as a medium for data transfer between dissimilar types of computer, the recording format must be to the appropriate ECMA/ANSI/QIC/DCAS standard to ensure compatibility. Where tape is used as a back-up medium for winchester disks, the data format does not need to comply with an international standard and a drive with suitable performance characteristics must be selected to suit the system requirements.

When selecting a back-up device for a winchester disk several factors must be borne in mind, including:

a) The ratio of formatted to unformatted capacity is different for disk drives, start-stop tape drives and streaming tape drives.

b) Although disk data transfer rates are higher than most tape transfer rates, disk access times and latency slow down overall data transfer rates.

c) Unless serpentine recording is adopted on the tape, it will be necessary to halt the transfer while the tape is rewound at the end of each track.

d) If disk capacity exceeds tape capacity, time must be lost exchanging tape media.

e) With start-stop recorders, total transfer time is proportional to the number of data blocks, the sum of inter-record gap times plus the data block recording time.

f) While data is output from the disk the streaming tape moves continuously but, when data is interrupted, the tape stops and must be rewound to a point where it can be accelerated to operating speed for

Table 7.2 Comparison of media to back up a 90 Mbyte winchester

	Flexible disk		*Quarter-inch tape cartridge*		*Half-inch reel-to-reel*	
	$5\frac{1}{4}$ inch	8 inch	Start/ Stop	Streaming	Start/ Stop	Streaming
Capacity (Mbytes)	0.5	1	15	20	45	90
Transfer rate (Kbyte/s)	30	60	24	90	120	160
Number of media changes	200	100	5	4	1	0
Media price (£ per 90 Mbyte)	1000	600	225	200	50	25
Peripheral price (£)	500	700	1200	800	3000	2000

the next part of the data transfer. Repositioning time may be more than one second with a high-speed streamer. Buffer memory may be used to reduce the number of occasions when a streamer is required to reposition.

When short disk records are employed, frequent repositioning may make dump time excessive with a streaming tape drive. In these circumstances a 64 Kbyte buffer may reduce dump time from 52 minutes to 5 minutes for a 90 IPS streaming tape drive. In the same circumstances a start-stop tape drive may be a more cost effective solution or a slower streaming tape drive may have a lower dump time because repositioning time is shorter.

The selection of a tape back-up system also requires system operation to be considered. If dumps are made as a mirror image of disk files, the disk characteristics may reduce the transfer rate to about 40% of the theoretical rate. If records are transferred using file management procedures, additional disk head movement is involved and the transfer rate may be less than 10% of the theoretical rate. Table 7.2 summarises typical performance and cost factors for alternative winchester back-up devices.

Quarter-inch tape cartridges are now available with capacities over 200 Mbytes: this exceeds the capacity of half-inch nine-track reel-to-reel streaming tape drives with a $10\frac{1}{2}$ inch reel. Data transfer rates up to 3 Mbyte/s are available from tape cartridges; this exceeds a typical data rate of 1.25 Mbyte/s for a half-inch reel-to-reel drive. Small 0.15 inch tape cassette drives are available with a storage capacity of 12 Mbytes for lower-capacity storage applications.

Six tape cartridge standards have been in common use since 1972; they share the same internal mechanism but differ in the length of tape and the coercivity of the magnetic material. These standards are

DC300 A	300 ft, 0.25 inch, 300 Oersted
DC300XL/P	450 ft, 0.25 inch, 300 Oersted
DC600A	600 ft, 0.25 inch, 550 Oersted
DC100A	140 ft, 0.15 inch, 300 Oersted
DC1000	185 ft, 0.15 inch, 550 Oersted
DC2000	205 ft, 0.125 inch, 550 Oersted

The DC600XTD standard is a more recent addition which permits track densities up to 128 tracks/inch which is double the track density supported by the other standards. The initial lack of standards for streaming tape drives prompted drive manufacturers to set up standardisation committees: QIC for quarter-inch cartridges, DCAS for data cassettes and HI/TC for half-inch tape cartridges. Several QIC standards have been defined and are being submitted to the American National Standards Institute (ANSI) and the European Computer Manufacturers Association (ECMA) for ratification as an industry standard.

QIC standards include:

a) QIC-24: quarter-inch tape format for four-track and nine-track serial streaming drives.
b) QIC-02: intelligent drive interface for QIC-24 streaming tape drives used with a host adaptor leading to a computer backplane.
c) QIC-36: basic non-intelligent drive interface for a small tape drive requiring a controller and a host adaptor leading to a computer backplane.

7.4 Disk controllers

7.4.1 Techniques which improve performance

A high-performance processor using a SCSI or IPI adaptor to interface with several disk and tape drives can achieve overlapped seeks but, if it is necessary to further optimise the performance of the disk system, a single disk controller may incorporate many features which improve overall data throughput.

In a multi-drive system the controller can overlap the seek operations to give a several hundred percentage improvement in average access time compared with sequential disk accesses. This improvement depends upon random disk file requests being received from the computer's operating system. If disk file requests are received consistently for one drive, there is little advantage to be gained by overlapping seeks. Some operating systems, including Unix, randomly select disks to store newly created files.

Average seek time can also be reduced by employing the elevator accessing technique. This technique sorts track accesses into those which use track numbers moving towards the disk spindle and those which move away from the spindle. The read/write heads thus first move in one direction accessing data on various tracks on the way, then move in the opposite direction avoiding random back-and-forth motion and significantly reducing seek time.

Disk transfers may be more efficient if data is transfered sequentially to or from sectors as the disk rotates. This technique is called *zero interleaved data transfer* and can avoid the need for interleaved sectors on the track which can double disk access time. Some form of first-in first-out buffer or dual buffer arrangement is required to implement zero interleaved data transfer. Disk controllers which implement performance optimisation techniques are much more complex than the single-chip VLSI controllers and are frequently constructed from bit-slice processors to achieve the required speed of operation.

Disks often have surface defects which make some blocks unusable, and to overcome this, operating systems usually incorporate a bad block remapping scheme. A disk can become fragmented because of bad block remapping, thus preventing large files being stored continuously and degrading system performance. To avoid this problem the disk controller may be designed to allocate spare sectors at the end of each track. Bad sectors have the header changed to cause the sector to be disregarded; all subsequent headers on the track are renamed and a spare sector is written with the last good header. Using this sector slip technique, tracks with bad sectors may be reformatted giving the appearance of being error free to the operating system. The order of headers on the disk is preserved and full track transfers may be achieved in one revolution regardless of bad sectors.

7.4.2 Disk cache

A disk data cache may be employed to reduce average access times by storing copies of disk data in a semiconductor memory. When the required data is held in cache the access time is considerably reduced. Disk caches can reduce average access times between two and nine times by eliminating head positioning delays. A cache may be used to give an inexpensive low-

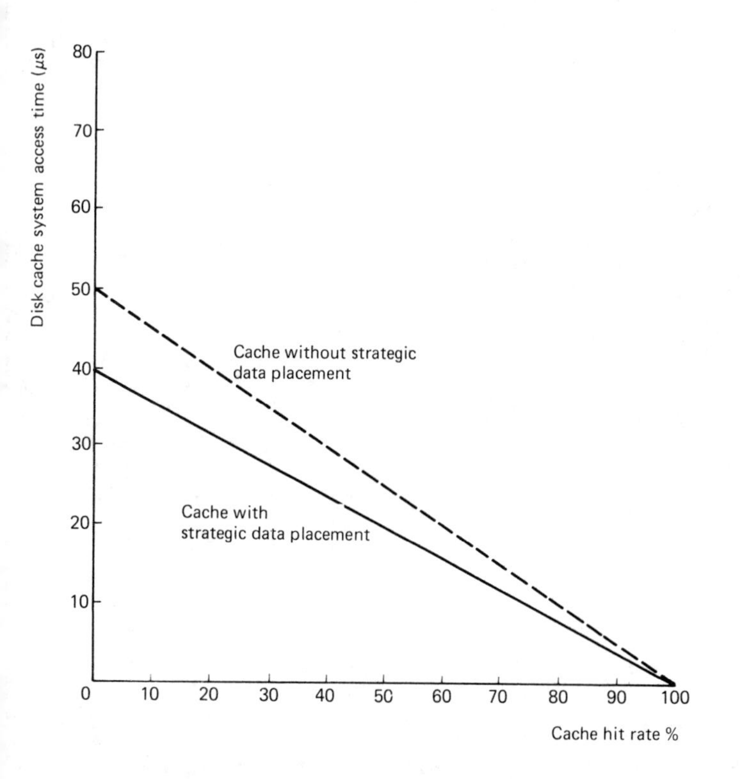

Fig. 7.12 The reduction in access time provided by strategic data placement in a disk cache system

performance disk a performance similar to an expensive high-performance disk.

A disk cache may be implemented by the operating system or by a dedicated cache controller. The implementation by the operating system requires additional software and memory space for the buffer. A dedicated cache controller takes cache requests from the operating system which would otherwise be routed to the disk controller. If the required data is in cache, it is passed to the system without involving the disk controller and, if the required data is not in cache, the cache controller passes the command to the disk controller. When the data is returned from the disk the cache controller also stores a copy in the cache.

The access time of a disk cache involved in random disk seeks may be reduced by strategic placement of information on the disk. The most frequently read data is placed on the outer tracks, close to the head's starting position, to shorten the average seek time. Strategic placement can reduce the disk access time by 20% but this advantage is reduced as the cache hit rate increases. (See Figure 7.12.)

8 Communications interfaces

8.1 Standards for computer communications and interfaces

The more common forms of communication interface found on microcomputers include:

a) Serial interfaces for local terminals.
b) Parallel interfaces for local peripherals (such as high-speed printers), other processors or instruments (using the IEEE 488 bus).
c) Local area network interfaces which permit communication with terminals, peripherals, other processors or remote networks (via network gateways).
d) Long-distance communications including wide area networks, commonly provided by synchronous serial interfaces connected to modems and using a communications protocol.

The adoption of standard interfaces makes it possible for a computer manufacturer to provide a small number of alternative interface types which will permit communication with many types of terminal, peripheral, instrument and other computer types. The electrical standards for serial and parallel interfaces were the first to be developed. The RS-232-C serial interface was published in 1969 and the higher-performance serial interface standards, RS-422 and RS-423, were published in 1975. The general-purpose functional and mechanical standard, RS-449 (which together with RS-422 and RS-423 was intended to replace RS-232-C as the specification for the interface between a data terminal equipment and a data circuit-terminating equipment [modem]), was published in 1977.

The IEEE 488 parallel interface bus standard was published in 1978 and was developed from the Hewlett Packard General Purpose Instrument Bus (GPIB). This is primarily an electrical and mechanical specification and does not give details of messages or in what format they should be sent over the bus. As a result, the different instrument manufacturers have defined their own codes and formats for data, and therefore test programs for computers connected to test instrumentation may have to be rewritten if a particular instrument is replaced by an equivalent from a different manufacturer. In an attempt to prevent these problems, an IEEE P981 task force is working on standards for the layers of protocol above those which are defined in IEEE 488.

The advent of Local Area Networks and Wide Area Networks in the

1970s resulted in the establishment of standards for physical (including electrical) and data link protocols. Examples include:

a) CCITT X25 interface for terminals in packet switched public data networks.
b) The Ethernet Local Area Network, later developed into the IEEE 802.3 standard.

In the late 1970s it was apparent that in order to utilise the full potential of computer networks, open international standards were required for the aspects of computer-to-computer data transfers above the physical and data link protocol aspects. Previously the only standards were closed ones, proprietary to a particular computer manufacturer such as IBM or DEC. The International Standards Organisation (ISO) initiated work into defining the requirements for *Open Systems Interconnection* (OSI) in 1977. In Spring 1983 the basic reference model for OSI (ISO 7498) became an international standard and work progressed into defining the standards for individual layers of the reference model.

The ISO 7498 reference model is a framework for coordinating the development of OSI standards; it uses a layered architecture to break up the problem into manageable pieces. The OSI reference model identified the functions required for computers to transfer information and to interwork for achieving common distributed goals. The functions were arranged into seven layers and the functions which each layer must perform were identified in an implementation-independent manner. Later ISO standards defined the implementations for each layer to ensure that full compatibility is achieved at each layer.

Figure 8.1 shows the OSI layers required in two interconnected systems; in practice some layers may not be required in certain applications and null layers may be included. The CCITT X25 standard may be used as layers 1, 2 and 3 or in a local area network, and IEEE 802.3 may be used as layers 1 and 2 with ISO standards for the higher layers.

Layer one, the *Physical Layer*, ensures compatibility of the hardware aspects. The specification of the interconnection media, electrical (or fibre-optic) connectors, data rates, signal levels, etc. are included.

Layer two, the *Data Link Layer*, ensures compatibility of the data link protocols used by the computers. The specification for the frames of data includes frame length and the composition of headers including addressing information and cyclic redundancy checks. The rules which govern the control of access to the media and the re-transmission of erroneous data are included.

Layer three, the *Network Layer*, sets up the procedure for communication between networks, the switching and routing of messages and the ordering of packets. Layer three is vital in packet switched networks and systems with gateways between separate networks, but may be unnecessary in an autonomous local area network.

Layer four, the *Transport Layer*, monitors quality and ensures that the complete message, consisting of many frames, reaches its destination reliably. The message must be broken into the frame lengths supported by

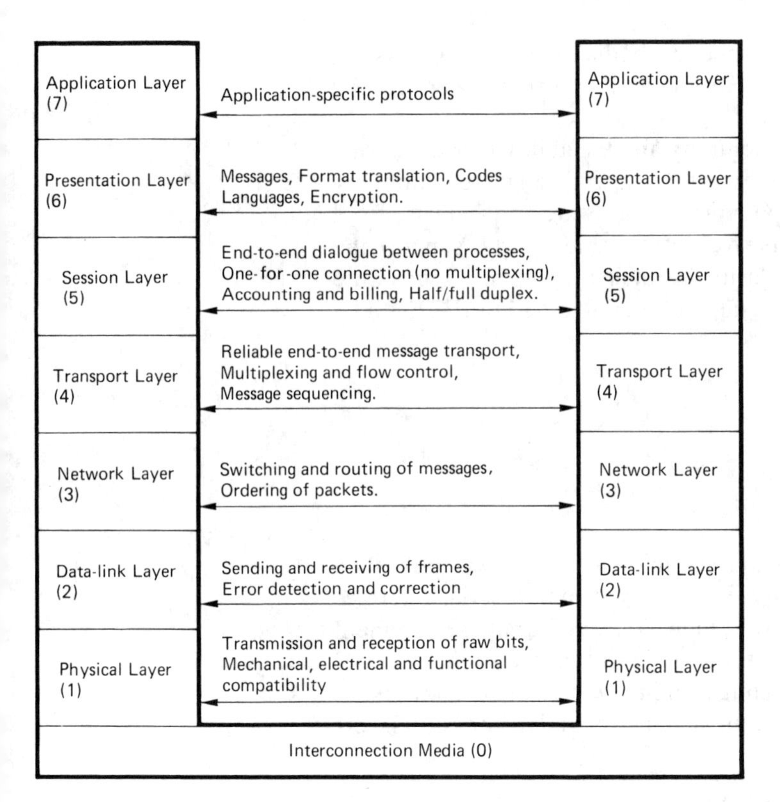

Fig. 8.1 OSI layers in two interconnected systems

the network layer and the data link layer and re-assembled upon arrival. The order in which frames arrive must be checked and acknowledgements transmitted when necessary. When re-transmission is requested the transport layer must repeat the appropriate message.

Layer five, the *Session Layer*, establishes and terminates the required half/full-duplex connections between systems, determining when to transmit and mapping logical names onto physical addresses. It is also responsible for accounting and billing for network usage.

Layer six, the *Presentation Layer*, converts the transmitted data into a form suitable for the receiving system. Data may require conversion from ASCII to EBCDIC or from fixed to floating point. If data must be encrypted for security before being transmitted over the network, the encryption and decryption may be carried out in the presentation layer. Virtual devices are supported at this layer.

Layer seven, the *Application Layer*, brings network services to the end user. These services may include: password checks, document or file transfers, log-in and file access checks. This is the highest layer and is the only one which is not completely transparent to the user. The application software in the host system is not part of the application layer but common application service elements such as X400 electronic mail standards may be included in layer seven.

When a message is transmitted, it passes from layer 7 to layer 1 at the sending system with each layer adding its own header to the message or processing the message in some way. The frames which make up the message are transmitted over the interconnection media to the receiving system where they travel through layers 1 to 7 having the headers removed and being re-assembled into the message.

The layered approach ensures modularity and the ability for networking software to be upgraded incrementally without introducing a revolutionary change. The modularity makes it possible for hardware and software from one vendor to work with products from other vendors who support the same standards at each layer. Modularity also makes it possible to substitute one form of media for another, for example to change X25 to IEEE 802.3, without changing layers 4 to 7.

8.2 Serial interfaces

8.2.1 RS-232-C and V24/28

The American Industries Association standard RS-232-C was published in 1969 and until the early 1980s was the only common serial interface standard for connecting computers or terminals (Data Terminal Equipment or DTE) to communications systems via modems (Data Communications Equipment or DCE) and for connecting terminals directly to computers.

RS-232-C defines the interconnection media layer and the physical layers of the interface by defining:

a) Electrical signal characteristics (Section 2)
b) Interface mechanical characteristics (Section 3)
c) Functional description of interface circuits (Section 4)
d) Standard interfaces for selected communications system configurations (Section 5).

The European CCITT equivalent of RS-232-C includes the mechanical characteristics (connector details and the functional description of interchange circuits) in the V24 standard and the electrical signal characteristics in the V28 standard. The designation of equivalent interchange circuits differs between RS-232-C and V24 as shown in Table 8.1

The standard connector for RS-232-C is a 25-pin D-type connector with a male plug on the DTE (terminal or computer) and a female socket on the modem. Peripherals such as printers usually have a female socket. A problem arises when a computer-to-computer connection is required because both computers will have a male plug and both will output data on pin 3 and input data in pin 2. In addition, each end expects particular voltage levels on various control pins. Figure 8.2 shows the cross-connections which may be necessary in a cable to link two computers together or to link a terminal to a computer. Linking a computer to a modem simply requires those pins which are in use to be linked to the equivalent pin number at the other end of the cable.

The maximum data rate specified in RS-232-C is 20 kbit/s and the maximum cable length is 50 ft. This length may however be exceeded and up to 150 ft of screened cable is usually satisfactory, depending upon the capacitance of the cable and the electrical noise in the environment.

Table 8.1 RS-232-C and V24 interchange circuits

Pin	RS-232-C Interchange	CCITT V24 Equivalent	Description	Gnd	Data		Control		Timing	
					From DCE	To DCE	From DCE	To DCE	From DCE	To DCE
1	AA	101	Protective Ground	X						
7	AB	102	Signal Ground/ Common Return	X						
2	BA	103	Transmitted Data			X				
3	BB	104	Received Data		X					
4	CA	105	Request to Send					X		
5	CB	106	Clear to Send				X			
6	CC	107	Data Set Ready				X			
20	CD	108.2	Data Terminal Ready					X		
22	CE	125	Ring Indicator				X			
8	CF	109	Received Line Signal Detector				X			
21	CG	110	Signal Quality Detector				X			
23	CH	111	Data Signal Rate Selector (DTE)					X		
23	CI	112	Data Signal Rate Selector (DCE)				X			
24	DA	113	Transmitter Signal Element Timing (DTE)							X
15	DB	114	Transmitter Signal Element Timing (DCE)						X	
17	DD	115	Receiver Signal Element Timing (DCE)						X	
14	SBA	118	Secondary Transmitted Data			X				
16	SBB	119	Secondary Received Data		X					
19	SCA	120	Secondary Request to Send					X		
13	SCB	121	Secondary Clear to Send				X			
12	SCF	122	Secondary Rec'd Line Signal Detector				X			

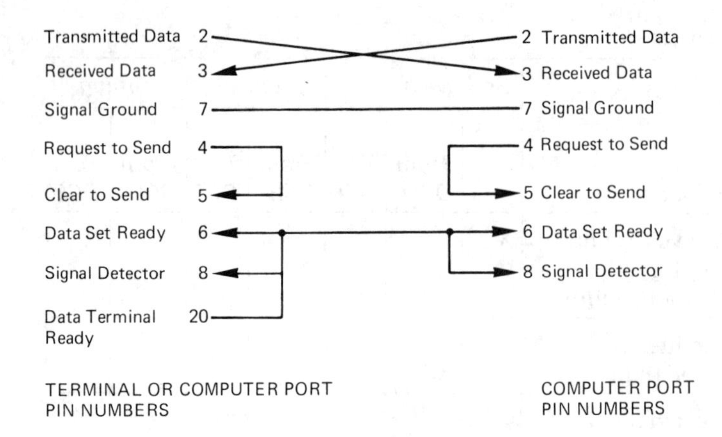

Fig. 8.2 Cable wiring to link the RS-232-C interface on a computer to a terminal or a second computer

The electrical signalling levels for RS-232-C are unbalanced, that is they are measured with respect to the signal ground reference. A positive voltage greater than 3 volts is interpreted as ON for control circuits and binary 0 (or space) for data circuits, while a negative voltage greater than 3 volts is interpreted as OFF or binary 1 (mark). Serial data is transmitted in a character code either synchronously (using the Transmitter Signal Element Timing clock signals) or asynchronously.

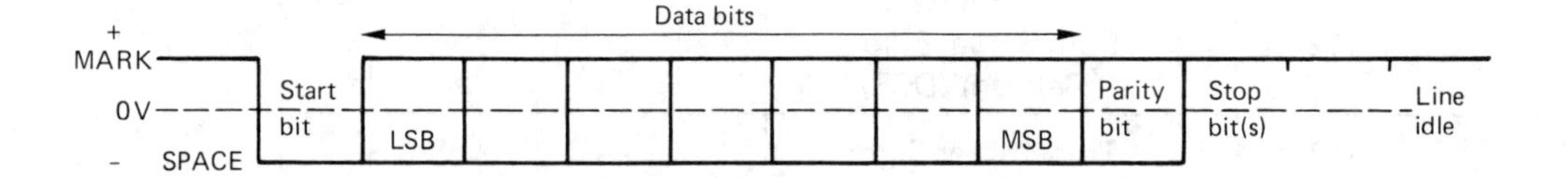

Fig. 8.3 A typical asynchronous frame

Serial asynchronous data is transmitted in frames containing a start bit, up to 8 data bits, a parity bit, and either 1 or 2 stop bits (see Figure 8.3). By convention, odd parity (in which the parity bit is set to produce an odd number of ones in the data plus parity block) is used on synchronous links and parity on asynchronous links. The start bit is used to synchronise the receiver with the sender by triggering a clock in the receiver which runs at approximately the same speed as the clock used to generate pulses at the sender.

8.2.2 RS-422, RS-423 and RS-485

In the early 1970s new serial interfaces were developed to overcome the limitations in speed and cable length imposed by RS-232-C. The EIA standards RS-422 and RS-423 were published in 1975. RS-422 defines the electrical characteristics of balanced voltage digital interface circuits and RS-423 defines the electrical characteristics of unbalanced voltage digital interface circuits.

Figure 8.4 compares RS-422 with RS-423 interfaces. Balanced interfaces use a voltage on one line with respect to another line to determine a mark signal, reversing the polarity to determine a space signal. Because no reference voltage is required, balanced interfaces are immune to errors caused

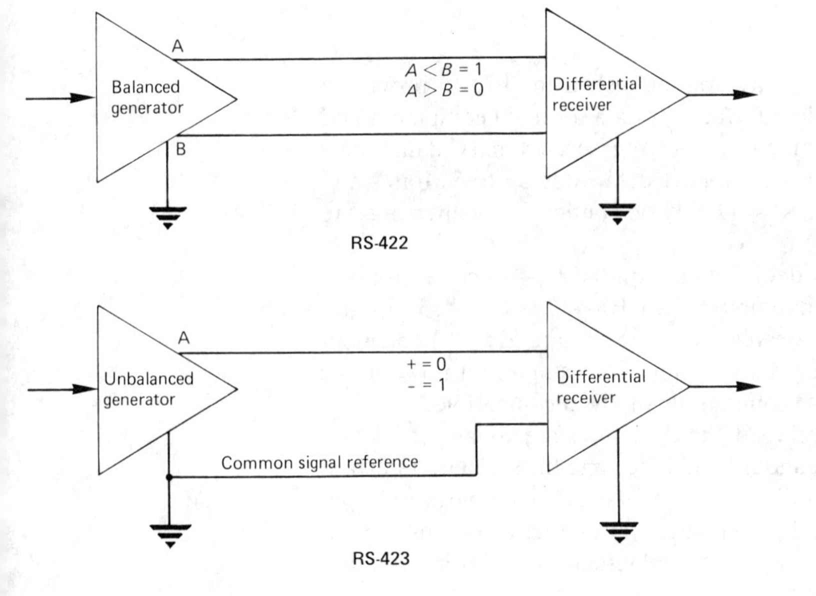

Fig. 8.4 Comparison of an RS-422 (balanced) interface with an RS-423 (unbalanced) interface

by differences in reference voltages and, since electrical noise affects both lines similarly, a much greater immunity to electrical noise corruption is achieved.

The same driver and receiver chips may be configured to provide either RS-422 or RS-423 interfaces. With suitable voltage levels, an RS-423 interface may be connected to an RS-232-C interface. The major parameters of RS-232-C, RS-422 and RS-423 are compared in Table 8.2. The more recent RS-485 standard permits tri-state driver outputs for multipoint or party line buses with up to 32 driver/receiver pairs. In other respects RS-485 is similar to RS-422 with a 10 Mbit/s maximum data rate and most RS-485 driver chips are pin-compatible with earlier RS-422 types to permit easy upgrading.

Table 8.2 Comparison of RS-232-C, RS-422 and RS-423

Parameter	*RS-232-C*	*RS-422*	*RS-423*
Maximum length	50 ft	1200 m (4000 ft)	1200 m (4000 ft)
Maximum speed	20K baud	10M baud	100K baud
Mark (Data 1)	−3 V	$A < B$	A Negative
Space (Data 0)	+3 V	$A > B$	A Positive
Maximum common mode voltage		−7 V to +7 V	
Open-circuit output voltage	3 V to 25 V (5 V to 15 V with 3 to 7 kΩ load)	<6 V	4 V–6 V
Minimum receiver input	±3 V	200 mV differential	200 mV differential

8.2.3 RS-449 and X21

The EIA RS-449 interface standard was published in 1977 to provide a general-purpose 37-pin or 9-pin interface for data terminal equipment and data circuit-terminating equipment employing serial binary data interchange. The RS-449 interface will support data rates up to 2 Mbit/s and cable lengths up to 60 metres. RS-449 may be configured to inter-operate with RS-232-C interfaces.

Each control function has a dedicated pin on the RS-449 connector and the electrical interface standards employed are RS-422 and RS-423. A minimum of 10 circuits, designated category 1, are required in all implementations; the rest of the 30 circuits are optional. This makes it possible for two devices which claim RS-449 compatibility to be incompatible.

The European CCITT developed the X21 interface as an alternative to its V24/28 serial interface standard and it became the standard interface for digital circuit-switched public data networks. X21 employs a 15-pin connector and all its control functions use the same circuit as user data, rather than separate pins. A separate control circuit identifies information as data or control (see Figure 8.5).

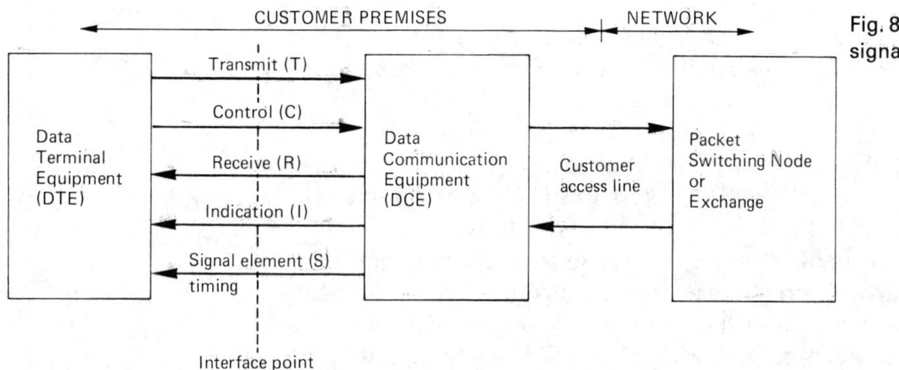

Fig. 8.5 X21 interface signals

Although some minor differences exist in receiver sensitivity, both the X21 standard and the RS-422 standard use similar electrical characteristics. X21 is capable of operating with cable lengths up to 1000 metres at speeds up to 10 Mbit/s. Figure 8.6 compares the transmission rate and distance capabilities of RS-232-C, RS-422, RS-423, RS-449 and X21.

8.2.4 Serial communications controllers

For local serial interfaces with terminals it is unusual to employ a data link protocol. Straightforward asynchronous communications with flow control (X on and X off) characters are commonly employed. Several different varieties of Dual Universal Asynchronous Receiver-Transmitter (DUART) chips are available which include all the circuitry required to interface two serial ports to an 8-bit bus. Facilities include bit-rate generators and a first-in first-out buffer memory for each channel. It is necessary only to provide suitable input and output chips for the required electrical interface standard.

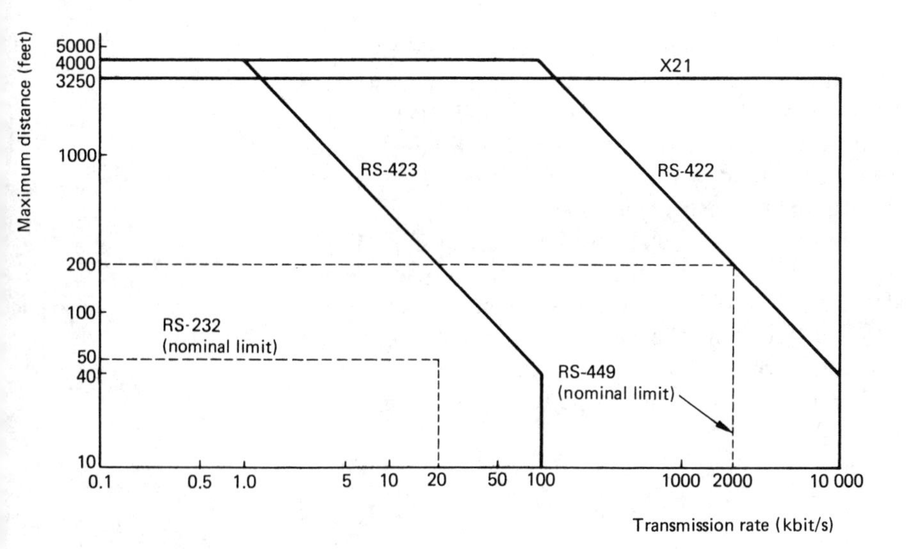

Fig. 8.6 Comparison of transmission rates and distance capabilities for RS-232-C,RS-422, RS-423, RS-449 and X21

A high-performance computer system would find the servicing of interrupts and input/output operations to DUART chips extremely time consuming and it has become common practice to employ an intelligent serial input/output controller board to handle the routine aspects of serial input and output and to transfer the accumulated data by DMA over a 16 or 32-bit system bus to the main processor or global memory.

Synchronous or asynchronous data links employing a variety of character and bit-oriented data link protocols may be interfaced by a suitable driver and receiver and a data-communication controller chip. Once configured for a particular protocol, data communications controllers perform many functions including:

a) Interfacing with a DMA controller
b) Vectored interrupt generation
c) Clock generation
d) Handling control characters for error control, etc.
e) Bit stuffing and other forms of data transparency
f) Data buffering
g) Clock synchronisation
h) Generating and checking cyclic redundancy codes
i) Loop back and auto-echo generation
j) Encoding and decoding of NRZI and FM data
k) Generating and monitoring modem control signals.

8.3 Parallel interfaces

Prior to 1978 the only parallel interface standards were for line printers for which two major manufacturers had evolved their own interface standards, Dataproducts and Centronics. These interfaces were basic single-direction interfaces unsuitable for general use. Most computer manufacturers provided a basic 16-bit TTL parallel interface, some had DMA capability and others were little more than a parallel I/O chip with TTL driver/receivers. In 1975 Hewlett Packard submitted their HPIB bus standard to the American Institute of Electrical & Electronic Engineers and in 1978 it was approved, after modification, as the IEEE 488 Standard Digital Interface for Programmable Instrumentation.

IEEE 488 has two groups of data lines: eight are for data transfers (DIO_1 to DIO_8) and eight are for control. A further eight lines provide signal ground returns and shielding. Up to 15 devices may be connected to the IEEE 488 bus and data transfers can take place at up to 1 Mbyte/s with a maximum bus length of 20 metres.

As shown in Figure 8.7 devices are able to perform one or more of the three basic functions:

a) Talking
b) Listening
c) Control.

A listener only accepts data from the bus, a talker sends data over the

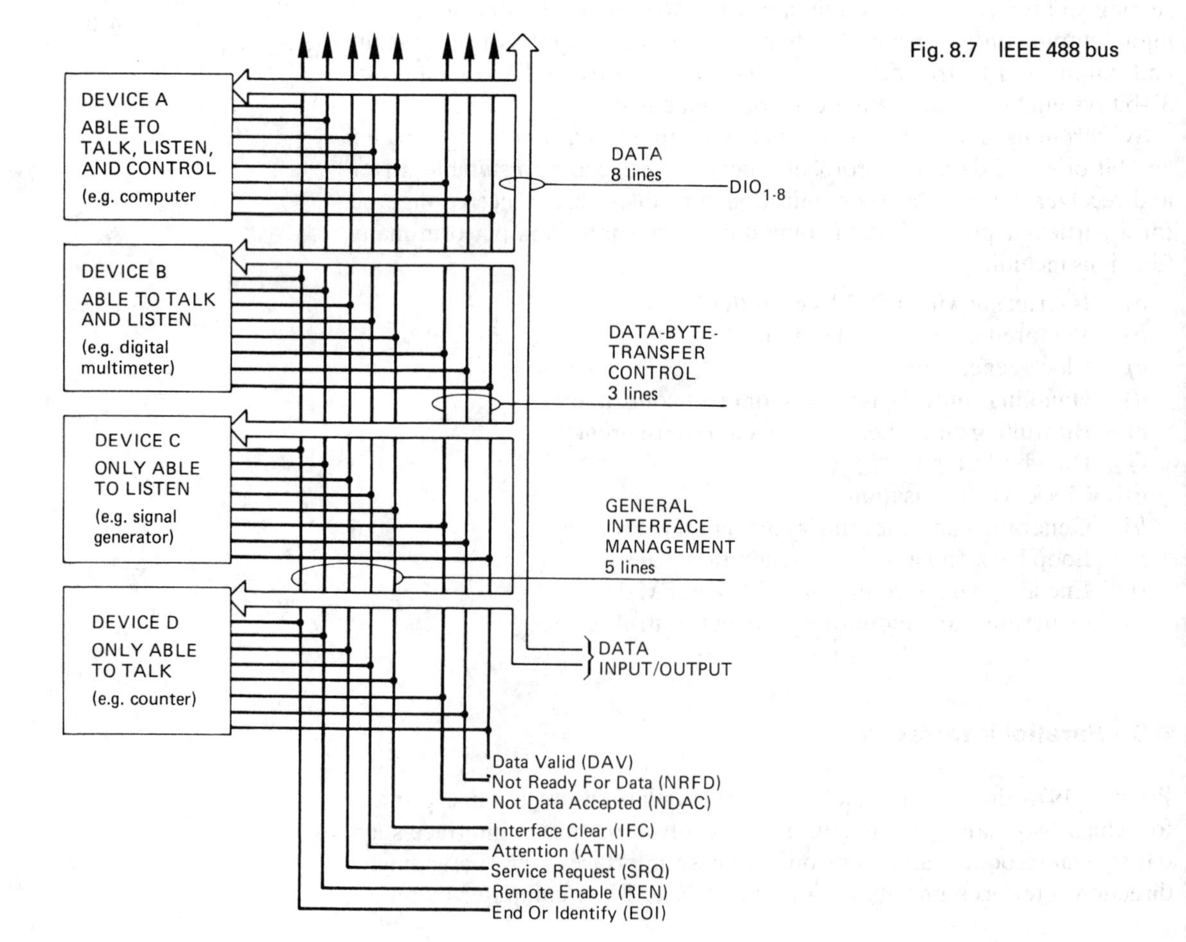

Fig. 8.7 IEEE 488 bus

bus, and the controller addresses other devices and grants permission for talkers to use the bus. Only one bus controller and one talker may be active at any time.

Devices all have unique addresses and the controller may address as many listeners as required in broadcast transmissions but typical operation is from one talker to one listener. A talker may initiate a serial poll sequence by sending a service-request message to the system controller. The controller responds by obtaining a status byte from all the devices in sequence to determine which one requested the bus. A parallel poll is also possible, in which devices on the bus report their status simultaneously to the controller. Byte-serial bit-parallel transmission is employed with negative logic TTL voltage levels. The eight control lines are made up of three data-byte transfer control lines which perform a handshake for each byte transfer and five general interface management lines.

IEEE 488 interface chips are available to minimise the amount of interface circuitry required and DMA interfaces may be constructed for high-speed applications. The most common applications of IEEE 488 are to connect instruments to computers or recording equipment and as an interface for peripherals such as high-speed printers and plotters.

8.4 Local area networks

8.4.1 Alternative local area networks

The use of a local area network to interconnect computers, terminals, workstations, data base servers, etc. within a building or local group of buildings has developed rapidly since 1980. Local area networks are expected to provide much greater data rates, faster responses and much lower error rates than wide area networks which use telecommunications lines to interconnect terminals and computers. For this reason, completely new transmission media, protocols and topologies have been developed for local area networks.

Four types of *transmission media* are commonly employed for local area networks:

1 *Twisted-pair electrical cable* which is limited to data rates up to 3 Mbit/s and has typical error rates around one in 100 000 when not screened.
2 *Baseband coaxial cable* for data rates up to 50 Mbit/s and typical error rates of 1 in 10 million.
3 *Broadband coaxial cable* for data rates (the sum of many channels) over 300 Mbit/s and typical error rates of 1 in 1000 million.
4 *Fibre-optic cable* for total data rates of more than 150 Mbit/s and extremely low error rates. The number of devices which may be attached to a fibre-optic bus is small and therefore the ring topology which uses fibre-optic links between access points is most suitable. Alternatively star couplers may be used to interconnect up to 64 devices in a star configuration.

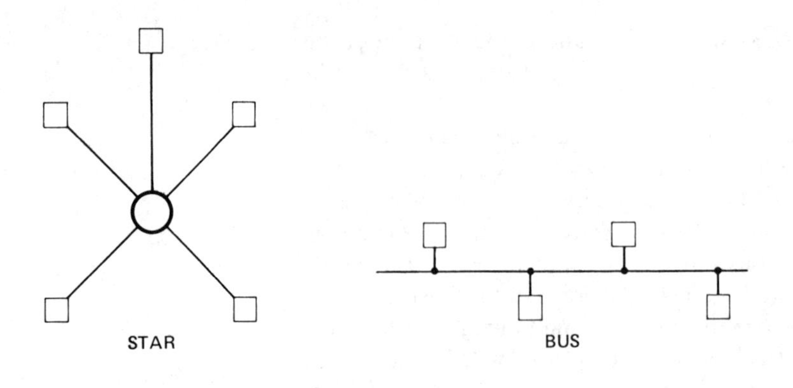

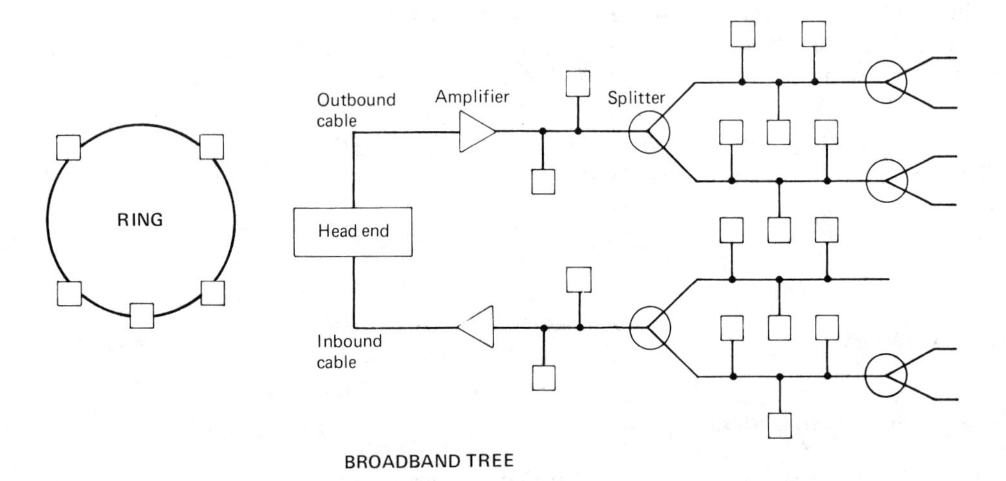

Fig. 8.8 Common local area network topologies

Four types of *network topology* (see Figure 8.8) are commonly employed for local area networks:

1 *Star networks* with either an active switch or a passive fibre-optic star coupler at the hub, directly connected to each station. A passive star coupler broadcasts data to all connected stations.
2 *Bus networks* in which stations tap onto a single cable. Several segments may be interconnected by repeaters or gateways to increase the distance covered or the number of stations. Information is broadcast to all connected stations.
3 *Ring networks* in which each station is connected to two adjacent stations and information is passed around the ring from one station to the next.
4 A *tree network* such as may be employed in a broadband system with a head amplifier (which changes the transmit frequencies to receive frequencies) connected by successive branches to a large user population.

Local area networks which time division multiplex a common communications channel must have a protocol which controls access to the channel. There are three basic forms of *access control* in common usage:

1 The use of a *bus controller* to poll each station in turn and invite/command transmission. This form of access control is most common on military data buses such as MIL-STD-1553 B and polled multidrop terminal connections.
2 *Carrier Sense Multiple Access with Collision Detection* (CSMA/CD) as used by Ethernet (IEEE 802.3). In this contention system, each station listens to the traffic on the bus. A station wishing to transmit waits until no traffic is detected before transmitting. If another station transmits simultaneously, both packets of data will be corrupted so a mechanism is included to detect the collision and abort both transmissions. Both stations then wait for a random period before transmitting again to minimise the probability of a repeated collision.
3 *Token passing* may be applied to a ring or a bus topology and employs a unique data packet (token) which allows the holder to transmit information. Any station wishing to transmit must wait until it receives the token. It then transmits its data and passes the token onto the next station in the sequence.

It is not intended here to describe the vast number of different local area networks but the four local area network standards adopted by the IEEE and ANSI will be briefly described because they are expected to have the greatest usage in the future and they each require a dedicated interface to the computer system at each station. These standards are

a) IEEE 802.3 (1985) Carrier Sense Multiple Access with Collision Detection (CSMA/CD). Access method and physical layer specification.
b) IEEE 802.4 (1985). Bus utilizing token passing as an access method.
c) IEEE 802.5 (1985). Ring utilizing token passing as the access method.
d) ANSI X3T9.5(b). Fibre Distributed Data Interface (FDDI).

8.4.2 IEEE 802.3

The IEEE 802.3 standard is based upon the Ethernet standard and uses CSMA/CD access control. The data rate is 10 Mbit/s using baseband coaxial cable with a bus topology.

As shown in Figure 8.9, the Data Terminal Equipment (DTE) is connected to the cable by a Media Access Unit (MAU) (known as a transceiver on Ethernet). An Access Unit Interface (AUI) cable connects the standard 15 pin connector on the DTE to the MAU. The MAU is connected to the medium which may consist of up to 500 metres of coaxial trunk cable in each segment. Repeater units may be used to extend the system topology by connecting trunk cable segments together up to the limit of 2.5 km between any two MAUs.

The maximum number of DTEs which may be connected to a single IEEE 802.3 network is 1024 but gateways may be used to link several networks together to exceed the length and DTE quantity limitations. A less-expensive B version of the physical layer specification (sometimes referred to as Cheapernet) is available which permits standard BNC-T connectors to be used in place of the MAU and RG58 coaxial cable to be

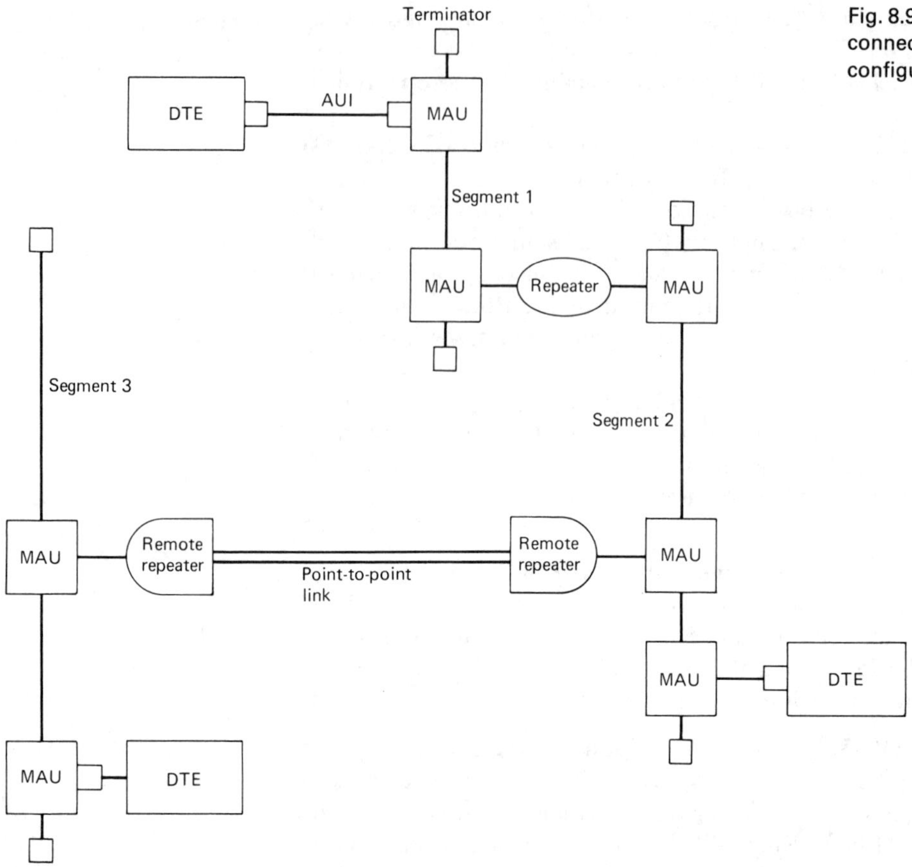

Fig. 8.9 IEEE 802.3 network connection and configuration

used in place of expensive trunk coax. This reduces the distances which may be supported on each segment but all other parameters are unchanged. Cheapernet dispenses with the separate MAU; to reduce costs the MAU is an integral part of the DTE.

Several chip sets are available to construct an IEEE 802.3 DTE. Figure 8.10 shows a typical DTE constructed from the LANCE chip set. The LANCE chip transfers data packets to and from the MAU and manages the data buffers in local memory, sharing DMA access to this memory with other bus master devices. In the transmitting mode, the LANCE transfers data from the current buffer to a 48-byte internal FIFO buffer. The output from this FIFO is serialised and sent to the Serial Interface Adaptor which encodes the data and passes it to the coax cable through the transceiver chip in the MAU.

In the receiving mode the serial interface adaptor decodes data and passes it to the FIFO buffer in the LANCE chip. The LANCE transfers the data from the FIFO buffer to the current buffer in local memory. The local

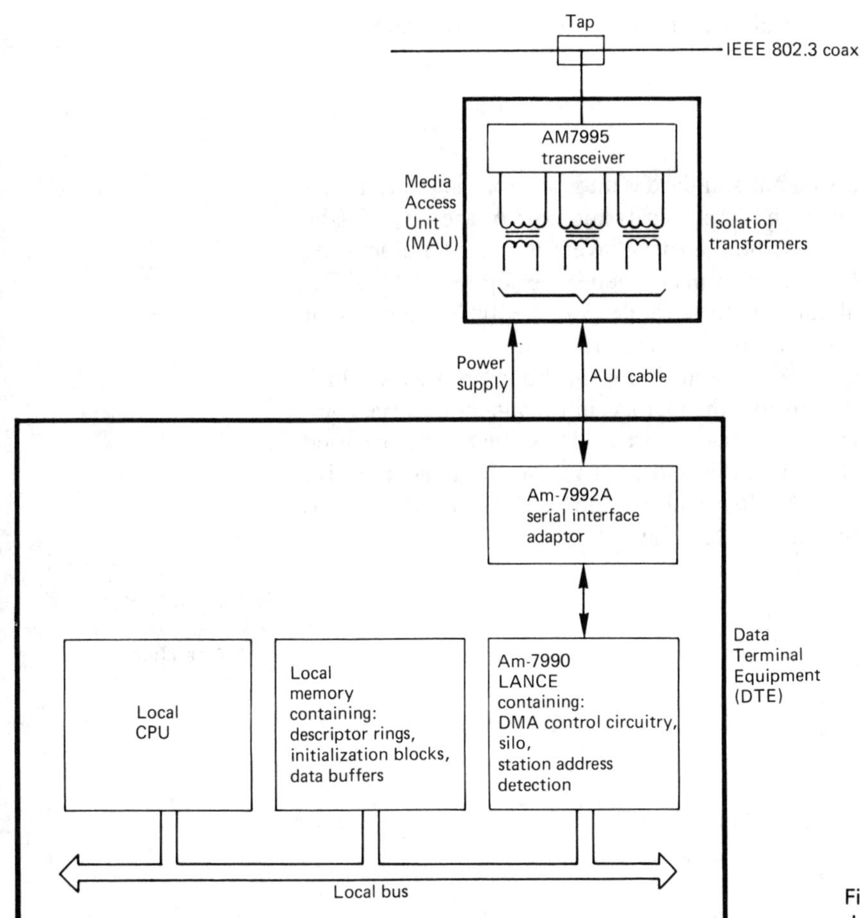

Fig. 8.10 An IEEE 802.3 data terminal equipment

CPU must provide the functions of OSI layers 3 to 7 and the logical link control part of layer 2 because IEEE 802.3 covers only the access method and the physical layer. The data link layer (layer 2) consists of the medium access control, which is defined in IEEE 802.3, and the logical link control, which is specified in IEEE 802.2.

The IEEE 802.2 network can transfer data at burst rates up to about 9 Mbit/s but this is considerably reduced if the network becomes heavily loaded and a large proportion of collisions occur. Repeated collisions become significant above 60% applied load on most systems. In these circumstances, transmission delay is unpredictable making IEEE 802.3 unsuitable for applications where guaranteed transmission delays are required. Polled systems and token passing techniques with priority mechanisms are more suitable. IEEE 802.3 has become extremely popular for office automation where response times are less critical and large numbers of users require occasional access to the media.

The transfer rate which may be sustained by an IEEE 802.3 user is frequently limited by the ability of the local processor to carry out the functions of OSI layers 2 to 7 rather than the ability of the network to transmit data or the DTE interface circuitry to transfer data into, or from, local memory.

8.4.3 IEEE 802.4

The IEEE 802.4 token passing bus standard is intended for factory automation applications and forms layer 1 (physical) and part of the layer 2 (the medium access control part of the data link layer) in the Manufacturing Automation Protocol, MAP. Two forms of media are supported by IEEE 802.4: broadband coaxial cable with several 5 or 10 Mbit/s channels or a single-channel medium using carrier band modulation.

The main network in a MAP system is the backbone network which covers the greatest distances around the factory, interconnecting large computers, gateways and subnetworks (see Figure 8.11). Subnetworks are used to connect small areas of automation and tend to use the less-expensive single-channel carrierband technology whereas the backbone network tends to use the more costly broadband technology.

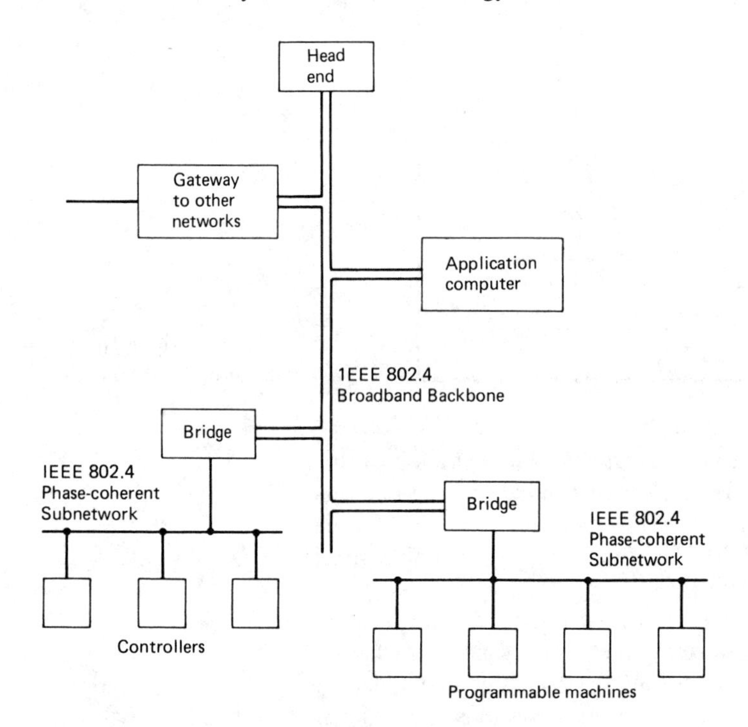

Fig. 8.11 IEEE 802.4 backbone and subnetworks in a MAP architecture

A single carrierband segment can accommodate up to 30 stations and 1 km of cable but repeaters may be used to extend these limits. Phase-coherent modulation (a form of frequency shift keying) with data rates of 5 and 10 Mbit/s is used at carrierband. A single-chip carrierband modem has been developed by Motorola and this may be connected to the MC 68824 Token Bus Controller chip to implement the IEEE 802.4 phase coherent physical layer standard (see Figure 8.12).

A local CPU is required to handle the logical link control part of layer 2 and all the higher MAP layers. The MC 68824 handles medium access

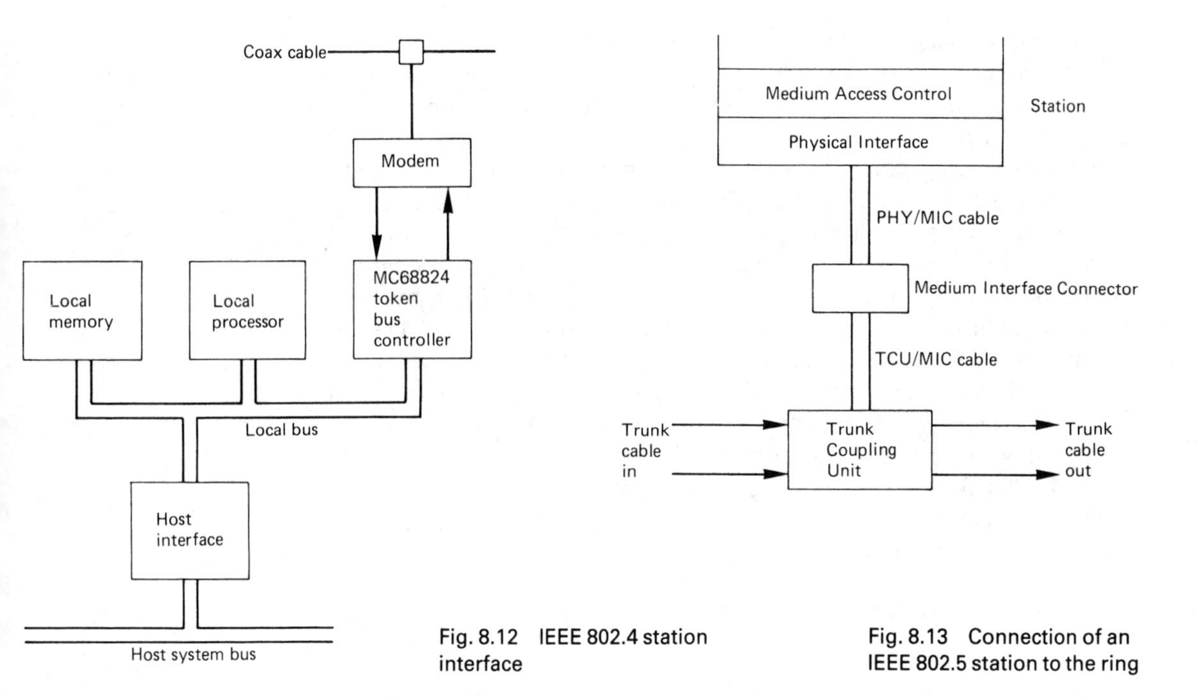

Fig. 8.12 IEEE 802.4 station interface

Fig. 8.13 Connection of an IEEE 802.5 station to the ring

control and the modem chip handles the physical layer. If the local CPU handles all the higher MAP layers, between 0.5 and 1 Mbyte of local memory may be required. If the host system provides some of these functions or if only a collapsed set of MAP services is required, the local processing and storage requirements will be reduced.

8.4.4 IEEE 802.5

IEEE 802.5 specifies a Token Ring Access Method and Physical Layer Specification similar to the IBM token ring network. The standard emphasises the externally visible characteristics needed for interconnection compatibility while avoiding unnecessary constraints on the processing equipment which is to be interconnected. The data signalling rate may be 1 Mbit/s or 4 Mbit/s and the error rate must be better than 1 in 100 million.

A standard medium interface connector is specified to link the station to the Trunk Coupling Unit (TCU) which is attached to the trunk cable (see Figure 8.13). An insertion/bypass switching mechanism is incorporated in the TCU and this permits the station to switch itself into the ring when necessary. Transmission is by baseband modulation on shielded, twisted-pair trunk cables linking successive stations in the ring. Repeaters may be used to extend the length of the trunk links but each repeater counts as one station from the maximum of 250 which may be connected.

Each station in the token ring transfers information bit-by-bit from one active station to the next. Upon receiving the token, a station transfers information onto the ring where it circulates. The addressed destination station copies the information as it passes and finally the station which transmitted the information removes the information from the ring and, after checking that the data was not corrupted in transmission, it initiates a new token which provides other stations with the opportunity to gain access to the ring.

A token holding timer controls the maximum period of time a station can use the medium before passing on the token. Multiple levels of priority may be assigned to each class of message and each station monitors the token rotation time. When the token rotation time exceeds certain thresholds, messages of lower priority are prevented from being transmitted. An error detection and recovery mechanism restores network operation when transmission errors or temporary medium faults are detected.

A typical station interface for IEEE 802.5 is shown in Figure 8.14. The TMS-38030 manages the transfer of data between the host system memory and the station local bus. The TMS-38010 processes and buffers data while the TMS-38020 manages the IEEE 802.5 protocols. The TMS-38051 and TMS-38052 monitor cable integrity, control network insertion and perform clocking and signal conditioning.

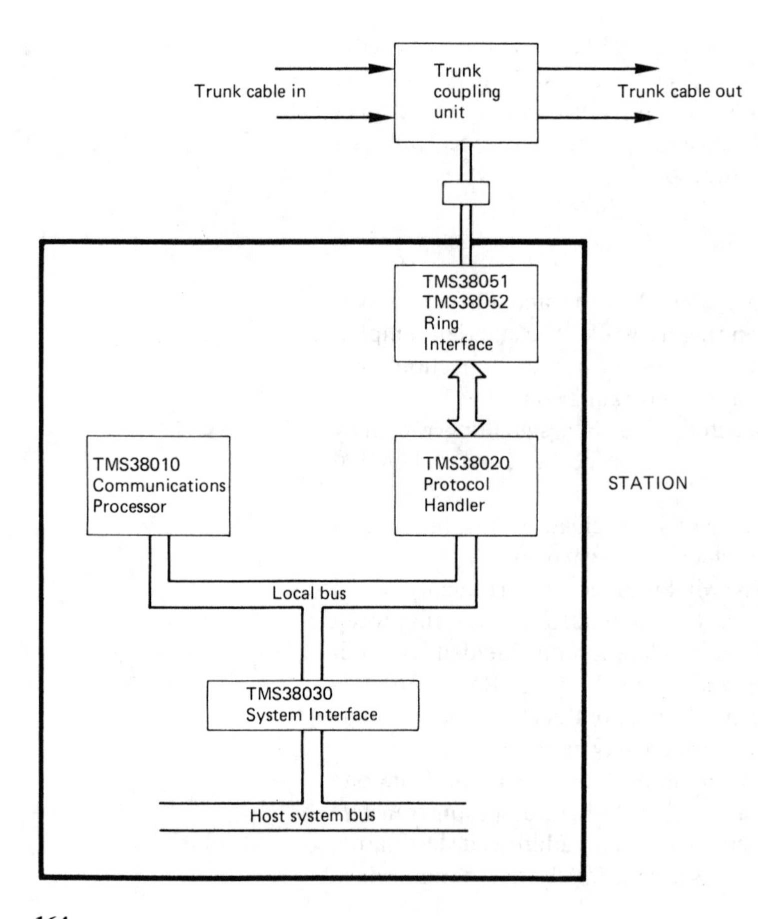

Fig. 8.14 IEEE 802.5 station interface using the TMS380 chip set

8.4.5 ANSI FDDI

The ANSI Fibre Distributed Data Interface standard specifies a fibre-optic token passing ring with a signalling rate of 100 Mbit/s. The 100 Mbit/s data rate is the practical maximum which can currently be achieved using relatively inexpensive PIN light-detecting diodes and light-emitting diodes with a highly efficient 4B/5B encoding scheme. This encoding scheme requires only 125 Mbaud pulses on the medium whereas the Manchester encoding scheme used on IEEE 802.3 and IEEE 802.5 would require 200 Mbaud for 100 Mbit/s data transmission.

A FDDI network can work with 2 km of fibre between nodes, a total circumference of 200 km of fibre and a maximum of 1000 nodes. Two classes of connection are defined. Class A nodes can take advantage of the dual-ring fault-tolerant capability but Class B nodes support only a single ring and may be routed to a wiring concentrator for connection to a dual ring (see Figure 8.15). If a Class B node fails, the wiring concentrator bypasses the node and keeps the ring operating.

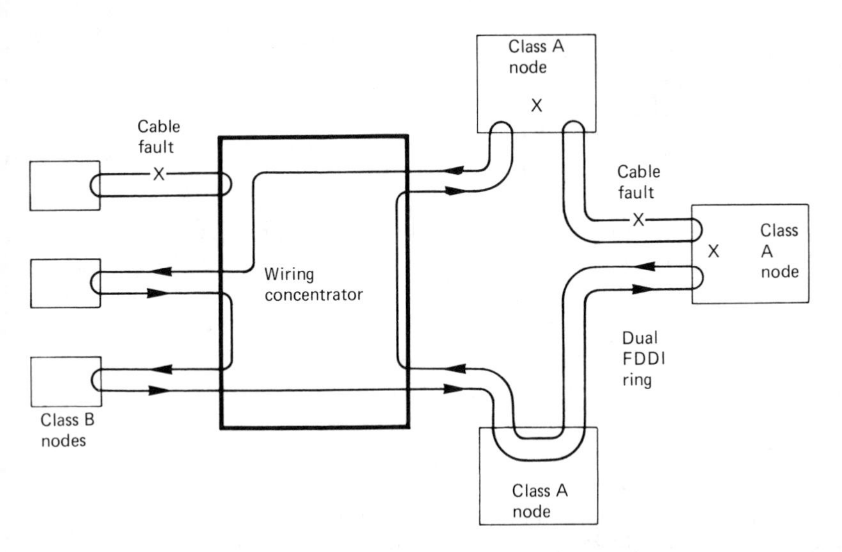

Fig. 8.15 Connection of class B nodes to a dual FDDI ring through a wiring concentrator

Fibre optic cables permit higher data rates and, because attenuation is lower than with electrical cables, larger distances may be covered. Further benefits include the immunity of the cable to electrical noise and lightning strikes (or the electro-magnetic pulse associated with a nuclear explosion). FDDI interfaces will inevitably be more expensive than IEEE 802.3 interfaces and the initial applications will probably be as a backbone network connecting high-performance computers and linking spur networks via gateways. Later applications may include the linking of high-performance CAD workstations which require high data rates to transfer graphics data.

FDDI uses two independent counter-rotating rings, each operating at 100 Mbit/s to increase system reliability. Automatic reconfiguration takes place when any part of a ring fails and loss of power to a node may switch an optical relay which bypasses that node. Single ring failures cause reconfiguration using appropriate paths on the second ring to keep the network running. A second ring failure will cause the ring to split into two smaller independent networks.

A Timed Token Passing system is used which permits each node to specify the token rotation time required. When a node determines that the target token rotation time has been exceeded, it inhibits the transmission of low-priority asynchronous messages to ensure that high-priority synchronous data (such as voice data) is transmitted within a specified period.

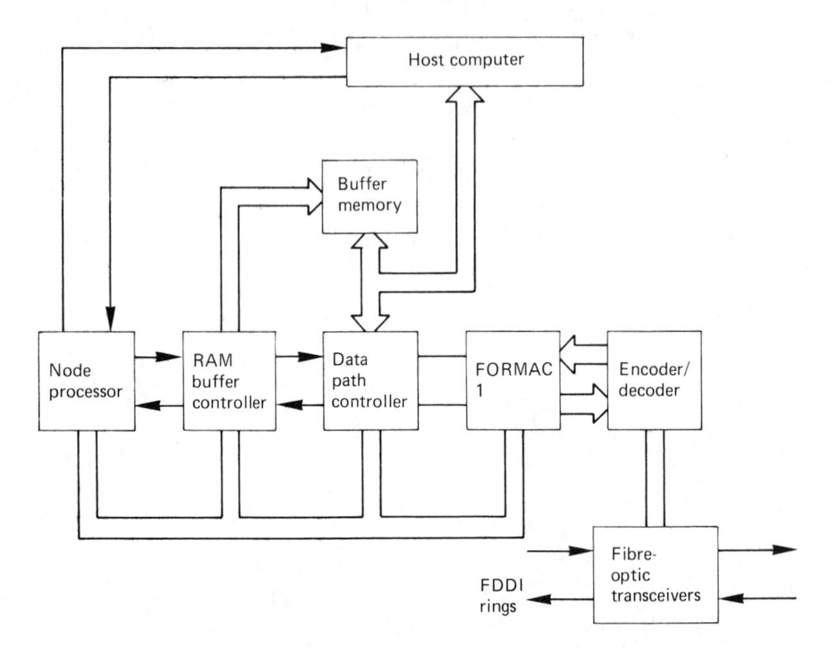

Fig. 8.16 FDDI interface using Supernet chips

Figure 8.16 shows a FDDI interface constructed using the AMD Supernet family of chips. The node processor off-loads the host system and must be a high-performance microprocessor in high-performance nodes. Its functions are to initialise and control the other chips and to handle higher OSI layers. The RAM Buffer Controller generates buffer memory addresses, configures the RAM to perform as FIFO buffers, and arbitrates for access to the buffer memory. The Data Path Controller converts data formats, performs reception and transmission of packets, generates/checks parity, and counts packet length, generating error status and interrupts when necessary. The FORMAC 1 chip is the Fibre Optic Ring Media Access Controller which implements the FDDI protocol. The Encoder/Decoder performs clock recovery, converts serial to parallel data, generates/checks parity, performs 4B/5B encoding and decoding, provides an elastic buffer, and implements the Connection Management (CMT) interface.

8.5 Long-distance communications

8.5.1 Long-distance communications options

Long-distance communications using telecommunications lines must cope with a different set of problems to those which local area networks experience. Data rates are lower, error rates are higher, transmission delays are greater, and national/international transmission standards must be complied with.

Long-distance communications most frequently use rented lines with modems operating at speeds up to 9.6 kbit/s but digital links at 64 kbit/s and 2 Mbit/s are also available (56 kbit/s and 1.54 Mbit/s in the USA). The design of synchronous modems to transmit data over these lines is constantly improving and new line transmission standards have been developed. The physical interface between the modem (Data Communication Equipment) and the Data Terminal Equipment consists of a serial interface standard such as X21, RS-232-C, or RS-449 but a data link protocol must be employed to ensure compatibility of format, meaning and timing of information exchanged between two communicating devices.

Packet switched networks are commonly used for national and international data communications and the X25 standard has been developed by CCITT to permit access to these networks. The IEEE is engaged in defining the 802.6 standard for Metropolitan Area Networks which will use fibre-optic links to interconnect buildings within an area up to 25 miles in diameter.

8.5.2 Data link control protocols

The problems which long-distance communications links experience must be overcome by the design of the data link protocol, layer 2 of the OSI model. Three categories of data link control protocols have been developed:

1. *Character Control* protocols such as ANSI X3.28 and IBM BISYNC.
2. *Character Count* protocols such as DEC DDCMP.
3. *Bit Oriented* protocols such as ANSI X3.66 (ADCCP), ISO HDLC, X25 LAP-B and IBM SDLC.

Bit oriented protocols are the most popular because they use a single-frame format, unrestricted information field length, any character code and only three reserved bit sequences. This makes them more efficient, reliable and easy to implement in software. A data link control protocol is responsible for five basic functions:

1. *Framing of the message block* by identifying groups of bits which act as message delimiters.
2. *Link management*, controlling transmission and reception.
3. Ensuring *message integrity* by using parity checks or cyclic redundancy checks and providing a retransmission scheme to correct data which is received with errors.
4. Ensuring *information transparency* by implementing a means of distinguishing between data and control characters.
5. *Bootstrapping secondary stations* onto a data link by permitting the primary station to set the initial states and control modes.

8.5.3 X25 packet switched network interface

The CCITT X25 standard covers the physical layer, data link layer and network layer of the OSI model. The physical layer is the X21 interface standard. The data link control layer is known as LAP-B which is compatible with the ISO High-level Data Link Control standard, HDLC. The network layer is called the Packet Level Logical Interface and supports switched virtual circuits and permanent virtual circuits.

Data is moved in packets through the network. Each packet comprises a header, containing control and destination fields, plus a data field. The principal task of the network is to route packets from source to destination and ensure that they are delivered in their original sequence. A permanent virtual circuit is a permanent association existing between two data terminal equipments analogous to a point-to-point private link. A switched virtual circuit is a temporary association between two data terminal equipments and is initiated by a call request from the sender to the network.

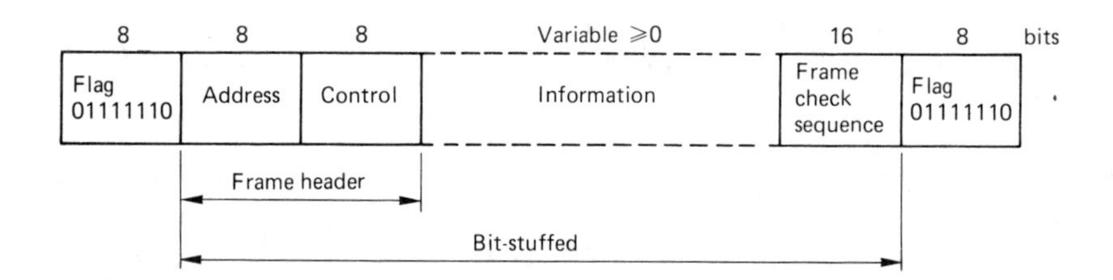

Fig. 8.17 An HDLC frame format

Figure 8.17 shows the format of the HDLC (LAP-B) frame. The synchronous modem provides bit timing but a flag consisting of the binary sequence 01111110 is added to the start and end of each frame to identify the limits of the frame and to identify the bits which constitute octets of data or address information. To allow transparent user data, any sequence of five ones causes a zero to be inserted and, whenever five ones are received followed by a zero, the zero is removed. This procedure is known as *bit stuffing*.

A computer which interfaces directly with the packet switched system must provide an X21 electrical interface and must implement the LAP-B data link control protocol. The use of a data communication controller chip considerably simplifies the implementation of LAP-B but some software involvement is required to manage the error correction and other functions at the data link control layer. The network layer is a software function and it may be necessary to provide an intelligent communications controller board to carry out these functions.

Asynchronous terminals with V24/28 interfaces may be connected to an X25 packet switched network by using the alternative CCITT standards, X3, X28 and X29, which define terminal and network interaction with a Packet Assembler/Disassembler (PAD). A PAD is a unit which buffers the asynchronous data from the terminal to form X25 packets and converts received packets into asynchronous data which may be accepted by an unintelligent terminal.

8.5.4 Metropolitan area networks

In 1981 the IEEE set up working group 802.6 to specify major functional capabilities needed by Metropolitan Area Networks (MANs). While LANs are limited to about 2 km, MANs span distances greater than 5 km and may include several transmission media. The favoured access control method is time-division multiple-access (TDMA) with channel reservation.

The IEEE 802.6 working group proposes the use of fibre-optic lines in several rings linked by bridges which transfer data from one ring to another. Each bridge contains templates which specify which channels on each ring are to be written into and read from. Three data rates may be employed: 11 Mbit/s, 44.7 Mbit/s and 200–250 Mbit/s.

Media access chips for IEEE 802.6 have been developed by Burroughs and future applications for MANs are expected to integrate voice, data and possibly video. These systems are likely to face competition from cable TV systems which also cover metropolitan areas up to 25 miles in diameter and MANs may be connected to national Integrated Services Digital Networks (ISDNs) planned to be introduced in the 1990s.

9 Software options and development systems

9.1 Introduction

The subject of software for use with advanced microprocessors warrants at least one book in its own right so this chapter attempts only to give a brief introduction to the types of operating systems, languages and development systems which may be used. It also briefly describes in-circuit emulators which are an invaluable development aid but which are more concerned with hardware development than software in most applications.

A few subjects have been given a more detailed description because they are relatively unknown or are vital to the understanding of some of the new types of advanced microprocessor. These subjects include:

a) Unix which is the only specific operating system described (not in much detail however). Unix is rapidly becoming a standard for many applications where a hardware manufacturer wishes to ensure compatibility of future products without retaining the same processor instruction set or where the user does not want to be committed to an operating system which is proprietary to one manufacturer.
b) Occam which is the only language currently available to fully support concurrent processing and is used by the transputer which is described in Chapter 5. Occam is described in greater depth to aid the understanding of concurrent systems.
c) Lisp and Prolog are described because they are the most popular languages for expert systems. Expert systems are expected to rapidly increase in importance as the subject develops and machines are now available to execute Lisp without compilers or interpreters. The Compact Lisp machine (CLM) is the first Lisp microprocessor and is described in Section 3.13.

9.2 Operating systems

9.2.1 Basic principles

An operating system has been defined in several ways:

a) As 'a set of manual and automatic procedures that enable a group of people to share a computer installation efficiently'.

b) As 'a collection of system software that permits users to interface with the machine hardware and interact with other tasks in a straightforward, efficient and safe manner'.
c) As 'software that enhances the functionality provided by the hardware in a way that creates a new virtual machine'.
d) As 'the first level of software (above the naked hardware) that provides an enriched environment for configuration.'

Operating systems tend to fall into three categories:

a) Stand-alone
b) Real-time
c) Multiple-user.

Stand-alone operating systems permit a single user to interface with the hardware in personal computers or workstations; typical examples are CP/M and MS-DOS. *Multi-user operating systems* were originally developed for mainframes and minicomputers but have now been adapted for 16 and 32-bit microcomputers. Multi-user operating systems typified by the Unix operating system and its many variants generally require large memories (at least 64 Kbytes of RAM) and rely heavily on fast disks and code swapping to and from disk. Interrupt response times are generally slow in multi-user operating systems. *Real-time operating systems* or *executives* are typically employed for control applications and are often small enough to fit into ROM. The term real-time is relative to the application but most real-time operating systems have interrupt response times in the range 50 to 250 μs.

As shown in Figure 9.1 the operating system kernel forms the interface with the bare machine and provides a basic set of operating system utilities which constitute a virtual machine. The kernel may be implemented in firmware, for example the Intel 80130 chip implements the iRMX-86 operating system in order to simplify hardware and software design. To permit customisation and upgrades to the firmware kernel, a configuration table is provided in RAM.

An operating system's capability may be defined in terms of

1 The *user interface* which comprises a command-interpreter program with a command set which may be interpreted by application programs.
2 The *application interface* comprising a set of system calls which an application program may use to access operating system functions such as accessing disk files.
3 The *device interface* which permits the peripheral's I/O routines to carry out I/O operations using a command set issued by the operating system.
4 The *media interface* which permits various media to be used to exchange data with other computer systems which share a media-dependent format.

Incompatibility between many implementations of real-time kernels and operating systems makes it difficult to run application software developed for one version of the operating system on another version. These incompa-

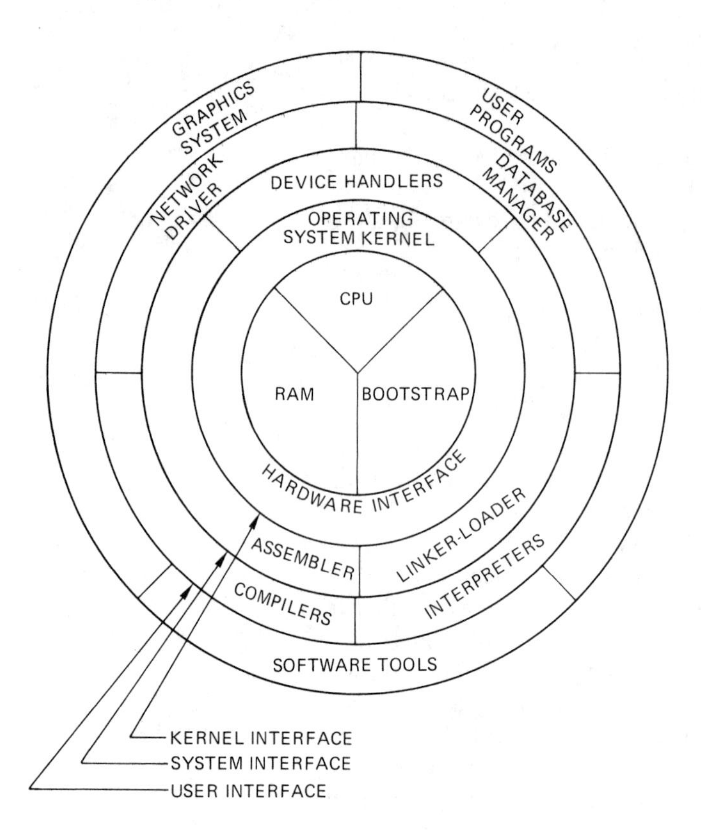

Fig. 9.1 Relationship of the operating system kernel to the hardware and other software

tibilities may be caused by the way the operating systems access hardware devices or have ROM-resident functions when implemented on a particular computer.

To make application programs less machine-specific the concept of *virtual machine operating systems* has been developed. This permits either the system calls provided by the operating system to be emulated or the operating system may be run as a process or task of the host operating system.

A single-user operating system dedicates all the system peripherals to a single application at any instant. Concurrent single-user operating systems share the system resources between the applications, storing the machine status for each application. Input/output functions are shared between applications and there is little interaction between applications.

Real-time operating system kernels divide the application into many concurrent activities and each high-speed interface has an interrupt service routine synchronised to the co-operating task (see Figure 9.2).

Peripherals such as disk controllers are handled in much the same way by real-time multi-tasking operating systems and multi-user operating systems. A real-time I/O system typically makes use of I/O system calls rather than interrupt service requests.

9.2.3 Unix

Unix was originally developed in the late 1960s by Bell Laboratories as an experimental single-user operating system (as its name suggests). During 1973, Unix was rewritten as a multi-user operating system in C, a high-level language suitable for use in systems programming. It was this feature which made Unix capable of simple adaptation to run on any computer and it is now available for a wider range of computers than any other operating system.

The core of Unix consists of the *kernel* which insulates the other parts of the system from the hardware. The kernel implements the file management system, data protection system, multi-user scheduling and input/output facilities. Applications programs interface with the kernel by using a set of about 60 system calls.

Outside the kernel is the Unix *shell* which provides the user interface. The shell uses about 200 standard system commands and additional shell commands to form special interfaces. User interaction is in the form of a dialogue with the shell. Commonly used sequences of shell commands may be stored in a file and invoked by using the file name.

Unix includes over 200 *utility programs* to support common requirements such as text editing and file copying. Application programs may be added to complement the utilities and the utilities may be combined to form more complex facilities such as the source-code control system which combines ten utilities to provide a powerful software development capability. A full implementation of Unix may consist of more than 8 Mbytes of code, more than 7 Mbytes consisting of utilities.

By using Unix, a hardware manufacturer can ensure compatibility of future products without retaining the same processor instruction set. If the system calls are standard on future versions of Unix, applications software will be capable of running on any Unix system. This capability makes a vast range of software packages available to any Unix system user, regardless of hardware type.

The latest AT&T version of Unix is System V which became available in 1983. For computers which are not supported by AT&T versions of Unix, a license may be granted to port the source code but these versions, some containing many enhancements, must be given an alternative name (e.g. Berkeley Unix) because the Unix trademark is not licensed. A royalty must be payed on every computer system sold with a Unix-based operating system. To avoid the need to pay royalties, several Unix lookalikes have been produced. These are based on new source code but the same system calls are used and they behave exactly like Unix which permits standard Unix applications software to be run without modification.

An IEEE standard for a Unix interface has been under consideration since 1981; this will ensure compatibility of system calls and kernel responses. Unix is already a favourite operating system for multi-user software development systems and Unix is predicted to become a standard for commercial software applications on super-microcomputers.

9.3 General-purpose languages

9.3.1 C

The C language which characterises Unix-based systems became increasingly popular throughout the early 1980s, largely at the expense of Pascal. There are four main reasons for the popularity of C:

a) The increased popularity of Unix-based operating systems.
b) There are not a large number of dialects of C, unlike Pascal and Basic.
c) C was designed as a system language to make system software easily transportable from one process to another.
d) C produces compact code.

C is a general-purpose programming language closely associated with the Unix operating system but not tied to any operating system or computer. Although it is described as a system language it may be used for other forms of program. C is a relatively low-level language because it can deal with the type of objects which are implemented directly by the machine but it provides no operations to handle composite objects such as character strings, sets, lists or complex arrays.

C does not define other than basic storage allocation facilities and it provides no input-output facilities such as read and write statements. Only single-thread control flow constructions such as tests, loops, grouping and sub-programs are provided. No multiprogramming, parallel operations, synchronisation or co-routines are available.

By excluding many high-level language functions the size of C code has been made compact and the language may be learned quickly. Compilers for a wide range of machines may be written quickly (as little as two months) using 80% of code which is common to other compilers. Apart from the code which supports assembly language and the I/O device handler, about 95% of C code is identical in compilers written for different machines.

Because C code is highly efficient, it is not usually necessary to write any software in assembly language. A Unix operating system for example uses only 800 lines of assembler code in 13 000 lines of system code.

9.3.2 Forth

Forth is a relatively new language which has little in common with the other general-purpose languages. Forth is a high-level language which embodies structured programming concepts for producing modular and portable programs. Forth programmers have access to primitive machine functions or a symbolic assembler if required.

The normal use of Forth is to interpret all inputs and to execute them directly but, if the input is enclosed within a colon, it is compiled into a compact threaded code. The interactive interpretive environment may be used for testing and debugging programs but the final program may be compiled for fast and efficient execution. Forth combines the advantages of interpreted Basic but can be compiled to run at ten times the speed, comparable to Pascal in run-time efficiency.

To reduce development and debugging time, Forth has the ability to extend the language by defining new words using the existing set and adding these new words to the dictionary. The new words may then be used to develop still more complex operations in a special vocabulary for a particular application. Most Forth systems have vocabularies for an editor, assembler and disk handler built in, making other development software unnecessary.

Typical Forth systems are smaller than 16 Kbytes making it possible to use a target machine as a development machine in many cases. Points against Forth are its use of integer arithmetic, unusual stack operations resulting in reverse Polish notation, and the difficulty which trained programmers may experience in learning the language.

9.3.3 Pascal

The first definition of Pascal came in the *Pascal User Manual and Report* published in 1975 by Jensen and Wirth. An *International Standard for Pascal* was published in 1981. There are however many different implementations of Pascal, mostly based on the *Pascal User Manual and Report* and each has its particular extensions and restrictions. To make a Pascal program portable from one computer to another it must avoid unofficial compiler extensions.

Pascal was the first language designed to support the concepts of structured programming proposed by Dijkstra. It was derived from Algol and is widely used in academic, scientific and business computing, particularly with microcomputers. Pascal was developed by Niklaus Wirth and was named after a French philosopher who developed one of the first digital computing devices.

Three main elements make Pascal a structured language:

a) Declarations which require the programmer to inform the compiler about the program structure.
b) Block structure which lets Pascal programs reflect a natural method of problem solving using structured sequences of conditional and repetitive execution of simpler instruction sequences.
c) Procedural code which decomposes a program into a number of smaller tasks with well-defined interfaces and interactions. Procedural code is the result of a top-down software design methodology.

9.3.4 COBOL

COBOL was developed for the US Department of Defense for data processing applications, its name being derived from Common Business Oriented Language. An ANSI committee produced a standard in 1974 (COBOL 74) and a later version in 1985 (COBOL X3.23 – 1985).

Many commercial software packages have been written in COBOL and the language is widely used on mainframes, minicomputers and microcomputers. Compilers are available for more than 100 different microcomputers. COBOL uses English-like words arranged in sentences with sentences grouped into paragraphs. COBOL can be learned quickly but it has many powerful features such as string handling statements, SORT statements and MERGE statements for file handling. Files containing complex data can be created, read and updated by easily understood English words.

COBOL 85 retains all the features of COBOL 74 but includes several improvements. Programs written in COBOL 74 require only minor changes to be compiled in COBOL 85. COBOL compilers include a variety of different screen handling extensions and this is the major impediment in portability of COBOL programs from one machine to another.

9.3.5 Ada

Ada was developed by the US Department of Defense as a universal standard to be employed on all Army, Navy and Air Force embedded computers. Development started in 1975 when the Higher-Order Language Working Group was set up. A language requirement was issued in 1977 and sixteen proposals were received of which four were funded for preliminary design. The winning design was selected in May 1979 and was named after Ada Augusta, Countess of Lovelace who was involved in the development of early computing equipment in the nineteenth century.

Ada is a structured, high-level programming language developed from Pascal with many improvements in control structures and sub-programs. The program structure of Ada allows the user to package logically related collections of resources and facilitates the definition of common data pools, collections of related subprograms and abstract data types.

Ada tasks may be executed concurrently. Each task can provide a set of resources to other tasks by means of a task specification which is independent of the implementation. The concurrent execution of tasks has been included to support shared-memory architectures and distributed processing architectures (without shared memory, where message passing is used for communication). To support these two forms of architecture, Ada performs two forms of communication between tasks:

a) Communication by shared non-local variables.
b) Communication by message passing.

The Ada language is defined in MIL-STD-1815 and all Ada compilers must be subjected to a stringent validation procedure before they may be sold as Ada compilers. The mandatory use of Ada for all military embedded computers in the US and UK forces is scheduled to become a requirement in defence contracts let from 1987.

9.3.6 Mixing assembly and high-level languages

Despite the efficiency of many compilers and the support provided for high-level languages by many 32-bit microprocessors, there are still instances where assembly language is regularly used; for example in interrupt service routines, I/O device handlers and other time or space critical

9.5.3 Prolog

The resolution principle, developed by Robinson in 1965, is the basis of Prolog and provides a formal means of drawing inferences and carrying a search forward.

Prolog has followed a development path similar to Lisp and has been used by a large number of European computer scientists who are refining the language and developing new applications. More recently Prolog has been adopted by Japanese and American computer scientists for artificial intelligence applications. Prolog has become much more well known since 1982 when its use in the Japanese Fifth Generation Computer project became known.

Prolog interpreters and compilers have been produced. Prolog compilers can be written in Prolog and are therefore suitable for self-compilation and optimisation. Prolog programs are usually 5 to 10 times shorter than programs written in other languages and the current VAX interpreters operate at 300 to 1000 lips (logical inferences per second) while some Prolog compilers can produce programs operating at 20 000 lips.

There are a number of ways of using Prolog to create programs with operations and instructions which can be executed in parallel. A language called Concurrent Prolog has been developed to produce parallel algorithms in systems programming and graph manipulation.

The special environments, consisting of suitable compilers, debuggers, editors, etc. required to produce extremely large programs in Prolog, are not yet available but it is probable that special Prolog workstations will be developed as has been the case with Lisp.

Some Prolog programs are able to perform inverse computation, for example a differentiation program could perform integration, and a compiler carefully written in Prolog can also be used for decomposing.

Prolog has several unique benefits including:

a) It encourages programmers to describe problems in a logical manner which simplifies checking and debugging.
b) The algorithms needed to interpret Prolog programs are capable of parallel processing.
c) Prolog programs are ideal for prototyping because their concise nature minimises development time.

As with Lisp, Prolog demands a high-power processor and a large virtual memory space which partly offsets the advantages in terms of shorter programs and shorter development time.

9.6 Development systems

9.6.1 Alternatives

Developing software for a 32-bit microprocessor will be different to what most programmers have previously experienced.

Programmers with experience of 8 or 16-bit microprocessors may find themselves working with much more complex hardware and software, using multiprocessor architectures, multi-tasking/multi-user software, memory management systems, coprocessors, pipelining and cache memories. The 32-bit buses and higher clock speeds will make many of the hardware-based development tools obsolete.

Users with previous experience of super-minicomputers and mainframes may wish to take advantage of the inexpensive, single-user 32-bit microprocessor development systems which permit much more interaction with the target system or they may even consider developing software on the target machine. Instead of several programmers sharing a multi-user super-minicomputer for high-level software development, it may be more economical to give each programmer a separate 32-bit development system.

High-level language programmers using super-minicomputers for software development have previously had to rely on symbolic debuggers and a monitor ROM in a target machine to set breakpoints, perform single stepping and to examine or change memory and registers. Hardware-based debugging tools are capable of handling interrupts, measuring execution times, performing sequential triggering on complex events and performing real-time tracing or trapping of complex software executing on the target machine.

Early users of 32-bit microprocessors are unlikely to need many hardware-based debugging tools such as in-circuit emulators because 32-bit microprocessors are expected to be used primarily for high-level software intensive applications. After the first year or two, 32-bit microprocessors will be used in many embedded processor designs which demand hardware-based debugging tools.

Cross-assemblers and cross-compilers with symbolic debugging facilities are available for the more popular 32-bit microprocessors. These permit software to be developed on a super-minicomputer such as a VAX and downloaded into a target machine containing a monitor program.

Several ROM-based operating systems are available for popular 32-bit microprocessors. In place of a simple monitor program those operating systems, with suitable peripherals, can turn the target system into a development system. ROM-based operating systems range from simple real-time operating system functions to a Forth development environment or a simple version of Unix.

The use of a predefined operating system for a target processor can save a lot of time and effort which may be involved in developing a custom operating system kernel. The production of a custom operating system for the target machine must be completed before application software can be tested, making any delay in development reflect on overall system development time scales. In addition, it is unlikely that a company with experience in developing only application software will have the necessary skills to develop an effective operating system in a reasonable period of time.

By using Forth development software on the target system, a considerable saving in development hardware may be made. Forth may be used as an interpreter for software development, thus reducing the development time, and all the resources of the target system are immediately available to the programmer. Many programmers with previous experience of high-level languages or assembly languages find Forth difficult to master. This may result in a long learning period before the advantages, in terms of efficient programs rapidly developed, are achieved.

9.6.2 In-circuit emulators

The Motorola HDS-400, in-circuit emulator, is a typical hardware-based development tool. Fitted with an MC68020 emulator pod, the HDS-400 can emulate a 68020 at 8 MHz clock speed with no wait states but a 16 MHz processor will run with one wait state for memory access. A plug on the emulator fits into the pin-grid-array socket on the target board in place of the MC68020 chip.

The HDS-400 has up to 256 Kbytes of emulation memory which can be mapped in 4-Kbyte increments over the memory address space of the target system. A contiguous 16 Mbyte sector of the target system's address space may be addressed by the emulator and cache memory may be controlled from the development system.

A logic state analyser is available and runs in parallel with the emulation facility to monitor up to 75 pins on the microprocessor and four uncommitted inputs from elsewhere on the target system. The analyser will operate without wait states on a 5 MHz bus but one wait state is introduced per bus cycle at 20 MHz. Separate breakpoints may be set for the emulator and the analyser. A pre-defined sequence of up to seven events may be used by the analyser to halt the target system where each event is a pattern on the inputs. The in-circuit emulator may be programmed to halt on any one of 16 events.

The analyser may be used to recognise the entry and exit points of a software routine and to measure the execution time to the nearest clock cycle. Software performance histograms may be produced for specified address ranges. This may be used to identify frequently used software modules which are likely candidates for assembly level coding to speed up execution or modules which are never used.

The National ICE32 provides three connectors, one for each of the CPU, memory management chip and clock chip. Several emulators are available to replace the ROM/PROM in a system with an external microcode ROM (such as the NCR-32) or an embedded 32-bit microprocessor with a PROM socket. The high speed of such ROMs makes it necessary for the emulator to operate at higher speeds than standard microprocessor in-circuit emulators. ROM emulators are available for cycle times down to 10 ns and, since most ROMs are similar, the emulators will handle a wide range of systems.

The major difference between in-circuit emulators and ROM emulators is that the in-circuit emulator has to switch the processor interface lines back and forth between the target system and the emulation memory, which slows down system performance, but the ROM emulator leaves the processor connected permanently to the emulation memory. The ROM emulator however does not see activity within the processor, it can only infer the activity of the processor, based on external events, and cause the processor state to be dumped off-line when the processor has halted. Many 32-bit microprocessors have debugging modes which permit single-step operation and register dumps. A ROM emulator can access the internal debugging facilities by replacing an instruction in the program under test with a jump instruction leading to a diagnostic routine or a halt instruction. Alternatively some ROM emulators include a logic analyser which can be used to gate the clock for the target system on and off.

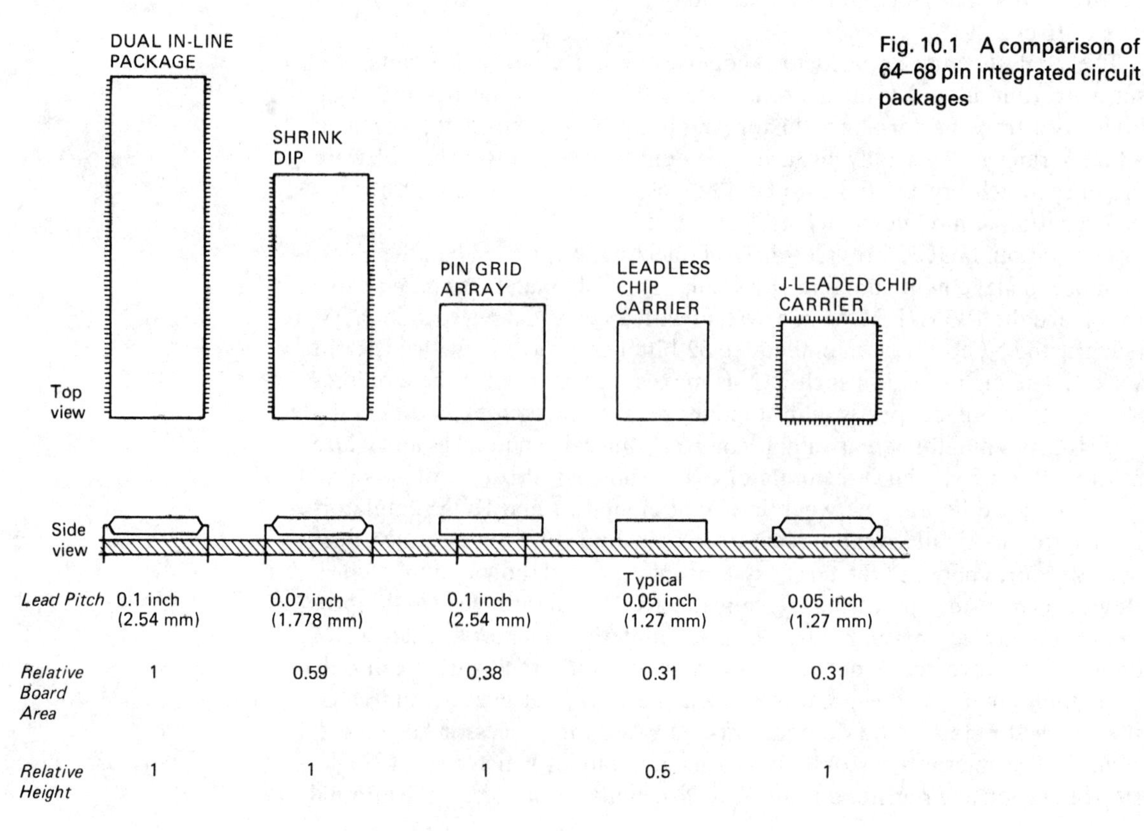

Fig. 10.1 A comparison of 64–68 pin integrated circuit packages

10 Design factors

10.1 Mechanical construction

10.1.1 Packages

Advanced microprocessors make it possible to fit the processing power which previously required a rack of equipment into a desk-top unit. To carry through this potential reduction in size to the complete equipment, new methods of packaging components have been developed. *Surface mounting* of components on multi-layer circuit boards is increasing in popularity where miniaturisation and low production costs are essential. At the other extreme, new packaging methods have been developed to reduce interconnection lengths and remove heat in high-speed computers. By these means it is possible to build supercomputers incorporating large arrays of microprocessor chips to achieve previously unattainable levels of processing power.

One of the most important aspects of packaging is the integrated circuit carrier. Larger chips and the need for greater numbers of leads has resulted in new forms of IC package (see Figure 10.1). The traditional dual in-line package with 0.1 inch (2.54 mm) lead pitch would be unacceptably long if used to accommodate 32-bit microprocessors. The shrink-DIP package which uses pins on a 0.07 inch (1.778 mm) pitch slightly reduces the length but most 32-bit microprocessors are packaged in J-leaded chip carriers or pin grid arrays.

Pin grid arrays retain the same 0.1 inch lead pitch as dual-in-line packages but the use of an array of pins beneath the package permits a much higher pin count and a smaller package area. Pin grid array packages may be dip-soldered or inserted in sockets. Earlier pin grid array packages were of ceramic construction but less expensive plastic versions have been developed.

Plastic chip carriers are available with J-shaped leads for surface mounting; leads are located around the four edges with 0.05 inch pitch. Leadless ceramic chip carriers have inset copper pads on the four edges which may be connected by a socket or by direct surface mounting. When surface mounted, the leadless ceramic chip carrier may suffer from cracked solder joints caused by the difference in thermal coefficients of the ceramic material and the epoxy-glass circuit board. This problem is avoided by the leaded chip carriers.

10.1.2 Printed circuit technology

Surface mounting is a production technique which has been used for manufacturing thick-film hybrid circuits for many years but it is predicted that 50% of electronic assembly will use surface mounting techniques by 1990. Components are soldered to pads on one side of a printed circuit board rather than having leads pushed through holes in the circuit board. The advantages of using surface mounting technology for general printed circuit applications are

a) Higher density of components
b) Lower assembly costs
c) Improved high-speed operation because of reduced lead inductance
d) Improved reliability.

Surface mounting demands expensive placement machines and components available in a suitable package. Standard IC packages suitable for surface mounting have been registered by JEDEC but these have not been adopted by all manufacturers. This can cause problems in second-sourcing components because the functional equivalent may not be compatible with the pads on a circuit board. If possible, it may be worth designing a circuit board with alternative pads to accept second-sourced components.

High-speed, high-density computer systems are suited to surface mounting techniques because track lengths are minimised. Polyimide is used in some high-speed circuit boards in place of the traditional epoxy-glass material because it has a low dielectric constant which reduces signal propagation delay and its smooth surface permits a high density of thin-film circuit tracks.

Some supercomputers use a composite substrate for surface mounting components. A ceramic multi-layer base may contain power and ground planes while several layers of wiring and ground planes may be located in polyimide, on top of the ceramic. Ceramic has a high thermal conductivity, which helps to remove heat from components, and polyimide makes it possible to cut circuit board tracks and add jumpers on the surface layers.

10.1.2 High-speed logical interconnections

There has been a trend in microprocessor design to develop complex systems using a black box approach. One consequence of this trend is that the fundamental problems associated with designing digital circuits are no longer considered and, all too often, board layouts and systems fail because the designer had insufficient experience in the fundamentals of high-speed logic design.

The trend with advanced microprocessors is to use higher clock speeds as the semiconductor technology improves. A relatively low clock speed version of current 32-bit microprocessors will operate at 12 MHz; this compares with a typical rate of 1 MHz ten years ago. The design of circuit boards and interconnections at these higher speeds demands careful consideration of the transmission line properties of signal paths and the characteristics of the logic family in use.

The early users of Schottky TTL tried to replace standard TTL with Schottky chips in critical timing paths on production circuit boards. The result was that various noise problems were caused by the faster switching edges and V_{CC} (power supply voltage) droop resulting from faster charging of load capacitance. To prevent these problems the circuits had to be modified by

a) Better bypassing to ground of V_{CC} to prevent droop.

b) Use of a ground plane to prevent coupling through common ground paths.

c) Providing a return beneath each signal line to minimise crosstalk by confining the radiated fields.

A common problem with bus driver packages is the generation of a large spike on ground strips when all the lines switch simultaneously. To minimise this problem, the buffer chips should be placed together at the edge of the circuit board and be fed from their own ground, brought from the backplane by a separate pin.

Jumper wires for V_{CC} and ground on breadboards are a potential source of inductance which causes ground spikes to be generated when one output changes, thus affecting the entire package. The inductance also increases the output rise and fall times which reduces the maximum circuit speed and may cause timing problems.

Good power distribution is essential in high-speed logic boards to prevent loss of supply voltage due to $I \times R$ drops, ground loop problems, noise and crosstalk problems. A ground plane reduces resistive voltage drops and reduces inductance. In multilayer boards the power voltage may also be distributed by a voltage plane giving similar advantages to a ground plane. Alternatively, laminated bus bars can be mounted on the printed circuit board for power distribution.

Low-inductance bypass capacitors varying between 0.01 and 0.001 μF must be provided for every 1 to 4 packages to minimise noise and switching transients. Power supply lines and grounds should be connected to multiple pins on an edge connector to maintain a low-inductance path to the power supply unit.

Signal transmission on printed circuit boards can be a major cause of problems in high-speed logic circuits and propagation times (30 cm in 1 ns) can be a major cause of delays in system operation. The two most common problems are ringing and crosstalk.

Figure 10.2 shows three common techniques for interconnections on printed circuit boards:

1 *Microstrip lines*, which are a strip of conductor separated from a ground plane by dielectric from which the board is made.

2 *Striplines*, which are a strip of conductor centred in a dielectric medium between two ground planes, constructed by multi-layer techniques. Striplines are less popular than microstrip lines because buried lines are hard to troubleshoot.

3 *Wire over ground*, which is a conductor in proximity to a voltage plane. Propagation delay and characteristic impedance are variable with distance from the ground plane, so performance is unpredictable unless implemented in a fixed medium, such as Multiwire.

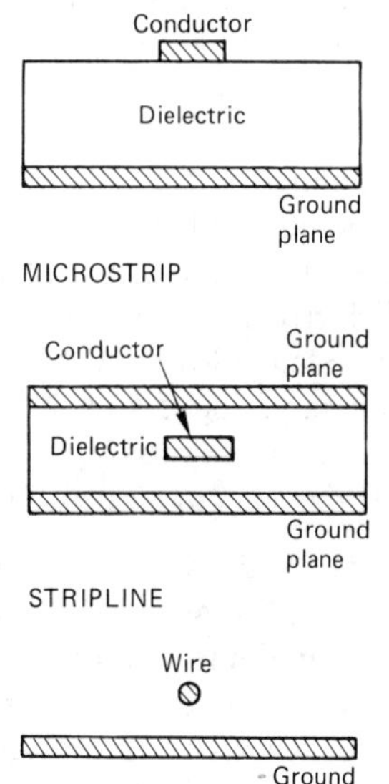

Fig. 10.2 Common interconnection techniques for printed circuit boards

Propagation velocity is determined by the formula:

$$V_p = c/\sqrt{K}$$

where c is the velocity of light in air and K is the effective relative dielectric constant of the media surrounding the transmission line.

The propagation delay of microstrip lines is typically 5.7 ns per metre and for stripline is 7.6 ns per metre. Propagation delay is particularly important on timing signals and clock lines. Characteristic impedance is important in preventing reflections or crosstalk and is related to line width and dielectric thickness (spacing from the ground planes).

Ringing is caused by reflections on the signal line due to loading and termination problems. Severe ringing can cause edge triggered circuits to be triggered falsely and performance is reduced because time is taken for the signal line to become stable. Reflections may be prevented by matching the load to the characteristic impedance of the line and minimising the capacitive loading of receiving devices on the line. Each input connection to the line reduces the characteristic impedance and takes or injects current.

To minimise reflections some practical guidelines may be followed:

a) Use short lines (in which the two-way propagation delay is less than the rise/fall time of the driver).

b) For longer lines, use a parallel termination consisting of low-inductance resistor(s) at the receiving end to match the line impedance.

c) For TTL it is often preferable to use series termination which consists of a series resistor at the sending end of the line (with a value which, when added to the source impedance, is equivalent to the line impedance) to prevent the signal reflected from the receiving end being further reflected. Series termination may be used to drive multiple lines by using a separate resistor per line.

Crosstalk between signal lines is caused by inductive and capacitive coupling of signal transitions. Capacitive coupling is called backward crosstalk and its coefficient K_B is a measure of coupling between two lines. Crosstalk is reduced if spacing between the lines is increased and the dielectric thickness of microstrip lines is reduced, making the characteristic impedance lower. Ground planes reduce crosstalk by reducing characteristic impedance and, if parallel runs are kept short, the crosstalk will not reach full amplitude.

Practical guidelines to minimise crosstalk include:

a) Make spaces between signal lines as large as possible.

b) Minimise the signal line to ground plane separation. Running a ground line next to, or between, the crosstalking lines can also help.

c) In multi-conductor cables, use twisted pair wires and, in ribbon cable, make every other conductor a ground.

d) Minimise the length of signal lines running in parallel. On multi-layer boards, run lines on adjacent planes in perpendicular directions.

e) In a multi-layer sandwich containing two or more signal planes, shielding is necessary to prevent coupling between lines travelling in the same direction in different planes.

f) Signal lines should not be run between power planes.

Board-to-board connectors may have a small physical size but their *effective electrical length*, or *rise length*, depends on other factors. The rise length of a signal, which defines a physical length associated with the risetime, depends on the risetime of the waveform multiplied by the propagation velocity. For example, a signal with 2 ns risetime and a propagation velocity of 10 cm/ns has a rise length of 20 cm.

The position of signal and ground contacts on a connector can influence performance because characteristic impedance and backward crosstalk increase as the signal is separated from the ground, possibly causing reflections. If the ground is taken by a longer physical path through a connector than the signal lines, this can increase characteristic impedance and backward crosstalk but, in addition, the effective electrical length of the connector becomes considerably greater than the physical length.

The use of unequal electrical lengths for signals and ground connections can introduce timing skew which may degrade system performance. If the electrical length of a longer ground path becomes a significant fraction of the rise length for the signals being transmitted, system problems may be experienced.

The assignment of signal and ground contacts on card edge connectors or two part connectors should be designed to give the minimum spacing between signals and grounds. The number of grounds required will depend on the risetime and noise immunity of the logic plus the number of connections in the signal path. Figure 10.3 shows several possible arrangements of grounds in a two-row connector; these arrangements give minimum separation of signals from grounds. The ratio of signal to ground contacts required for risetimes below 2 ns may be 1:1 or 3:1 but a 5:1 ratio may be adequate for signals with risetimes between 2 and 10 ns. Slower signals may require only one ground.

The most common form of crosstalk is on backplane wiring, in which the conductors travel in parallel for considerable distances. The use of a ground plane and intervening ground wires between signal wires can

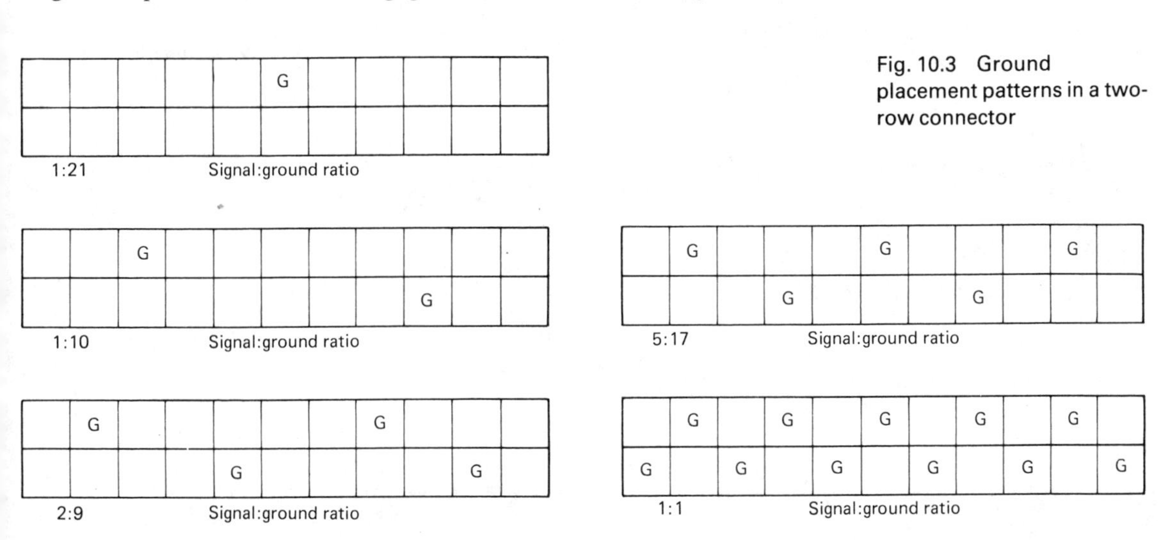

Fig. 10.3 Ground placement patterns in a two-row connector

reduce crosstalk to tolerable levels. The intervening grounds act as favoured ground returns and as shields between the signal conductors.

Termination of both ends of a backplane is essential. Typically, a terminating resistor of twice the line impedance reduces the noise amplitude by one third and a matched termination halves the noise amplitude, compared with an unterminated backplane. A Thevenin split resistor termination gives a better impedance match than a pull-up resistor but increases the load on the bus drivers.

10.2 Reliability and maintainability

10.2.1 Estimating reliability

Many equipment specifications require a Mean Time Between Failures (MTBF) and an availability figure to be met. Demonstrating the MTBF and availability figures requires faults to be monitored over a long period of time but at the design stage it is possible to predict the MTBF and to modify the design until the predicted figure meets the requirement.

The most common standard for reliability prediction is MIL-HDBK-217 produced by the US Department of Defense which contains predicted failure rates (over a range of temperatures and forms of stress) for many generic types of component. By adding together the failure rates (multiplied by the stress factors) for each component, the system failure rate may be calculated on the assumption that the system fails if any component fails.

The figures provided in MIL-HDBK-217 are for the linear portion of the bathtub reliability curve (see Figure 10.4). Early failures, caused by manufacturing and constructional faults and failures which occur after the operational lifetime of the components, have been excluded from the reliability calculation. The intermediate region of the curve exhibits a constant failure rate which may be used in reliability estimation.

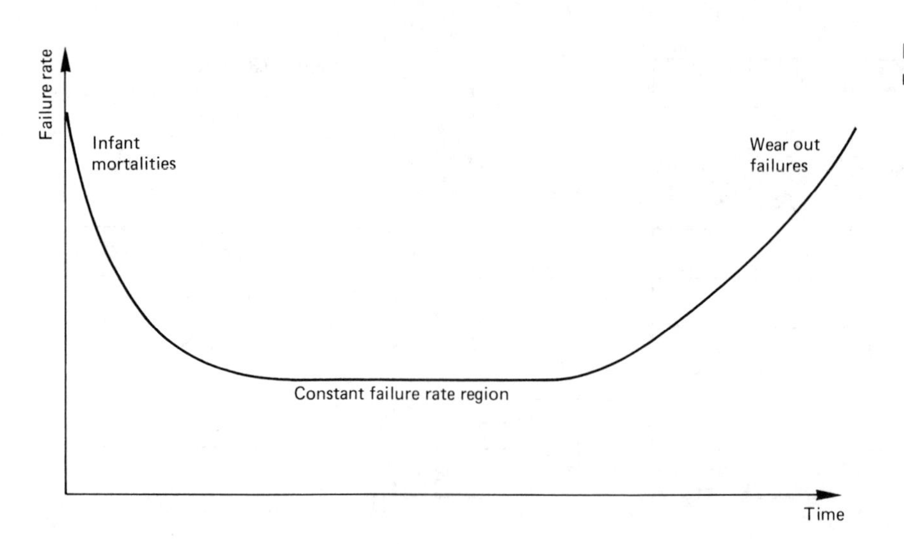

Fig. 10.4 The bathtub reliability curve

If the *reliability factor* $R(t)$ is defined as the probability that an item will perform satisfactorily for a stated period of time, then for a large number of similar items, the reliability factor $R(t)$ at time t may be calculated from

$$R(t) = \frac{\text{The number surviving at instant } t}{\text{Number of items when } t = 0}$$

When the failure rate λ is constant and N is the number surviving at time t, then

$$\frac{dN}{dt} = -\lambda N$$

and $$R(t) = \frac{N}{N_0} = e^{-\lambda t}$$

Thus for a constant failure rate λ, the reliability factor decreases exponentially. The term mean time between failures (MTBF), which is $1/\lambda$, is commonly employed where the equipment is repaired after failures. If the equipment is not repaired and put back into service after failure, the term Mean Time To Failure (MTTF) is used.

Example 1 To find the probability that an equipment with an MTBF of 2000 hours will function satisfactorily for 1 week (168 hours):

$$R(t) = e^{-(168/2000)} = 0.92 \text{ or } 92\%$$

If two subsystems are connected in parallel, A being operational and B being a working spare, the reliability factor for the pair of subsystems is

$$R = 1 - (1 - R_A)(1 - R_B)$$

where R_A is the reliability factor for system A alone over period t
R_B is the reliability factor for system B alone over period t.

Example 2 To find the reliability factor (over a one-week period) of a single computer with two disk drives, one being a working spare, the formula used is

$$R = R_C[1 - (1 - R_D)(1 - R_D)]$$

where R_C is the reliability factor of the computer alone over period t
R_D is the reliability factor of the disk drive alone over period t.

If M_C = MTBF of the computer = 15 000 hours
M_D = MTBF of the disc drive = 2500 hours

then

$$R_C = e^{-t/Mc} = e^{-168/15\,000} = 0.989$$

$$R_D = e^{-t/Md} = e^{-168/2500} = 0.935$$

$$R = 0.989\,[1 - (1 - 0.935)^2] = 0.985 \text{ or } 98.5\%$$

MIL-HDBK-217 describes two methods of predicting system reliability:

a) The parts stress analysis which may only be performed when the design is at an advanced stage because detailed information on component specifications and operating conditions is required.
b) The parts count analysis which may be performed at the preliminary design stage before component stresses are known.

The parts count analysis gives an *equipment failure rate* of

$$\lambda_E = \sum_{i=1}^{i=n} N_i (\lambda_G \pi_Q \pi_L)i$$

where λ_G = generic failure rate for the *i*th generic part
π_Q = quality factor for the *i*th generic part
π_L = the learning factor for the *i*th generic part (used for microelectronic devices, set to 10 for new devices and 1 for established devices).
N_i = number of components in the equipment of the *i*th generic part
n = number of different generic part categories.

Table 10.1 provides an example of λ_E calculation by the parts count method using figures for failures per 10^6 hours given in MIL-HDBK-217 for each component. Established components of commercial quality are used and no redundant components are included.

Table 10.1 Calculation of MTBF by MIL-HDBK-217 parts count method

	Generic part	N_i	λ_G	π_Q	π_L	$N_i(\lambda_G, \pi_Q, \pi_L)$
1	Integrated circuit	10	0.15	75	1	112.50
2	Transistor (Si)	4	0.98	1	1	3.92
3	Diodes (Si)	4	0.68	1	1	2.72
4	Resistors	16	0.04	1	1	0.64
5	Capacitors	5	0.10	1	1	0.50

Total λ_E *(failures per 10^6 hours) = 120.28*

$\therefore$ *MTBF = $10^6/\lambda_E$ = 8314 hours*

Operation of components at elevated temperatures reduces the life and increases the failure rate. A typical increase in failure rate of ×1.9 may be found for an integrated circuit operating at 40°C ambient temperature compared with 25°C. The Arrhenius model may be used to predict the increase in failure rate with ambient temperature:

$$\lambda_T = Ae^{-E_A/K}\left(\frac{1}{T} \cdot \frac{1}{T_0}\right)$$

where λ_T = temperature-related failure rate
E_A = activation energy or the slope of the $\Delta\lambda_T/\Delta_T$ curve.
K = Boltzmann's constant
T = temperature
T_0 = reference temperature.

The parts stress method in MIL-HDBK-217 takes account of the Arrhenius model. *Component failure rate* is given by

$$\lambda_p = \pi_Q [C_1 \pi_T \pi_V + (C_2 + C_3)\, \pi_E]\, \pi_L$$

where π_Q = quality factor
C_1, C_2, C_3 = complexity factors, determined by the number of gates in an integrated circuit
π_T = temperature factor (junction temperature of the integrated circuit)
π_V = voltage stress factor
π_E = mechanical stress factor
π_L = learning factor.

10.2.2 Estimating availability

The *availability* of a system is the proportion of time for which the system is expected to be fully operational:

$$\text{Availability} = \frac{\text{MTBF}}{\text{MTBF} + \text{MTTR}}$$

where MTTR is the mean time to repair the fault, including fault diagnosis.

Preventive maintenance must also be included in availability calculations. For example, a system which requires 30 minutes preventive maintenance every 1000 hours of operation, and has a computer with an MTBF of 15 000 hours with an MTTR of 1 hour and a disk with an MTBF of 2000 hours and an MTTR of 2 hours, has an availability of

$$A = \frac{1000}{1000 + 0.5} \times \frac{15\,000}{15\,000 + 1} \times \frac{2000}{2000 + 2}$$

$$= 0.99843 \text{ or } 99.843\%$$

10.2.3 Improving maintainability

Repair time can consist of several factors:

a) Fault detection time
b) Preparation time
c) Fault isolation time
d) Disassembly time
e) Replacement time
f) Reassembly time
g) Alignment time
h) Checkout time.

The *design of equipment* should take account of all these activities in order to reduce the repair time and hence improve the maintainability. Modular design with easily removable modules can reduce the time required to replace the faulty component. The design of an equipment enclosure determines the disassembly time and reassembly time, while the use of built-in test facilities consisting of hardware and/or software can reduce the fault detection time, fault isolation time and checkout time.

There are several practices in *circuit design* which can improve testability:

a) Dividing complex functions into functionally-complete, smaller sections.
b) Provide edge terminated test/control points on boards.
c) Provide a means of isolating each logic section from a common bus.
d) Provide a means of substituting an external clock.
e) Use sockets for complex integrated circuits.
f) Provide tester access to all inputs and outputs.
g) Provide a means of initialising all storage elements.
h) Provide a means of breaking all feedback loops.
i) Avoid logical redundancy.
j) Avoid the use of monostable circuits and asynchronous logic.
k) Avoid excessive gate fan-out.

Relatively inexpensive *signature analysis test equipment* may be used to diagnose faults in complex digital circuits, including memory. Signature analysis is a data compression technique which uses a cyclic redundancy check produced by a pseudo-random binary-sequence generator operating on a serial bit stream. By checking the signatures at various points on a faulty digital circuit board and comparing them with the signatures produced by a good board, it is often possible to track down the source of a fault much more rapidly than with other forms of test equipment. To permit the use of signature analysis, an adequate number of easily accessible test points and a means of disabling bus drivers are required.

10.3 Environmental factors

10.3.1 Temperature

For static applications, temperature is the most important environmental factor in the design of a computer system. If the components run at an excessive temperature, their reliability and life will be impaired, as described in Section 10.2.1. Most commercial components are specified to operate between 0°C and 65°C and integrated circuits are specified for the range 0°C to 70°C. Industrial and military temperature range components are available. Some military components operate between −50°C and +125°C but a considerable cost increase is incurred in using these selected components.

Many peripherals and storage media have narrow temperature ranges. Disk drives are sensitive to changes in temperature because head misalignment occurs when the casting expands at a greater rate than other components. For immunity to a wide operating temperature range and the resultant mechanical shifts within the device, a closed loop servo is preferable and an embedded servo is ideal.

To compensate for changes in media coercivity with temperature, the better disk drives use write current temperature compensation. This allows data written at one temperature extreme to be read at the other. The storage media in most winchester disk drives has a maximum operational temperature of 65°C while flexible disk recording media has a typical maximum operational temperature of +55°C and a storage temperature range of −62°C to +75°C. The DC300 tape cartridge has an operational/non-operational temperature range of +5°C to +45°C and a humidity range of 20–80%.

Heat losses within an equipment enclosure cause the internal ambient temperature to rise until an equilibrium is reached between heat generated and heat dissipated. When internal heat loss is low, it can often be dissipated by natural convection from the equipment surface to the external air. Typical heat losses of $10\,W/m^2K$ can be dissipated by natural convection and this may be increased by providing cooling fins to increase the effective equipment surface area. Cooling slits which permit cooling air to pass directly over the hot components improve the heat loss. By using a fan, the air flow is increased in comparison to that achieved by natural convection and the heat dissipation is greatly increased making the internal temperature lower.

To calculate the required airflow V to dissipate a given heat loss W the formula used is

$$V = \frac{W}{C\rho\Delta t}$$

where V is the volume of airflow in m^3/s
W is the heat loss in watts
C is the specific thermal capacity of air, 1010 W s/kg K
ρ is the density of air, roughly $1\,kg/m^3$
Δt is the heating of the airflow in K ($t_{out} - t_{in}$).

Δt should be limited to 10–20 K because the temperature of internal components rises with Δt. For example, a computer with a consumption of 360 W and $\Delta t = 15°C$ would require an airflow of

$$V = \frac{360}{1010 \times 1 \times 15} = 24 \times 10^{-3}\,m^3/s$$

Components will have a higher temperature than the temperature of air flowing past them; this is caused by component heat loss and thermal resistance (which depends on the thermal conductivity between the chip and the package surface and an external factor which depends on the quantity of heat transferred from the surface to the cooling air). Turbulent air flow increases heat transfer from the component and the thermal resistance of a component in still air can be reduced to one third with an air flow velocity of 4–5 m/s.

A suitable fan may be selected to suit the calculated volume of air flow V and pressure rise ΔP. The static differential pressure rise ΔP_f required to drive the cooling flow through the equipment should be measured, if

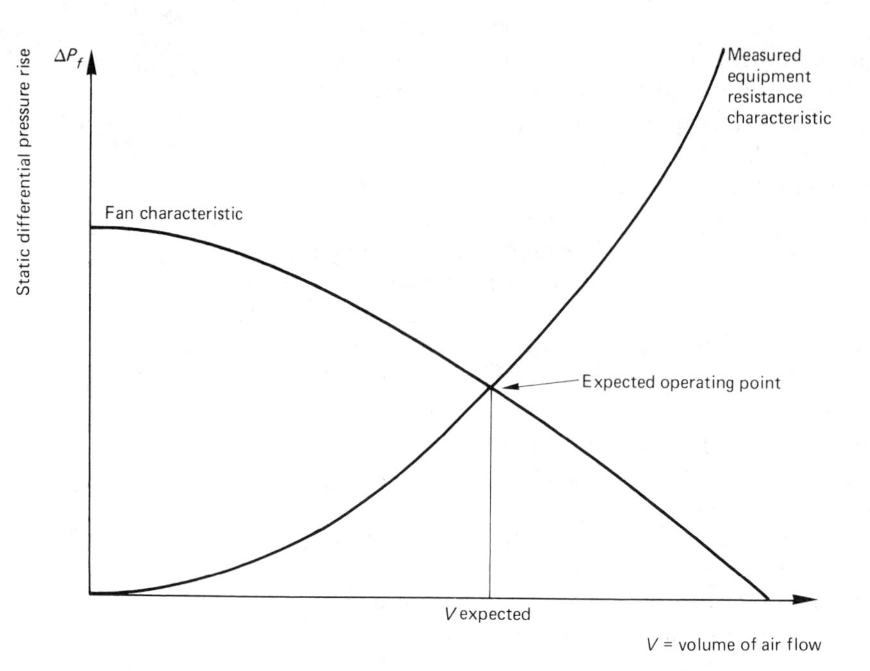

Fig. 10.5 ΔP_f against V characteristic for a fan, with required characteristics superimposed

reasonable accuracy in the selection of a suitable fan is expected. Each fan has a characteristic P_f against V characteristic (see Figure 10.5) and the measured equipment resistance characteristic should be superimposed to determine the expected volume of air flow.

Air filters are often required and these introduce additional pressure losses, especially when dirty. There are two major disadvantages caused by using cooling fans in electronic equipment:

a) Reliability reduction
b) Acoustic noise produced.

If the equipment requires the fan to be working in order to maintain satisfactory operation, the MTBF of the fan must be included in the system reliability calculation, if necessary fitting a second redundant fan to meet the reliability targets. Some systems find it desirable to fit a temperature sensor to raise an alarm or switch off the power supply when the maximum internal temperature is exceeded, possibly as a result of the fan failing.

In a quiet environment, the noise produced by a fan can be unacceptable. By careful design of the cooling arrangements, selection of a quiet type of fan, careful positioning of air entry and exit points, and fitting of sound-absorbant material, it may be possible to achieve an acceptable level of sound output. If not, the heat dissipation must be reduced to avoid the need for fan cooling. Some improvement in internal cooling may be achieved by ensuring a uniformly distributed air flow, by mounting boards vertically and fitting boards in unused slots in a backplane.

10.3.2 Air filtration

The air contains a variety of dust particles, smoke particles and other contaminants which may include corrosive or conductive agents in an industrial environment. High-velocity air flow from a fan will import those contaminants to the equipment. If sensitive disk drives are included in the equipment, an efficient filter will be required on the air intake to remove particles down to 1 μ-inch diameter. The efficiency of the filter at the required particle size must be matched to the requirements of the disk drive.

Filters are more efficient at low air velocities, and a large-area filter reduces the air velocity. If a positive pressure is maintained within the equipment, dust will not enter the equipment through small holes and cracks and, if the equipment includes a door, the fans should be positioned to prevent dust entering when the door is open. Corrosive atmospheres cannot be filtered out by using conventional filters; sealed equipment is the best solution in this kind of environment.

10.3.3 Humidity

The major problem occurs when surface temperatures of circuit boards or disk drives are below the dewpoint of the surrounding air. This is a temperature at which the relative humidity is 100% and condensation starts to occur. Unprotected electronic equipment generally works between 0 and 80% relative humidity where no condensation occurs. At low humidity levels, problems caused by static electricity may be encountered.

Condensation on a disk or tape media surface can be a serious problem when inserting a cold, recently transported cartridge into a hot drive. A standby/warm-up control can be useful in rapidly pre-heating and purging such a cartridge.

When moisture condenses on metal surfaces, corrosion can result and circuit boards may experience leakage of current and sparking in high voltage circuits. Conformal coatings may be applied to circuit boards to prevent moisture affecting the circuitry but this can cause maintenance difficulties by making it impossible to monitor signals on the board and making component replacement difficult. Conformal coatings can also reduce the heat loss from components.

An internal heater may be used to prevent the temperature falling below the dewpoint when the equipment is switched off. Internal heat dissipation may be adequate to prevent condensation in normal operation but previous chilling of circuit boards and an accumulation of dust can cause condensation problems when the equipment is first switched on.

10.3.4 Shock and vibration

Equipment which is transported by land, sea or air experiences levels of shock and vibration which most commercial equipment is not able to survive without protective packaging. Equipment which is required to operate when on the move, or to be portable, must have additional protection because it will not be provided with protective packaging.

The levels of shock experienced when an equipment is dropped from 30 inches can subject the structure to hundreds of *g*s but a suitable shock mount could reduce the shock level experienced by internal units to survivable levels. Components such as circuit boards, fans and power supplies frequently survive high levels of shock and vibration but winchester disks are damaged by high levels of vibration and floppy disks may survive but not operate in high levels of vibration.

Moving-head disk drives employ various methods of positioning the read/write heads. Closed loop servo positioners using linear or rotary voice coil actuators have more resistance to mechanical shock than the open loop designs using rotary stepper motors found on small, inexpensive disk drives. Designs which use embedded servo data within the data track will outperform those which use a separate servo surface in an environment with high shock and vibration.

Many disk drives are more vulnerable when power is removed than when the disks are rotating and the heads are flying. When in use, the air will provide a stiff head-bearing surface to protect the recording area of the disks. Disk drives which allow the recording heads to contact the media when stationary may allow the heads to slide over the data area, but this may cause wear to the head and recording surface under shock and vibration.

Components on circuit boards may move under vibration, causing the leads to fracture. To prevent this, all relatively heavy components must be securely fixed to the circuit board. Under vibration, circuit boards flex and movement is greatest at the natural resonant frequency of the board. Resonance can cause damage to tracks or components and the board may work out of its connectors, components may work out of sockets, and cable connectors may work free or break due to fatigue. To prevent these problems, the boards and cables should be firmly fixed in place, not relying on a connector on one edge. All connectors should be of a type which can be locked together or held with clips or foam.

All heavy components must be securely attached to the main structure and sensitive components such as disk drives should be provided with shock mountings to keep the applied level of acceleration below 10–20 *g*. If operation is required at acceleration levels above 1 *g*, any form of disk drive, except a special ruggedised unit, should be fitted with shock mounts.

Shock and vibration isolators are available; these allow relative movement which reduces the applied force by distributing it over a longer time. Energy is absorbed by the isolator in the form of hysteresis loss in rubber or friction between the coils, depending upon the form of construction.

Isolators have a natural frequency of oscillation which depends on the mass of the supported object and the stiffness of the vibration isolator. At this resonant frequency, vibration will be amplified but, at other frequencies, the amplitude of vibration will be reduced (see Figure 10.6). For transport over rough roads or in aircraft, an isolator with a resonant frequency of 12 to 14 Hz is suitable because this corresponds to a frequency range which is not typically found at high acceleration levels in road vehicles or aircraft. At frequencies above about 40 Hz, which are present at high acceleration levels in road vehicles and aircraft, the isolator shown in Figure

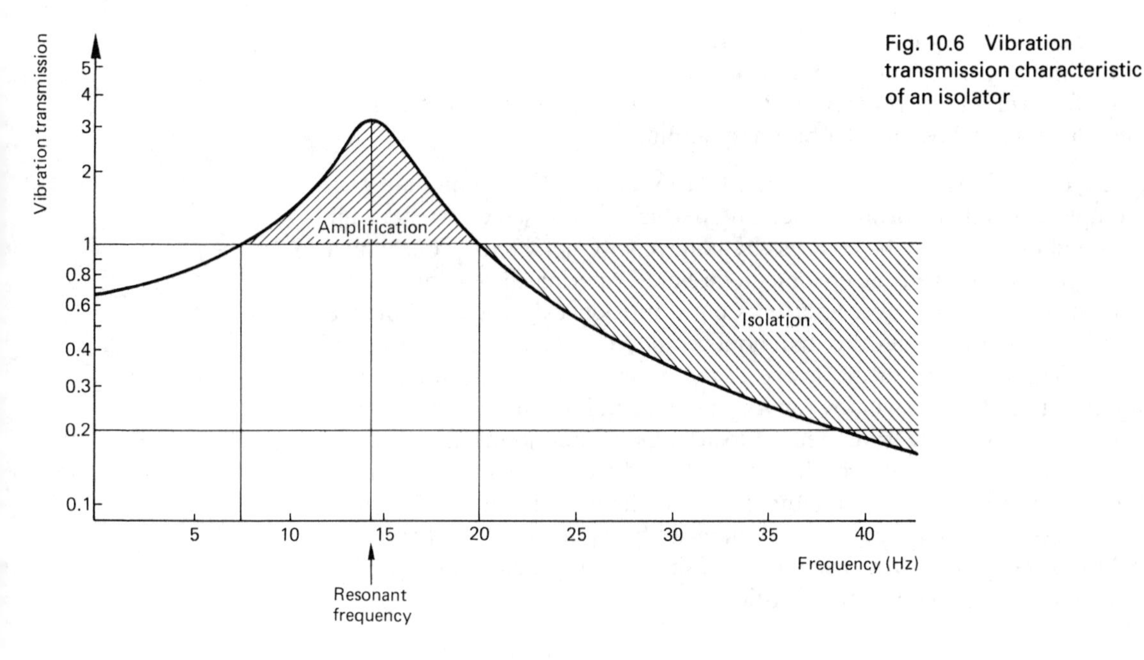

Fig. 10.6 Vibration transmission characteristic of an isolator

10.6 will transmit less than 20% of the applied g forces. For shipboard applications, an isolator with a lower resonant frequency would be required because acceleration levels increase rapidly above 10 Hz.

10.3.5 Electromagnetic interference

All electronic equipment is capable of generating electromagnetic interference and is also a potential victim of electromagnetic radiation from other equipment or natural phenomena such as lightning. The FCC regulations define the levels of radiation which are permitted from computing devices (with a clock rate above 10 kHz) in the USA and other specifications apply elsewhere, for example the West German VDE-0871 standard. Specific military or industrial applications may require more stringent electromagnetic interference standards.

Electromagnetic interference may be radiated through free space or conducted down the power and signal cables. Emission of, and susceptibility to, electromagnetic radiation may be reduced by effective screening of the equipment and its connecting cables, while transmission of, and susceptibility to, conducted interference may be reduced by providing filters in the power input circuitry and possibly the signal cable interfaces.

In a factory, voltage spikes up to 10 kV for 1 ms may be experienced on power supplies and equipment connected to power lines, and external communications cables may experience lightning strikes. Military equipment may have to survive the electromagnetic pulse (EMP) which accompanies a nuclear explosion and can destroy electronic equipment over several thousand miles while the other effects of an exo-atmospheric nuclear explosion have little effect. The most common means of protecting an equipment from these effects is to

a) Screen the equipment and cables.
b) Filter the input and output lines.
c) Fit overvoltage protection devices, such as transzorbs, varistors or gas discharge tubes, on all inputs and outputs.

Effective screening may be accomplished by enclosing the equipment in a complete metal enclosure. Essential apertures in the screen, such as air inlets and outlets, may be covered by honeycomb metal extrusions which let air pass but prevent electromagnetic fields entering or leaving. Metal mesh may be used to cover apertures but it introduces greater turbulence in air flow and is less effective than honeycombs at attenuating electromagnetic radiation. Holes for displays or screens may be covered with a transparent thin metal film window or a window containing a fine metal mesh which is bonded to the grounded enclosure. Doors and joints in the enclosure should be fitted with conductive gaskets. Steel is the ideal screening material but it is heavier than aluminium. As shown in Figure 10.7, aluminium is less effective at screening frequencies below about 100 kHz. Plastic enclosures can be given a measure of screening by lining them with grounded metal foil or using a conductive plastic.

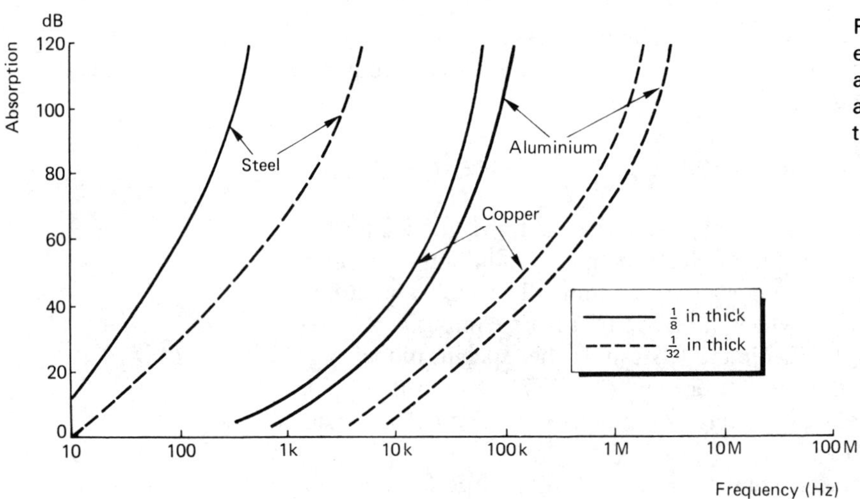

Fig. 10.7 Comparison of electromagnetic signal absorption by steel, copper and aluminium of varying thickness

Common mode ground noise is a frequent cause of radiated emissions from computers. This is produced by signals, such as that on the clock driver ground pin, exciting the logic ground system and causing radiation from any wire connected to the logic ground. Inductance in long printed circuit tracks connected to ground and power pins, combined with current transients in the circuit, are the main cause of common mode noise. The problem may be reduced by minimising the length of supply and ground tracks, adding more decoupling capacitors, or shielding the cables which are connected to the logic ground. If this fails it may be necessary to use lower-speed bipolar or CMOS logic which produces less radiation.

An equipment design must take into consideration the emission standards of every country in which the equipment may be operated. The FCC regulations define conducted and radiated emission levels for two classes of equipment:

a) *Class A* Computing devices used primarily in commercial, business or industrial environments.
b) *Class B* Computing devices intended for home use.

Table 10.2 Radiated and conducted emission limits for FCC Part 15/J

Radiated limits

Frequency Range (MHz)	*Class A (μV/m at 30 m)*	*Class B (μV/m at 3 m)*
30–88	30	100
88–216	50	150
216–1000	70	200

Conducted limits

Frequency range (MHz)	*Class A (μV)*	*Class B (μV)*
0.45–1.6	1000	250
0.6–30	3000	250

As shown in Table 10.2, the FCC limits for Class B equipment are more stringent than Class A for both radiated emissions and conducted emissions.

When tested, equipment must be configured and operated in the manner which will maximise emissions. For Class B equipment, radiation measurements may be made at a distance of 3–10 m but the results must be extrapolated to 3 m using the inverse-inductance linear relationship (20 dB/octave). For Class A equipment, measurements may be made at distances less than 30 m and extrapolated accordingly. The West German VDE-0871 and VDE-0875 emission standards are compared with the FCC standards in Figure 10.8.

The selection of suitable susceptibility levels for equipment is up to the designer. Electromagnetic radiation is generally well below 1 V/m except when radio transmitters are operated nearby. The European Economic Community directive 78/766 defines power line susceptibility levels:

100% voltage reduction for about 10 ms
50% voltage reduction for about 20 ms
20% voltage reduction for about 50 ms

with at least 10 seconds interval between interruptions. Supply over-voltage levels are shown in Table 10.3.

The radiated susceptibility levels in EEC-78/766 are

a) An induction field of 60 A/m and 50 Hz obtained from a typical cable carrying 10 A at 2.5 cm.
b) An electromagnetic radiation field strength of 10 V/m at frequencies between 100 kHz and 500 MHz and a field strength of 1 V/m at frequencies between 500 MHz and 1000 MHz.

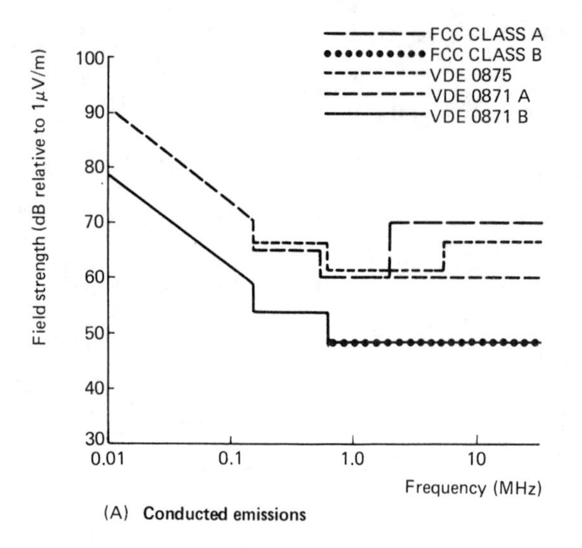

(A) **Conducted emissions**

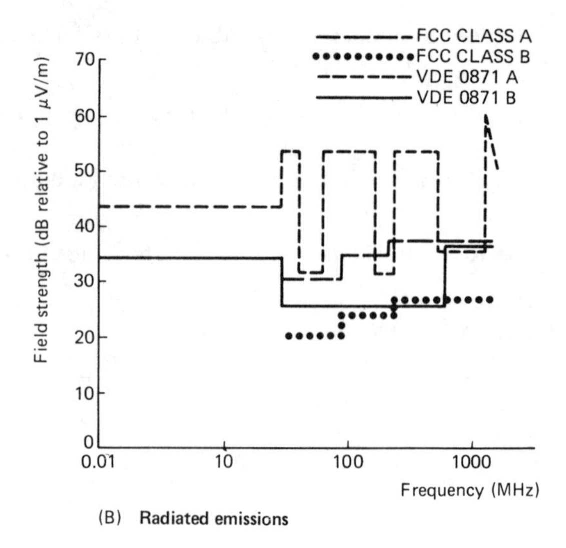

(B) **Radiated emissions**

Fig. 10.8 Comparison of FCC and VDE standards for conducted and radiated emissions

Electrostatic discharges of 6 kV with an energy of 2 mJ on an earthed chassis may be expected with a minimum of 10 seconds between individual discharges. With a relative humidity of 10–20%, electrostatic voltages up to 20 kV may be generated by picking up a plastic bag and 35 kV may be generated by walking across a vinyl floor (1.5 kV with 70–90% RH).

Unprotected MOS devices can be damaged by electrostatic voltages below 1 kV. CMOS, NMOS and PMOS integrated circuits with internal protection may be able to survive 1 to 4 kV while low-speed bipolar logic, such as TTL, may not be damaged by electrostatic voltages up to 15 kV.

10.3.6 Radiation hardness

For most commercial applications the immunity of components to ionising radiation is not an important factor but equipment which is intended for military applications, for use in the nuclear industry or in spacecraft must have a specified level of immunity to ionising radiation.

An exception to this generalisation is the occurrence of soft errors (or single-event upsets) in semiconductor memories caused by cosmic rays or an alpha particle passing through the integrated circuit. If the alpha particle has adequate charge to upset the stored charges in a dynamic RAM, the data will be corrupted. Traces of thorium or uranium in the packaging material may emit alpha particles which cause soft errors in memory devices with small feature sizes. This problem became significant when dynamic memory cells were reduced in size to produce 16 Kbit devices but has become less significant as new packaging materials, which do not produce alpha particles, have been introduced. It has also been found that beyond 16 Kbits, dynamic RAM increases its radiation harness becoming an order of magnitude better at 64 Kbits.

The radiation effects on VLSI devices are caused by

Table 10.3 EEC 78/766 transient overvoltage levels (of either polarity from a 50 Ω source)

Amplitude (V)	*Risetime*	*Half-amplitude duration*	*Repetition rate*
500 V	2 ns	100 ns	10 Hz
1500 V	25 ns	1 μs	<12 Hz
300 V	1 ms burst of 1 Mhz pulses		<12 Hz
5% of nominal	Sinewave superimposed on supply		30–150 kHz
1 V	Sinewave superimposed on supply		150 kHz–400 MHz

Table 10.4 Comparison of semiconductor technologies for use in a radiation environment

Technology	*Total dose* (rads)	*Neutrons* (cm^{-2})	*Single event upset/bit.day*	*Problems*
NMOS	10^{14}–10^{15}	$>10^{15}$	Sensitive	Power
CMOS	10^{5}–$\geqslant 10^{7}$	$>10^{15}$	10^{-5}–10^{-7}	Latch-up
CMOS/SOS	$\geqslant 10^{6}$	$>10^{15}$	$<10^{-8}$	Cost, availability
Bipolar	10^{4}–$>10^{6}$	10^{13}–$>10^{14}$	$>10^{-5}$	Power
GaAs	$\geqslant 10^{7}$	$>10^{15}$	3×10^{-6}	No VLSI, high cost

a) Ionisation resulting in trapped charge enhancement in dielectrics and photocurrents in semiconductors.
b) Atomic displacement which causes modification of semiconductor properties.

Photons (X-rays and gamma rays) and charged particles (electrons and cosmic rays) produce both radiation effects but ionisation is the most significant consequence. Neutron radiation mostly causes atomic displacement. Total radiation dose requirements vary from 10^3 to 10^6 rads and dose rate requirements vary from about 10^3 rad/s to over 10^8 rad/s. Neutron tolerance requirements may be up to $10^{14}/cm^2$. Cosmic ray fluences in satellites are typically 1 to $10/cm^2/day$. Some systems are required to function immediately after exposure to radiation while others must function after annealing effects have subsided.

Table 10.4 compares the semiconductor technologies for use in radiation environments.

For many years it was believed that NMOS VLSI components would become more susceptible to total dose and ionising dose rate radiation induced effects as the level of integration was increased but this has proved not to be the case. NMOS hardness levels to gamma and other ionising radiations have increased from about 10^3 rads to about 10^5 rads for static HMOS III. As shown in Figure 10.9 this compares well with the trend for advanced VLSI bipolar integrated circuits which have decreased by about two orders of magnitude in ionising radiation hardness because parasitic MOS devices have been introduced in the sidewall oxide isolation process.

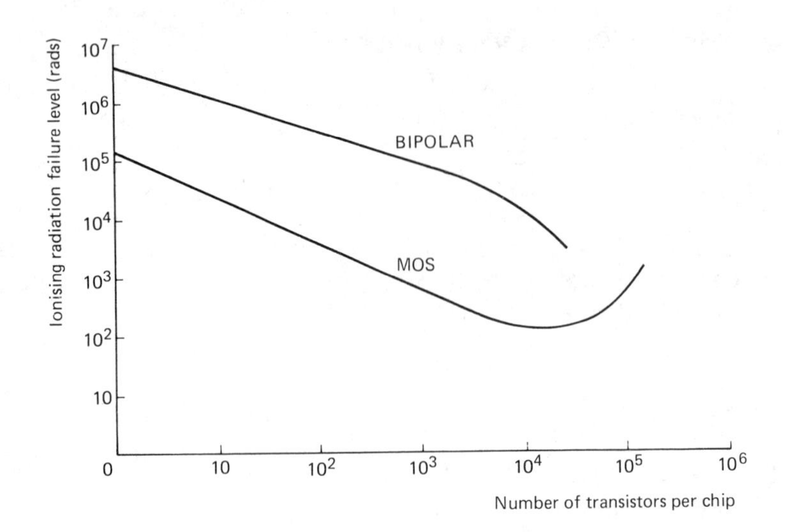

Fig. 10.9 Total dose ionising radiation hardness trends for commercial bipolar and MOS semiconductors

CMOS is the preferred technology for most high radiation applications because it has a much lower power consumption and this is an overriding factor in space applications. CMOS exhibits latch-up caused by parasitic SCR action at high radiation levels; this results in excessive current consumption and destruction of the device unless current limiting resistors are used in the supply line. Special radiation-hardened CMOS devices are available to overcome the latch-up problem and CMOS with a silicon-on-sapphire substrate does not suffer from latch-up.

Circumvention techniques may be employed to prevent damage to components which would otherwise be damaged by high radiation levels if powered-up during exposure to radiation. By sensing the onset of high radiation levels, possibly by using a fast-switching SCR, it is possible to quickly remove power from the circuit by firing SCR devices connected across the supply on each circuit board. These will rapidly discharge the energy stored in on-board capacitors. The radiation levels which many devices can survive when unpowered can be more than three orders of magnitude greater than the powered survival levels.

10.4 Cost considerations

10.4.1 Cost trends

The semiconductor industry is exceptional in that it is able to reduce the cost of achieving the same level of microprocessor computing power and data storage capacity as each new generation of VLSI components become available. Alternatively, a higher level of performance and storage capacity is available for the same price from each new generation of VLSI chips (see Figure 10.10).

As each new generation of VLSI product becomes available, the manufacturers are able to charge high prices because it is still competing with

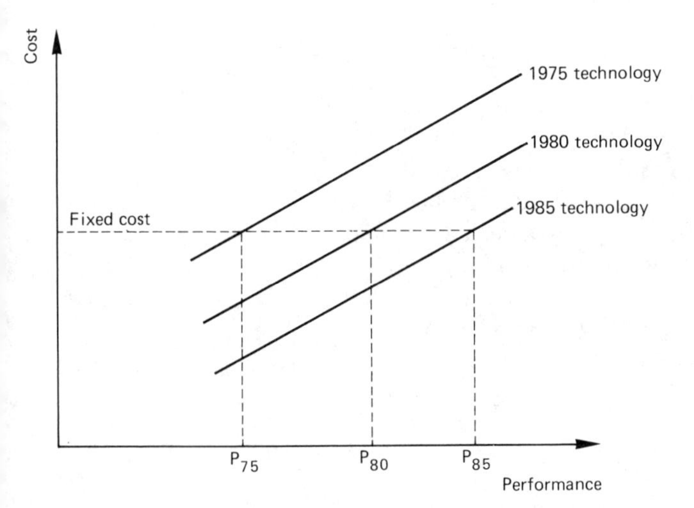

Fig. 10.10 Cost/performance relationships for VLSI technology

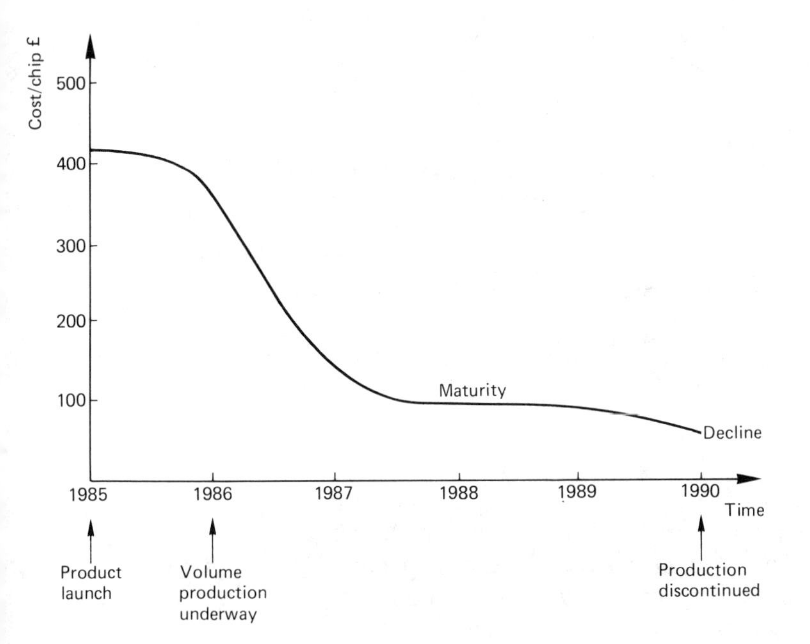

Fig. 10.11 Typical changes in component cost through the product life cycle

products from the last generation and buyers are prepared to pay more for superior performance. As shown in Figure 10.11, this initial period of high prices soon gives way to lower prices, based more on production costs, as the product becomes mature. There are usually several similar products competing during maturity and high-volume production is then underway so prices can, and do, fall. During the declining phase of a product's lifetime, the price tends to fall further because a new generation of higher-performance devices are now competing. A typical cost for 32-bit microprocessors was £400 ($600) in 1985 but this fell below £200 ($300) by 1987 when these components were almost at the mature stage of their life cycle.

10.4.2 Life cycle costs

Systems using microprocessors, particularly those for military and industrial applications, follow a life cycle similar to that shown in Figure 10.12. After the conceptual research and development phase, costs increase as advanced development models are produced and engineering development progresses. Once production commences, costs increase to a peak as the maximum delivery rate is reached, then decline as the production requirement is completed. From the date when the first units are in service, the operating and support costs increase, then level off when all the units are in service, finally declining when the equipment becomes obsolete and is taken out of service.

Fig. 10.12 Costs throughout a typical system life cycle

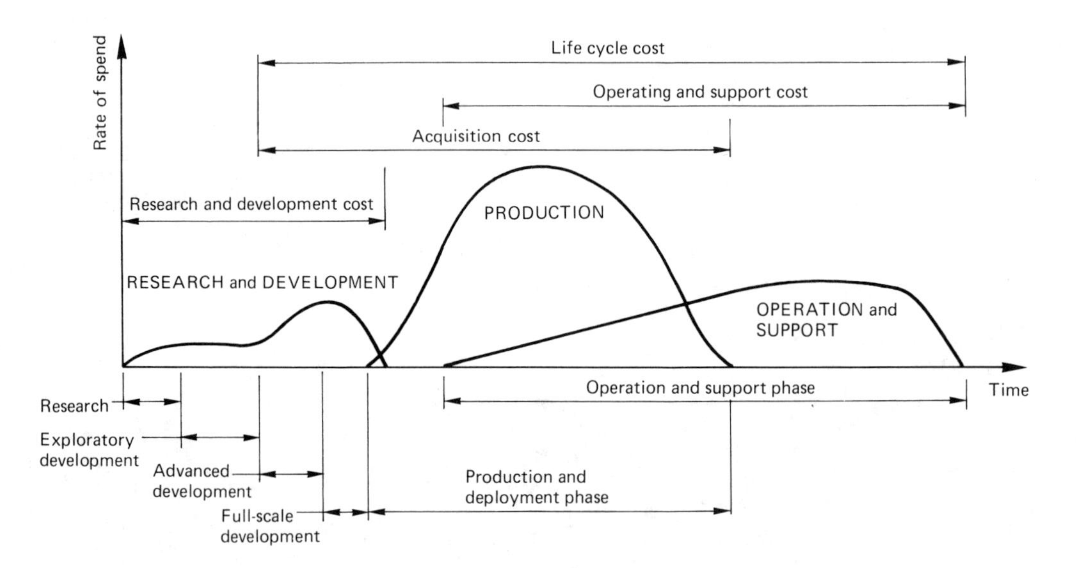

When a user is able to influence the design of a system, the life cycle costs may become the major consideration rather than the acquisition cost. When this is the case it is necessary to consider the savings in operation and support cost which may be achieved by increasing the acquisition costs, in order to increase the MTBF, improve maintainability, and reduce the operation costs in terms of manpower, consumables, etc. Figure 10.13 shows the trade-off results obtained for a US military computer. To minimise life cycle costs, an MTBF of 800 hours was required which increased acquisition costs by $3 million over the acquisition cost of a computer with 200 hours MTBF. The total saving over the 10-year life cycle was $12 million.

10.4.3 System design trade-offs

A system designer may construct a computer system from custom VLSI, microprocessor chips, single board computers, or complete microcomputer boxes. In deciding what level of construction is appropriate for a product, it is necessary to consider the trade-offs between development cost, product cost and time required to have the product on the market. The user influenc-

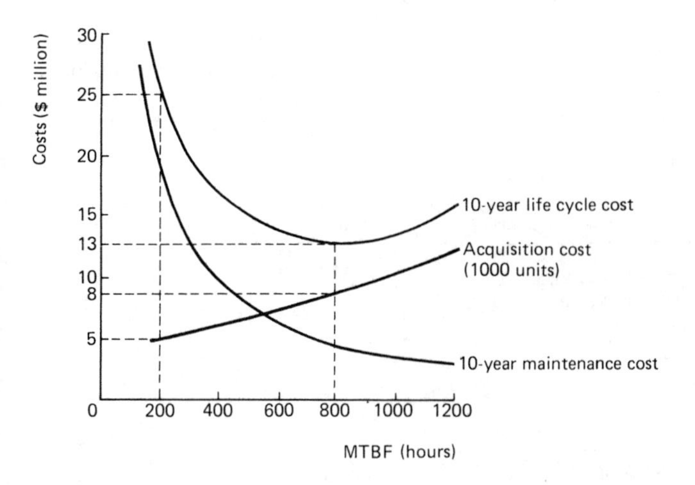

Fig. 10.13 Relationships between 10-year life cycle cost, 10-year maintenance cost and acquisition cost against MTBF for a military computer

ing design would want the operating and support costs included in the trade-off but if the product is to compete on an open market this would probably be secondary to the product cost in relation to competitive products and the time to hit the market.

Figure 10.14 shows a typical relationship between development cost, product cost and time to reach the market for solutions using custom VLSI, chip level design, board level design and microcomputer boxes. A more precise analysis of the options may be carried out as shown in Figure 10.15 which compares the cost of constructing a computer board using microprocessor chips with the cost of using a single board computer from a board manufacturer. The costs plotted should include amortized development costs and production costs, both of which change with the number of units produced. A crossover point will be found and, if the production required lies above this point, it is less expensive to develop a computer board using microprocessor chips than to use a ready-made single board computer.

Software development is a major part of the development cost and it is worth considering the savings which could be made by buying better software development facilities and using high-level languages to improve

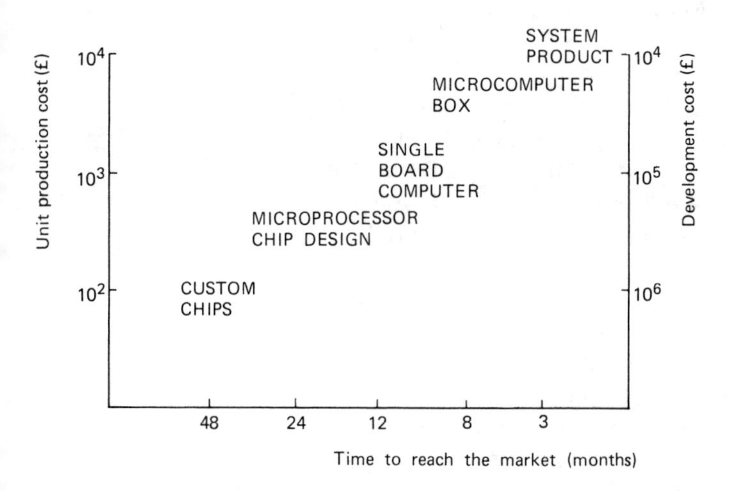

Fig. 10.14 Relationship between development cost, production cost and time to reach market for various levels of system integration

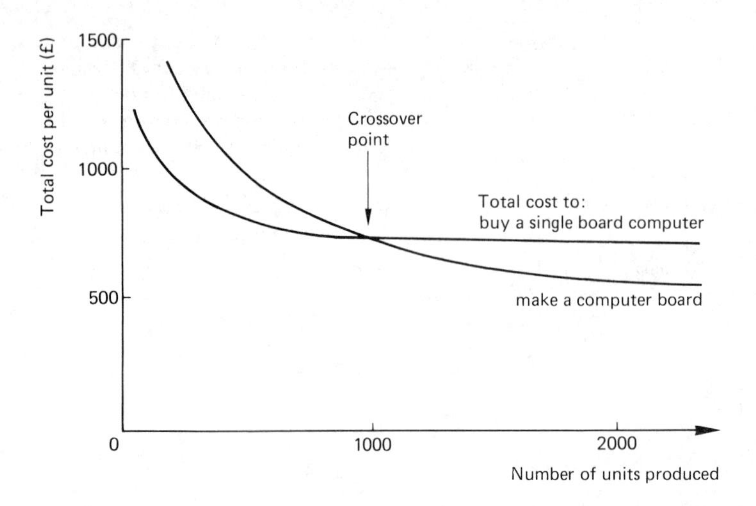

Fig. 10.15 Comparison of production cost for building a computer board or using a single board computer

the productivity of programmers. High-level languages require more processing power and more memory but for most low-quantity applications of advanced microprocessors, it will be found that the additional cost of more memory and more processing power will be saved by reductions in software development and maintenance costs. The cost of producing each line of code is increasing rapidly (see Figure 10.16) while the cost of processing power and memory is reducing rapidly. The proportion of costs required to develop and maintain software is therefore increasing and it is wise to take all reasonable steps to reduce software costs.

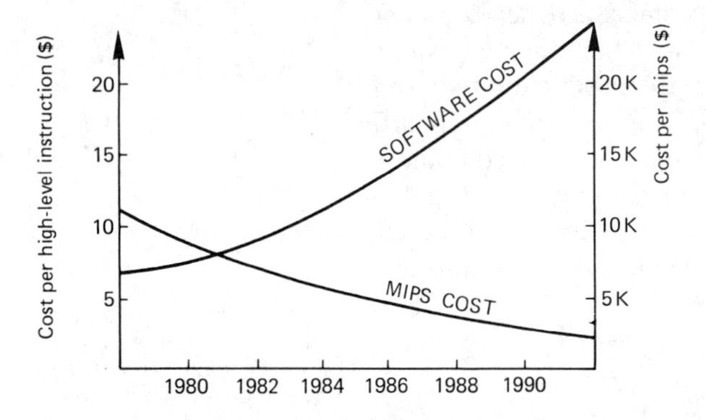

Fig. 10.16 Software and hardware cost trend

When selecting the program memory for a microcomputer, the reduced cost of mask programmed ROM at high volumes should be traded-off against the versatility of EPROM or EEPROM, taking into account the mask-making charge for the ROM. Figure 10.17 illustrates the volume relationship and the additional cost if two program changes are required.

10.4.4 Risk analysis

It is often necessary to make decisions on design alternatives when the risk associated with one alternative must be evaluated against other lower-risk but higher-cost options. A fault tree may be used to quantify the overall risk associated with each option, or combination of options, to estimate

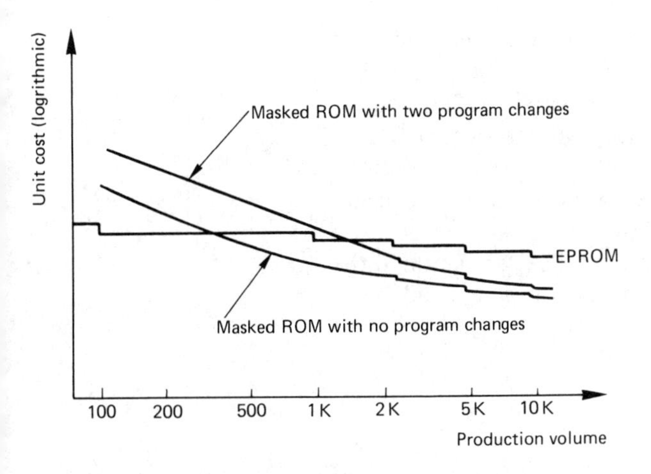

Fig. 10.17 Comparison of costs for EPROM and masked ROM with zero and two program changes

the additional costs and delays which may occur as a result of each possible outcome and the probability of each outcome occurring.

Figure 10.18 shows a fault tree used to analyse the risk probability, delay and cost of each possible outcome when comparing two microprocessors for an application. Microprocessor A has a 50% probability that no suitable software is available and, if it were not available, the cost of developing the software would be £40k but no delay is incurred. There is also a 20% risk of delay if modifications are required after integration; these would cost £10k and take 3 months.

Microprocessor B has a 50% probability of being available late; this would cause a 3-month delay and incur £30k of additional cost. If it is late there is a 16% probability that modifications may be required after integration, taking 2 months and costing £10k but there is also a 4% probability that the microprocessor is not viable. This would cause 13 months delay and cost £500k.

Fig. 10.18 A fault tree used to analyse the risk, delay and cost associated with two alternative microprocessors

Branch	Outcome	*Probability %*	*Months delay*	*Additional cost £K*
MICROPROCESSOR A — 50% software available	integration OK (80%)	40	0	0
MICROPROCESSOR A — 50% software available	mod's required (20%) (£10 K) (3 months)	10	3	10
MICROPROCESSOR A — 50% develop software (£40 K)	integration OK (80%)	40	0	40
MICROPROCESSOR A — 50% develop software (£40 K)	mod's required (20%) (£10 K) (3 months)	10	3	50
MICROPROCESSOR B — 50% on time	integration OK (90%)	45	0	0
MICROPROCESSOR B — 50% on time	mod's required (10%) (£15 K) (2 months)	5	2	15
MICROPROCESSOR B — 50% available late (£30 K) (3 months)	integration OK (80%)	40	3	30
MICROPROCESSOR B — 50% available late (£30 K) (3 months)	mod's required (16%) (£10 K) (2 months)	8	5	40
MICROPROCESSOR B — 50% available late (£30 K) (3 months)	not viable (4%) (£500 K) (13 months)	2	16	530

The fault tree analysis shows that if microprocessor A is used, the most probable outcomes (40% each) incur no delay and one outcome incurs an additional cost of £40k to develop software. The worst-case alternative incurrs £50k additional cost and 3 months delay. Microprocessor B has a 45% probability of incurring no delay or additional costs but there is a worst-case 2% probability that the microprocessor may prove to be unsuitable incurring a delay of 16 months and a cost of £530k. The decision may still be difficult to make but the fault tree analysis has quantified the probabilities and possible outcomes based on the best estimates available.

11 Alternative system architectures

11.1 General comments

Chapter 2 described several 'new' architectures and design features which are used in advanced microprocessors, microcomputers and other forms of computer including supercomputers. Many of the architectural alternatives have been known for many years but the new generation of advanced microprocessors has made it practical and economical to use these architectures for a variety of applications.

This chapter considers the suitability of several alternative architectures for a range of applications. Particular attention is given to those architectures which are compatible with the use of existing microprocessors described in Chapters 3, 4 and 5.

11.2 Summary of computer classification

11.2.1 Supercomputers

Supercomputers are the most powerful class of computer. Computer power includes speed of operation, storage capacity and precision. Most supercomputers use 64-bit data words and perform floating-point operations at speeds between 100 Mflops and 10 Gflops.

Supercomputers cost several millions of pounds and are primarily used for scientific and engineering applications where vector processing with a SIMD or MIMD architecture is desirable. Several vector processors may be incorporated, each permitting a single instruction to operate on several data elements.

The design of conventional supercomputers such as those manufactured by CRAY and NEC depends upon the use of high-speed circuitry which is tightly packed to minimise propagation delay. This results in heat dissipation problems which demand a complex heat removal system using, for example, liquid nitrogen, baths of inert liquids or water cooling.

The use of parallel processing, particularly concurrent processing networks, is having a considerable impact on the design of supercomputers and mini-supercomputers because they permit much higher levels of performance to be achieved at a lower cost than more traditional vector processors. The current problem lies in the design of suitable algorithms and software to exploit the vast potential performance of parallel processors.

11.2.2 Mini-supercomputers

Mini-supercomputers were first introduced in the early 1980s to provide high-performance computing for scientific and engineering applications with a performance approaching that of supercomputers but at a price similar to that of super-minicomputers. Several forms of parallel architecture and vector processing architecture have been used, most providing 64-bit data words to give adequate precision in floating-point arithmetic.

Typical performance of mini-supercomputers is in the range 20 to 500 Mflops.

11.2.3 Array processors

Array processors are optimised for the execution of processing algorithms which operate on arrays (regular structures) of input data. They were introduced in the mid-1970s as fixed program units which could be attached to general-purpose computers but have now been developed to include a high degree of program flexibility. Many array processors work only as attached processors for a general-purpose host computer.

Most array processors perform 32-bit floating-point operations at a rate between 5 and 50 Mflops and have high-speed data ports to accept input data directly without host processor intervention. Array processors range from single cards which fit inside a computer to multi-cabinet units which are almost pipelined supercomputers.

Typical applications for array processors are seismic signal processing, sonar signal processing, and speech recognition where operations such as fast Fourier transforms, digital filtering and matrix operations are required. The smaller, more economical array processors employ bit-slice ALU segments, often with a vector processor constructed from a bipolar floating-point processor chip.

Future array processors are likely to use arrays of processors to increase performance beyond the limits of a bus-based architecture.

11.2.4 Mega-mainframes

Mega-mainframes were introduced in the mid-1980s to permit the expansion of mainframe processing power without frequent computer replacement. Incremental processing power and memory capacity enhancements are provided by adding more processors (up to a total of four) giving up to 100 Mips floating point performance and 256 Mbytes main memory capacity. Architectures are optimised for scalar processing which consists of serial operations on single data elements. Scientific applications frequently require long strings of iterative calculations to be performed on large arrays of data but commercial data processing needs a computer which is optimised for the performance of file manipulations and handling I/O to a variety of peripherals and remote terminals.

To meet the requirements of both scientific and commercial processing, the basic scalar architecture of most mega-mainframes is enhanced by a vector processor or attached array processor.

11.2.5 Mainframes

Mainframes have been the mainstay of commercial automatic data processing since the early valve machines in the 1950s. The second generation of mainframes used discrete transistors and a third generation, using LSI logic, was introduced in the 1960s.

There is a fine line between current mainframes and super-minicomputers, but a mainframe may be described as a computer with high processing power (3 to 30 Mips) intended to form a central facility for many users. Mainframes are frequently used for commercial data processing and many mainframes are plug-compatible with IBM machines.

11.2.6 Super-minicomputers

Super-minicomputers are high-performance minicomputers (1 to 15 Mips) with a word length of at least 32-bits, used for a wide range of scientific, engineering and commercial applications. Architectures tend to be scalar and several dual-processor super-minicomputers are available at the upper end of the performance range. Microcomputers based on multiple 32-bit general-purpose microprocessors are expected to replace super-minicomputers, initially at the low performance end of the market, but as microprocessor speed increases, the entire super-minicomputer market may be vulnerable.

11.2.7 Minicomputers

Minicomputers were first developed in the 1960s as small, inexpensive alternatives to mainframes and throughout the 1970s minicomputers became extremely popular but in the 1980s they are being replaced by microcomputers in most applications.

Minicomputers are mostly constructed from discrete LSI logic and bit-slice ALU elements. Many minicomputer families have been replaced by microcomputers with the same internal architecture, e.g. the DEC PDP11 range has been superseded by the Micro-PDP range.

11.2.8 Microcomputers

Microcomputers may be defined as small computers using one or more microprocessors as the processing element. Many specialised forms of microcomputer have been developed including personal computers, workstations, control computers, communications processors, and digital signal processors.

11.2.9 Digital signal processors

Digital signal processors are computers which accept digitised signal information and perform mathematical operations on it before outputting the results in digital or analog form. A single specialised digital signal processing chip is frequently employed but computer arrays are becoming viable alternatives for high-performance applications where a high degree of parallelism exists.

11.3 Summary of computer architectures

11.3.1 Scalar and vector architectures

The major architectural difference between conventional scientific and commercial computers is that commercial computers (minicomputers, superminicomputers, mainframes and mega-mainframes) mainly have a scalar architecture and scientific computers (supercomputers, mini-supercomputers and array processors) have a vector architecture.

A scalar architecture (see Figure 11.1) is based upon the conventional von Neumann or SISD design which has a single data bus and executes single data elements (scalars) in sequence. A vector machine (see Figure 11.2) employs separate vector processors, or pipelines, to make a single instruction operate on several data elements (vectors). Vector architectures are mostly of the SIMD type but some could fall in the MIMD classification. Vector processing increases the performance of the processing elements but does not permit other than fine-grain parallelism in the processing task.

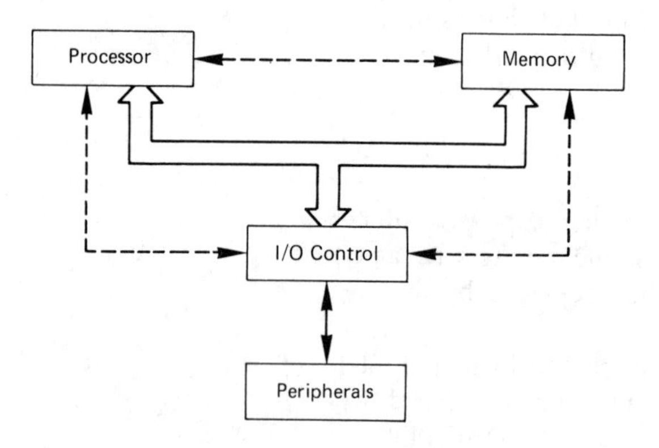

Fig. 11.1 A scalar computer

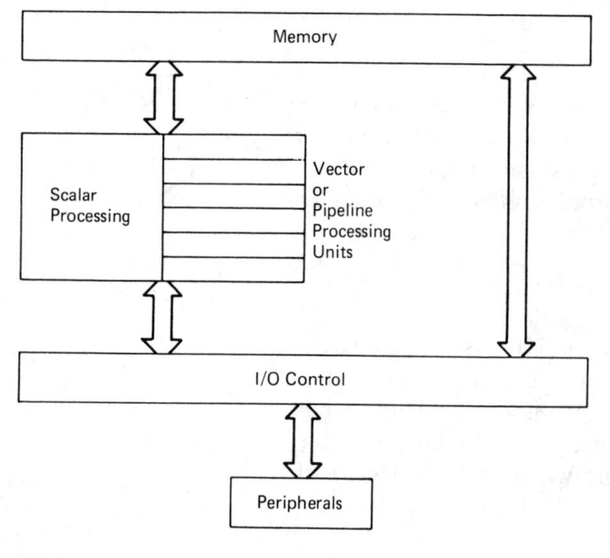

Fig. 11.2 A vector computer

11.3.2 Parallel system architectures

Parallelism may be used to improve the performance of computers at several levels:

a) Between jobs or phases of a job
b) Between parts of a program or within DO loops
c) Between phases of instruction execution
d) Between elements of a vector operation or within arithmetic logic circuits.

Categories *a* and *b* fall within the scope of what may be called parallel computers but *c* and *d* are a fine-grain form of parallelism which may be used in sequential processing units and are often implemented by a pipelined processor.

Basic forms of parallel multiprocessor architecture currently in use or being developed include:

1 *Control-flow*, which uses a control processor to send instructions to many processing elements, each consisting of a processor and associated memory. (See Figure 11.3.)

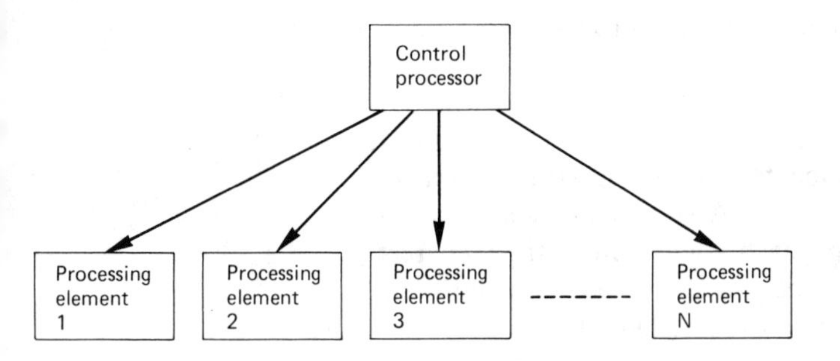

Fig. 11.3 A control-flow architecture

2 *Dataflow*, which is highly decentralised with parallel instructions sent along with data to many equivalent processing elements.
3 *Demand-driven*, which breaks tasks into less-complicated sub-tasks which, after processing, are recombined to produce the final result. The instruction to be executed is identified when its result is needed by another active instruction.
4 *Pattern-driven*, which breaks tasks into less-complicated sub-tasks which, after processing, are recombined to produce the final result. The instruction to be executed is identified when some enabling pattern or condition is matched. Typical applications are in pattern recognition using cellular arrays of processing elements.
5 *Shared-memory computers*, which employ some form of interconnection system to link processors with memory. Interconnection systems include buses, rings, cubes, caches, or cross-bar switches. (See Figure 11.4.)
6 *Concurrent processors*, which employ a high-level form of parallelism to permit independent operation of several computing activities on several processors. The hypercube or binary-n cube is a popular form of concurrent processing structure using message-passing point-to-point links between

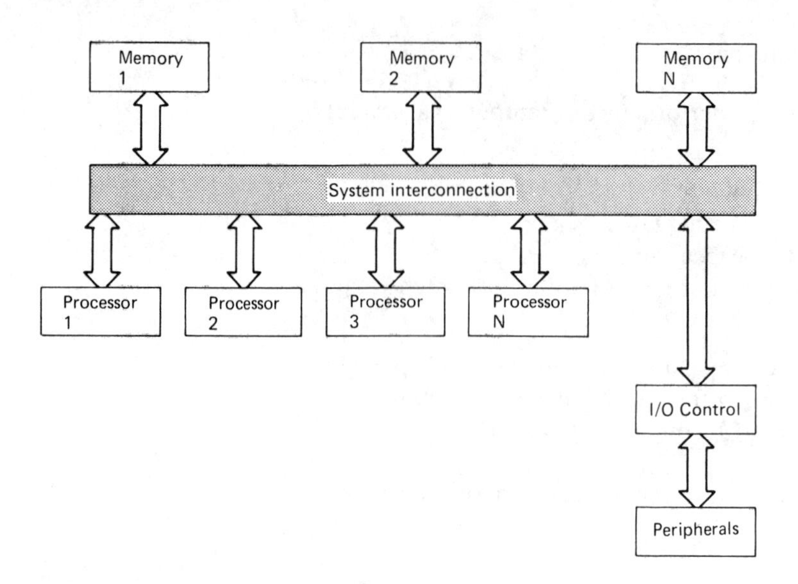

Fig. 11.4 A shared-memory parallel processor

computing nodes. A 16-node cube links each node to its four nearest neighbours.

(Shared memory computers may also be concurrent processors.)

11.3.3 Computer arrays

MIMD arrays or processors may be connected as systolic arrays or wavefront arrays for signal processing applications. A *systolic array* is an array of individual processing nodes which are each connected to their nearest neighbours in a regular lattice. Most of the processors perform the same basic operation and the signal processing task is distributed across the processor array in a highly pipelined fashion. The processors operate synchronously using a globally distributed clock.

A *wavefront array* distributes the processing function across the array, like the systolic array, but it does not operate synchronously from a global clock. Each processor is controlled locally and depends on the necessary input data being available from the appropriate neighbouring processor. The resulting processing wavefront develops across the array as input data is processed and passed on to other processors in the array.

11.3.4 Achievable performance

A single processor is unlikely to be able to achieve more than 2 Gflops before the common bus and the CPU become overloaded. A high-performance computer must therefore make use of some form of parallelism. The potential increase in performance which may be achieved by a parallel processing system depends upon the fraction of the computation which can be performed in parallel. Figure 11.5 shows performance improvement which may be achieved by various numbers of processors in parallel against the fraction P of parallel processing possible. The relationship between

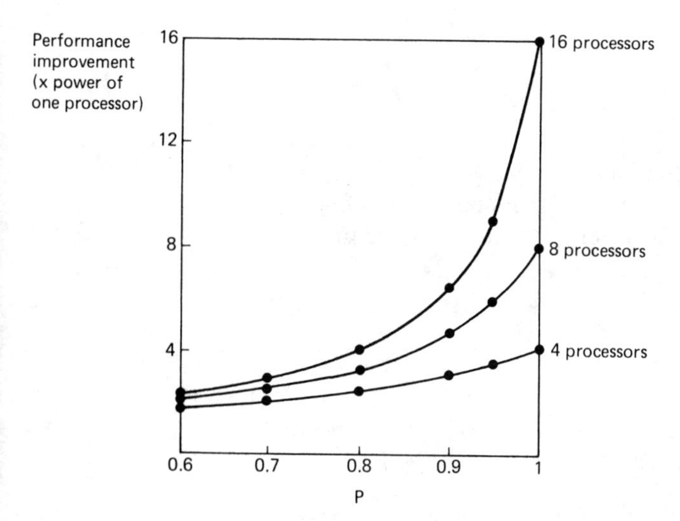

Fig. 11.5 Typical performance improvement achieved by parallel processors against the fraction *P* of computation which can be performed in parallel

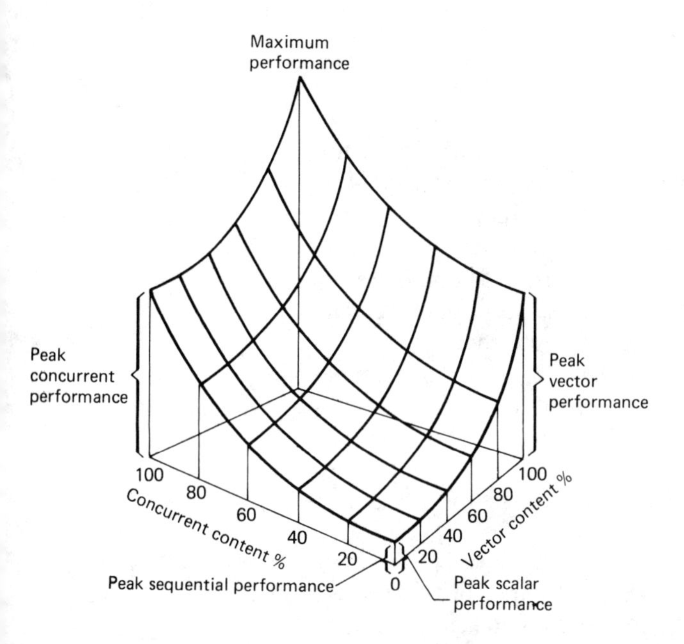

Fig. 11.6 Relationship between a computer's vector, concurrent and scalar processing performance

a computer's ability to perform vector, concurrent and scalar operations is shown in Figure 11.6. The increase in performance achieved from vector and concurrent processing is multiplicative so computing algorithms which demonstrate both forms of parallelism are considerably speeded-up.

Scientific processing frequently has a large vector and concurrent processing element and therefore a concurrent processing system with vector processing capability (to speed up the operation of each processor) may be used to achieve levels of performance much greater than the theoretical 2 Gflops limit of a single processor. Commercial processing, on the other hand, tends to be mostly scalar and there is therefore less scope for increasing the power of mainframes and mega-mainframes by the use of parallel processing.

11.4 Communicating process computers

11.4.1 Alternative structures

Concurrent computers which are built from large numbers of processors, each with private memory and using interprocessor links for communication between processes, can be interconnected in several topological structures including:

a) Tree networks
b) Buses
c) Pipelines
d) FFT butterfly connections
e) Shuffle exchange networks
f) Hypercubes
g) Meshes or arrays in 1, 2, 3 or more dimensions
h) Rings
i) Cylinders
j) Toroids
k) Pyramid networks.

These structures may be compared in terms of: the ease with which the structure may be constructed from practical devices such as the transputer; the complexity of the interconnection network; the ease with which the structure can be extended; and the compatibility between the application algorithm and the structure. For specific applications, the topology may easily be tailored to the algorithm but a general-purpose machine may find other factors more important than matching the algorithm.

Figure 11.7 shows a selection of topologies which may be found suitable for some practical algorithms. The *tree network* suffers from variable delays as more nodes are added to a sub-tree when data from all the nodes in one sub-tree must be passed to another sub-tree. A *bus network* is susceptible to overloading when all the connected nodes wish to transmit and an arbitration mechanism is required.

The throughput of a *pipeline* is limited by the throughput of the slowest part of the pipeline. For example, an N-stage pipeline would have a processing time of $N \times$ the longest time taken for any stage. An equivalent parallel element implementation would require a processing time which is the sum of the times taken for each stage. A pipeline also requires processing time to pass messages from one stage to the next. There may however be sequential dependencies in the data which make a parallel element implementation impractical in which case the performance of a pipeline may be the same yet the code size may be much smaller because the sequential dependencies require no additional processing.

To overcome some of the limitations of the traditional communications networks, high-flux networks have been developed. *Flux* is a measure of the ability of a network to transfer data from one arbitrary point to another. Three high-flux networks have been found suitable for *concurrent* applications:

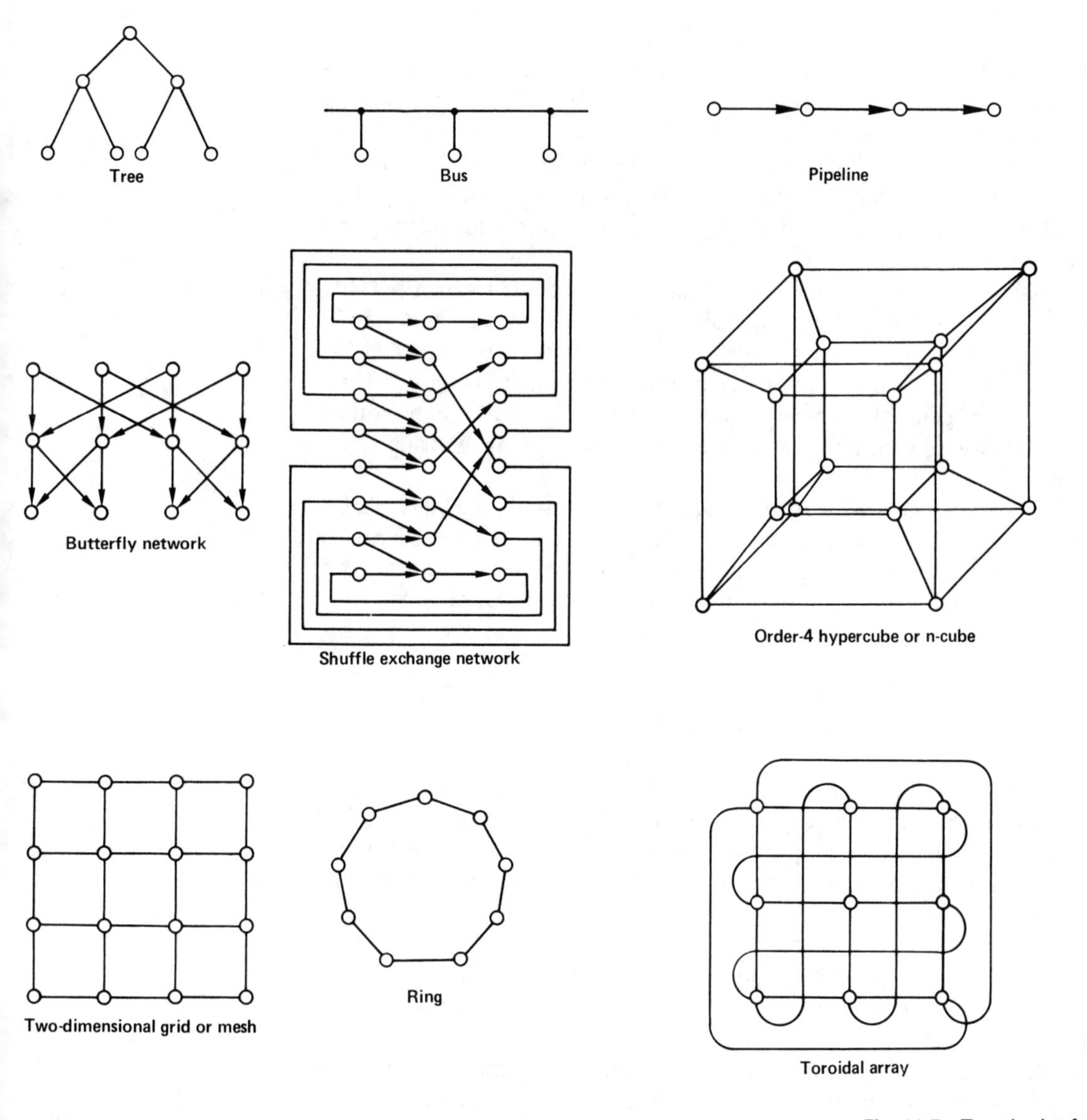

Fig. 11.7 Topologies for concurrent processors

a) The butterfly network
b) The shuffle exchange network
c) The hypercube

The *butterfly network* developed by Rabiner and Gold in the late 1960s increases the speed of calculating fast Fourier transforms (FFTs). Each pass of the butterfly algorithm requires four multiplications and six additions for complex variables. To perform an N-point complex FFT, the butterfly algorithm must be executed $N/2 \log_2 N$ times which is a considerable improvement on the digital Fourier transform algorithm which requires $4N^2$ multiplications and $4N^2$ additions.

The *shuffle exchange network* was developed in the late 1960s by M. C. Pease and H. S. Stone working independently and offers an alternative connection network to the butterfly for performing fast Fourier transforms and other signal processing algorithms. To perform an FFT the shuffle network combines pairs of elements with indices that differ by four in their binary expansions. After one shuffle, the pairs differ by two and, after the final iteration, by one. The shuffle network requires $\log_2 N$ steps to complete an N-point FFT.

The *hypercube* or *binary N-cube* is a theoretical concept which permits extension to more than three dimensions. An n-dimension cube has 2^n nodes. Where nodes are numbered 0 to 2^{n-1} each node is connected to all other nodes which differ in number by one binary digit. The hypercube is suitable for general-purpose computer arrays because many other network topologies can be mapped onto the hypercube by ignoring some connections.

Grid or mesh networks are arrays in one, two or more dimensions. These networks are suited to systolic and wavefront arrays where each cell is connected to its nearest neighbours in each dimension. Cylinders and toroids are variations on the mesh network where the number of dimensions used and the surface topology are selected to match the application algorithm.

11.4.2 Communication requirements

Many applications are insensitive to the structure of the processors on which they are run, subject to the availability of adequate communication bandwidth. Pipelines and simple two-dimensional arrays can most easily be implemented and extended while more complex arrays and hypercubes become more difficult to implement as the number of dimensions increases. With more than 1000 nodes, the communications required between non-adjacent nodes in a hypercube imposes overheads and the number of links required by each node must be at least as great as the dimension of the hypercube.

To overcome limitations in the number of links available on each node of a hypercube, each node may be constructed as a ring of processors such as the transputer (known as cube connected cycles) which makes more links available for hypercube connections.

When two non-adjacent nodes need to communicate via intermediate nodes, the network should desirably make the worst-case path between the nodes (called the network diameter) as small as possible in relation to the total number of nodes. A one-dimensional array, with a diameter which is equal to the number of nodes, is the worst case. More suitable structures include:

a) Hypercubes with a diameter $n-1$ and size 2^n.
b) Cube-connected cycles with a diameter $(n \times 5)/2$ and size $n \times 2^n$.
c) Folded trees with a diameter n and size $n \times 2^{n-1}$.

In each intermediate node some form of message-routing algorithm will be required. A simple routing algorithm may be implemented in a transputer. This algorithm examines the first word of a message, from a link or a co-resident process, to determine the destination and uses a routing table to determine whether to send the message to a local process or to send the message down a link. The processing load imposed by this routing algorithm is small because, once the data transfer has been initiated, the links operate autonomously. It is therefore desirable to minimise the number of messages and to maximise the length of each message except when message delay is an important consideration.

It is desirable to organise numerical problems to make computing time much greater than communication time. For example, a problem which inputs two $n \times n$ arrays and outputs the product requires $3 \times n^2$ communication operations but the computation involves n^3 operations.

11.4.3 Some applications of transputer arrays

The Royal Signals and Radar Establishment in Malvern, England has undertaken an evaluation of transputer arrays for signal processing applications. Some of the conclusions from a paper by J. G. Harp, J. B. G. Roberts and J. S. Ward are described here.

It has been found that a simple two-dimensional array of transputers provides ample scope for indirect routing of messages without a significant reduction in data rates, assuming relatively short block lengths (up to 10 words of 16 bits) are used. This makes it practical to implement self-routing around congested sections of an array. Where a tree or pyramid network may seem appropriate for an algorithm, a standard array is acceptable because messages may be routed indirectly rather than through direct connections and self-routing may be adopted to avoid congestion.

Images of 256×256 pixels from a frame store may be partitioned into 32×32 pixel sub-images which are stored and processed by an individual transputer in a two-dimensional 8×8 array (see Figure 11.8). Additional transputers are used for global operations, accepting images and formatting them for display. Images are fed to each column of the array from the frame store and each processor passes appropriate sub-image data to other processors in the column.

Various image processing algorithms have been performed on smaller arrays with the following predicted execution times (excluding data input time) relating to an array of 64 transputers, each using a 20 MHz clock:

a) 3×3 convolution, as used for image smoothing and edge detection, takes 16 ms.

b) 3×3 median filtering, as used for noise reduction without edge degradation, takes 2 ms.

c) Producing a local histogram (32×32 pixels), as used for segmentation of threshold values or object classification, takes 44 μs.

d) Producing a global histogram (256×256 pixels) and distributing this to each processor to set image thresholds takes 3 ms.

e) Normalisation to stretch the intensity in each local area of the image, to match the display luminance range and to determine the global maximum, takes 3 ms.

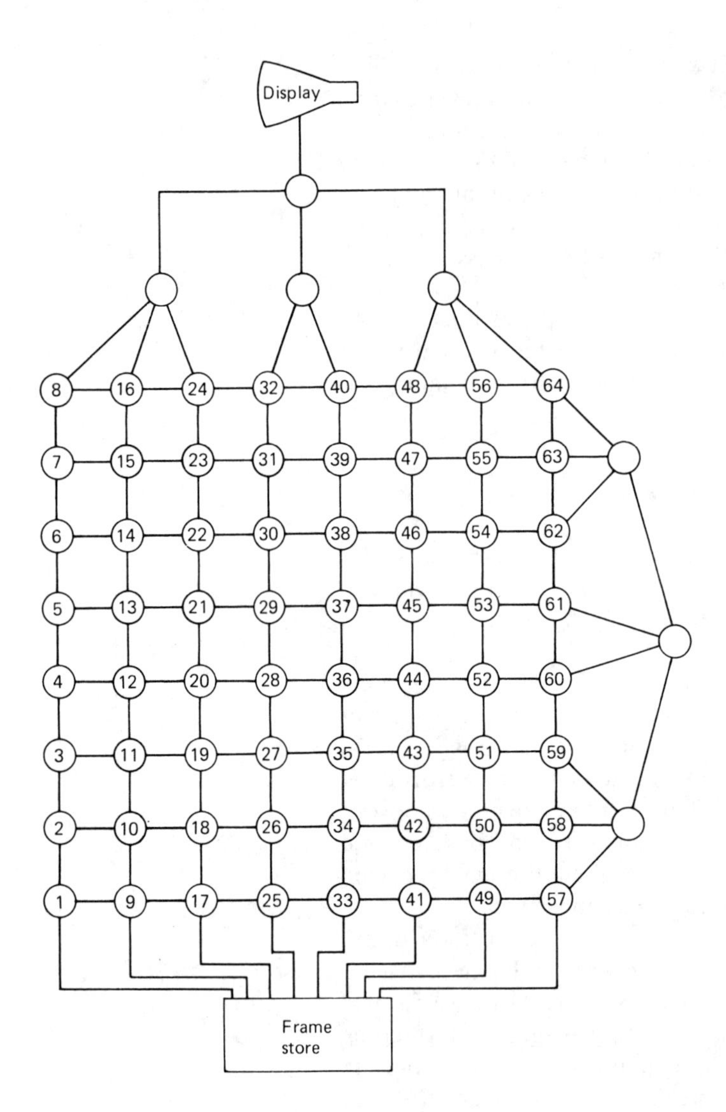

Fig. 11.8 An image processing array of 64 transputers

f) Producing a binary image for each pixel, based on a threshold value which is a local mean intensity level, takes 800 μs.
g) Binary image thinning, which reduces objects in a binary image to pixel-wide skeletons for object classification, takes 16 ms maximum.

From these results it was concluded that the array of 64 transputers can perform image processing on real time television images, and communication times are small compared with processing times.

For fast Fourier transforms, a single transputer with a 4 Kbyte on-chip memory can store up to 256 points without requiring external memory. Using integer arithmetic, a 20 MHz transputer using pre-calculated twiddle factors and both data and program stored in on-chip memory is expected to perform an N-point complex FFT in

$$2.1 + \log_2 2N(2.9 + 9.3N)\ \mu s$$

For a 128-point transform the data rate may be 15.3 k samples / second assuming a butterfly execution time of 17 μs.

A pipeline of $\log_2 N + 1$ transputers can be employed to perform fast Fourier transforms with each transputer performing $N/2$ butterflies. The time between successive transforms is $(9.3N + 4.0)$ μs and throughput is limited by the slowest stage in the pipeline. Eight transputers can perform a 128-point FFT at 107 k samples/second.

An alternative FFT implementation is the constant geometry form which uses $N/2$ transputers to perform one pass of the FFT and this is repeated $\log_2 N$ times to form the result. By this method the transputer only has to store data for one butterfly at a time so no restriction applies to the number of points. The time between successive transforms is 13.3 $\log_2 N$ μs. Sixty-four transputers could perform a 128-point FFT at 1.37 M samples/second.

The most computer-intensive implementation of the FFT uses one transputer per butterfly; this reduces the time between transforms to 12.6 μs and 448 transputers could perform a 128-point transform at 10 M samples/second.

A wavefront array of transputers has been constructed to perform least squares minimisation. Each processor is connected to its nearest neighbours as shown in Figure 11.9. Unlike the systolic array, no global clock is used and the speed of operation is not limited by the slowest processor in the array. The boundary nodes perform one part of the computation while the internal nodes perform the second operation. The data generator generates simulated data and the lower node receives the result and formats it for display.

The asynchronous wavefront processor has demonstrated a higher throughput than an equivalent synchronous systolic array. A systolic array of 20 MHz transputers is expected to be capable of 70 kHz throughout.

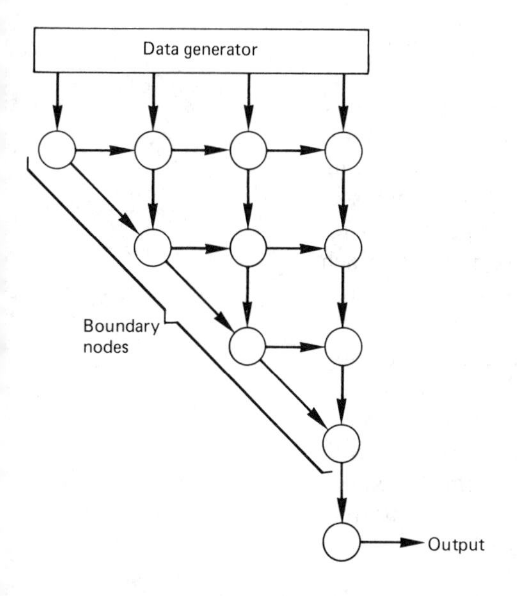

Fig. 11.9 A wavefront array for least squares minimisation

11.4.4 The Meiko computing surface

Meiko was set up by engineers and programmers who had worked on the development of the Inmos transputer; their objective was to exploit the transputer to produce a flexible, expansible, concurrent mini-supercomputer with a cost/Mips of around $250 and a maximum performance over 1000 Mips.

Meiko rejected rigid fixed topologies for the computing surface because they considered them to be compromises which prevent complete flexibility. Different applications require different solutions; the optimum topology differs between problems and different resources may be required. For instance, some applications are computing-intensive and others require rapid database access.

The computing surface retains its flexibility by providing a set of modular subsystems which may be configured into any topology to suit the application. The computing surface can be treated as a processor farm, operated as a multi-task environment with a separate, independent task per computing element. In this case many existing applications can be run with virtually no modification. Alternatively the machine's innate concurrency can be adopted in an application which views the machine as a homogeneous processing resource.

A support infrastructure is provided to enable a host computer to build a physical map of the entire computing surface. Using this map and electronic configuration, it wires a machine topology to a high-level specification derived from the application program which is to be loaded. Software specifies both the application program and the machine on which it will be executed. Programs may be written in Occam or in other languages such as Fortran, C, Pascal, etc. These programs run in an Occam harness to handle communication with other processors which may be executing copies of the same program.

The development process provides support for hierarchical program source management, automatic recompilation, run-time error reporting, and the loading and running of distributed multiprocessor programs using single-function key commands.

The small desktop M10 computing surface can provide 250 Mips and is suitable for personal, workstation or development use. Larger systems use the M40 module, a single one of which can yield configurations ranging from a compute engine giving an aggregate 1100 Mips with 42 Mbytes of concurrently addressed dynamic RAM, to a database machine with 315 Mbytes of store, 400 Mips and over 75 Mbyte/s disk bandwidth. Each M40 is a small module 40 inch × 20 inch × 20 inch and as many as required may be interconnected with unrestricted connectivity.

Several boards and subsystems are available to create a customised computing surface module. All computing elements conform to the same generic model (see Figure 11.10) to provide a logically consistent interface to the application programmer. Each element is based upon a transputer with its own interface to the global supervisory bus and a private local memory in addition to specialised function units. Every element has eight unidirectional serial communication channels operating at 10 or 20 Mbit/s.

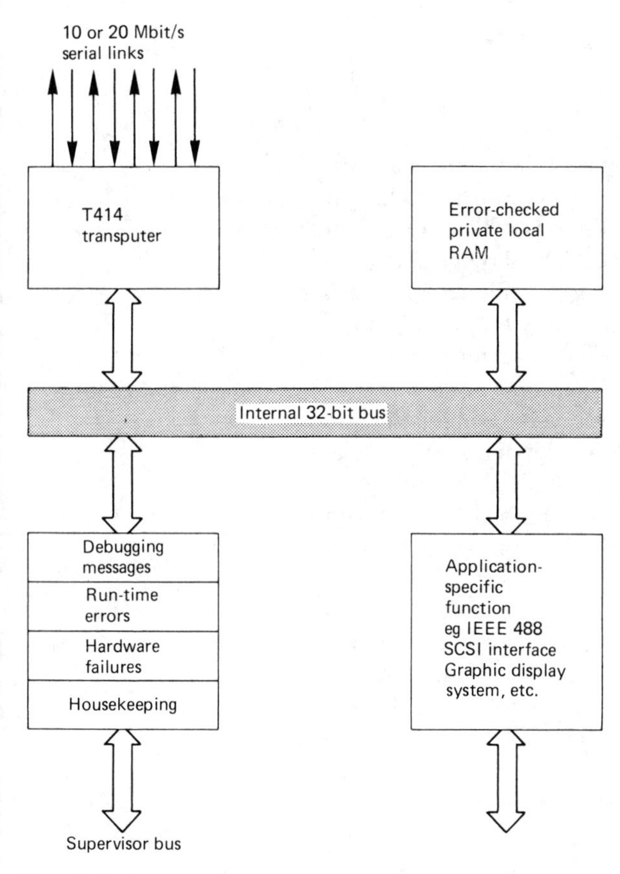

Fig. 11.10 Generic model for a computing element of the Meiko Computing Surface

Specialised function boards include:

a) *Quad Computing Element* containing four computing elements each with a T414 transputer, 256 Kbytes of error checked RAM, eight unidirectional serial links, and an interface to the supervisory bus.

b) *Mass Store* containing a T414 transputer, 8 Mbytes of error checked RAM, eight unidirectional serial links, an interface to the supervisory bus, and a 2 Mbyte/s DMA-controlled SCSI peripheral interface. 500 Mbyte winchester disks and 2 Gbyte laser disks are available for connection to this interface.

c) *Local Host* (IEEE 488) containing a T414 transputer, 3 Mbytes of error checked RAM, 128 Kbytes of EPROM, eight unidirectional serial links, an interface to the supervisory bus, an IEEE 488 parallel interface, and dual RS-232 serial interfaces.

d) *Display Element* containing a T414 transputer, 128 Kbytes of private static RAM, 1.5 Mbytes of dual ported display store, eight unidirectional serial links, an interface to the supervisory bus, a 70 MHz pixel rate (200 Mbyte/s) external pixel highway, and a CCIR/RS-343 compatible colour video generator. Multiple display elements may be ganged to provide a larger-format frame store or to increase drawing bandwidth.

Higher-performance computing elements are available using the T800 transputer which has an improved floating-point capability and 4 Kbytes of on-chip RAM.

11.5 Hypercube architectures for supercomputers

11.5.1 The hypercube or binary N-cube

The hypercube architecture was originally developed at the California Institute of Technology and uses many individual microprocessors, each with associated local memory, to form computational nodes which are linked together by point-to-point communication channels. A hypercube of dimension n connects together $N = 2^n$ nodes which operate independently on a part of the overall program. For example, a binary-6 cube connects together 64 nodes with each node connected to six adjacent neighbours in a 6-dimensional hypercube.

Data may be entered into a node by messages sent on the communication channels from processes in other nodes or from a cube manager. Special operating system primitives are used to direct the sending and receiving of messages. The communication bandwidth of a hypercube increases with the number of nodes (proportional to $N \log_2 N$) and the worst-case message latency is $\log_2 N$.

A hypercube can be defined inductively; a hypercube of order $n+1$ may be constructed by duplicating a hypercube of order n and connecting the two sets of nodes together. This makes it possible to write software for a hypercube of any dimensions; the dimension need only be defined at run-time. It is also possible to split a large hypercube machine into sub-cubes, to allocate the maximum effective number of nodes to each program, and to use the surplus nodes on another program rather than leaving them unused.

The hypercube is the most densely connected network which may be scaled up to thousands of processors because only one additional communications channel must be added to each node in order to double the number of processors. The dense interconnection of nodes makes it practical to assume full connectivity which is an important approximation for parallel computation because the communication pattern is frequently not predictable.

If the nodes are numbered 0 to 2^{n-1}, each processor is directly connected to all others whose numbers differ by one binary digit. Many other network topologies can be mapped onto a hypercube by ignoring some of the hypercube connections. These topologies include:

a) Grids or meshes up to dimension N
b) Rings
c) Cylinders
d) Toroids
e) FFT butterfly connections.

A hypercube uses a high-level form of parallelism known as concurrent processing which allows asynchronous operation of processors in a multiprocessor system. Vector processing may also be employed to increase the performance of individual nodes where a high vector processing content is present in the application. As shown in Figure 11.6 the maximum performance which may be achieved by such a computer system is the product of the concurrent, vector and scalar performance for the particular application. A concurrent processing language such as Occam should be used to achieve the maximum performance feasible within the limitation imposed by the concurrent content of the application.

11.5.2 The Intel iPSC-VX hypercube

The Intel iPSC was one of the first hypercube systems made available commercially and has a maximum performance of 424 Mflops. Subsequent hypercube systems intended for scientific applications include:

a) Floating Point Systems T-series which has a maximum performance of 262 Gflops.
b) N Cube / Ten which has a maximum performance of 500 Mflops.
c) Thinking Machines Connection Machine expected to have a maximum integer performance of 2 billion additions per second.

The Intel iPSC-VX uses a standard 80286 microprocessor with an 80287 numeric coprocessor, an 82586 LAN coprocessor, seven serial I/O channels, 512 Kbytes of dynamic RAM, and 64 Kbytes of EPROM on a circuit board which functions as a node in the hypercube. (See Figure 11.11.) More memory may be added to a node using a local bus extension (iLBX-II)

Fig. 11.11 An iPSC-VX node

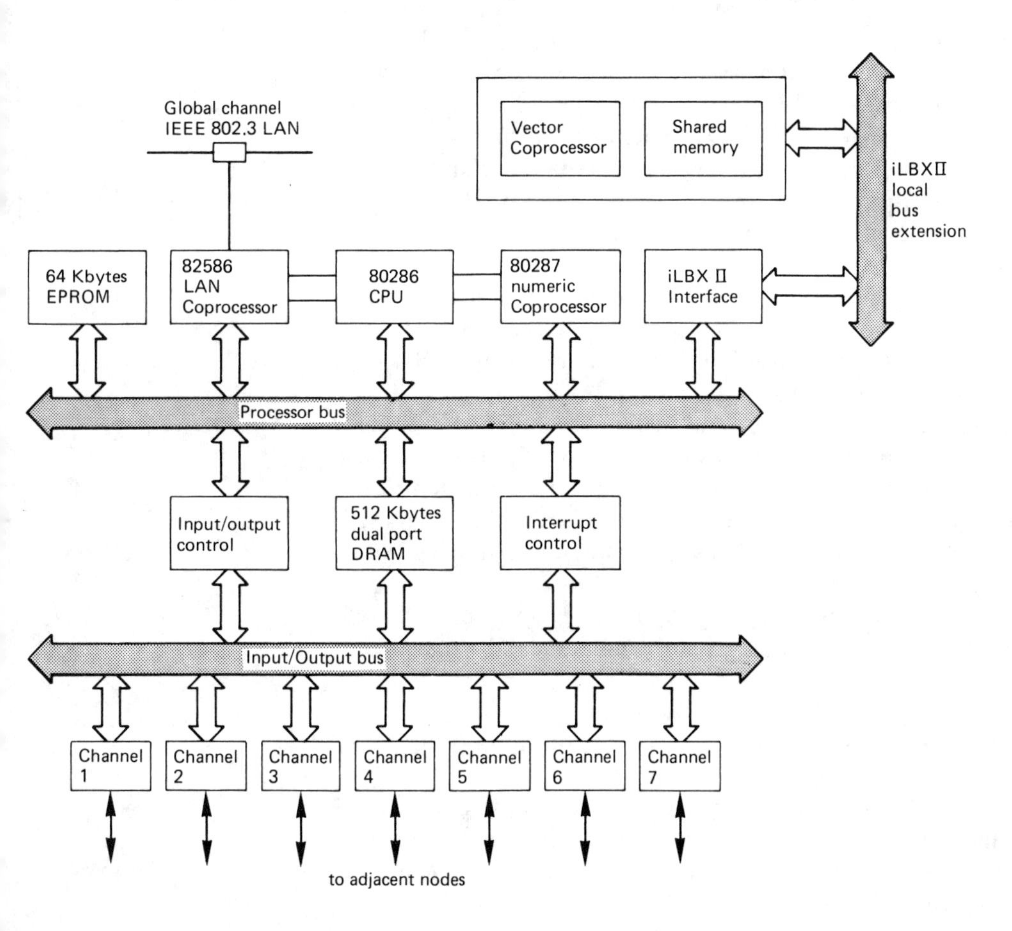

bus interface. The VX version has a second board connected by a shared memory interface; this board has a vector coprocessor which enhances the performance of the node by a factor of up to 100 times for 64-bit vector operations and up to 10 times for 64-bit scalar operations.

The iPSC-VX system can be expanded in groups of 16, 32 or 64 nodes accommodated in one, two or four computational units, respectively. A cube manager, which is an Intel system 286/310 microcomputer, is connected to each node by an IEEE 802.3 local area network (the global channel) and provides a system interface plus a Xenix-based software development system. Point-to-point links between the nodes are provided by the seven serial I/O channels and these carry the majority of message transfers. Seven links per node permit a maximum hypercube of $N = 2^7 = 128$ nodes.

The node operating system kernel is held in RAM and provides basic services such as interprocess communication, process management, physical memory management and protected address space. A monitor program is held in EPROM, and is used to initialise the node at power-up or reset. Once the monitor has verified that the node is operable, it loads the kernel and application software from the cube manager.

The communication primitives provided by the operating system are the same whether the processes are in the same node or elsewhere. A common message format is used for all functions. Messages may be queued but are always received in the order generated by the sending process. Message routing is performed by the operating system using channels, and a process sends or receives a message by invoking operating system calls. Messages over 1 Kbyte in length are automatically split up into smaller messages and reassembled at the destination without user intervention. Point-to-point transmission between adjacent nodes incorporates end-to-end acknowledgements but this is not provided between more distant nodes.

To program an application for the hypercube, an algorithm must be developed to define the discrete processes which make up the application. Process descriptions are assigned to specific nodes by the programmer in a manner which models the application as well as is possible. Software may be written in Fortran, C or ASM 286.

Most applications have both vector and scalar elements and each node of a concurrent processing system solves a portion of the vector element and a portion of the scalar element. When vector and concurrent forms of parallelism are present in a problem, vector-concurrent computers such as the iPSC-VX can achieve superior performance compared with pure vector or concurrent processors.

Unlike pure vector supercomputers, the hypercube can be used to solve non-numerical problems such as event-driven simulation and artificial intelligence applications.

11.5.3 The FPS T-series homogeneous vector supercomputer

The Floating Point Systems Inc. T-series offered potential performance greater than any other supercomputer at its time of introduction in 1986. The top end of the series, the T/40 000, has 16 384 nodes, each incorporating an Inmos T414 transputer and a 16 Mflop 64-bit floating-point vector processor to give a maximum potential power of 262 Gflops and up to 16 Gbytes of main memory.

A smaller T/20 system with 256 Mflop performance, achieved by connecting sixteen processing nodes, sells for a small fraction of the cost of an equivalent supercomputer. The size, power consumption and cooling requirements are also much smaller than an equivalent vector supercomputer. The T/20 requires only one equipment cabinet and a normal office environment.

Software for the T-series is in the Occam parallel processing language which includes channel commands to transfer data between concurrent processes. Occam is able to specify or program the control and data flow for virtually any scientific computing algorithm and to control the operation of the vector arithmetic unit in each node. A library of mathematical subroutines, vector processor support, a communications library, system downloading and uploading functions, file system support and run-time diagnostics have all been added to the Occam development system.

Each node contains one T414 transputer (referred to as a control processor), a 64-bit floating-point vector processor, 1 Mbyte of dual-port RAM, and sixteen serial links, on a single circuit board. Eight node boards are connected to each other and to a system board to form a module. The system board has a disk interface to record memory snapshots for error recovery. Two modules, each containing eight nodes, are accommodated in a self-contained 19-inch rack-mounted assembly with disks and power supplies. To form larger systems, cabinets are interconnected by cables up to 40 ft in length.

The capability of each module is 128 Mflops peak floating-point performance and it can accommodate 8 Mbytes of RAM. The local inter-node communications bandwidth is 12 Mbyte/s and the system board has a bandwidth of 0.5 Mbyte/s available for external connections.

Figure 11.12 shows the major components of a node processor board. The T414 transputer (control processor) executes system and user applications code in scalar, integer arithmetic and sends vector operands to the floating-point vector arithmetic processor where they may be processed in parallel with the operation of the control processor. The 1 Mbyte dual-port memory is constructed from dynamic RAM and may be accessed by the control processor using a 32-bit random access port.

The vector processor accesses memory by a set of vector registers which are closely coupled to the memory and can access a 1024-byte row of memory in the same time as a single random access by the control processor. The vector processor accesses memory as two banks of vectors with 256 in one bank and 768 in the other. A vector is 256 elements long for 32-bit operations and 128 elements long for 64-bit operations. By using two memory banks, two memory accesses may be made by the arithmetic unit in a 125 ns ALU cycle. Some operations are able to progress at full ALU speed without being constrained by memory bandwidth.

The control processor is used to collect operands into contiguous vectors and to scatter the results back into various memory locations. The time taken to move a 64-bit operand from one memory location to another is 1.6 μs, in which time two 32-bit reads and two 32-bit writes are performed by the control processor. A 32-bit operand requires 0.8 μs per element. In 1.6 μs about 13 vector operations can take place while operation of the control processor and vector processor is overlapped.

A row of 1024 bytes of data can be moved into or out of a vector register in 400 ns making the effective bandwidth between memory and the vector register 2650 Mbyte/s. The vector registers can each supply data to the

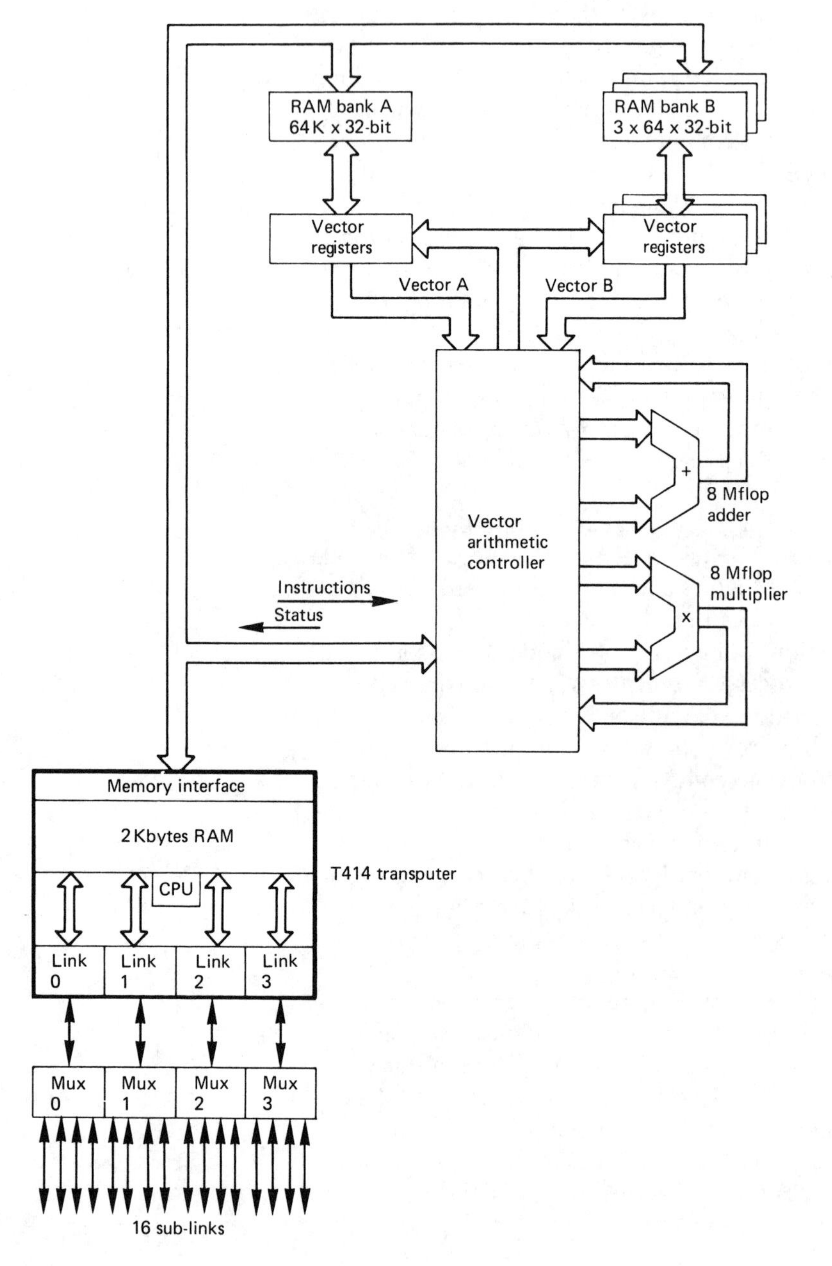

Fig. 11.12 A node processor board of the FPS T-series

ALU at 62.5 ns intervals for 32-bit words or 125 ns for 64-bit words. Two vector inputs and one vector output may be performed every 125 ns making the maximum bandwidth between the vector registers and the ALU 192 Mbyte/s.

The vector processor incorporates a floating-point adder and a floating-point multiplier which can each produce a 32 or 64-bit result every 125 ns. This is equivalent to 16 Mflops peak performance. Sixty-four-bit floating-point gives about 15 decimal digits precision and the 11-bit binary exponent gives a dynamic range of 10^{-308} to 10^{+308}. The adder has a six-stage pipeline but the multiplier has a five-stage pipeline in 32-bit mode and a seven-stage pipeline in 64-bit mode.

A micro-sequencer controls the adder and multiplier, translating the input and output vector and the form of vector operation required into the required sequence of activities. Scalars may be held in the floating-point input registers and the outputs may be fed back as inputs to perform dot product and sum operations. The vector processor interrupts the control processor when the vector operation is complete or if an error has occurred.

The four serial links on the T414 have a maximum data rate of 0.5 Mbyte/s when the overhead bits are taken into account. Each link is multiplexed

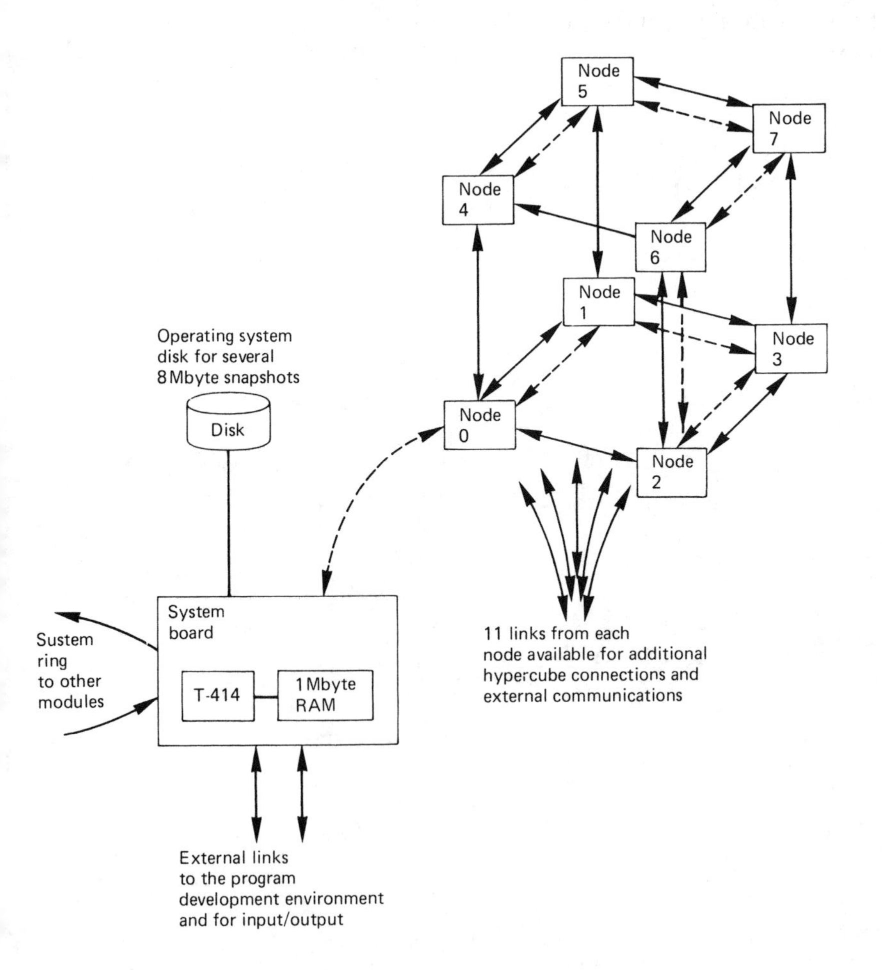

Fig. 11.13 System board connections within a module of the FPS T-series

four ways to provide sixteen bi-directional sub-links per node, each with a maximum bandwidth of 0.125 Mbyte/s. This rate of transfer between nodes permits about 100 vector operations to be performed for every 64-bit word which is moved between nodes over a link.

The system board is connected to each node within the module by a chain of communications links as shown in Figure 11.13. The system ring, which links all system boards in the computer, is independent of the hypercube network which interconnects the processor nodes. Each node uses three links for intra-module hypercube communication and the system board requires two links from each node, leaving eleven links for further hypercube and external communications.

Probably the largest practical system, a 12-cube, consisting of 4096 nodes may be constructed using 256 cabinets (512 modules) to provide over 65 Gflops peak processing performance and 4 Gbytes of RAM. Such a system would consume about 256 kW of electrical power and would therefore require special accommodation, whereas smaller systems require no special accommodation. Because each module is identical and has identical connections to other modules, a completely homogeneous system is produced and programming is greatly simplified. To construct a 14-cube with 16 384 nodes, the two links per node required for external input/output and mass storage must be dedicated to hypercube links, making the system unsuitable for many practical applications.

Standards and References

MC68020 32-Bit Microprocessor User's Manual, Motorola Ref: MC68020-UM(ADI).

Transputer Reference Manual, Inmos: 72 TRN04801.

Transputer Compiler Writer's Guide (Draft), 19 February 1986.

The OSI Reference Model, *Proceedings of the IEEE*, Vol. 71, No. 12, December 1983.

IEEE Std. 488–1978, *IEEE Standard Digital Interface for Programmable Instrumentation*.

EIA Standard RS-232-C (August 1969), *Interface between Data Terminal Equipment and Data Communication Equipment Employing Serial Binary Data Interchange*.

EIA Standard RS-422 (April 1975), *Electrical Characteristics of Balanced Voltage Digital Interface Circuits*.

EIA Standard RS-423 (April 1975), *Electrical Characteristics of Unbalanced Voltage Digital Interface Circuits*.

EIA Standard RS-449 (November 1977), *General-purpose 37-position and 9-position Interface for Data Terminal Equipment and Data Circuit-terminating Equipment Employing Serial Binary Data Interchange*.

ANSI/IEEE Std. 802.3-1985, *Carrier Sense Multiple Access with Collision Detection (CSMA/CD): Access Method and Physical Layer Specifications*.

ANSI/IEEE Std. 802.4-1985, *Token Bus Access Method and Physical Layer Specifications*.

ANSI/IEEE Std. 802.5-1985, *Token Ring Access Method and Physical Layer Specifications*.

ANSI X3T9.5, *Fiber Distributed Data Interface* (FDDI).

J. G. Harp, J. B. G. Roberts and J. S. Ward (Royal Signals and Radar Establishment Malvern, Worcestershire, England), Signal Processing with Transputer Arrays (TRAPS), *Computer Physics Communications*, 1985.

Appendix A Motorola MC68020 data

This information is selected from Motorola product data on the MC68020, MC68881 and MC68851.

TABLE 5 — SIGNAL INDEX

Signal Name	Mnemonic	Function
Address Bus	A0-A31	32-bit address bus used to address any of 4,294,967,296 bytes.
Data Bus	D0-D31	32-bit data bus used to transfer 8, 16, 24, or 32 bits of data per bus cycle.
Function Codes	FC0-FC2	3-bit function code used to identify the address space of each bus cycle.
Size	SIZ0 SIZ1	Indicates the number of bytes remaining to be transferred for this cycle. These signals, together with A0 and A1, define the active sections of the data bus.
Read-Modify-Write Cycle	$\overline{RMC}$	Provides an indicator that the current bus cycle is part of an indivisible read-modify-write operation
External Cycle Start	$\overline{ECS}$	Provides an indication that a bus cycle is beginning.
Operand Cycle Start	$\overline{OCS}$	Identical operation to that of $\overline{ECS}$ except that $\overline{OCS}$ is asserted only during the first bus cycle of an operand transfer.
Address Strobe	$\overline{AS}$	Indicates that a valid address is on the bus.
Data Strobe	$\overline{DS}$	Indicates that valid data is to be placed on the data bus by an external device or has been placed on the data bus by the MC68020.
Read/Write	R/$\overline{W}$	Defines the bus transfer as an MPU read or write.
Data Buffer Enable	$\overline{DBEN}$	Provides an enable signal for external data buffers.
Data Transfer and Size Acknowledge	$\overline{DSACK0}$ $\overline{DSACK1}$	Bus response signals that indicate the requested data transfer operation is completed. In addition, these two lines indicate the size of the external bus port on a cycle-by-cycle basis.
Cache Disable	$\overline{CDIS}$	Dynamically disables the on-chip cache to assist emulator support.
Interrupt Priority Level	$\overline{IPL0}$-$\overline{IPL2}$	Provides an encoded interrupt level to the processor.
Autovector	$\overline{AVEC}$	Requests an autovector during an interrupt acknowledge cycle.
Interrupt Pending	$\overline{IPEND}$	Indicates that an interrupt is pending.
Bus Request	$\overline{BR}$	Indicates that an external device requires bus mastership.
Bus Grant	$\overline{BG}$	Indicates that an external device may assume bus mastership.
Bus Grant Acknowledge	$\overline{BGACK}$	Indicates that an external device has assumed bus mastership.
Reset	$\overline{RESET}$	System reset.
Halt	$\overline{HALT}$	Indicates that the processor should suspend bus activity.
Bus Error	$\overline{BERR}$	Indicates an invalid or illegal bus operation is being attempted.
Clock	CLK	Clock input to the processor.
Power Supply	V_{CC}	+5 ±5% volt power supply.
Ground	GND	Ground connection.

MC68020 Technical Summary

32-BIT VIRTUAL MEMORY MICROPROCESSOR

This document contains both a summary of the MC68020 as well as a detailed set of parametrics. The purpose is twofold – to provide an introduction to the MC68020 and support for the sophisticated user. For detailed information on the MC68020 refer to the *MC68020 User's Manual.*

The MC68020 is the first full 32-bit implementation of the M68000 Family of microprocessors from Motorola. Using VLSI technology, the MC68020 is implemented with 32-bit registers and data paths, 32-bit addresses, a rich basic instruction set, and versatile addressing modes. The resources available to the MC68020 user consist of the following:

- Virtual Memory/Machine Support
- Sixteen 32-Bit General-Purpose Data and Address Registers
- Two 32-Bit Supervisor Stack Pointers
- Five Special Purpose Control Registers
- 4 Gigabyte Direct Addressing Range
- 18 Addressing Modes
- Memory Mapped I/O
- Coprocessor Interface
- High Performance On-Chip Instruction Cache
- Operations on Seven Data Types
- Complete Floating-Point Support via MC68881 Coprocessor

FIGURE 1 — FUNCTIONAL SIGNAL GROUPS

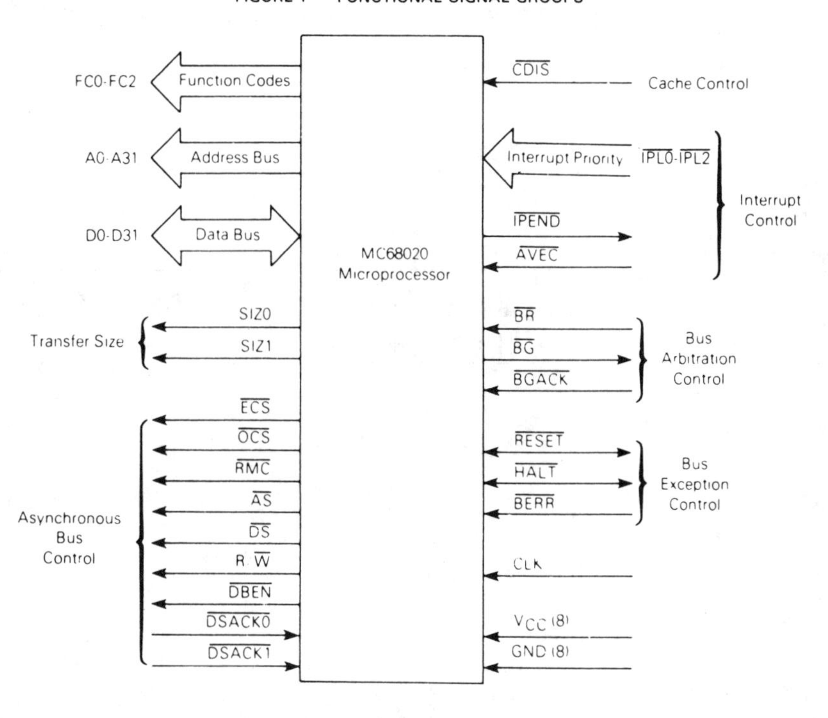

MECHANICAL DATA AND ORDERING INFORMATION

MC68020
RC Suffix Package
Preliminary Mechanical Detail

DIM	INCHES		INCHES	
	MIN	MAX	MIN	MAX
A	34.18	34.90	1.345	1.375
B	34.18	34.90	1.345	1.375
C	2.67	3.17	.100	.150
D0	.46	.51	.017	.019
G	2.54 BSC		.100 BSC	
K	4.32	4.82	.170	.190
V	1.74	2.28	.065	.095

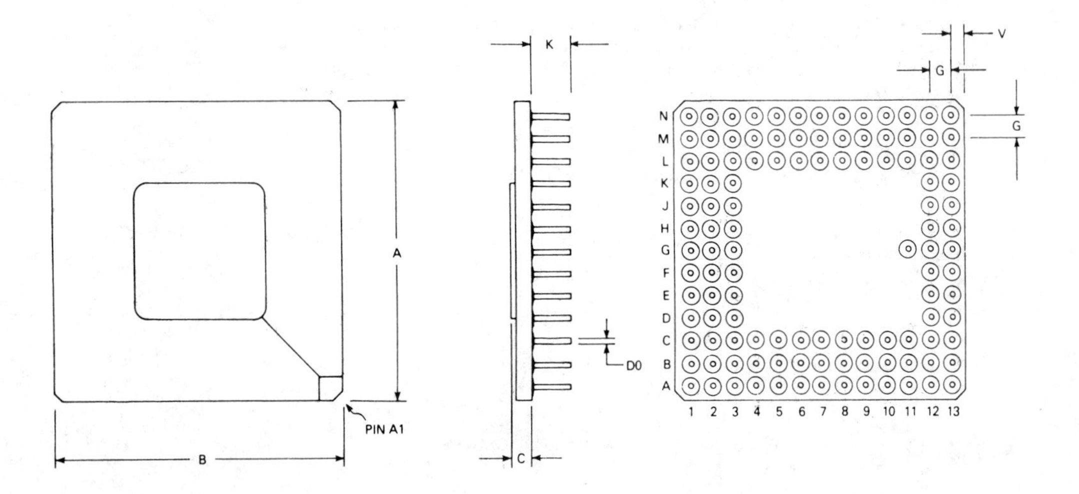

ORDERING INFORMATION

Package Type	Frequency (MHz)	Temperature	Order Number
Pin Grid Array RC Suffix	12.5 16.7	0°C to 70°C 0°C to 70°C	MC68020R12 MC68020R16

Pin Number	Function
A1	$\overline{BGACK}$
A2	A1
A3	A31
A4	A28
A5	A26
A6	A23
A7	A22
A8	A19
A9	V_{CC}
A10	GND
A11	A14
A12	A11
A13	A8
B1	N.C.
B2	$\overline{BG}$
B3	$\overline{BR}$
B4	A30
B5	A27
B6	A24
B7	A20
B8	A18
B9	GND
B10	A15
B11	A13
B12	A10
B13	A6
C1	$\overline{RESET}$
C2	CLOCK
C3	N.C.
C4	A0
C5	A29
C6	A25
C7	A21
C8	A17
C9	A16
C10	A12
C11	A9
C12	A7
C13	A5

Pin Number	Function
D1	V_{CC}
D2	V_{CC}
D3	N.C.
D4-D11	–
D12	A4
D13	A3
E1	FC0
E2	$\overline{RMC}$
E3	V_{CC}
E4-E11	–
E12	A2
E13	$\overline{OCS}$
F1	SIZ0
F2	FC2
F3	FC1
F4-F11	–
F12	N.C.
F13	$\overline{IPEND}$
G1	$\overline{ECS}$
G2	SIZ1
G3	$\overline{DBEN}$
G4-G10	–
G11	V_{CC}
G12	GND
G13	V_{CC}
H1	$\overline{CDIS}$
H2	$\overline{AVEC}$
H3	$\overline{DSACK0}$
H4-H11	–
H12	IPL2
H13	GND
J1	$\overline{DSACK1}$
J2	$\overline{BERR}$
J3	GND
J4-J11	–
J12	$\overline{IPL0}$
J13	$\overline{IPL1}$

Pin Number	Function
K1	GND
K2	$\overline{HALT}$
K3	N.C.
K4-K11	–
K12	D1
K13	D0
L1	$\overline{AS}$
L2	$R/\overline{W}$
L3	D30
L4	D27
L5	D23
L6	D19
L7	GND
L8	D15
L9	D11
L10	D7
L11	N.C.
L12	D3
L13	D2
M1	$\overline{DS}$
M2	D29
M3	D26
M4	D24
M5	D21
M6	D18
M7	D16
M8	V_{CC}
M9	D13
M10	D10
M11	D6
M12	D5
M13	D4
N1	D31
N2	D28
N3	D25
N4	D22
N5	D20
N6	D17
N7	GND
N8	V_{CC}
N9	D14
N10	D12
N11	D9
N12	D8
N13	N.C.

The V_{CC} and GND pins are separated into three groups to provide individual power supply connections for the address bus buffers, data bus buffers, and all other output buffers and internal logic.

Group	V_{CC}	GND
Address Bus	A9	A10, B9
Data Bus	M8, N8	L7, N7
Logic	D1, D2, E3, G11, G13	G12, H13, J3, K1

PRELIMINARY AC ELECTRICAL SPECIFICATIONS — CLOCK INPUT (See Figure 11)

Num	Characteristic	Symbol	MC68020R12		MC68020R16		Unit
			Min	Max	Min	Max	
	Frequency of Operation	f	8	12.5	8	16.7	MHz
1	Cycle Time	t_{cyc}	80	125	60	125	ns
2, 3	Clock Pulse Width	t_{CL}, t_{CH}	35	125	25	95	ns
4, 5	Rise and Fall Times	t_{Cr}, t_{Cf}	–	5	–	5	ns

FIGURE 11 — CLOCK INPUT TIMING DIAGRAM

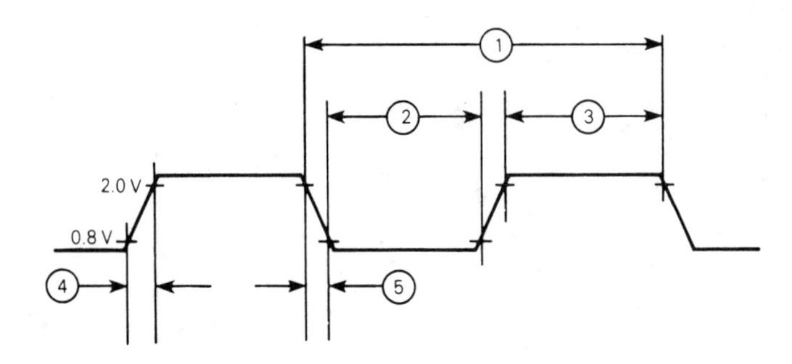

NOTE:
Timing measurements are referenced to and from a low voltage of 0.8 volts and a high voltage of 2.0 volts, unless otherwise noted. The voltage swing through this range should start outside, and pass through, the range such that the rise or fall will be linear between 0.8 volts and 2.0 volts.

PRELIMINARY AC ELECTRICAL SPECIFICATIONS — READ AND WRITE CYCLES (V_{CC} = 5.0 Vdc ± 5%; V_{SS} = 0 Vdc; T_A = 0 to 70°C; see Figures 12, 13, and 14)

Num	Characteristic	Symbol	MC68020R12		MC68020R16		Unit
			Min	Max	Min	Max	
6	Clock High to Address/FC/Size Valid	t_{CHAV}	0	40	0	30	ns
6A	Clock High to $\overline{ECS}$, $\overline{OCS}$, $\overline{HALT}$, $\overline{RESET}$ Asserted	t_{CHEV}	0	30	0	20	ns
7	Clock High to Address, Data, FC, Size High Impedance	t_{CHAZx}	0	80	0	60	ns
8	Clock High to Address/FC/Size Invalid	t_{CHAZn}	0	–	0	–	ns
9	Clock Low to $\overline{AS}$, $\overline{DS}$ Asserted	t_{CLSA}	0	40	0	30	ns
9A[1]	$\overline{AS}$ to $\overline{DS}$ Assertion (Read) (Skew)	t_{STSA}	– 20	20	– 15	15	ns
10	$\overline{ECS}$ Width Asserted	t_{ECSA}	25	–	20	–	ns
10A	$\overline{OCS}$ Width Asserted	t_{OCSA}	25	–	20	–	ns
11[6]	Address/FC/Size Valid to $\overline{AS}$ and $\overline{DS}$ Asserted (Read)	t_{AVSA}	20	–	15	–	ns
12	Clock Low to $\overline{AS}$, $\overline{DS}$ Negated	t_{CLSN}	0	40	0	30	ns
12A	Clock Low to $\overline{ECS}$/$\overline{OCS}$ Negated	t_{CLEN}	0	40	0	30	ns
13	$\overline{AS}$, $\overline{DS}$ Negated to Address, FC, Size Invalid	t_{SNAI}	20	–	15	–	ns
14	$\overline{AS}$ and $\overline{DS}$ Read Width Asserted	t_{SWA}	120	–	100	–	ns
14A	$\overline{DS}$ Width Asserted Write	t_{SWAW}	50	–	40	–	ns
15	$\overline{AS}$, $\overline{DS}$ Width Negated	t_{SN}	50	–	40	–	ns
16	Clock High to $\overline{AS}$, $\overline{DS}$, R/$\overline{W}$, $\overline{DBEN}$ High Impedance	t_{CSZ}	–	80	–	60	ns
17[6]	$\overline{AS}$, $\overline{DS}$ Negated to R/$\overline{W}$ High	t_{SNRN}	20	–	15	–	ns
18	Clock High to R/$\overline{W}$ High	t_{CHRH}	0	40	0	30	ns
20	Clock High to R/$\overline{W}$ Low	t_{CHRL}	0	40	0	30	ns
21[6]	R/$\overline{W}$ High to $\overline{AS}$ Asserted	t_{RAAA}	20	–	15	–	ns
22[6]	R/$\overline{W}$ Low to $\overline{DS}$ Asserted (Write)	t_{RASA}	90	–	70	–	ns

PRELIMINARY AC ELECTRICAL SPECIFICATIONS — READ AND WRITE CYCLES (CONTINUED)

Num	Characteristic	Symbol	MC68020R12 Min	MC68020R12 Max	MC68020R16 Min	MC68020R16 Max	Unit
23	Clock High to Data Out Valid	t_{CHDO}	–	40	–	30	ns
25[6]	$\overline{\mathrm{DS}}$ Negated to Data Out Invalid	t_{SNDI}	20	–	15	–	ns
26[6]	Data Out Valid to $\overline{\mathrm{DS}}$ Asserted (Write)	t_{DVSA}	20	–	15	–	ns
27	Data-In Valid to Clock Low (Data Setup)	t_{DICL}	10	–	5	–	ns
27A	Late $\overline{\mathrm{BERR}}$/$\overline{\mathrm{HALT}}$ Asserted to Clock Low Setup Time	t_{BELCL}	25	–	20	–	ns
28	$\overline{\mathrm{AS}}$, $\overline{\mathrm{DS}}$ Negated to $\overline{\mathrm{DSACKx}}$ Negated	t_{SNDN}	–	80	–	80	ns
29	$\overline{\mathrm{DS}}$ Negated to Data-In Invalid (Data-In Hold Time)	t_{SNDI}	0	–	0	–	ns
29A	$\overline{\mathrm{DS}}$ Negated to Data-In (High Impedance)	t_{SNDI}	–	60	–	60	ns
31[2]	$\overline{\mathrm{DSACKx}}$ Asserted to Data-In Valid	t_{DADI}	–	60	–	50	ns
31A[3]	$\overline{\mathrm{DSACKx}}$ Asserted to $\overline{\mathrm{DSACKx}}$ Valid ($\overline{\mathrm{DSACK}}$ Asserted Skew)	t_{DADV}	–	20	–	15	ns
32	$\overline{\mathrm{HALT}}$, $\overline{\mathrm{RESET}}$ Input Transition Time	t_{HRrf}	–	200	–	200	ns
33	Clock Low to $\overline{\mathrm{BG}}$ Asserted	t_{CLBA}	0	40	0	30	ns
34	Clock Low to $\overline{\mathrm{BG}}$ Negated	t_{CLBN}	0	40	0	30	ns
35	$\overline{\mathrm{BR}}$ Asserted to $\overline{\mathrm{BG}}$ Asserted ($\overline{\mathrm{RMC}}$ Not Asserted)	t_{BRAGA}	1.5	3.5	1.5	3.5	Clk Per
37	$\overline{\mathrm{BGACK}}$ Asserted to $\overline{\mathrm{BG}}$ Negated	t_{GAGN}	1.5	3.5	1.5	3.5	Clk Per
39	$\overline{\mathrm{BG}}$ Width Negated	t_{GN}	160	–	150	–	ns
39A	$\overline{\mathrm{BG}}$ Width Asserted	t_{GA}	160	–	150	–	ns
40	Clock High to $\overline{\mathrm{DBEN}}$ Asserted (Read)	t_{CHDAR}	0	40	0	30	ns
41	Clock Low to $\overline{\mathrm{DBEN}}$ Negated (Read)	t_{CLDNR}	0	40	0	30	ns
42	Clock Low to $\overline{\mathrm{DBEN}}$ Asserted (Write)	t_{CLDAW}	0	40	0	30	ns
43	Clock High to $\overline{\mathrm{DBEN}}$ Negated (Write)	t_{CHDNW}	0	40	0	30	ns
44[6]	R/$\overline{\mathrm{W}}$ High to $\overline{\mathrm{DBEN}}$ Asserted	t_{RADA}	20	–	15	–	ns
45[5]	$\overline{\mathrm{DBEN}}$ Width Asserted — Read Write	t_{DA}	80 160	– –	60 120	– –	ns
46	R/$\overline{\mathrm{W}}$ Width Asserted (Write or Read)	t_{RWA}	180	–	150	–	ns
47a	Asynchronous Input Setup Time	t_{AIST}	10	–	5	–	ns
47b	Asynchronous Input Hold Time	t_{AIHT}	20	–	15	–	ns
48[4]	$\overline{\mathrm{DSACKx}}$ Asserted to $\overline{\mathrm{BERR}}$ Asserted	t_{DABA}	–	25	–	30	ns
53	Data Out Hold from Clock High	t_{DOCH}	0	–	0	–	ns
55	R/$\overline{\mathrm{W}}$ Asserted to Data Bus Impedance Change	t_{RADC}	40	–	40	–	ns
56	$\overline{\mathrm{RESET}}$ Pulse Width (Reset Instruction)	t_{HRPW}	512	–	512	–	Clks

NOTES:
1. This number can be reduced to 5 nanoseconds if strobes have equal loads.
2. If the asynchronous setup time (#47) requirements are satisfied, the $\overline{\mathrm{DSACKx}}$ low to data setup time (#31) and $\overline{\mathrm{DSACKx}}$ low to $\overline{\mathrm{BERR}}$ low setup time (#48) can be ignored. The data must only satisfy the data-in to clock low setup time (#27) for the following clock cycle, $\overline{\mathrm{BERR}}$ must only satisfy the late $\overline{\mathrm{BERR}}$ low to clock low setup time (#27A) for the following clock cycle.
3. This parameter specifies the maximum allowable skew between $\overline{\mathrm{DSACK0}}$ to $\overline{\mathrm{DSACK1}}$ asserted or $\overline{\mathrm{DSACK1}}$ to $\overline{\mathrm{DSACK0}}$ asserted, specification #47 must be met by $\overline{\mathrm{DSACK0}}$ or $\overline{\mathrm{DSACK1}}$.
4. In the absence of $\overline{\mathrm{DSACKx}}$, $\overline{\mathrm{BERR}}$ is an asynchronous input using the asynchronous input setup time (#47).
5. $\overline{\mathrm{DBEN}}$ may stay asserted on consecutive write cycles.
6. Actual value depends on the clock input waveform.

FIGURE 12 — BUS ARBITRATION TIMING DIAGRAM

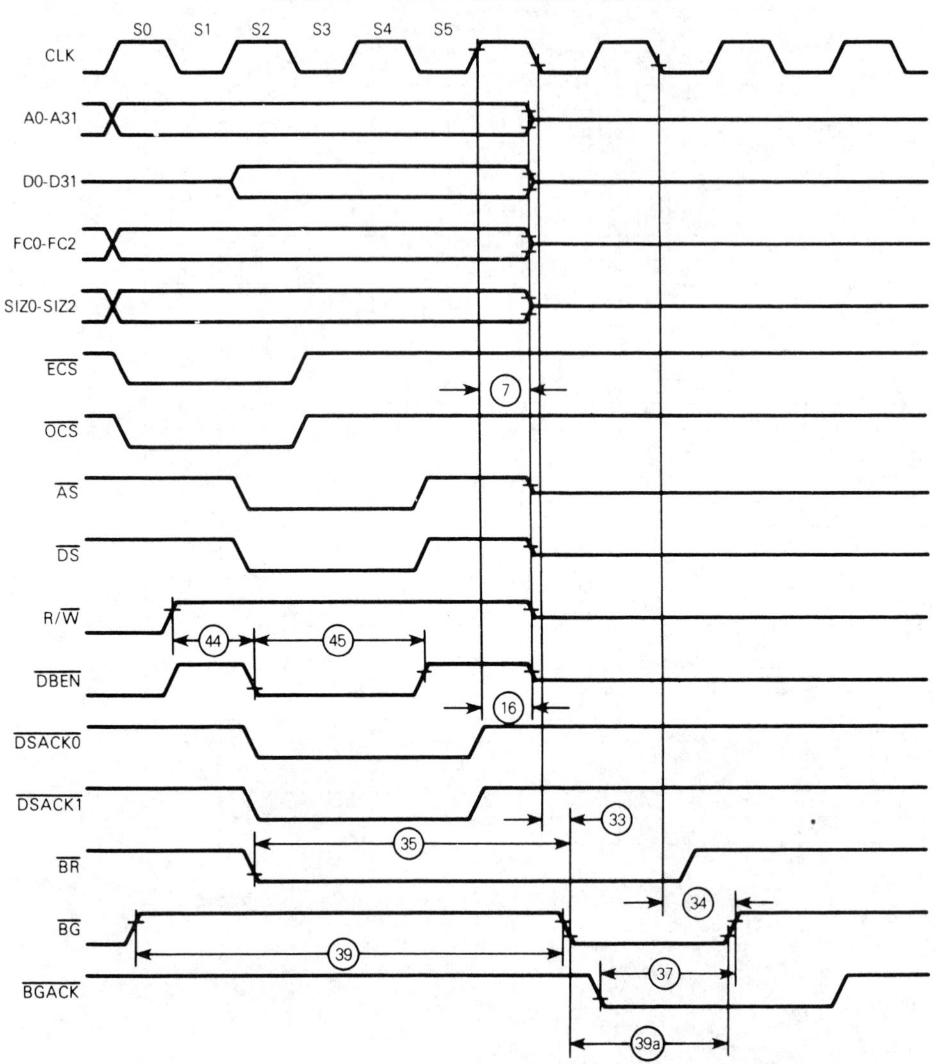

NOTE: Timing measurements are referenced to and from a low voltage of 0.8 volts and a high voltage of 2.0 volts, unless otherwise noted. The voltage swing through this range should start outside and pass through the range such that the rise or fall will be linear between 0.8 volts and 2.0 volts.

FIGURE 13 — READ CYCLE TIMING DIAGRAM

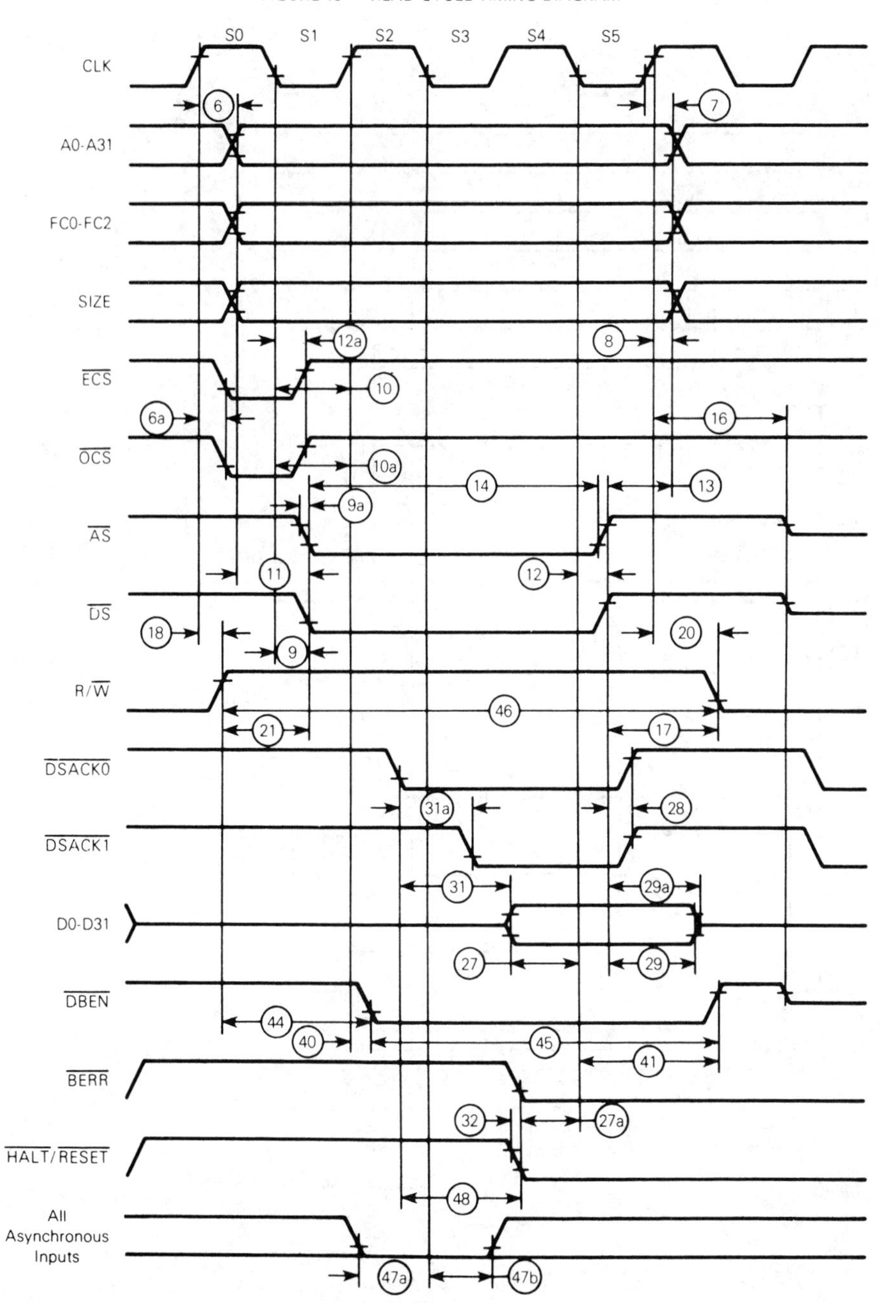

NOTE:
Timing measurements are referenced to and from a low voltage of 0.8 volts and a high voltage of 2.0 volts, unless otherwise noted. The voltage swing through this range should start outside and pass through the range such that the rise or fall will be linear between 0.8 volts and 2.0 volts.

FIGURE 14 — WRITE CYCLE TIMING DIAGRAM

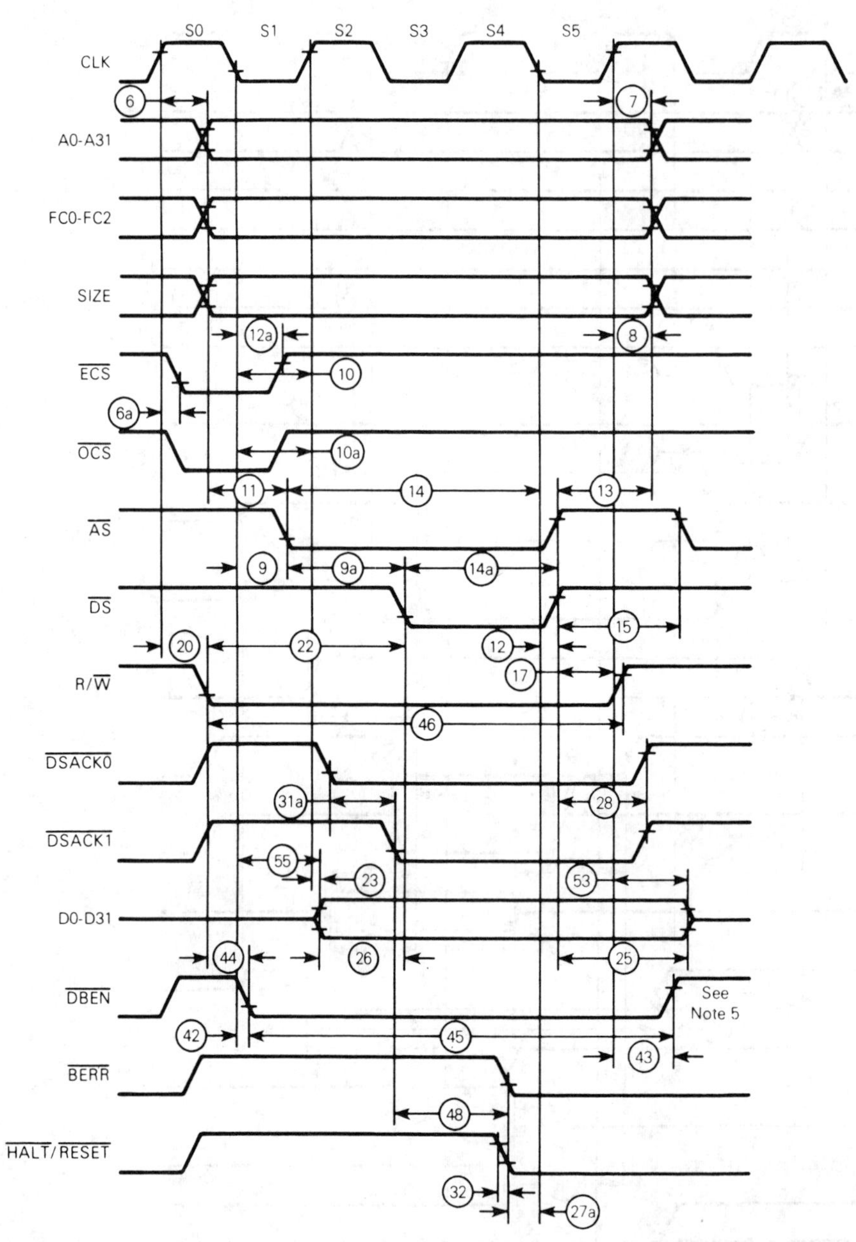

NOTE:
Timing measurements are referenced to and from a low voltage of 0.8 volts and a high voltage of 2.0 volts, unless otherwise noted. The voltage swing through this range should start outside and pass through the range such that the rise or fall will be linear between 0.8 volts and 2.0 volts.

MC68881

Product Preview

THE MC68881 FLOATING-POINT CO-PROCESSOR

The MC68881 is a high-performance HMOS floating-point processor designed to interface with the advanced MC68020 microprocessor. It can also be used as a peripheral in systems with other processors. The MC68881 is a comprehensive floating-point co-processor that provides a wide range of floating point capabilities seldom found even in a large main frame computer. System performance with the MC68020 is the overriding design goal of the MC68881.

ARCHITECTURE

The architecture of the MC68881 was defined as an extension to the architecture of the M68000 Family. It is a register-oriented processor. The programmer's model for the MC68881 is shown in Figure 1.

FIGURE 1 — PROGRAMMER'S MODEL

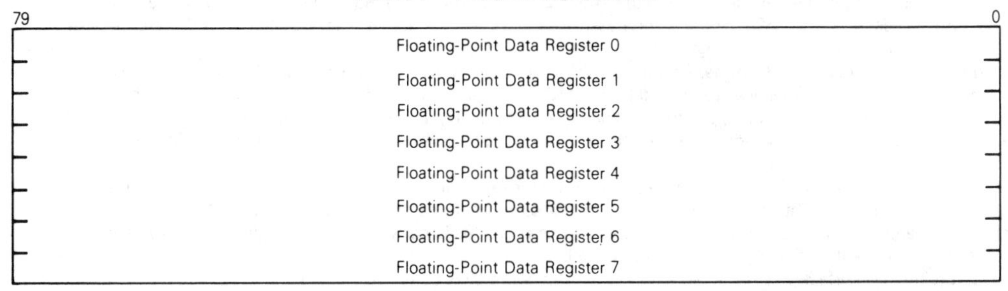

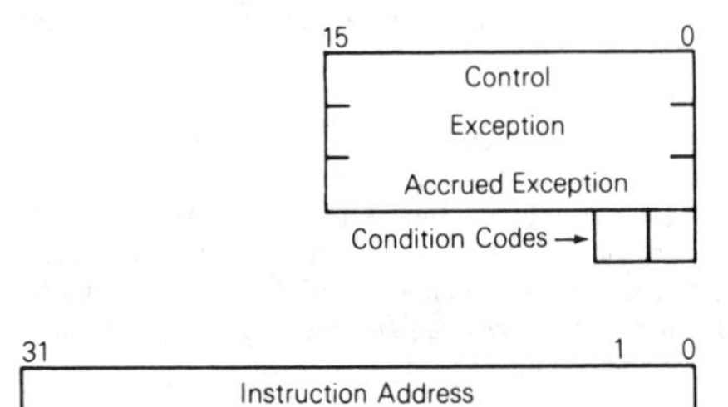

31 1 0

Instruction Address

There are eight 80-bit floating-point data registers. These registers always hold full extended precision numbers.

The control word contains the user selectable modes. The accrued exception word contains the logical inclusive OR of the exceptions for all operations since the last clear of the accrued exception register. The exception word contains the exception(s) of the last operation only. The condition code register holds the result of the last compare instruction.

The instruction address register contains the address in main processor memory of the last instruction executed by the co-processor. This address can be used during an error trap to determine the address of the faulty instruction.

ARCHITECTURAL DETAILS

Data Types

The MC68881 incorporates four new data types. They are:

Single Precision Real (S)
Double Precision Real (D)
Double-Extended Precision Real (X)
Packed Real BCD String (P)

In the assembly language syntax these new data types are handled in the same manner as the existing byte, word, and long word data types. The suffixes S, D, X, and P are appended to the opcode.

Operation Types

The operations on the MC68881 can be broken into five major types. They are:

Dyadic Operations (2 operands)
Monadic Operations (1 operand)
Moves and Conversions
Conditional Tests
Control Operations

Dyadic Operations — All dyadic operations have as their source argument a MC68020 memory location, a MC68020 data register, or a floating-point data register. The source is converted to double-extended precision, if not already such. The destination argument is always a floating-point data register. The result is returned to the floating-point data register defined as the destination argument.

Monadic Operations — The monadic instructions only have one argument. It is either in MC68020 memory, an MC68020 data register, or in a floating-point register. It is always converted to double-extended precision format, if it is not already. The destination is always a floating-point register.

Moves and Conversions — Conversion to double-extended precision format is implicit in the move-in portion of the dyadic or monadic operation. Similarly, data contained in floating-point registers may be converted to other formats as operands are moved out of the MC68881.

Conditional Test — The conditional instructions are the FBcc and FScc which are identical to the M68000 Family instructions Bcc and Scc except they use the MC68881's condition codes for determining the truth of the condition.

Control Operations — The control instructions are used to set modes in the control register and to read the exception, accrued exception, and instruction address registers.

Co-Processor Interface

The co-processor interface designed by Motorola is an integral part of the design of both the MC68020 and the MC68881 design. The interface is clean and simple with the MC68020 and MC68881 sharing the tasks of the interface. The MC68020 provides services for the MC68881 at the co-processor's request. The services provided by the MC68020 are the ones done more efficiently by the main processor.

On the other hand, the MC68881 does not depend on the MC68020 for all services as do some co-processor schemes. Once the MC68020 has provided the services requested by the MC68881 (which may be none) it is free to continue processing. Thus the choice of concurrency or non-currency is determined on an instruction-by-instruction basis and is determined by the co-processor. The great majority of MC68881 instructions are in fact overlapped in execution with MC68020 instructions.

Since the co-processor interface is simple and flexible, it opens up the possibility of user-created co-processors. For this and other reasons the co-processor interface allows multiple co-processors in a system. Furthermore, the same handshaking that occurs between the main CPU and the co-processor can be simulated in software on CPUs that do not have the co-processor interface, by treating the MC68881 as a peripheral.

Lastly, the co-processor interface was designed with the ever growing M68000 Family in mind. The MC68881 is fully compatible with all future and existing M68000 parts including the M68450 DMA Controller, the M68451 Memory Management Unit, and the MC68020's cache memory. It also supports true virtual memory.

Implementation

The MC68881 is a microcoded processor whose complexity is on the order of the MC68020 itself. It will be built using Motorola's advanced HMOS III process.

The hardware consists of a high-speed 67-bit ALU for manipulating mantissa bits. The hardware also includes a barrel shifter that can shift from 1 bit to 67 bits in one machine cycle. The barrel shifter not only speeds up standard arithmetic functions, but is also a fundamental part of transcendental function implementation. Since argument reduction for transcendental functions will be performed by the microcode, the number of functions provided will be dependent on the available microcode space.

THE IEEE FLOATING POINT STANDARD

The MC68881 is a conforming implementation of the proposed standard. In fact it not only supports all the *required* features and functions of the proposed standard, but also implements most of the *suggested* features as well. Further, the MC68881 conforms without the need for any software external to the processor. All operations take place in high-speed hardware.

Data Format Conformance

The MC68881 supports three data sizes defined by the proposed standard. They are single, double, and double-extended. (The single-extended type is redundant when these three are included; all references in this document which refer to "extended" imply "double-extended".) The format for all three data types has the basic organization of:

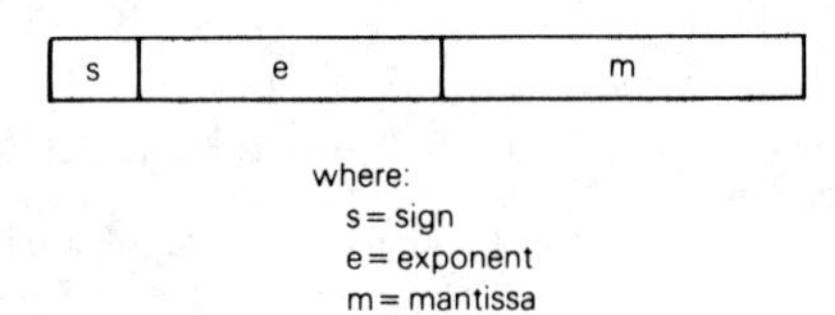

where:
s = sign
e = exponent
m = mantissa

The sizes of each field for the three floating-point formats are:

	Size in Bits		
	Single	Double	Extended
Sign	1	1	1
Exponent	8	11	15
Mantissa	23	52	64
Total	32	64	80

The three formats described above are the formats which are assumed by floating-point numbers in user's memory. Each time one of these numbers is transferred to the MC68881 it is converted into an extended real number. Thereafter, all operations in the co-processor take place with full extended precision. Even integers and BCD strings are converted into 80-bit numbers when they are loaded into an MC68881 data register. This means that the MC68881 supports mixed mode arithmetic.

Data Type Conformance

The proposed standard requires that not only must normalized numbers be recognized, but that special data types must also be recognized. The largest and smallest exponents are reserved for these special data types:

Positive True Zero
Negative True Zero
Plus Infinity
Minus Infinity
Denormalized Numbers
Not-a-Number (NaN's)

Operation Conformance

All operations specified by the proposed standard are supplied in full precision by the MC68881. The arithmetic operations provided are:

Add
Subtract
Multiply
Divide
Remainder
Compare
Square Root
Integer Part

MODE CONFORMANCE

Rounding Modes — The MC68881 supports all four rounding modes specified in the standard:

Round to Nearest
Round Towards Plus Infinity
Round Towards Minus Infinity
Round Towards Zero

Rounding Precisions — Even though the MC68881 does all arithmetic to full 80-bit precision, sometimes it is desirable to round the 80-bit result to the precision of a single or double result. The three choices are:

Round to Extended (Default)
Round to Double
Round to Single

Infinity Closures — Two types of infinity closures are also defined by the standard and supported in the MC68881. *Affine* closure defines a number system where both plus and minus infinity exist and are at opposite ends of the number line.

In *projective* closure, infinity is unsigned and the number system can be thought of as a circle which includes all numbers.

Error Handling Conformance

The proposed standard provides for the hardware to trap if an error occurs. On the MC68020/MC68881 if an error occurs on an enabled trap, the MC68881 will signal the MC68020 to take a trap and will supply a vector number. In other words, floating point exception traps are handled just like any other MC68020 traps. No external glue parts are required and there is no possibility of dead-lock.

BEYOND THE IEEE PROPOSAL

The MC68881 offers many features and functions beyond those required or suggested by the IEEE.

Additional Instructions

Some of the additional instructions provided in the MC68881 are:

Absolute Value
Negate
Scale Exponent
Set Byte determined by Floating-Point Condition
Branch on Floating-Point Condition
Get Index Based on Floating-Point Type
Move Constant to Floating-Point Register
Get Fraction of Floating-Point Number
Get Exponent of Floating-Point Number
Modulo

Transcendentals

The MC68881 includes on-chip hardware for evaluation of transcendental functions. The functions planned are:

Sine x
Cosine x
Arc Tangent x
Log Base 2
e^x
Log Base e

The following functions will also be provided if there is adequate space in the microcode after the above functions are included:

Tangent x
Hyperbolic Arc Tangent
Hyperbolic Sine
Hyperbolic Cosine
Hyperbolic Tangent
Log Base 10
Log Base 2
10^x
y^x

Each of these functions is calculated to double-extended precision.

SUMMARY

The MC68881 is the most comprehensive floating-point processor. It provides all the required functions and features of the proposed IEEE standard in hardware. In addition many other functions are provided to round out the support necessary in most numeric programs. The architecture is a logical extension to the M68000 Family architecture and is clean and easy to use. Furthermore, it lends itself to being moved onto the main processor in the future. The co-processor interface was designed with a great deal of thought; not only to allow it to work well with the MC68881, but also to allow for future co-processors, multiple co-processors, and user defined co-processors. Lastly, the MC68881 is being designed with state-of-the-art hardware and all-out performance as the primary design goal.

MC68851

Product Preview

THE MC68851 HCMOS PAGED MEMORY MANAGEMENT UNIT (PMMU)

The MC68851 is a high-performance HCMOS paged memory management unit (PMMU) designed to efficiently support a demand paged virtual memory environment as a coprocessor with the MC68020 advanced microprocessor. The MC68851 can also be used as a peripheral with other processors, especially the MC68010. The MC68851 provides an efficient means of paging and access control. The implementation of a comprehensive paged memory management system is facilitated by utilizing the following MC68851 features:

- Very Fast Logical-to-Physical Address Translation
- Logical Address Consists of a 4-Bit Function Code and a 32-Bit Address
- Full 32-Bit Physical Address
- Eight Available Page Sizes from 256 to 32K Bytes
- Fully Associative 64 Entry On-Chip Translation Cache
- Translation Cache Can Hold Descriptors for Multiple Processes
- Internal Hardware Maintains Translation Tables and On-Board Cache
- MC68020 Instruction Set Extension and Instruction Oriented Interface Using M68000 Family Coprocessor Interface
- Supports Linear Address Space of 4 Gigabytes or a Hierarchical Protection Mechanism with Eight Levels of Privilege/Protection
- Supports Multiple Logical and/or Physical Bus Masters
- Supports Logical and/or Physical Data Cache
- Supports Instruction Breakpoints for Software Debugging and Program Control

The primary system functions of the MC68851 are to provide logical-to-physical address translation, to monitor and enforce the protection/privilege mechanism, and to support the breakpoint operations. The MC68851 also supports the M68000 Family coprocessor interface in order to simplify processor/coprocessor communication.

ADDRESS TRANSLATION

Logical-to-physical address translation is the most frequently executed operation of the MC68851 and, as such, this task has been optimized and requires minimal processor intervention. The logical address operated on by the MC68851 consists of the 32-bit incoming logical address and a 4-bit function code.

The MC68851 initiates an address translation by searching for the page descriptor corresponding to the logical-to-physical mapping in the on-chip translation-lookaside module (TLM). The TLM is a very fast 64-entry fully-associative cache memory which stores recently used page descriptors. If the descriptor does not reside in the TLM, then the bus cycle of the logical bus master is aborted and the MC68851 executes bus cycles to search the translation table in physical memory. The translation table is a hierarchical structure in main memory that, at its lowest level, contains the page descriptors controlling the logical-to-physical address translations. The 64-bit primary root pointer registers in the MC68851 (see Figure 1) point to the head of these translation tables. The page descriptor is loaded into the TLM and the logical bus master is allowed to retry its bus cycle, which should now be correctly translated.

PROTECTION MECHANISM

The MC68851 hierarchical protection mechanism provides cycle-by-cycle examination and enforcement of the access rights of the currently executing process. There are eight distinct levels in the privilege hierarchy and these levels are encoded in the upper three bits of the incoming logical address LA (31-29). The MC68851 compares these bits against the value in the current access level register (CAL in Figure 1). If the priority level of the incoming address is less than the current access level, then the bus cycle is requesting a higher privilege than allowed and the MC68851 will terminate this access as a fault. The MC68851 will not assert a physical address strobe during a bus cycle resulting in a privilege violation.

The MC68851 completely supports the MC68020 module call and return functions (CALLM/RTM), which include a mechanism to change privilege levels during module operation.

BREAKPOINTS

The MC68851 provides a breakpoint acknowledge facility to support the MC68020 and other processors with on-chip cache memory. When the MC68020 encounters a breakpoint instruction it executes a breakpoint acknowledge cycle by reading a particular address in CPU address space. The PMMU decodes this address and responds by either providing a replacement opcode for the breakpoint opcode and asserting the data size and acknowledge outputs or by asserting bus error to initiate illegal instruction processing. The PMMU can be programmed to signal the illegal instruction exception or to provide the replacement opcode n times ($1 \leq n \geq 255$) before signaling the exception.

This document contains information on a product under development. Motorola reserves the right to change or discontinue this product without notice.

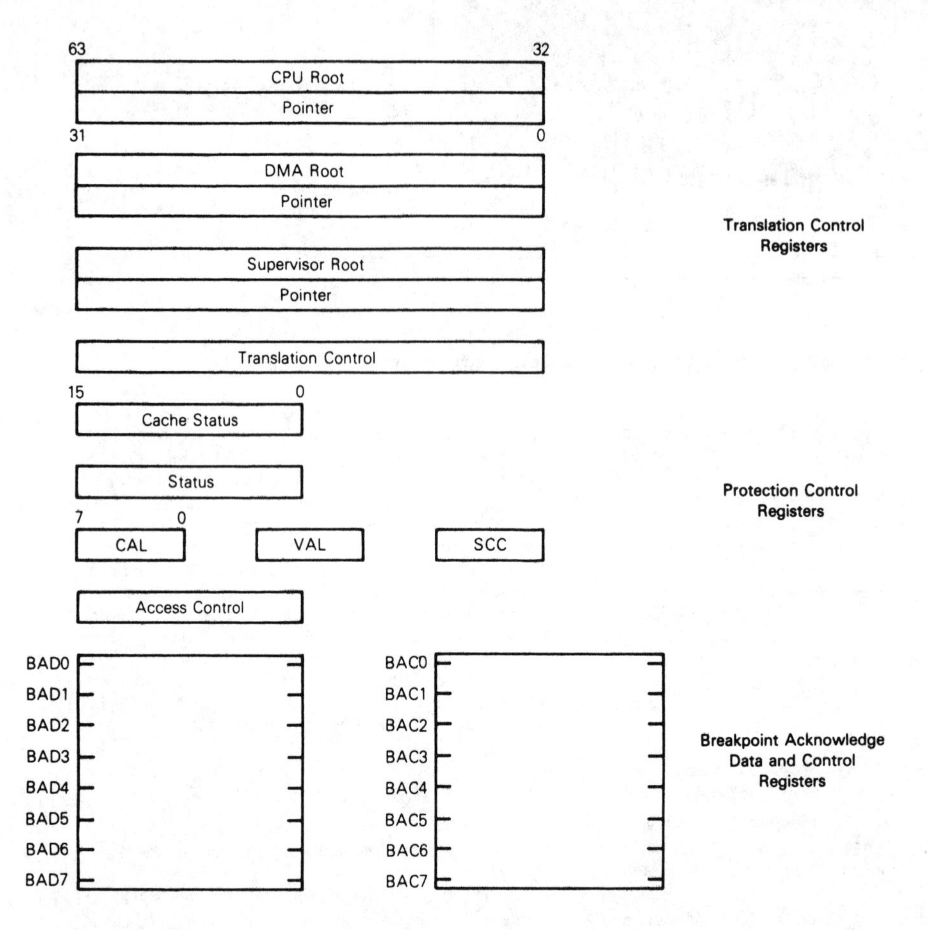

COPROCESSOR INTERFACE

The M68000 Family coprocessor interface is an integral part of the design of the MC68020 advanced microprocessor, the MC68881 floating-point processor, and the MC68851 paged memory management unit. The coprocessor interface allows the execution of special purpose instructions which are not executable by the processor. Each coprocessor (e.g., MC68851 or MC68881) has an instruction set that reflects its special function. These instructions may be executed merely by placing the instruction opcode and parameters in the MC68020 instruction stream. The MC68020 decodes the coprocessor instruction and performs bus communication with the coprocessor registers specifying the nature of the action to be taken. Both the MC68020 and the coprocessor will execute parts of the instruction depending on which is best suited to handle a particular task.

The interchange of information and the division of responsibility between the processor and the coprocessor are controlled by the coprocessor interface and this process is transparent to the user. The addition of a coprocessing unit to an MC68020 system simply complements the instruction set executable by the processor.

The coprocessor interface was designed to be flexible, functional, and expandable. The interface is intended to support the M68000 Family of devices and future extensions to the Motorola coprocessor family, as well as user defined coprocessors in single or multiple coprocessor systems.

M68000 FAMILY INSTRUCTION SET EXTENSION

The MC68851 implements an extension of the current M68000 Family instruction set using the M68000 Family coprocessor interface. These instructions provide control functions for:

1. loading and storing of MMU registers,
2. testing access rights and conditionals based on the result of these tests, and
3. MMU control functions.

The instruction set extension is as follows:

PMOVE – Moves data to/from MC68851 register.

PVALID – Compares access rights requested by logical address and traps if it is less than the current access level.

PTEST – Searches the translation tables to determine the access rights to an effective address. Sets the MC68851 status register according to the results.

PFLUSH – Flush translation cache entries by root pointer; by root pointer and effective address; or by root pointer, effective address, and function code.

PSAVE – Saves the internal state of the MC68851 coprocessor interface in order to support the MC68020 virtual memory capabilities.

PRESTORE – Restores the state of the coprocessor interface stored by the PSAVE instruction.

PBcc – Branches conditionally on MC68851 condition.

PDBcc – Tests MC68851 condition, decrements, and branches.

PScc – Tests operand according to MC68851 condition.

PTRAPcc – Traps on MC68851 condition.

Appendix B
Inmos T414 data

The performance of the transputer is measured in terms of the number of bytes required for the program, and the number of (internal) processor cycles required to execute the program.

The figures here relate to occam programs. For the same function, other languages should achieve approximately the same performance as occam.

7.1 T414 speed selections

The following table illustrates the designation of the T414 speed selections.

Designation	Instruction throughput	Processor clock speed	Processor cycle time	Input clock frequency
IMS T414-15	7.5 MIPS	15 MHz	67 ns	5 MHz
IMS T414-20	10 MIPS	20 MHz	50 ns	5 MHz

7.2 Performance overview

These figures are averages obtained from detailed simulation, and should be used only as an initial guide. The following abbreviations are used to represent the quantities indicated

np number of component processes
ne number of processes earlier in queue
r 1 if INT or array parameter, 0 if not
ts number of table entries (table size)
w width of constant in nibbles
p number of places to shift
Eg expression used in a guard
Et timer expression used in a guard

	size bytes	**time** cycles
Names		
variables		
in expression	1.1+**r**	2.1+2(**r**)
assigned to or input to	1.1+**r**	1.1+(**r**)
in **PROC** call, corresponding to an **INT** parameter	1.1+**r**	1.1+(**r**)
channels	1.1	2.1
Array Variables		
constant subscript	0	0
variable subscript	5.3	7.3
expression subscript	5.3	7.3
Declarations		
CHAN OF *type*	3.1	3.1
[size]CHAN OF *type*	9.4	2.2 + 20.2*__size__
PROC	body+2	0
Primitives		
assignment	0	0
input	4	26.5
output	1	26
STOP	2	25
SKIP	0	0

Arithmetic operators		
+, -	1	1
*	2	39
/	2	40
REM	2	38
>>, <<	2	3+**p**
Boolean operators		
OR	4	8
AND, **NOT**	1	2
Comparison operators		
= constant	0	1
= variable	2	3
<> constant	1	3
<> variable	3	5
>, <	1	2
>=, <=	2	4
Bit operators		
/\, \/, ><, ~	2	2
Expressions		
constant in expression	**w**	**w**
check if error	4	6
Timers		
timer input	2	3
timer **AFTER**		
if past time	2	4
with empty queue	2	31
non-empty queue	2	38+**ne***9
ALT (timer)		
with empty queue	6	52
non-empty queue	6	59+**ne***9
timer alt guard	8+2**Eg**+2**Et**	34+2**Eg**+2**Et**
Constructs		
SEQ	0	0
IF	1.3	1.4
if guard	3	4.3
ALT (non timer)	6	26
alt channel guard	10.2+2**Eg**	20+2**Eg**
skip alt guard	8+2**Eg**	10+2**Eg**
PAR	11.5+(**np**-1)*7.5	19.5+(**np**-1)*30.5
WHILE	4	12
Procedure call		
	3.5+(nparams-2)*1.1 +nvecparams*2.3	16.5+(nparams-2)*1.1 +nvecparams*2.3
Replicators		
replicated **SEQ**	7.3{+5.1}	(-3.8)+15.1*count{+7.1}
replicated **IF**	12.3{+5.1}	(-2.6)+19.4*count{+7.1}
replicated **ALT**	24.8{+10.2}	25.4+33.4*count{+14.2}
replicated timer **ALT**	24.8{+10.2}	62.4+33.4*count{+14.2}
replicated **PAR**	39.1{+5.1}	(-6.4)+70.9*count{+7.1}

Figures in curly brackets are not necessary if the number of replications is a compile time constant.

To estimate performance, add together the time for the variable references and the time for the operation.

When calculating the time of the predefined maths elementary function library procedures no time needs to be added for procedure calling overhead. These procedures are compiled directly into special purpose instructions which are designed to support the efficient implementation of multiple length and floating point arithmetic. Refer to the documentation on the *Elementary Function Libraries* in the occam programming manual (supplied with INMOS software products and available as a separate publication).

7.2.1 Floating point operations

Floating point operations are provided by a run-time package, which requires approximately 400 bytes of memory for the single length arithmetic operations, and 2500 bytes for the double length arithmetic operations. The following table summarizes the estimated performance of the package.

		Processor cycles (typical)	**Processor cycles** (worst)
`REAL32`	+, -	230	300
	*	200	240
	/	245	280
	<, >, =, >=, <=, <>	60	60
`REAL64`	+, -	565	700
	*	760	940
	/	1115	1420
	<, >, =, >=, <=, <>	60	60

7.2.2 Effect of external memory

Extra processor cycles may be needed when program and/or data are held in external memory, depending both on the operation being performed, and on the speed of the external memory. After a processor cycle which initiates a write to memory, the processor continues execution at full speed until at least the next memory access.

Whilst a reasonable estimate may be made of the effect of external memory, the actual performance will depend upon the exact nature of the given sequence of operations.

External memory is characterized by the number of extra processor cycles per external memory cycle, denoted as **e**. The value of **e** is 2 for the fastest external memory; a typical value for a large external memory is 5.

The number of additional cycles required to access data in external memory is **e**. If program is stored in external memory, and **e** has the value 2 or 3, then no extra cycles need be estimated for linear code sequences. For larger values of **e**, the number of extra cycles required for linear code sequences may be estimated at (**e** - 3)/4 per byte of program. A transfer of control may be estimated as requiring **e** + 3 cycles.

These estimates may be refined for various constructs. In the following table, **n** denotes the number of components in a construct. In the case of `IF`, the **n**'th conditional is the first to evaluate to `TRUE`, and the costs include the costs of the conditionals tested. The number of bytes in an array assignment or communication is denoted by **b**.

	Program off chip	**Data off chip**
Boolean expressions	**e**-2	0
`IF`	3**en**-8	**en**
Replicated `IF`	(6**e**-4)**n**+7	(5**e**-2)**n**+8
Replicated `SEQ`	(3**e**-3)**n**+2	(4**e**-2)**n**
`PAR`	(3**e**-1)**n**+8	3**en**+4
Replicated `PAR`	(10**e**-8)**n**+8	16**en**-12
`ALT`	(2**e**-4)**n**+6**e**	(2**e**-2)**n**+10**e**-8
array assignment and communication in one transputer	0	max (2**e**, **e**(**b**/2))

The effective rate of INMOS links is slowed down by external memory if all four links are operating in both directions simultaneously and **e** has a value of 6 or greater.

The following simulation results illustrate the effect of storing program and/or data in external memory. The results are normalized to 1 for both program and data on chip. The first program (Sieve of Erastosthenes) is an extreme case as it is dominated by small, data access intensive, loops; it contains no concurrency, communication, or even multiplication or division. The second program is the pipeline algorithm for Newton Raphson square root computation.

	e	2	3	4	5	**on chip**
Program off chip	(1)	1.3	1.5	1.7	1.9	1
	(2)	1.1	1.2	1.2	1.3	1
Data off chip	(1)	1.5	1.8	2.1	2.3	1
	(2)	1.2	1.4	1.6	1.7	1
Program and data off chip	(1)	1.8	2.2	2.7	3.2	1
	(2)	1.3	1.6	1.8	2.0	1

8.8 Peripheral interfacing AC characteristics

Event signals waveforms

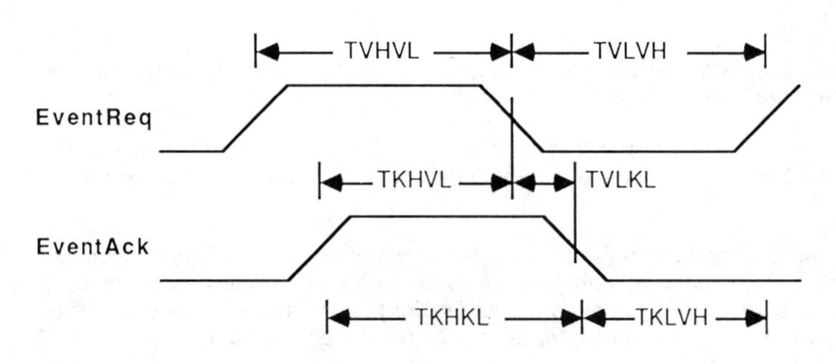

Parameter		Min	Max	Unit
TVHVL	**EventReq** pulse width high	2		processor cycles
TVLVH	**EventReq** pulse width low	2		processor cycles
TVLKL	Falling edge delay from **EventReq** to **EventAck**	0	2	processor cycles
TKHKL	**EventAck** pulse width high	2		processor cycles
TKHVL	Delay from **EventAck** to falling edge of **EventReq**	0		
TKLVH	Delay from falling edge of **EventAck** to next **EventReq**	0		

9 T414 signal summary

Full details of each signal are provided in the referenced section.

Analyse

Signal used to investigate the state of a T414. The signal brings the processor, links and clocks to a halt within approx three timeslice periods (approx 2.5 milliseconds). **Reset** may then be applied, which will not destroy state information nor reinitialise the memory interface. After **Reset** has been taken low, **Analyse** may be taken low after which the processor will execute its bootstrap routine.

Input

BootFromROM

If this is held to **VCC**, then the boot program is taken from ROM. Otherwise the T414 awaits a bootstrap message from a link.
Input

CapMinus

The negative terminal of an internal power supply used for the internal clocks. This must be connected via a 1 microfarad capacitor to **CapPlus**. If a tantalum capicitor is used **CapMinus** should be connected to the negative terminal.

CapPlus

The positive terminal of an internal power supply used for the internal clocks. This must be connected via a 1 microfarad capacitor to **CapMinus**. If a tantalum capicitor is used **CapPlus** should be connected to the positive terminal.

ClockIn

Input clock from which all internal clocks are generated. The nominal input clock frequency for all transputers, of whatever wordlength and speed, is 5 MHz.
Input

DoNotWire

These are output pins reserved for INMOS use. They should be left unconnected.
Output

Error

The processor has detected an error and remains high until **Reset**. Errors result from arithmetic overflow, by array bounds violations or by divide by zero. The **Error** flag can also be set by an instruction, to allow other forms of software detected error.
Output

EventAck

The **EventReq** and **EventAck** are a pair of handshake signals for external events. External logic takes **EventReq** high when the logic wishes to communicate with a process in the T414. The rising edge of **EventReq** causes a process to be scheduled. The processor takes **EventAck** high when the process is scheduled. At any time after this point the external logic may take **EventReq** low, following which the processor will set **EventAck** low.
Output

EventReq

Request external event. See description of **EventAck** above.
Input

GND

Power supply return and logic reference, 0 V. There are several **GND** pins to minimize inductance within the package.

HoldToGND

These are input pins reserved for INMOS use. They should be held to ground either directly or through a resistor of less than 10K ohms.
Input

LinkIn0 - 3

Input pins of the standard links. A **LinkIn** pin receives a serial stream of bits including protocol bits and data bits. Link inputs must be connected to another Link output or tied to **GND**. The Link input must not be tied high or left floating.
Input

LinkOut0 - 3

Output pins of each of the standard links. A **LinkOut** pin may be left floating or may be connected to one (and only one) **LinkIn** pin. As long as the skew specification is met, the connection may be via buffers.
Output

LinkSpecial

LinkSpecial selects the non-standard speed to be either 20MBits/sec when high or 5MBits/sec when low.
Input

Link0Special

Link 0 operates at the non-standard speed selected by **LinkSpecial** if this pin is wired high.
Input

Link123Special

Links 1, 2 and 3 operate at the non-standard speed selected by **LinkSpecial** if this pin is wired high.
Input

MemAD

32-bit wide multiplexed external memory address and data bus.
Input/Output

MemConfig

The **MemConfig** input determines how the external memory interface is to be configured. It may be connected to any of the **MemAd** pins directly, or to the output of an inverter which takes its input from any of the **MemAD** pins in order to select the required memory configuration.
Input

MemReq

This input is used by external devices to access the memory interface **MemAD**. When **MemReq** is sampled high, and if there is no refresh cycle outstanding, the **MemAD** signals are taken high impedance. **MemGranted** is taken high one period **Tm** later. If a refresh cycle is outstanding when **MemReq** is sampled, the refresh cycle is completed before access to the memory interface is granted.
Input

MemGranted

See description below of **MemReq**.
Output

While **MemGranted** is high, **MemReq** is sampled every alternate clock period **Tm**; if it is found to be low, **MemGranted** is taken low two periods **Tm** later, and any pending transputer interface cycle can start.

MemWait

Wait input for the memory interface. The **MemWait** signal is sampled synchronously just before the end of **T4**. If, at the time **MemWait** is sampled, the input is low, the interface cycle proceeds. Otherwise, the interface is held in **T4** until the input is sampled and found to be low; one period **Tm** later the interface cycle proceeds to **T5**.
Input

notMemRd

Used for Read Data, Read Enable, Output Enable for external memory. The **notMemRd** signal is taken low during read cycles, including those which occur during configuration, at the start of **T4**, and is taken high at the start of **T6**.
Output

notMemRf

Refresh indicator. **notMemRf** goes low a processor cycle before **T1** and remains low until the end of **T6**.
Output

notMemS0

AddressValid strobe, LatchEnable, or ChipEnable for external memory. The **notMemS0** signal goes low at the start of **T2** and goes high at the start of **T6**.
Output

notMemS1

External memory strobe with configurable width, normally used for RowAddressStrobe, AddressLatchEnable, or ChipEnable.
Output

notMemS2 - S4

Three separate external memory strobes with configurable delay. Their falling edge can be configured to go low between zero and 31 periods **Tm** after the start of **T2**, and they go high at the start of **T6**. The conventional use suggested for the strobes is:

notMemS2 use as AddressMultiplex for dynamic RAMs

notMemS3 use as CAS for dynamic RAMs

notMemS4 use as wait state generator

If the system does not use dynamic RAMs, **notMemS2** and **notMemS3** may be used as wait state generators with different delays from **notMemS4**.
Output

notMemWrB0 - B3

Separate write strobe for each byte of external memory. The **notMemWrB** signal for each byte only goes low if the relevant byte is to be written. The write strobes may be configured to be either early or late. Early write strobes allow a wide write pulse to static RAM and allow common I/O for dynamic RAM. Late writes allow the data to be strobed by either the falling edge or the rising edge of **notMemWrB**.

Output

ProcClockOut

The processor clock output, in phase with the memory interface. The processor clock frequency is a multiple of the input clock frequency. The multiple differs for different speed parts.
Output

Reset

The falling edge of **Reset** initialises the T414, triggers the sequence which configures the memory interface and then starts the processor executing a bootstrap routine. If **Analyse** is asserted during reset, then the memory interface is not reconfigured, and sufficient state is preserved to permit software analysis.

Input

VCC

Power supply, nominally 5 V. There are several **VCC** pins to minimize inductance within the package. **VCC** should be decoupled to **GND** by at least one 100 nF low inductance (such as ceramic) capacitor.

The T414 is available in an 84 pin J-Lead chip carrier or 84 pin Grid Array.

10.1 J-Lead chip carrier

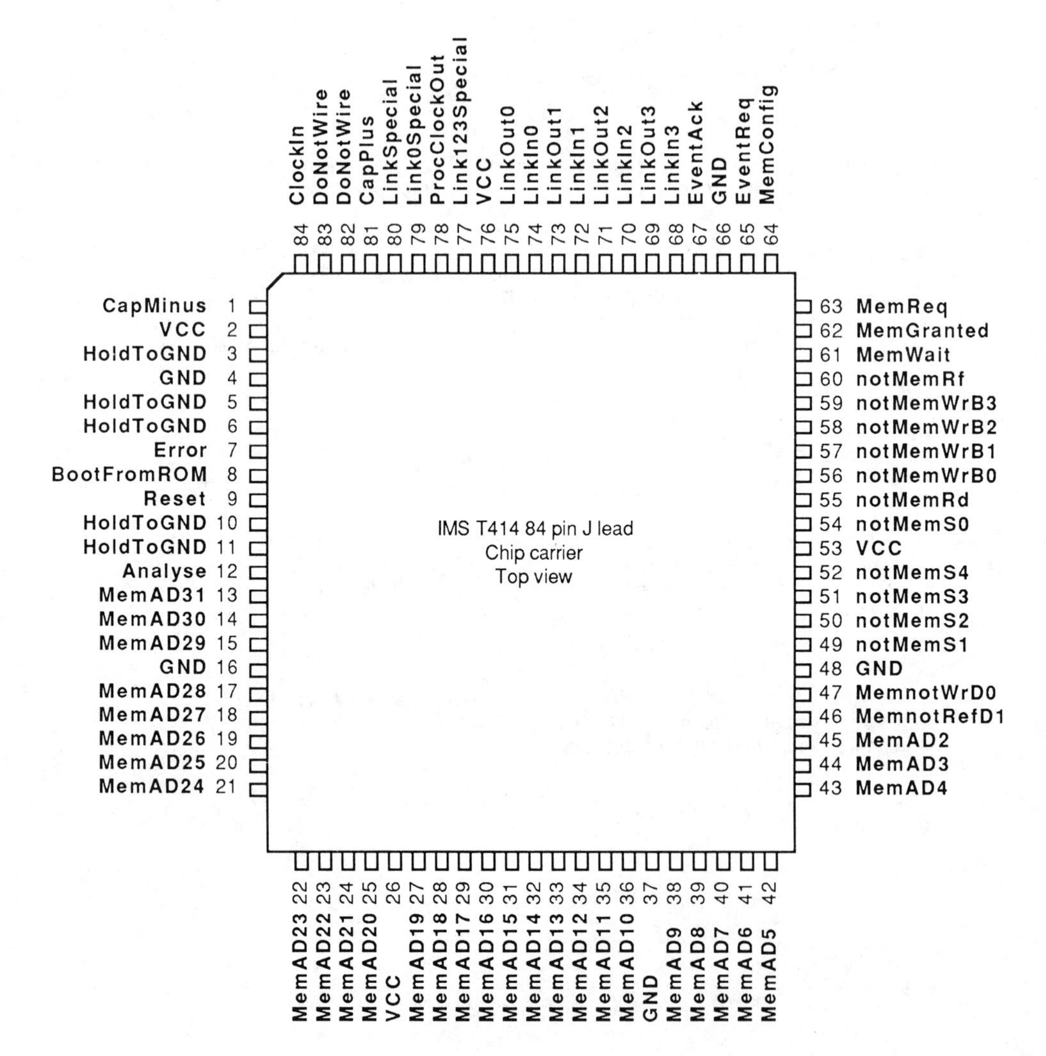

10.2 Pin Grid Array

	1	2	3	4	5	6	7	8	9	10
A	DoNot Wire	Link Special	ProcClock Out	L123 Special	LinkIn0	LinkOut1	LinkIn2	EventAck	GND	MemWait
B	HoldTo GND	ClockIn	DoNot Wire	L0Special	LinkOut0	LinkOut2	LinkOut3	EventReq	MemReq	notMem WrB3
C	GND	VCC	CapMinus	CapPlus	VCC	LinkIn1	LinkIn3	Mem Config	Mem Granted	notMem WrB1
D	Error	HoldTo GND	HoldTo GND					notMem Rf	notMem WrB2	notMem WrB0
E	HoldTo GND	BootFrom ROM	Reset					notMem Rd	notMem S0	VCC
F	HoldTo GND	Analyse	Mem AD31					notMem S3	notMem S2	notMem S4
G	Mem AD30	GND	Mem AD27					Memnot WrD0	GND	notMem S1
H	Mem AD29	Mem AD25	Mem AD23	VCC	Mem AD16	Mem AD12	Mem AD8	MemAD4	MemAD3	Memnot RfD1
J	Mem AD28	Mem AD24	Mem AD22	Mem AD19	Mem AD17	Mem AD13	GND	MemAD6	MemAD5	MemAD2
K	Mem AD26	Mem AD21	Mem AD20	Mem AD18	Mem AD15	Mem AD14	Mem AD11	Mem AD10	MemAD9	MemAD7

Index

T414 84 Pin Grid Array
Top View

IMS C011 link adaptor

Mode 1 Block Diagram

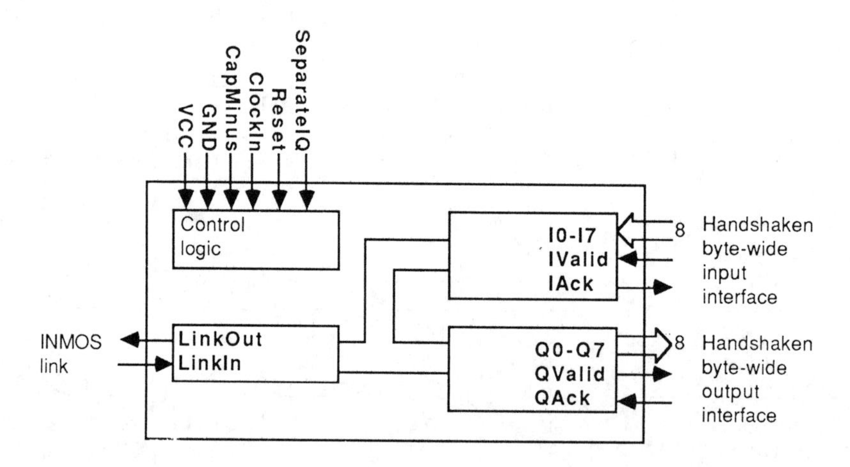

In mode 1 the link adaptor converts between an INMOS serial link and two independent fully handshaken byte-wide interfaces. One interface is for data coming from the serial link and one for data going to the serial link.

The serial link enables the link adaptor to communicate with another link adaptor, a transputer or an INMOS peripheral processor. Data reception is asynchronous which allows communication to be independent of clock phase. Transfers may proceed in both directions at the same time.

This mode provides programmable I/O pins for a transputer.

The serial links can be operated at differing speeds; when connected by their parallel ports two C011 link adaptors can connect high and low speed links whilst maintaining the synchronised message transmission provided by the link protocol.

The IMS C011 converts the bidirectional serial link data into parallel data streams. It can be used to fully interconnect transputers, INMOS peripheral controllers, I/O subsystems, and microprocessors of different families.

Mode 2 Block Diagram

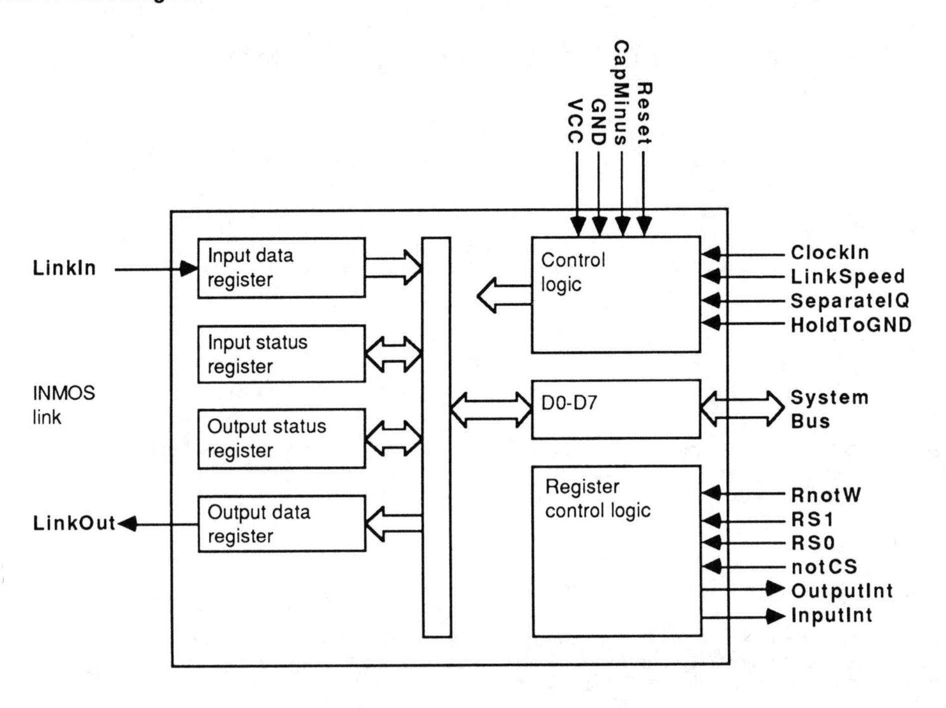

In mode 2 the link adaptor provides an interface between an INMOS serial link and a microprocessor system bus, via an 8-bit bi-directional interface.

This mode has status/control and data registers for both input and output. Any of these can be accessed by the byte wide interface at any time. Two interrupt lines are provided, each gated by an interrupt enable flag. One presents an interrupt on output ready, and the other on data present.

The IMS C011 converts the bidirectional serial link data into parallel data streams. It can be used to fully interconnect transputers, INMOS peripheral controllers, I/O subsystems, and microprocessors of different families.

4 The INMOS serial link interface

Standard Clock Input

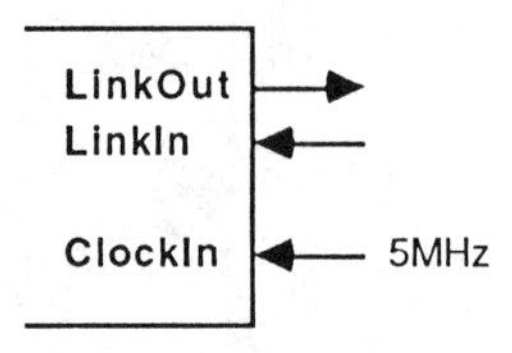

The INMOS serial links are standard across all products in the transputer product range. All transputers will support a standard communications frequency of 10 Mbits/sec, regardless of processor performance. Thus transputers of different performance can be connected directly and future transputer systems will be able to communicate directly with those of today.

Each link consists of a serial input and a serial output, both of which are used to carry data and link control information.

Link protocol

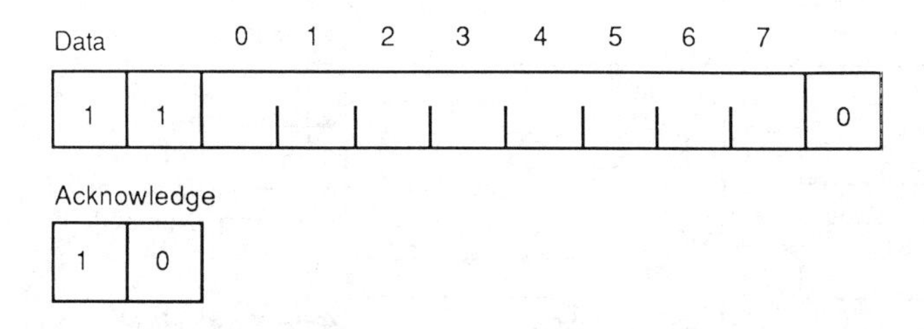

A message is transmitted as a sequence of bytes. After transmitting a data byte, the sender waits until an acknowledge has been received, signifying that the receiver is ready to receive another byte. The receiver can transmit an acknowledge as soon as it starts to receive a data byte, so that transmission can be continuous. This protocol provides handshaken communication of each byte of data, ensuring that slow and fast transputers communicate reliably.

When there is no activity on the links they remain at logic 0, **GND** potential.

A 5 MHz input clock is used, from which internal timings are generated. Link communication is not sensitive to clock phase. Thus, communication can be achieved between independently clocked systems as long as the communications frequency is within the specified tolerance.

5 Functional description mode 1

Output to link

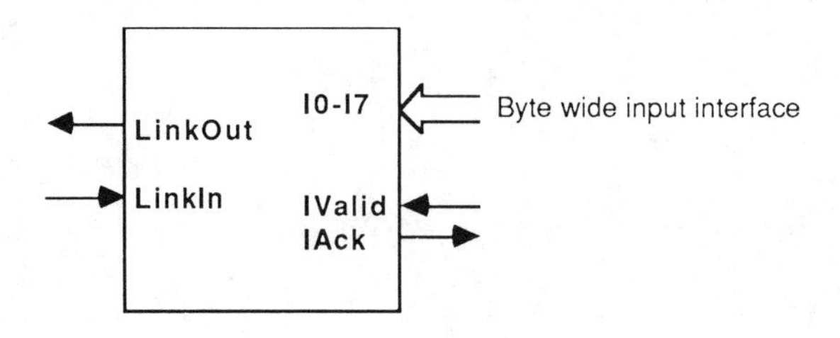

Timing of output to link

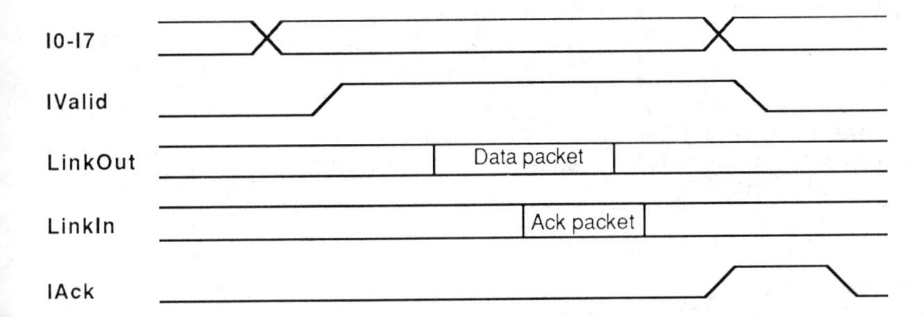

IValid and **IAck** provide a simple two wire handshake. Data is presented to the link adaptor on **I0-I7**, and **IValid** is taken high to commence the handshake. The link adaptor transmits the data through the serial link, and acknowledges receipt of the data on **IAck** when it has received the acknowledgment from the serial link **IValid** is then taken low, and the link adaptor completes the handshake by taking **IAck** low.

Input from link

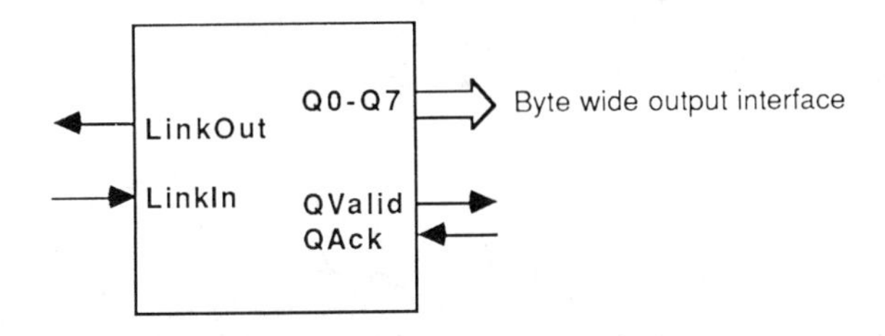

Timing of input from link

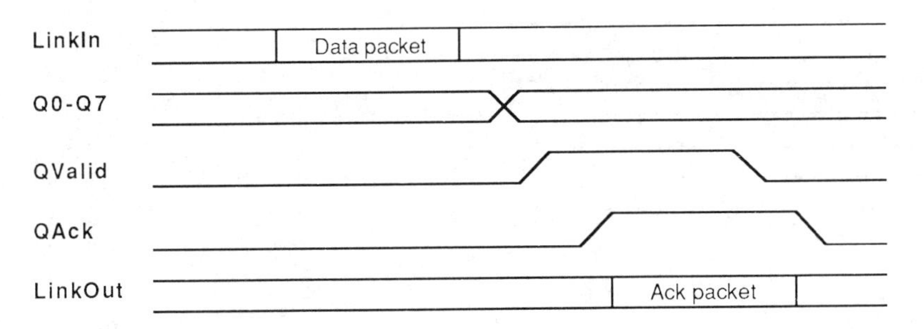

The link adaptor receives data from the serial link, presents it on **Q0-Q7**, and takes **QValid** high to commence the handshake. Receipt of the data is acknowledged on **QAck**, and the link adaptor then transmits an acknowledgement on the serial link. The link adaptor takes **QValid** low and the handshake is completed by taking **QAck** low.

6 Functional description mode 2

In mode 2 the link adaptor is controlled at the parallel interface by reading and writing status/control registers, and by reading and writing data registers. Two interrupt lines are provided. One indicates that the link adaptor is ready to output a byte to the link, and the other indicates that it is holding a byte which it has read from the link.

Parallel interface

One of the four registers is selected by **RS0** and **RS1**. If a new value is to be written into the selected registers, it is set up on **D0-D7** and **RnotW** is taken low. **notCS** is then taken low. On read cycles, the current value of the selected register is placed on **D0-D7**.

RS1	RS0	RnotW	Function
0	0	1	**D0-D7** := input data register
0	1	0	output data register := **D0-D7**
1	0	1	**D0-D7** := input status register
1	0	0	input status register := **D0-D7**
1	1	1	**D0-D7** := output status register
1	1	0	output status register := **D0-D7**

Note : Writing to the input data register has no effect and reading the output data register will result in undefined data on the data bus. Unused bit positions must be set to zero in both the input status register and the output status register.

Read register timing diagram

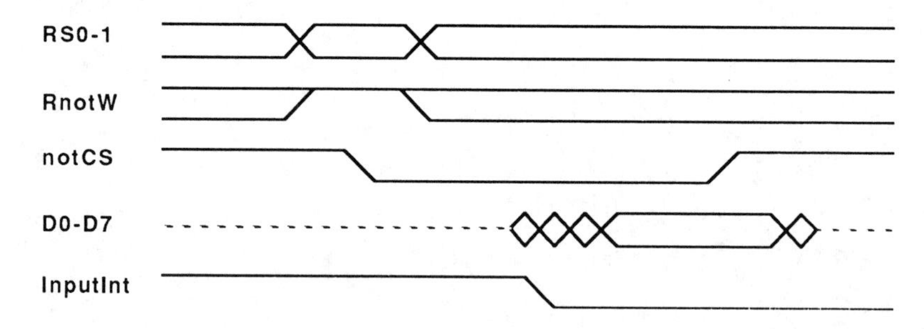

Write register timing diagram

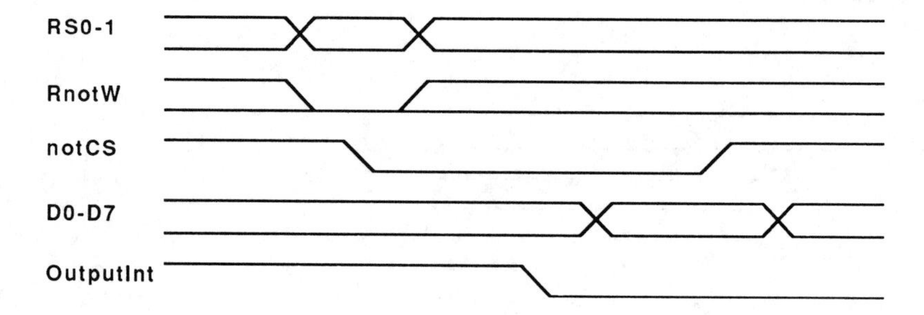

Output to link

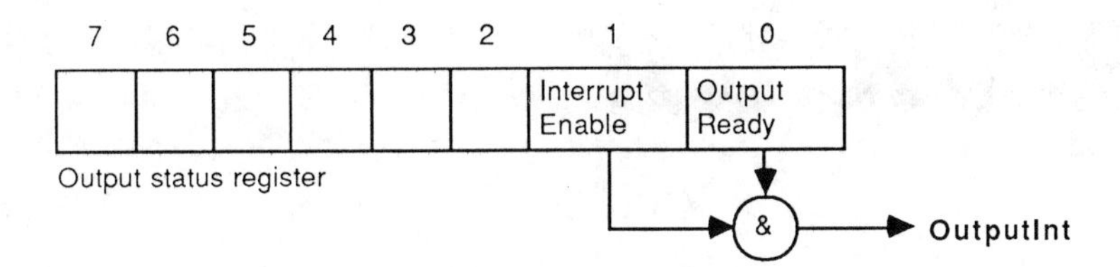

The output ready status bit indicates that the serial link is ready to send a byte of data. The bit is set high on reset, and when the link adaptor receives an acknowledgement from the serial link. It is reset low when a data byte is written to the output data register on the parallel interface. **OutputInt** is set high if both output ready and interrupt enable are set high. Output interrupt enable is set low on reset.

Input from link

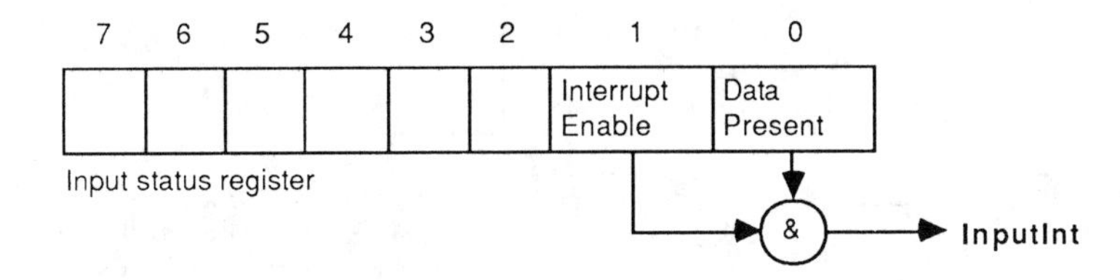

The data present status bit indicates that the serial link has received a byte of data. The bit is reset low when the data byte is read from the input data register on the parallel interface, this causes an acknowledgement to be transmitted on the serial link. **InputInt** is set high if both data present and interrupt enable are set high. Input interrupt enable and **data present** are both set low on reset.

IMS C012 link adaptor

C012 Block Diagram

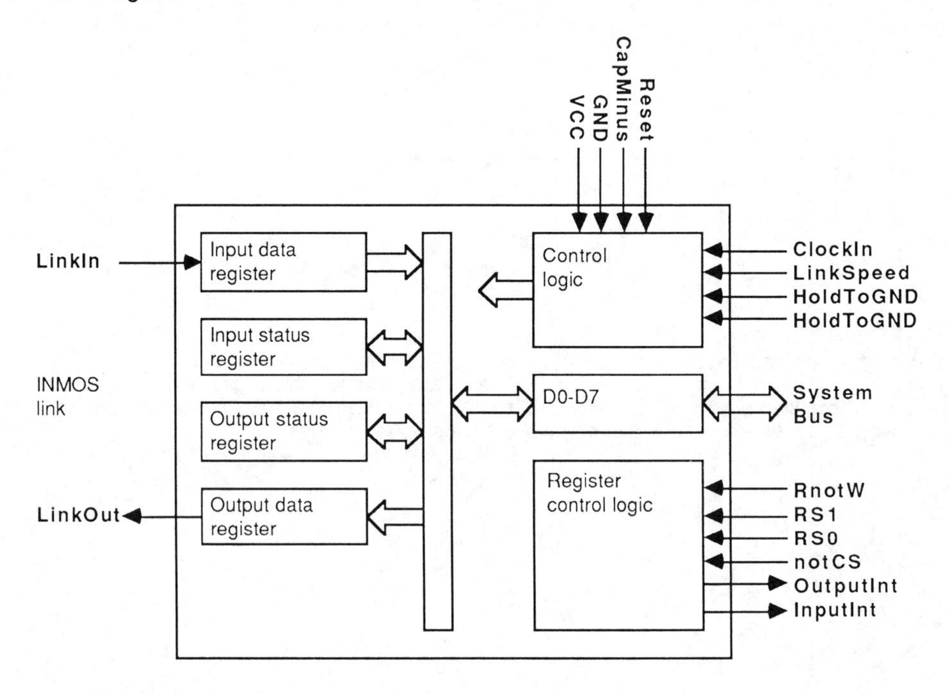

The C012 link adaptor provides an interface between an INMOS serial link and a microprocessor system bus, via an 8-bit bi-directional interface.

The device provides status/control and data registers for both input and output. Any of these can be accessed by the byte wide interface at any time. Two interrupt lines are provided, each gated by an interrupt enable flag. One presents an interrupt on output ready, and the other on data present.

The IMS C012 converts the bidirectional serial link data into parallel data streams. It can be used to fully interconnect transputers, INMOS peripheral controllers, I/O subsystems, and microprocessors of different families.

3 Functional description

The IMS C012 link adaptor is controlled at the parallel interface by reading and writing status/control registers, and by reading and writing data registers. Two interrupt lines are provided. One indicates that the link adaptor is ready to output a byte to the link, and the other indicates that it is holding a byte which it has read from the link.

Parallel interface

One of the four registers is selected by **RS0** and **RS1**. If a new value is to be written into the selected registers, it is set up on **D0-D7** and **RnotW** is taken low. **notCS** is then taken low. On read cycles, the current value of the selected register is placed on **D0-D7**.

RS1	RS0	RnotW	Function
0	0	1	**D0-D7** := input data register
0	1	0	output data register := **D0-D7**
1	0	1	**D0-D7** := input status register
1	0	0	input status register := **D0-D7**
1	1	1	**D0-D7** := output status register
1	1	0	output status register := **D0-D7**

Note : Writing to the input data register has no effect and reading the output data register will result in undefined data on the data bus. Unused bit positions must be set to zero in both the input status register and the output status register.

Read register timing diagram

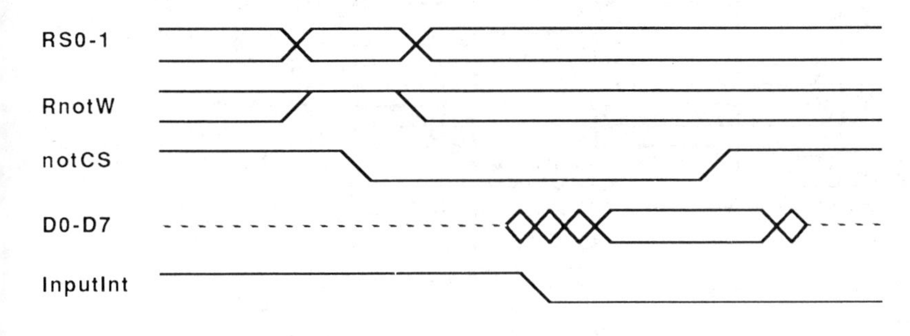

Write register timing diagram

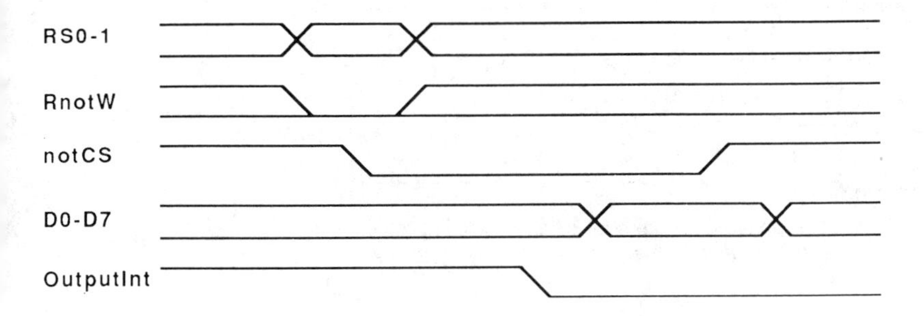

IMS 212 disk processor

2.4 Signal designations and connection diagram

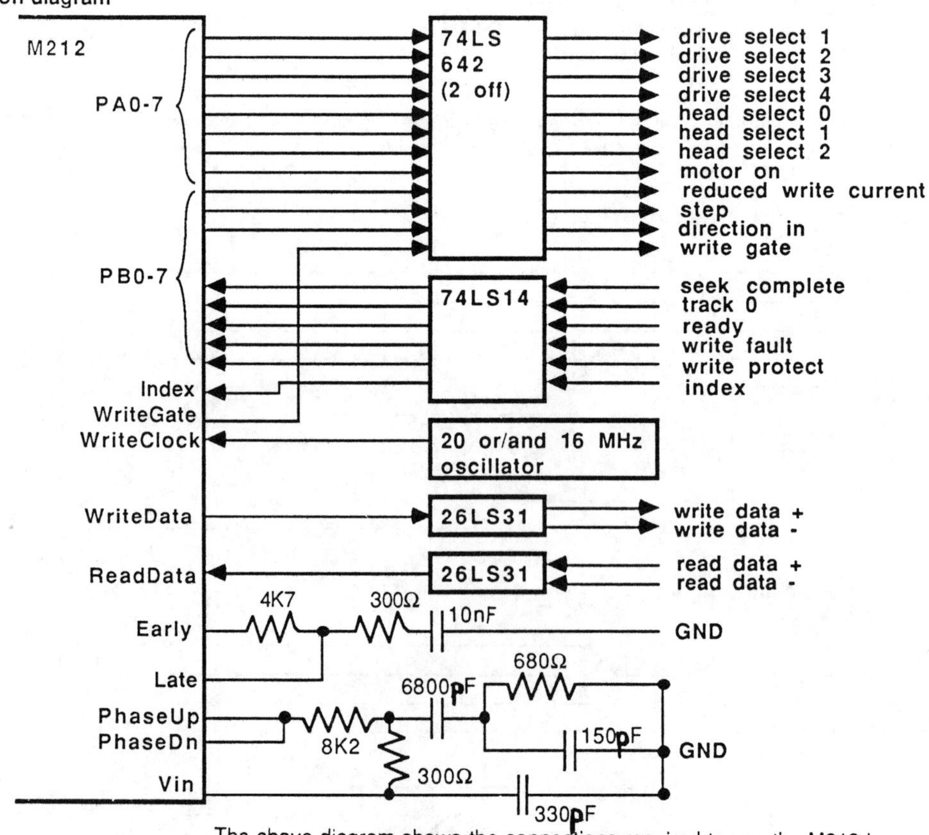

The above diagram shows the connections required to use the M212 in conjunction with the internal ROM procedures.

When using the M212 ROM process, the signal designations for the M212 are as follows.

Signal	I/O	Designation
A0 - 7	O	8-bit wide lower byte address bus for external memory expansion.
AD0 - 7	I/O	8-bit wide multiplexed upper byte address bus and data bus for external memory expansion.
ALE	O	Latches the multiplexed address during an external memory cycle.
Analyse	I	Signal used to investigate the state of the M212.
BootFromROM	I	This must be held to **VCC** to use the internal ROM process. Otherwise the M212 awaits a bootstrap message from a link.
CapMinus		The more negative terminal of an internal power supply used for the internal clocks The signal must be connected to the negative terminal of a capacitor of nominal value 1 microfarad.
CapPlus		This pin must be connected to the more positive terminal of the 1 microfarad capacitor connected to **CapMinus**.
ClockIn	I	Input clock from which all internal clocks are generated. The nominal input clock frequency for all transputers, of whatever wordlength and speed is 5 MHz.
DisIntROM	I	This pin should be held low in order to use the ROM disk procedures.
Early		Provides connection to a filter for the on-chip precompensation. See connection diagram.
Error	O	The processor has detected an error. Errors result from arithmetic overflow, by array bounds violations or by divide by zero. The error flag can also be set by an instruction, to allow other forms of software detected error.
EventAck	O	**EventReq** and **EventAck** are a pair of handshake signals for external events.
EventReq	I	Request external event.
GND		Power supply return and logic reference 0V.
HoldToGND	I	These are input pins reserved for INMOS use. They should be held to ground either directly or through a resistor of less than 10K ohms.
Index	I	This is a timing reference signal from the disk drive occurring once every revolution.
Late		Provides connection to a filter for the on-chip precompensation. See connection diagram.
LinkIn0 - 1	I	Input pins of the standard links. The **LinkIn** pin receives a serial stream of bits including protocol bits and data bits. Link inputs should not be left floating. Unused pins should be tied low.
LinkOut0 - 1	O	Output pins of each of the standard links. A **LinkOut** pin may be left floating or may be connected to one (and only one) **LinkIn** pin. As long as the skew specification is met, the connection may be via buffers.
LinkSpeed	I	This signal effects the speed of the links.
notCE	O	This active low pin provides a chip enable for the external memory system.

Signal	I/O	Designation
PA 0-3	O	Drive select
PA 4-6	O	Head select
PA 7	O	Motor on (floppy only)
PB 0	O	Reduced write current
PB 1	O	Step
PB 2	O	Direction in
PB 3	I	Seek complete
PB 4	I	Track zero
PB 5	I	Ready
PB 6	I	Write fault
PB 7	I	Write protect (floppy only)
PhaseUp/Dn	O	These signals provide connection to an external filter for an on-chip data separator. See diagram.
ProcClockOut	O	The processor clock which is output in phase with the memory interface.
ReadData	I	This is used to input raw data from the disk drive.
Reset	I	The falling edge of **Reset** initializes the M212 and then starts the processor executing a bootstrap routine.
RnotW	O	When high, this signal denotes a read operation, when low, a write.
VCC		Power supply, nominally 5 V. **VCC** should be decoupled to **GND** by at least one 100 nF low inductance (such as ceramic) capacitor.
Vin	I	This pin provides connection to an external filter for an on-chip data separator.
Wait	I	If, at the time **Wait** is sampled, the input is low, the interface cycle proceeds. Otherwise the interface is held until the input is sampled and found to be low.
WriteClock	I	This is a reference frequency to the disk hardware during writing. Frequency should be 20 MHz for a winchester drive and 16 MHz for a floppy and must be applied continuously.
WriteData	O	This pin is used to output serial data to the disk drive.
WriteGate	O	This indicates to the disk drive that valid write data is being output from the controller.

Pin numbers are given in section 12.

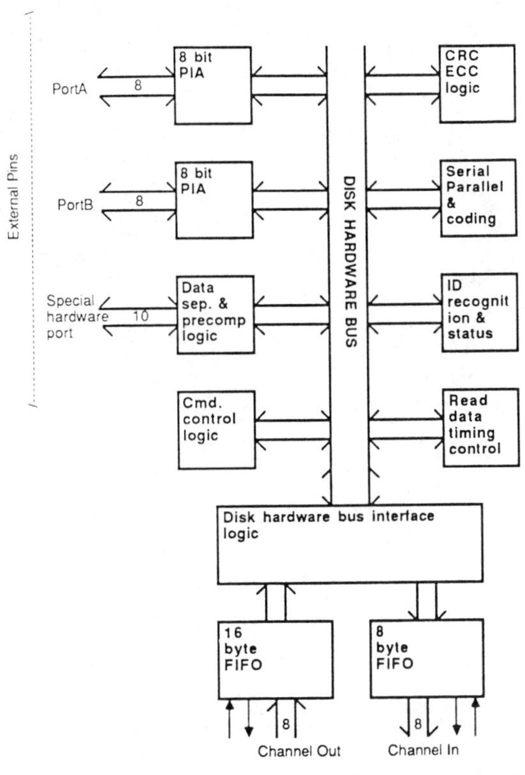

The M212 has been designed to allow as many tasks as possible to be performed by the on-chip processor. This ensures optimum flexibility in the design of a disk controller. There are, however, certain functions involved when interfacing to a disk drive that require specific hardware, and the above diagram shows the modules that contain this hardware.

Each module contains one or more registers which control its operation and are accessed from the channels connecting the disk hardware to the processor.

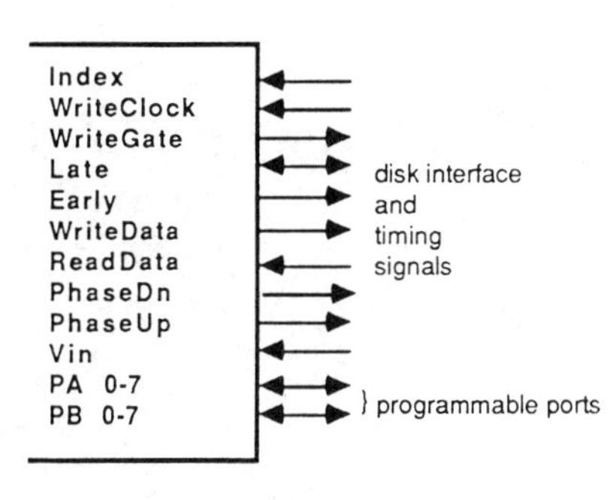

The bus interface logic interprets the command and data bytes and synchronises them to the disk hardware. It also controls all the interfacing between the disk logic and the channels.

The programmable PIA ports **PA0-7** and **PB0-7** interface to the control port of the disk drive. The data to these ports and the direction of each pin is controlled by the processor.

The data separation and precompensation logic provides connection to the remaining disk interface signals. An incoming data stream is separated into data and clock information by this module. An on-chip, self-calibrating delay circuit implements write precompensation.

The serial data from the disk is converted into parallel byte-wide format and the necessary address and ID field comparisons are performed. Encoding and decoding of FM or MFM data, and the necessary Cyclic Redundancy Check or Error Correction Check are all performed by the disk hardware.

The disk hardware communicates with the processor via a pair of byte-wide channels. These on-chip channels transfer control and data using specific protocol in the form of control codes and they communicate with the bus interface logic via a pair of FIFO buffers. The control codes and their format are set out in the table below. Full details can be obtained from INMOS and its franchised distributors.

Code type	Byte pattern	Function
Read register	11AAAAAA	Reads the register addressed by the field **AAAAAA**. This code is not followed by any data byte.
Write register	10AAAAAA	Writes the register addressed by the field **AAAAAA**. This code is followed immediately by a single data byte.
Implicit	000BBBBB	Performs the instruction **BBBBB**. This code is not followed by any data on the channel.
Single data	001CCCCC	Performs the instruction **CCCCC**. This code is followed by a single data byte.
Repeat data	010XXXXX	Outputs a single data byte **XXXXX** times before another control code.
Multiple data	011XXXXX	Outputs the following **XXXXX** bytes before the the next control code.

BBBBB is encoded as follows:

00000	NOP
00001	start
00100	switch off write gate
00101	set test mode
00110	reset test mode
00111	set external clock
01000	set internal clock
1XXXX	append **XXXX** syndrome bytes where **XXXX** has the same meaning as for **repeat data** with the msb equal to **0** (i.e 1-16).

CCCCC is encoded as follows:

10001	miss data address mark
10101	miss ID address mark
11001	miss index address mark
00000	toggle ID field.

XXXXX is encoded as follows:

If the most significant bit is **0** the value of **XXXXX** is the value of the bottom 4 bits, with the exception that 00000 has the value of sixteen. If the most significant bit is **1** the value of **XXXXX** is 2 to the power of the bottom 4 bits.

e.g 00011 has a value of 3, and 10011 has a value of 8.

The M212 is available in an 68 pin J-Lead chip carrier or 68 pin Grid Array

68 pin J-Lead chip carrier

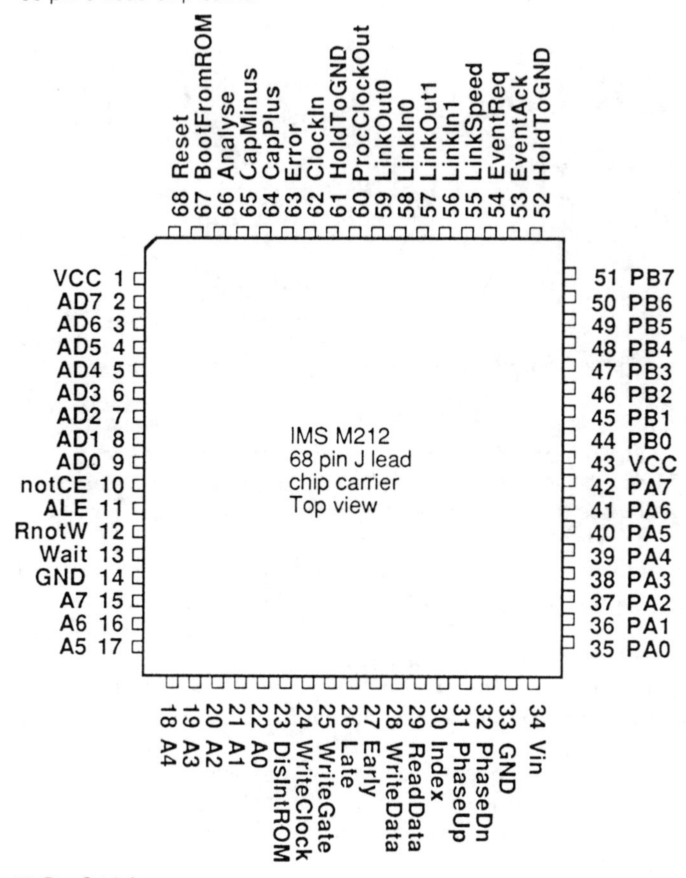

68 Pin Grid Array

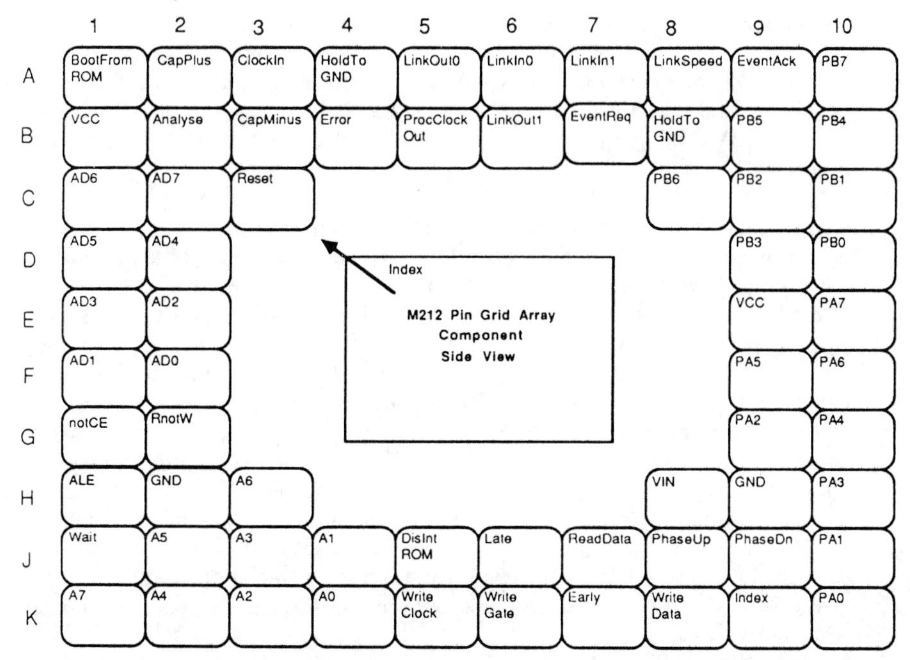

Appendix C Glossary of micro-processor terminology

Access Time The time between enabling a memory circuit and the data appearing on the output.

Accumulator A register in a central processing unit which accumulates the output of the arithmetic logic unit.

Address Bus The wires or conducting paths used by a processor (or DMA controller) to transmit signals which contain address information. The width (number of lines) of the address bus determines the address space (e.g. 16 lines give 64 K address space).

Address Space The number of addresses that can be uniquely specified. The maximum amount of memory (usually in bytes) a processor can handle (e.g. 16 Mbytes).

Architecture A representation of the hardware and software components of a system and their interrelationships, considered from the viewpoint of the whole system, as opposed to that of a single part.

Arithmetic Logic Unit (ALU) The portion of a computer central processing unit which performs the Boolean and arithmetic operations on data inputs. The accumulator acts as the storage location for the results of these operations. Typical elements consist of an adder and shift register.

Array Processor A processor which is optimised for the execution of processing algorithms which operate on arrays (regular structures) of input data.

Assembly Language The specific mnemonics which are supplied as data to an assembler program to produce the machine code for a specific computer.

Asynchronous An event which is not coordinated with or controlled by the clock.

Auto-increment Addressing An addressing mode whereby the register used to generate the effective address (usually an index register) is incremented before (pre-incremented) or after (post-incremented) an instruction that uses auto-increment addressing is executed.

Barrel Shifter A shift register which will perform multiple numbers of shift positions in a single operation. A combinatorial logic device without input clocks to determine shift positions.

Bit Slice Architecture A high-performance CPU composed of several smaller, high-speed processing elements called bit slices. A bit slice element can perform basic arithmetic and Boolean operations on part of the data word, typically four bits. The slices are connected together to allow arbitrary CPU wordlengths.

Bootstrap A program located in the memory location which the central processing element accesses when power is applied. Its purpose is to provide enough logic to allow the CPU to load a program into memory from a storage device, thereby minimising the amount of memory used for permanent program storage.

Breakpoint A pointer to a memory location which is used for debugging. When a program under test addresses the location to which the breakpoint is pointing, processing is interrupted and control is returned to a monitor program.

Buffer An array of memory locations used for the temporary storage and accumulation of data. Also a circuit which is used to provide additional drive (fan-out) or isolation.

Bus Transceiver A logic circuit used to increase bus drive and provide isolation, similar to a bus driver but bi-directional. A control line determines which direction the information is flowing.

Cache A very-high-speed memory which provides a buffer between the CPU and main memory. A cache can provide increased throughput by pre-fetching instructions and data and making them available to the CPU in a shorter time than main memory.

Central Processing Unit (CPU) The functional unit of the computer which contains the arithmetic logic unit and its support circuitry, and may include a coprocessor or memory. It can be composed of a microprocessor or bit-slice elements.

CHMOS Acronym for complementary high performance metal oxide semiconductor.

Clock Cycle The period of the computer clock, frequently used as a frequency-independent measure of instruction execution time.

CMOS Acronym for complementary metal oxide semiconductor. A semiconductor process which produces integrated circuits with low power consumption by using gates containing both NMOS and PMOS transistors.

Compiler A program which translates a high-level language program (source) either into intermediate form or directly to machine code (object).

Concurrent Processor A multiprocessor which uses concurrency, a high-level global form of parallelism which permits independent operation of several computing activities.

Conditional Branching A program branch which occurs only if a certain condition (e.g. zero or overflow) is true. Otherwise the next program step is executed.

Context Switching The operation to save the state of a currently operating task and the restoration of the state of a previously operating task. This usually requires the saving of all CPU registers and sometimes the return address.

Coprocessor A processing unit which acts in parallel with the central processing unit and uses the same instruction stream as the central processing unit, but is otherwise independent.

Cycle Time The time it takes the processor to execute its simplest instruction. Also the time it takes a memory to perform and recover from an access.

Cyclic Redundancy Check (CRC) An error detecting and correcting technique which is usually employed on transmitted messages and disk records.

Dataflow Processor A parallel processor with decentralised processing elements communicating by packets containing instructions and data.

Daisy Chain Priority A priority arbitration scheme for bus access or interrupts whereby contending devices are strung together in a serial fashion from high to low priority. When the highest priority device is inactive it passes control to the next device, and so on down the chain.

Data Bus The signal paths for information which the central processing unit assumes to be data. The width of this bus determines the computer classification as 16 or 32 bits.

Debugger A small program, usually implemented in ROM, which provides examination and alteration of machine registers. It is usually used for debugging programs written in assembly or machine language. Provision for breakpoint insertions are usually found.

Demand-driven Processor A parallel processor which breaks tasks into sub-tasks which are separately processed and combined for the final result. Instructions are executed when the result is demanded by an active instruction.

Digital Signal Processor A computer consisting of discrete circuitry or a single chip which accepts digitised signal information and performs mathematical operations on it before outputting in digital or analog form.

Direct Memory Access (DMA) A high-speed data transfer method which permits data to be directly read (or written) from memory without processor intervention. A processor responds to a DMA request by floating the address and data lines and relinquishing control of the memory to the DMA device.

Dynamic Memory A type of read/write memory which is volatile and requires periodic refreshing in order to maintain the information stored.

ECC	Acronym for error checking and correcting computer hardware which checks for errors and corrects them as part of the memory access.
EEPROM	Acronym for electrically erasable PROM. A PROM that can be erased by the application of voltage pulses prior to re-programming.
EPROM	Acronym for erasable programmable read only memory. A PROM that can be erased, usually by the application of ultra violet light. It can then be reprogrammed.
Executive	A program which provides control of the execution of programs in a computer system. It creates and removes tasks, controls the sequence of task execution, handles interrupts and errors, allocates hardware resources among tasks, provides access to software resources, provides protection, access control, and security for information, and provides a means of communicating information among tasks, and between the system and its peripherals.
FIFO	Acronym for first-in first-out. A memory buffer technique where the first word written is the first word read. Also called an elastic buffer.
Floating-point Processor	A specialised coprocessor or peripheral which performs floating-point operations.
Flops	Acronym for floating-point operations per second. The number of floating-point operations that can be performed in one second.
Full Duplex	A communication system in which terminals are capable of simultaneously transmitting and receiving (i.e. simultaneous transmission in two directions is possible).
Half Duplex	Operation of a data transfer system in one direction at a time over a single bi-directional channel.
Hardwired	Control which is determined by the interconnection of the hardware and cannot be altered by software.
Harvard Architecture	An enhanced von Neumann architecture with separate data and instruction paths to reduce the bottleneck caused by a common bus.
HMOS	An acronym for a high-performance MOS process used in the manufacturing of VLSI components.
In-circuit Emulation (ICE)	The replacing of the microprocessor unit with a device which emulates its signals.
Index Register	A register whose contents can be added automatically to an address field contained in an instruction to generate a particular address.
Interpreter	A program which executes a sequence of commands which are not in machine code. Interpreters can execute commands typed in from a keyboard or programs in BASIC.
Interrupt Controller	A device which attaches to a processor to arbitrate among interrupt lines from other devices. The controller then interrupts the processor and provides it with information necessary to identify the interrupting device.
I/O	Acronym for input/output.
Latency	Refers to delay (latency) which is experienced when accessing a disk due to the time it takes the disk to go through a revolution. Can also refer to the time it takes a processor to respond to an interrupt. In general, any delay due to information flow and reaction time.
Logical Address	The address of a location in logical memory. Logical memory is associated with the program and is subsequently mapped into physical memory. The process of calculating the real physical address is called address mapping or translating.
Magnetic Bubble Memory	A memory technology which uses magnetic domains for information storage.
Mainframe	A computer with high processing power intended to form a central facility for many users, frequently used for commercial data processing. A fine line exists between mainframes and super-minicomputers.
Maskable Interrupt	An interrupt which may be disabled and ignored under processor control.
Mask Programmable	A ROM whose bit pattern is established when the chip is manufactured.
Memory Interleaving	A technique where several memory words are simultaneously accessed to reduce memory access time.
Microcomputer	A computer using one or more microprocessors as the processing element.

Microinstruction — An instruction which is executed internal to the CPU as a result of an externally fetched machine instruction. A microinstruction contains many bits for control of internal CPU register and buses. Several microinstructions are executed during a typical single machine instruction execution.

Microprocessor — An integrated circuit containing the processing element for a computer but not the program and data memory.

Microprogram — The program executed by the central processing unit when it receives an instruction. The microprogram is composed of microcode.

Microprogram Sequencer — The element of the central processing unit which causes sequential execution of the CPU microcode. Usually a single device in bit-slice processors, and integral to monolithic microprocessors.

MIMD — Multiple Instruction-stream, Multiple Data-stream computer using duplicated processor-memory pairs and no central control.

Mini-supercomputer — A computer intended for high-performance scientific and engineering applications with performance approaching that of a supercomputer at a price similar to that of a super-minicomputer.

MISD — Multiple Instruction-stream, Single Data-stream computer, not a popular architecture but may be applied to applications with a single data input (e.g. radar).

Mnemonic — Symbolic representation of an instruction, e.g. ADD, SUB, LDA, etc., used in assembly language programming.

Modem — A term for a modulator/demodulator. A device used to convert digital information to analog form (modulator) and the analog form to digital form (demodulator).

Monitor — A small program which enables primitive programming (usually in machine code) with examination and alteration of CPU registers. Similar to a debugger.

Multiplex — A means of integrating a multiple number of signals onto a single signal path.

Multiprocessing — A term referring to the use of more than one processing element on a given bus. This may be more than one CPU internal to a computer or multiple computers connected by a communications bus.

Multi-tasking — An operating system or executive which can support simultaneous execution of tasks.

Multi-user — An operating system or executive which can support several users simultaneously. Each user has a set of tasks which are associated with it.

Nibble — A collection of four bits or half of a byte.

Non-maskable Interrupt (NMI) — A special high-priority interrupt which cannot be disabled (masked) by a processor. NMI is usually used to warn the processor of a fault condition or impending disaster (e.g. loss of power).

Non-volatile — A logic circuit, especially a memory, which will retain stored data even when no power is applied to the device.

Object-oriented Machine — A machine which deals with objects (arbitrary collections of bits) rather than words. Addresses are generally not seen by the programmer, only references to objects. This architecture is suited particularly for high-level language programming.

Opcode — Part of a machine instruction which represents the specific operation to be performed. (The rest of the instruction may be an operand.)

Operand — An entity such as a byte, word or address which is operated upon during the execution of an instruction (the opcode).

Operating System — A computer program which provides the functions of a monitor and can also provide software tools such as compilers, editors, and file maintenance. An operating system provides the input/output interface from a program to the actual computer environment.

Page — A contiguous block of memory which is aligned to an address boundary which is a multiple of this standard size.

Paged Addressing — An addressing mode which decreases execution time and code size by using a page register to supply part of the address.

Parity — An encoding technique which adds extra information to the digital data being processed or transferred to facilitate error detection. The typical application is single-bit parity which may be even parity or odd parity. The parity bit is set to make the number of logic 1 bits in the monitored data even (for even parity) or odd (for odd parity). In either case, even multiples of bit errors will not be detected.

Peripherals — At the system level, the printer, disks, and I/O devices which surround the computer. Alternatively the circuits which control the system-level peripherals in the computer.

Physical Address — An actual location or address to which a memory cell or device responds. The true location of a memory cell with respect to the hardware.

Pipelined Processor — A processor using pipelines to execute different operations from several sequential instructions or instruction cycles simultaneously, thereby eliminating lost processing time.

Pipelining — The separation of processing into several stages. Each stage is always active and passes results to the next stage at regular intervals. This allows throughput for repetitive calculations to be much higher than for a similar processor without pipelining.

PLA — Acronym for programmable logic array. A regular structure of AND and OR gates which allow mapping of sum-of-product terms (i.e. combinatorial expressions) of inputs into the outputs. This is a regular structure in an integrated circuit intended to replace combinatorial circuits normally implemented in random logic.

Port — A functional element of a computer which acts as an I/O channel for peripheral device(s)

Position Independent Code (PIC) — A program which contains no absolute references to memory, only relative ones. Thus, the program can be located at any physical address and still operate properly.

Program Counter — A register whose contents are an address which points to the next instruction to be executed.

Programmable Read Only Memory (PROM) — A variant of ROM which is field-programmable.

Protocol — A set of terms or definitions which determine the structure of information to be transferred between two or more points in a system.

Random Access Memory (RAM) — A type of memory which allows alteration to the information stored within it. A memory which can be written to or read from. Also referred to as read/write memory.

Random Logic — Refers to the lack of a regular organisation or structure in a logic network.

Read — With respect to the processor, the action of acquiring the contents of a particular address (memory location) which will be used within the processor.

Read-Modify-Write — A single instruction which simultaneously reads a memory location and replaces it with a new value.

Read Only Memory (ROM) — A non-volatile memory which allows only reading of the information stored within it.

Real Time Operating System — An operating system tailored to have small latency with respect to interrupt requests.

Reduced Instruction Set Computer (RISC) — A computer which executes a simple instruction set at high speed giving simplification of design.

Re-entrant — An attribute of a program which allows several tasks to simultaneously execute the same code. This means that the code cannot be self-modifying and all data references occur with respect to a stack or a variable data pointer.

Refresh — In dynamic RAMs, the process by which the charges which represent the logic states are renewed. In a dynamic RAM this requires periodic read or refresh cycles for each internal memory row or column.

Relative Addressing — An addressing mode in which references to memory or operands are made relative to some register (usually the program counter for branch instructions). The register provides an absolute address pointing to memory. An instruction employing relative addressing adds or subtracts displacements to this pointer.

Scalar Processor A conventional (von Neumann or SISD) processor which executes single data elements (scalars) in sequence.

Scheduler That part of an operating system or executive that decides the order in which tasks will be executed.

Segment A logical or physical grouping of code or data in memory. Some machines support segmentation which is a general form of paging. The segments can be of variable length and location.

Semaphore A bit or word which indicates whether a system resource (e.g. peripheral) is being used by a task in a multi-tasking or multiprocessor system. Using a read-modify-write instruction is one of the ways to manage semaphores in order to prevent two tasks claiming control of a device.

SIMD Single Instruction-stream, Multiple Data-stream computer characterised by vector processing; requires central control of processing elements.

Single Board Computer A computer, usually a microcomputer, which contains its functional elements on a single printed circuit board, i.e. CPU, memory and I/O.

Single Chip Computer A microcomputer which contains it functional elements on a single monolithic substrate (CPU, program memory, data memory and I/O circuitry).

Single Step A process used in program debugging where instructions are executed one at a time, allowing inspection of registers and buses between each instruction.

Stack A buffer or segment of computer memory which is reserved for use by the central processing unit. Normally used for saving state information resulting from context switching.

Stack Pointer The register in the central processing unit which contains an address within the stack.

Static A device which does not require refreshing of internal logic states, i.e. it contains no dynamic logic.

Status Register A register internal to the central processing unit which maintains information on the results of the central processor operations.

String A linear collection of bytes whose contents are interpreted as characters.

Strobe A signal line which enables a gate or register. Typically refers to the signal which causes a register to store the data present at its input.

Supercomputer The most powerful computer class at the time of introduction.

Super-minicomputer A high-performance minicomputer with a word length of at least 32 bits, arbitrarily defined as having a processing rate in the range 0.5 to 15 Mips.

Synchronous An event which occurs in conjunction with the computer clock and can be timed relative to the clock.

Task A program or subroutine. Any autonomously executing set of code.

Trap A system-level interrupt structure normally used for processing errors during program execution.

Tri-state The output of a logic circuit which can have three states: on (1), off (0) or a high impedence state (z). The z state allows other outputs connected together to establish the state of the line.

TTL Acronym for transistor transistor logic. A bipolar logic family operating from a 5 V supply with defined interface characteristics.

UART Acronym for universal asynchronous receiver transmitter. A UART is a device which performs serial-to-parallel and parallel-to-serial conversions for serial computer I/O.

USART Acronym for universal synchronous/asynchronous receiver transmitter. A serial communication protocol device which implements a synchronous protocol or an asynchronous protocol.

UVPROM A PROM which may be erased by the application of ultra-violet light through a transparent window covering the IC. The PROM can then be reprogrammed.

Vector Computer A computer which uses vector processing to make a single instruction operate on several data elements or vectors. (Similar to pipelines.) SIMD classification by Flynn.

Vectored Interrupt An interrupt to the central processing unit which causes the flow of execution to go to the address contained in the location defined by the interrupt.

Very-large-scale Integration (VLSI) VLSI usually refers to integrated circuits with a level of complexity greater than 10 000 devices per monolithic substrate.

Virtual Memory A mechanism which allows the apparent (virtual) memory size to exceed the actual (physical) memory size. This allows programs to appear to use more memory than is actually resident in the computer.

Von Neumann (SISD) The basic digital computer architecture which has a Single Instruction-stream and a Single Data-stream. (It fetches instructions and data sequentially.)

Wait State Extra clock cycles added to a processor which cause it to wait for a slow memory or peripheral, or for the completion of a DMA activity.

Writable Control Store A very-high-speed RAM which can contain user-programmed microinstructions.

Index